STRAIGHT
AND TRUE

STRAIGHT AND TRUE

A History of
Royal Air Force Leeming

by

Peter Coupland

LEO COOPER
LONDON

First published in Great Britain in hardback in 1997 by

Leo Cooper
190 Shaftesbury Avenue, London WC2H 8JL

an imprint of
Pen & Sword Books Ltd,
47 Church Street,
Barnsley, South Yorkshire S70 2AS

A CIP record for this book is available from the British Library

ISBN 0 8502 569 1

Designed and typeset by Phoenix Typesetting,
Ilkley, West Yorkshire

Printed in England by Redwood Books,
Trowbridge, Wiltshire

CONTENTS

BUCKINGHAM PALACE

RAF Leeming was built as a result of "warning time". In 1938 a year before the outbreak of the Second World War the Air Ministry took over the land and built the air station.

Throughout the war Leeming housed bombers from the RAF and later in the war, from Canada. After the end of the Second World War, the Air Force changed its role to training in which it remained until July 1988. Since then, it has been the operational base for two squadrons of the air defence variant of the Tornado.

Warrant Officer Coupland's excellent work is reflected in the collection of the facts, figures, photographs and anecdotes which make up this most readable account of an air station which has featured in so many people's lives. It is as a student of the Royal Navy Elementary Flying Training School that I best remember Leeming not least from trying not to get lost whilst learning to fly and reinforcing the Royal Navy's presence at Leeming and its satellite airfield at Topcliffe.

My memories of Leeming both then and more recently, passing through in various capacities, is of a vibrant air station bonded by a strong relationship within the community surrounding it. I enjoyed the time I served at RAF Leeming and this book will, I hope, give you some insight into its unique character.

GLOSSARY

AA	Anti-aircraft
AAA	Amateur Athletics Association
ADR	Airfield Damage Repair
AI	Airborne Intercept
AIP	Any invasion port as a bombing target
ALTENT	Type of corrugated iron shelter
AMO	Any military objective as a bombing target
AMWD	Air Ministry Works Department
AOC	Air Officer Commanding
AOC in C	Air Officer Commanding in Chief
ARI	Airborne Radar Intercept
ATC	Air Traffic Control
ATC	Air Training Corps
AVTAG	Aviation Fuel
AVTUR	Aviation fuel (jet aircraft)
AWAC	Airborne (Early) Warning Aircraft
BA	Bomb Aimer (same as air bomber)
BULLSEYE	Night flying training exercise around the UK which was also used to keep the British air defences in practice and later as a feint to simulate a bombing raid while the real attack went in elsewhere
CAT 5	Scrap (aircraft)
CHAFF	Originally American version of "window", but term is now used universally for metallised strip reflector radar counter measure
CFI	Chief Flying Instructor
CFS	Central Flying School
CO	Commanding Officer
DECKER	Codename for a small type of incendiary bomb
E/A	Enemy aircraft
ENSA	Entertainments National Service Association – an organisation during World War II for entertaining the Services and war workers
ETA	Estimated Time of Arrival
FAW	Fighter All Weather
FEAF	Far East Air Force

FLAK	Abbreviation referring to German anti-aircraft artillery – from *Fliegerabwehrkanonen*
FTR	Failed To Return (from an operation)
FTS	Flying Training School
GARDENING	Sea minelaying from aircraft
GCA	Ground Control Approach (radar)
GCI	Ground Control Intercept (radar)
GEE	Navigation system using wireless pulse transmissions
GOODWOOD	Codename for the British attack to take Caen on 18 July 1944
GP CAPT	Group Captain
H2S	Airborne blind bombing and navigational aid radar that showed up ground features such as towns
HAS	Hardened aircraft shelter
IaW	In accordance with
IBs	Inboards (engines on 4 engined aircraft)
IFF	Identification Friend or Foe – an airborne transmitter/receiver which, when interrogated, distinguishes between friendly and enemy aircraft
KINSMAN	A dispersal exercise devised to acquaint V Force aircrew and groundcrew with their dispersal station
LAA	Light anti-aircraft (cannon)
LB	Light Bomber
MiD	Mentioned in Dispatches
MPBW	Ministry of Public Building and Works
MEDA	Master Emergency Diversion Airfield
MONICA	Codeword for tail warning radar. Later quickly removed when it was discovered that it also led the German night-fighters to the aircraft
MOPA	Military objective previously attacked (in a bombing raid)
MQ	Married Quarter
MT	Motor Transport
MUG	Mid upper gunner
NAAFI	Navy Army Air Force Institute
NCO	Non Commissioned Officer
NF	Night-fighter
NICKEL	Codename for leaflet drops
OBOE	Codeword for a blind bombing aid fitted to aircraft but ground controlled; could also be used as an aid to navigation
OC	Officer Commanding
OCU	Operational Conversion Unit
ORB	Operations Record Book
OTU	Operational Training Unit
PFF	Pathfinder Force
POW	Prisoner of War
PSA	Public Services Agency
QRA(I)	Quick Reaction Alert (Intercept)

QCVSA	Queen's Commendation for Valuable Service in the Air
RAFA	The Royal Air Forces Association
RAFVR	Royal Air Force Volunteer Reserve
RAZZLE	Codename for a very small type of incendiary bomb
RDF	Radio Direction Finding (the original British term for radar)
R/G	Rear gunner
RLG	Relief Landing Ground
RNethAF	Royal Netherlands Air Force
RNAS	Royal Naval Air Service
R/T	Radio Transmitter
SACEUR	Supreme Allied Commander Europe
SACLANT	Supreme Allied Commander Atlantic
SAM	Surface to Air Missile
SCHRÄGE-MUSIK	Upward (45°) firing cannon fitted to certain types of German night-fighter
SECO	A type of prefabricated building
SEMO	Self evident military objective (for bombers)
SHQ	Station Headquarters
SNCO	Senior Non Commissioned Officer
SQN CDR	Squadron commander – usually a Wing Commander in rank
SWO	Station Warrant Officer
TACEVAL	Tactical Evaluation
TFR	Terrain Following Radar
TRACTABLE	Codename for the operation by the Canadians to take Falaise on 14 August 1944
u/c	Undercarriage
u/s	Unserviceable
u/t	Under training
UHF	Ultra High Frequency (radio)
V-1	German flying bomb powered by a ramjet – from *Vergeltungs* (retaliation)
V-2	German long range rocket
VEGETABLES	Codename for air dropped mines
VGO	Vickers Gas Operated – a machine gun with pan type magazine and a very high rate of fire
VHF	Very High Frequency (radio)
WAAF	Women's Auxiliary Air Force
WINDOW	A radar counter-measure where metallised strips were dropped to confuse German early warning systems. It also affected radar controlled guns and searchlights, as well as ground control and intercept radar.
WRAF	Women's Royal Air Force
YMCA	Young Men's Christian Association

ACKNOWLEDGEMENTS

Soon after Group Captain E J Black RAF arrived at Royal Air Force Leeming to take up the post of Station Commander, he asked if it was feasible to publish a book on the history of the Station. I was somewhat taken aback at his question, because for more years than I care to remember I have wondered about the lack of such records on the history of the Stations in the RAF. Granted, books about aircraft abound, accounts of individual or collective acts of heroism are generally well documented, and almost everyone will have heard of the fighter pilots of the Battle of Britain. They will also know of the Dam-Busters, if not the Squadron number, but little is known about the stations from whence the crews came, many not to return, and where thousands of others have worked towards the defence of the United Kingdom. Relatively few RAF Stations are known to anyone from outside their immediate area, and though it is true to say that some histories have been written in recent years, the majority remain an unknown quantity to the public at large.

When the question about publication was posed to me, I knew that a basis for a book was already in existence, so while I had absolutely no idea what would be necessary to complete the task, my answer was a very positive 'Yes.' The original work, of which much is extant in this book, was the accomplishment of Squadron Leader Marion Cunningham MA RAF, who before her retirement in 1981 was an education officer at RAF Leeming. She, in essence, prepared the way for me when she compiled a history, when she built on a diary of important events which had already been prepared in 1968. I have expanded on that work, but it was her labour that gave me the confidence to begin, and it became the framework around which this book was written. However, I am keenly aware that I may not have taken on the task without her comprehensively researched effort, and I freely acknowledge how invaluable her achievement was in the preparation of this book.

I am also indebted to the Ministry of Defence (Air Historical Branch) for the access given to the records kept there, but in particular to Mike Hatch for his repeated assistance, as well as for making me welcome during my visits. The staff at the Public Record Office, Kew, are also duly acknowledged, especially for the assistance given on my first trip when I was a complete beginner to the task of research. The detail obtained from all of my visits has been taken from a variety of official records, and at times in using the statements made by so many unknown authors in the Operations Record Books I have done so because I feel they still retain their immediacy, and are more appropriate than any attempt at rework from me. In acknowledging their work, I would add that where such accounts are used they have been included in their original form, with no additions or alterations. A third major source of information was more local, and in thanking those at the Yorkshire Air Museum for allowing me repeated access to their archives, I must give specific recognition to Peter Slee, both for his assistance and his ever cheerful manner, even at 7 a.m.!

The book also bears witness to the generous contributions given by many people who supplied me with all manner of information, and I would like to thank them all for taking the time to write to me. I would also like to take the opportunity to say that whatever form their aid took, all of it helped in some way in the compilation of this history. It now seems an age ago, but in fact it is a little over two years since I made my first approach to someone about writing the book. That was to Derek Reed in the 'Cockpit' of his well known book store in York, and he got me 'up and running' by providing a list of people to contact. This list included: Kenneth Cothliff, the Chairman of 6 (RCAF) Group Bomber Command Association; Doug Dent, the Chairman of 10 Squadron Association; Harry Shinkfield, the historian of No 77 Squadron Association, and Norman Spence, the News Editor of the Yorkshire Air Museum. I am grateful for the help they gave, as well as for passing on my request for assistance to the members of their respective associations. I was also fortunate enough to be contacted by a local man, John Thompson, who was brought up on the farm that would provide much of the land for RAF Leeming, and whose remarkable memory was of great help in setting the scene with the pre-war landing ground at Londonderry. Perhaps his memory for detail could only be bettered by Mrs E M Wood-Clark, who retired from RAF Leeming in 1984 after more than 26 years employment at the Station. Her assistance was invaluable, particularly regarding the period when 3 FTS was in residence, as well as for her gift of a set of programmes from the Presentation of Wings Parade for each of the 62 courses that passed out from pilot training at Leeming. My thanks also go to Mr E Garvey, Bill Hird, Gordon Skellhorn, and

Bill Neal, stationed at Leeming in 1941, 1942, 1945/46, and 1950/51 respectively for their contributions. The photographs have come from various sources, and where it has been possible recognition is given alongside each picture, but I must make special mention of Charles Appleton from British Columbia. As a Halifax pilot in the RCAF he was stationed at Skipton-on-Swale in 1944, so not only was he able to give me the particulars of the 'bombed' Halifax, U for Uncle, he was also kind enough to supply me with a copy of a photograph of the bomber, taken when the damage was being inspected by the King.

In summation, I would like to extend my appreciation to Bill Chorley for his permission to extract from the meticulous research carried out by him for his first four volumes on the Bomber Command Losses of the Second World War. His work, when complete, must surely become *the* definitive account of the real cost of the Bomber Command offensive!

At the preparation stage I would not have been able to include the 'Squadron Badges', nor the maps, without the skill and patience of Angela Thompson, who worked many hours in their preparation. My sincere thanks must also go to another volunteer helper, Mandy Burges, who gave up much of her time in proof reading my drafts, an onerous task at the best of times, and probably more so on this occasion! In addition, mention must be made of the enthusiasm of her husband, Squadron Leader R (Budgie) Burges, whose continued advice and assistance have been of inestimable value to me. Finally, I must thank Group Captain Black for his continued support, without it this would not have been possible.

Peter Coupland
March 1997

THE FIRST OF MANY

On Sunday 5 October 1930, the quiet of a small corner of North Yorkshire was disturbed by the sound of an aeroplane circling the village of Londonderry. The people in the region were not unfamiliar with the sight and sound of aircraft passing overhead, but on this occasion, to the surprise of those watching, this one came in to land. The aircraft, a de Havilland Puss Moth was being flown by a Captain Ambler when it made its landing in the 34 acre field adjoining Clapham Lodge Farm which was farmed at the time by the Thompson family. The pilot was intending to take lunch at the nearby Newton House Hotel, but as he slowed to a halt he found that both he and his most up-to-date means of transport were the centre of attraction for a crowd of locals who had been drawn by the sight or sound of his approach and landing. Among those present was John Thompson who, as one of the farmer's sons, was able to be quickly on the scene, and once there he struck up a conversation with the unexpected visitor. The Captain was friendly but carried some sombre news; the Airship R101, while on its way to India, had crashed that day in France and Lord Thompson the Air Secretary was one of the many fatalities. The calamity was seen as a national one that made newspaper headlines for days, but within months the disaster had an even greater impact when it spelled the end of Airship design and development in Great Britain, affecting even the privately built and successful R100 which was grounded and then broken up. However, the decisions on the future of Airship travel were still to be made when Ambler brought his aircraft to Londonderry, but it was still a remarkable coincidence that the news of what in effect was the demise of one means of air transport was first brought to the region by one example of what had been its main rival. Furthermore, the arrival of this small, high winged monoplane was in itself an occasion of some distinction, because when it touched down it was as the first in a long line of aircraft that were to make countless other landings in the area that was to become known as Royal Air Force Leeming.

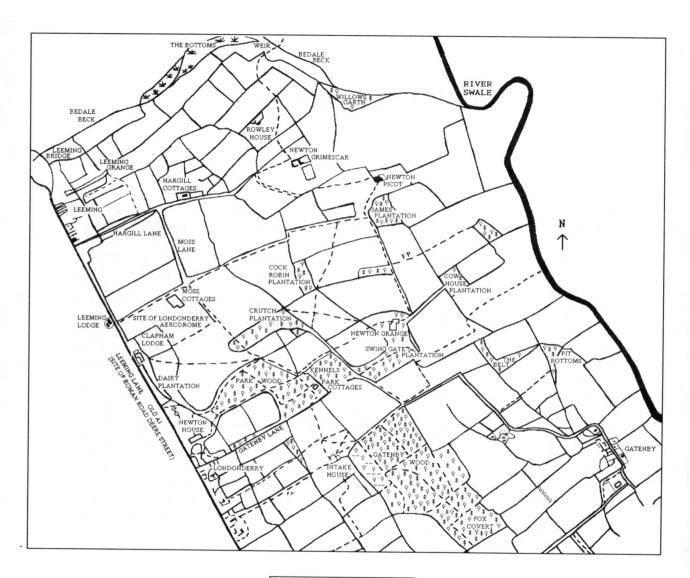

THE BOTTOMS
WEIR
BEDALE BECK
RIVER SWALE
WILLOWS GARTH
BEDALE BECK
ROWLEY HOUSE
NEWTON GRIMESCAR
LEEMING BRIDGE
LEEMING GRANGE
HARGILL COTTAGES
NEWTON PICOT
JAMES PLANTATION
LEEMING
N
HARGILL LANE
MOSS LANE
FP
COCK ROBIN PLANTATION
COW HOUSE PLANTATION
MOSS COTTAGES
CRUTCH PLANTATION
LEEMING LODGE
SITE OF LONDONDERRY AERODROME
NEWTON GRANGE
CLAPHAM LODGE
SWING GATE PLANTATION
THE BELT
PIT BOTTOMS
LEEMING LANE (SITE OF ROMAN ROAD DEERE STREET)
OLD A1
DAIRY PLANTATION
KENNELS
PARK WOOD
PARK COTTAGES
NEWTON HOUSE
GATENBY LANE
GATENBY WOOD
GATENBY
LONDONDERRY
INTAKE HOUSE
FP
FOX COVERT

LEEMING c 1910

EARLY DAYS

Through the Vale of York for centuries has run the main highway between the North and South of England. Watling Street, from Roman Britain, known between Aysclough and Catterick as Deere Street, came this way; later this route was overlaid by the Great North Road which in recent times became what is now known as the old A1. On this road, seven miles south of Catterick, lies the old village of Leeming and about a mile further south the newer settlement of Londonderry. To the east of this stretch of road, known locally as Leeming Lane, lay a stretch of agricultural land, roughly square in shape, bounded on the north by Bedale Beck. This ran from west to east through Leeming, on the east by the River Swale of which Bedale Beck is a tributary and on the south by Gatenby Lane which ran east from Londonderry. Enclosed within these boundaries were a number of farms: Leeming Grange (Wilson's), Newton Grimescar, Newton Picot (where Joe Langthorne farmed), Newton Grange, Clapham Lodge, to name but a few; farm cottages such as Moss Cottages, which were demolished to make way for the airfield, plus several plantations of trees with evocative names such as Cock Robin, Crutch, Cow House, Swing Gate, James, Dolly, Far Fairy and Near Fairy, all linked by numerous footpaths or country lanes. In the south-west corner of this area, on the northern edge of Londonderry was the mansion of Newton House, built as a Hunting Lodge at the end of the 18th century by Lord Darlington, later Duke of Cleveland. Within the 25 acres of garden and 45 acres of parkland were stables, coach houses, gate

lodges, the gamekeeper's house known as Park Cottage, and of course the Kennels which provided the last word in canine comfort for the small pack of hounds. Park Cottage and the kennels were the last to go sometime in the late 1980s, with the derelict Intake House being all that remains of the original estate.

Occasionally enlivened by a meet of the local Bedale Hunt and Point to Point Races at Newton House, life in this rural community continued peacefully into the 1920s. Among the older generation of local inhabitants are nostalgic memories of Sunday walks in the woods, of rhododendron plantations or skating on the frozen pond in winter. However, after the end of the First World War, things began to change.

With the increased use of the motor car, traffic along what was then the Great North Road increased in volume and noise and worse still to many, the flying machine began to appear with increasing frequency in the vicinity of Newton House. One of the fields nearby had been set aside as a landing ground for visitors, and local farmers noted with mixed feelings odd looking machines "buzzing" in over their fields. These were the days when "little men with red flags sprang from nowhere to guide you on take-off across the rough cart tracks as to where the main pot holes were." However, notwithstanding the random nature of these visits, they were in fact the true precursors of all that was to come.

In 1927 the last of the Cleveland Heirs, Miss M E Russell, died, the Newton House Estate was sold to William Jackson, Sunderland Ltd and the house itself became a hotel. The landing ground, to the north and east of Clapham Lodge was developed further for the use of the guests and became known as Londonderry Aerodrome. Local legend has numerous memories of this period in the early thirties. There was one enthusiast who built his own "Flying Flea" and employed local small boys to help with "assisted" take-off. The flying club held rallies and Alan Cobham's Flying Circus was an occasional visitor, tempting the more adventurous into the air at *5 shillings a flip*. The popularity of flying at the time helped Londonderry Aerodrome become commercially viable in the mid thirties, with the formation of "The Yorkshire Aviation Services Country Club Ltd - School of Flying, Sales and Air Services; Managing Director, Lieutenant Commander C W Croxford, DSC, RN (Retd), Secretary, W K Liversidge." This was one of the first flying clubs in England and the aerodrome, then with three small hangars found that business was brisk. A Mr Pick was one of the first pilots operating from Londonderry and Mr Pepper, as chief mechanic, was helped by a local lad, Jim Gothorpe. Cost for tuition was 35 shillings per hour or £1 for young John Thompson, but he couldn't afford it!

However, in the late 1930s, events in Europe began to cast a long shadow over all this enterprise. The rather belated expansion of the Royal Air Force which began to develop in '37 and '38 produced plans for a chain of airfields, suitable for bombers, to be built across the Vale of York. As a consequence, in 1938 the Crown purchased most of the land within the Leeming Lane, Gatenby Lane, River Swale and Bedale Beck boundaries, with contractors moving in during the Autumn of the same year. The area included that used by the Flying Club, as well as the land on the south western perimeter, owned by Newton House and used as a cricket green by the Yorkshire Gentlemen. Things were clearly getting serious! Buildings were to be cleared, land drained and levelled, trees removed and a start made on the erection of what amounted to a small town, a town to be known as Royal Air Force Leeming. Airmen's Married Quarters, No 1 Hangar and the Bomb Dump were the first structures to be erected, to be followed in quick succession by Barrack Blocks A to G, the Sergeants' Mess, Officers' Mess and various technical buildings, each building under construction in parallel with the others. Work continued throughout 1939 and Hangars, numbered 2, 3, 4 and 5, along with their adjoining structures, were completed. The Station was planned and built as a "standard" bomber airfield, where the type C1 hangars were on the south east side of the landing ground and barrack blocks were brick built, with even a decoy site prepared nearby at Burneston, near Bedale. Finally, the erection of the Control Tower and the Water Tower early in 1940 marked the completion of Phase 1 of building and the commissioning of Leeming as a functional airfield.

CHAPTER ONE

ROYAL AIR FORCE LEEMING
June 1940 to December 1942

On 3 June 1940, Royal Air Force Leeming was taken over from the contractors by No.4 Group, Bomber Command, the Headquarters of which was at Heslington Hall, on the southern boundary of York. The first Commanding Officer was Wg Cdr K E Ward, in charge of the party detached from No.78 Squadron at Dishforth for the purpose of establishing the necessary administrative organisation at the new Station. The first "Daily Routine Orders", issued on 3 June 1940, specified amongst other things the working day for the airmen of the detachment, and it is interesting to note that they had four meals a day, plus a longer break at mid-day than the modern day Royal Air Force!

0630	Reveille
0715	Breakfast
0800	First Working Parade
0800	Sick Parade
1000-1015	Break
1230-1345	Dinner
1345	Second Working Parade
1630	Tea
1930	Supper
2130	Tattoo Roll Call
2200	Staff Parade
2215	Lights Out

From 28 June 1940, when 31 airmen were posted in, personnel forming the permanent cadre of Leeming began to arrive in increasing numbers, allowing those detached from 78 Sqn to return to Dishforth in early July, although Wg Cdr Ward remained in command. There are no strength figures available for this period but it is perhaps indicative of the size of the total that the Airmen's Married Quarters, which had then been built but were not in use, were taken over to accommodate the overflow. On the administrative side, entries in "Daily Routine Orders" over the next three to four months indicate the speed with which the Station settled down to its task. There were the usual *classics* which sound vaguely familiar even today; one example in July being:

> . . . The practice of using Fire Buckets for washing down cars and other purposes must cease forthwith.

Somewhat more drastic on 14 October was the advice that:

> . . . Exit and entrance from and to the Station is to be by the Main Gate only. Recently at another Station an airman was shot and killed while attempting unauthorised entry.

Interspaced in these orders with the calls for volunteers to form a Station dance band, football team, rugby team etc, were such grim reminders of the times as:

> . . . Air Raid Warning – one maroon, or an explosion, or an enemy bomb dropping. All Clear Signal – bugle call.

The precautions to be taken in the event of an air raid had a particular relevance to those at Leeming, and its significance was not just the fact that Britain was at war with Germany. Prior to the war the propagandist William Joyce (Lord Haw-Haw) had often stayed at nearby Scruton House, from where he had seen the first stages of the construction of the airfield. Consequently in the first year of the war he gave the Station specific mention in some of his transmissions, stating that though an airfield was being built at Leeming it would be flattened as soon as it was finished. Assertions such as this, implying some form of inside information, appeared to many as evidence of a vast espionage "ring", and it was not until later in the war that his broadcasts became objects of amusement and derision.

Additionally, in the confused aftermath of Dunkirk came the call for:

> ...All ex BEF personnel are to hand in their names to SHQ at 0830 hrs on 27 July 1940. Any airman of this unit who knows of the present whereabouts of any airman on the following list, (which contained 54 names), or any of his movements since 1 June 1940, is to give full particulars at once to SHQ Orderly Room.

Then late in November, as the Blitz on London developed:

> ...Airmen wishing to make enquiries about relations in the Metropolitan area, are advised to contact SHQ.

With a little imagination when "reading between the lines", especially with the last two "orders", the parlous state of things in Britain in 1940 can be readily seen, and in some ways at Leeming they were to get worse.

THE FIRST AIRCRAFT

However, regardless of the problems being encountered at that stage of the war, the main task for RAF Leeming was always to become operational as soon as possible, and not surprisingly this happened with remarkable speed. In 1940 there was as yet no concrete runway but the grass field was adequate for operational use, and even before the arrival of the first resident operational bomber squadron, the airfield was used "in anger" by the Blenheim Mk.1F of No.219 Squadron, normally based at its Sector HQ at Catterick. The Squadron, under the command of Sqn Ldr J H Little, had originally detached aircraft into Leeming on 3 June 1940, but throughout the Battle of Britain, because of overcrowding at Catterick, the whole Squadron operated from its new base airfield until it returned to Catterick at the beginning of October. The crews, flying in the night-fighter role, had no successes during their stay but had the dubious honour of providing the first serious aircraft accident to be seen at Leeming. This occurred in August, when L8692 finished up on the edge of the Great North Road. The pilot had misjudged a practice flapless landing, then found he was going too fast to stop in time so he deliberately raised the undercarriage and finally halted with the aircraft's nose through the boundary hedge of the airfield. It could be termed "a good landing" in that he and the two others in the crew were able to walk away, although the Blenheim was a write-off!

NO.10 SQUADRON.

The first squadron actually to be assigned to Leeming had made its appearance some weeks before the accident, when the advance party from No.10 Squadron equipped with the Whitley Mark V and coded "ZA" arrived on 10 July 1940. Originally formed at Farnborough on 1 January 1915, the Squadron was disbanded in February

1919 and then reformed in January 1928. Based at Dishforth since 1937, and by the outbreak of the Second World War equipped with the Armstrong Whitworth Whitley Mk IV, the Squadron had provided detachments to France at various times up to March 1940 and to Kinloss on loan to 18 Group Coastal Command in the last two months of 1939. It had also achieved the distinction, though some of those in the crews may have judged it a somewhat dubious one, of providing the first aircraft from the RAF to visit Berlin in wartime, when three out of four Whitleys made a leaflet raid in very bad weather on the night of 1/2 October 1939.

Almost immediately after its arrival at Leeming, the Squadron CO, Wg Cdr Staton, was promoted to Group Captain, before taking over command of the Station on 12 July 1940. Sqn Ldr Whitworth assumed temporary command of 10 Sqn, allowing Wg Cdr Ward to return to Dishforth. Little time was lost on the settling-in process, and on 20 July 1940, the first Operations Order was issued from RAF Leeming. The new Station Commander was a large and very forceful man who was nicknamed *King Kong* by his crews. He had flown as a scout pilot with the Royal Flying Corps in the Great War, became an ace, won the Military Cross and was well known for his belligerent approach in taking the fight to the Germans, in both wars! A first class shot, seldom seen without his pipe or dog, he always tried to attend the short voluntary service held each morning at the hangars. He was not one to sit and wait, a fact recognised by his Air Officer Commanding, who on more than one occasion had to prevent him from joining his crews on operations.

At that juncture of the war, Command HQ would give the group commanders the targets for the night, which would then be allotted by telephone to the stations, where the station and squadron commanders would work out their own operation order. They had a relatively free hand in this area and would choose their own route for the operation, the heights to be flown, as well as the time at which the crews should be over the target, subject only to their interpretation of the Met forecasts. The crews and aircraft would be chosen and lists displayed in the Messes and crew rooms. The station itself would already have begun to prepare the aircraft, furnish their bomb loads and carry out all of the relevant equipment checks. The crews would receive a formal briefing during the afternoon and find where the operation would be; flying kit would then be issued and the crews would prepare to be transported to their aircraft at the times allotted to them. However, in those early days at Leeming, until work was finally completed on both buildings and tarmac, prior to each operation, the aircraft were required to fly to Topcliffe or Linton-on-Ouse for bombing-up. After the operation they would return to Leeming unless returning during darkness when they were diverted to Dishforth.

FIRST OPERATIONS.

Operation Order 1 RAF Leeming   **20 July 1940**

MSI	A/C	CAPTAIN	TIME OFF	TIME OVER TARGET
DT 1	E	S/L Hanafin	2119	00.05
DT 2	D	FO Nixon	2120	
DT 3	S	S/L Whitworth	2121	
DT 4	F	FO Henry	2122	
DT 5	O	Sgt Johnson	2123	to
DT 6	R	FO Prior	2124	
DT 7	N	Sgt Hillary	2125	
DT 8	H	Sgt Green	2126	
DT 9	J	PO Somerville	2127	00.55

The initial Operations Order had an aircraft factory at Wenzendorf as the primary target, with the alternate, an oil refinery in Hamburg. If crews were unable to bomb either of these, then the last resort target was to be the aerodrome at Borge. All aircraft returned safely home to base after three aircraft located and bombed the primary target, four others hit the alternate, and the remaining two brought their bombs back home after failing to locate any of the three areas. There were virtually no enemy night-fighters to worry about but there was an ever increasing volume of anti-aircraft fire to contend with, especially around the estuaries and rivers that were used as aids to navigation. Within four months of this initial raid, all of the aircraft captains who took part in it had been decorated for gallantry, that is with the exception of Sgt Green, who was a POW after being shot down on the night of 15-16 August after carrying out a raid on an aircraft factory in Milan.

Irrespective of the claims made by the crews after that first operation, it had already become apparent to some senior officers in Bomber Command that night bombing was largely ineffective. Accurate bombing required that the target be found, although initially, lacking the sophisticated navigational aids of later years, finding the correct target presented major difficulties. Crews were under strict instructions from the Air Ministry as to where they could drop their bombs, and notwithstanding the inherent dangers of landing with a fused bomb load, doing just that was not an uncommon occurrence at that time. Navigation in the early part of the war relied on dead reckoning and the visual observation of landmarks, railway lines, rivers, lakes and coastlines. Sextants could be used if the night was clear enough, but accurate weather information over Europe was simply non-existent and as a result the "Weather" became the controlling factor. Frequently, when cloud obscured the target, bombs were dropped on an ETA basis, which meant that a navigational calculation was used to estimate the supposed time of arrival over the bombing area, and given the limitations of the Met information available about the weather over Europe, the accuracy of this method was often suspect. In fact, even when flying by day over cloud, dead reckoning (calculation of position by reference to compass course, ground speed and drift due to the wind), had a margin of error of at least 50 miles. The occasional vague definition of alternate targets as, "any military objective which can be identified as such", perhaps recognised the problem, although assessing the extent of damage inflicted beyond the description "large fires and explosions" was practically impossible.

The aircraft with which 10 Sqn was equipped at that time was the Merlin powered Whitley V, which cruised at about 180mph. When carrying a bomb load of 3,000lb it had a range of 1,650 miles, and although an improvement over the Mark IV, it still had its problems. The crews, notwithstanding their layers of clothing, had to withstand the intense cold for periods of up to eight hours and sometimes even longer. The cold froze any food and drink even as it was being consumed, and with the sanitary arrangements relying on a chemical lavatory or a bottle, any form of comfort was almost impossible. The air gunner in the rear turret, apart from being isolated from the rest of the crew, had possibly the most dangerous position and certainly the coldest. In an attempt to improve matters they wore a one-piece sheep-skin suit containing plugs for heated gloves and boots, which when connected to the aircraft's power system, gave some form of extra warmth – when they worked! With only very basic anti-icing systems the aircraft surfaces iced up and control became increasingly difficult. Radios had a very restricted range and were constantly breaking down; the generators were not up to the demands placed on them and the oxygen supply was often insufficient for long, high altitude flights. Adding to the difficulty, particularly with targets at the limit of aircraft range, was the long return trip over hostile territory, along with the fact that the prevailing westerly winds often meant that an aircraft took longer to return home than it had taken to do the outward trip. Fog, low cloud and industrial pollution, encountered by many on return from raids made it difficult to locate the homing beacons at base. Unfortunately, this meant that many crashes were caused when aircraft ran out of fuel while searching for a landing ground. In addition to the beacon,

Leeming, like many other airfields, used "glim lamps" along the edges of the landing ground, and though the pin-points of light were not as visible as the older gooseneck paraffin flares they were still a welcome sight for many returning crews. However, the distances involved in returning to Leeming, meant that many aircraft, frequently lacking sufficient fuel to reach home, landed at whatever was the nearest base to their point of crossing the English coast. Unfortunately, as a number of crews found to their cost, locating the "coast" was not always that easy, with some crews who were lost without trace possibly flying past the UK, sometimes even across it, without ever realising their position. Happily for one crew from 10 Sqn who had lost their way while returning from a raid on Berlin, they survived unhurt after coming down in the Irish Sea following more than 12 hours in the air, and then were doubly fortunate in being rescued soon afterwards by a trawler which happened to be in the vicinity. When appraising all of the difficulties and dangers faced by the crews, it can be seen that even after combating many of the aforementioned problems, when they reached the Vale of York the danger, especially in bad weather, was still acute, and without a wireless fix – a common occurrence with the unreliable equipment of the day – "letting down" could be extremely unnerving. The position of RAF Leeming, sited between the North Yorkshire Moors and the Yorkshire Dales, was guaranteed to make a return through cloud or bad weather an extremely risky business. This then would be the final hurdle from a list of many harsh realities that were faced by the crews from Leeming as they carried the war to the enemy during the latter half of 1940.

The morning after the first raid, indications of the *big picture* were brought home to those at Leeming by the request from 4 Group HQ for six aircraft to be held on stand-by for use in the event of the expected German invasion. These invasion alerts were to continue at frequent intervals until the end of October 1940, but following more closely behind the first alarm came the arrival on 22 July 1940, of a new CO for the Squadron, Wg Cdr S O Bufton.[1] Sid Bufton had escaped from France on 17 June at the time of the final French collapse and made his first appearance to the adjutant of 10 Sqn by climbing through the hangar window, having been unable to find the door!

For the remainder of July and into August 1940, the targets continued to be mainly industrial: oil refineries and storage tanks, aircraft factories, power stations, marshalling yards, airfields etc, located in such places as Bremen, Hamburg, Wismar (Dornier factory), Dortmund and Essen (Krupps armaments). In the same category, Operation Orders 10 (13 August), 15 (24 August), and 16 (26 August), detailed the plans for attacks further afield on Milan (Caproni Aircraft Works) and Turin (Fiat Aircraft Factory). At this time, Whitleys were the only aircraft available with sufficient range to reach Italy from the UK, but even so they were only able to carry a light bomb load and they had to operate from a forward base such as Abingdon. The Milan Operation on 24 August 1940, was fairly typical of the period, and of the 10 aircraft supplied by Leeming: three returned early because of mechanical problems, one abandoned the mission because of a misread signal, five attacked various targets in Italy (one of which was identified as Sesto Calende), which left just one crew to claim an attack on Milan itself. Fortunately, notwithstanding the problems encountered on the raid, on this occasion all aircraft returned safely to an assortment of airfields in the South of England. The assessment of the debrief must have looked at the operation in general terms because the official view was that the raid had met with limited success, but even that appraisal must be debatable.

One variation from the industrial type of target attacked at that time is worthy of mention, if only for the frequency that another type of target was pursued. On 24 July 1940, nine Whitleys from 10 Sqn were detailed to join in the attack on Hamburg harbour where the brand new German battleship, "Bismarck", was lying accompanied by the large merchant ships, "Europa" and "Bremen". As an alternative there was the "Tirpitz", berthed at Wilhelmshaven. The aircraft were bombed up with 4 x 500lb and 6 x 250lb semi-armour piercing bombs and the crews were advised that:

> ... The best bombing height was 6000 ft to get reasonable penetration with greatest accuracy. If conditions permit, bombs are to be dropped in two sticks, spacing 30 yards. Best angle of approach 30° to 45° to fore and aft line of ship.

This procedure, although ideal in theory, clearly forgot that the Germans would be involved, and its implementation was ruined by the one factor which could not be predicted with any accuracy. This of course was the weather, and on that day it was decidedly unpleasant with heavy cloud, electrical storms and severe icing. The raid was not a success although all nine aircraft were able to return safely to RAF Leeming, because only one, piloted by Plt Off Parsons,[2] was able to locate and attack any of the targets given. This was the harbour at Wilhelmshaven where the Tirpitz was lying, although he only found the port after the flares he dropped on dead reckoning caused the ground defences to open fire. On investigation Wilhemshaven was identified, but owing to the weather conditions the bombs were dropped in a single attack and no results were observed.

Occasionally, additional *sideshows* were added to the main bombing operations. Like most of the other bomber squadrons, 10 Sqn had taken part in many "Nickel" operations where leaflets, using varying forms of propaganda, were dropped in the rather vain hope of undermining the morale of the German people. It must be remembered that at this time the German forces had been totally victorious in almost every venture, and the leaflets themselves must have had little or no effect on the troops or the civilian population. In fact, after the war when discussing the value of the nickel raids, *Bomber* Harris, went on to say that the purpose they chiefly served was:

> . . . to supply the Continent's requirements of toilet paper for the five long years of war.

This perhaps was a little simplistic, because as the war wore on the effect would have become more marked, but the RAF never had much belief in the value of the leaflets. The real benefit obtained from these raids was recognised in the training that crews received in the much neglected art of night flying, skills that were steadily being built up for use in the four engined bombers being built at that time. Propaganda was considered important though, and an even more obscure exercise in this aspect of the war was carried out in the autumn of 1940, when 10 Sqn crews, in an attempt to show that Britain was not suffering from shortages, threw bags of tea out over occupied countries whilst on raids to other areas!

Then on 11 August 1940, while engaged in attacks on Krefeld and Remscheid, the Squadron was required to exercise one of the war's slightly more exotic ideas – a "Razzle" operation. The smallest incendiary device developed then deployed operationally was a type given this codename, and it was probably the least successful, depending upon phosphorus pellets drying out and igniting spontaneously. The objects to be dropped consisted of a sandwich of two sheets of celluloid about 3 inches by 1 inch, with a piece of phosphorus surrounded by damp cotton-wool sandwiched between them. When the cotton-wool dried out the phosphorus began to smoulder and eventually ignited the celluloid, which would then burn fiercely for about 10 seconds. This device was rushed into production during the summer of 1940 in time to attack the German harvest.[3] The theory was, that if dropped in woodland or cornfields, they would set fire to the surrounding vegetation, which would not only deprive the German economy of valuable timber or grain but might also destroy hidden supply depots and ammunition dumps. Burning time was increased in the device codenamed "Decker", by introducing latex rubber into the sandwich and increasing the size to a four inch square. They were carried to the target in tins of alcohol and water, each containing about 500 leaves and dropped by being poured down the flare chutes. German reports indicated that Razzle burnt out very quickly but Decker burned fiercely for up to 15 minutes – once they dried out. This fact gave the local population time to search and collect the leaves before they had time to ignite. A considerable number were dropped, but despite reasonably dry conditions, apart from isolated fires, they were only a minor nuisance causing little damage to the Germans – except for those who might have pocketed one as a souvenir! In fact, German reports commented on the fact that their war effort benefitted from the salvaged latex rubber! Needless to say, this aspect of an operation was not a favourite pastime for the crews, since diverting over forest areas meant more time spent over enemy territory, and moreover, the loading of these devices occasionally caused fires in and around the aircraft. If this were not enough, they frequently got caught up in the tailplanes after emerging from the flare chutes, and often burst into flames after the landing! Fortunately, to the relief of the crews, this type of operation was soon abandoned and the stocks of Razzle and Decker were later used to supplement other incendiaries during raids on German cities.

Between August and October 1940, Bomber Command switched a large part of its effort to attacks on the German preparations for "Operation Sealion" – the invasion of Britain. This action was later styled, "The Battle of the Barges", where a series of raids on invasion ports and their surrounds were mounted with 10 Sqn taking part in a large number of them. Examples of the diversity of such raids found in the Operation Records are:

14 Sep – Raid against motor vessels and barges in Antwerp dock area.

30 Sep – Reich Air Ministry in Berlin.

7 Oct – Fokker aircraft factory in Amsterdam, Schipol aerodrome, railway yards at Dieppe and docks at Lorient, Le Havre and Cherbourg.

14 Oct – Synthetic oil plant in Stettin, oil refinery in Hamburg, Le Havre docks.

24 Oct – Hamburg shipbuilding yards.

The raids on all types of shipping continued into the winter, and although it has been estimated that only about one in eight of the invasion fleet had been destroyed by air attacks, Hitler's order for the dispersal of the armada assembled in the Channel ports,

... so that the loss of shipping space caused by enemy air attacks could be reduced to a minimum,

indicated that he had constantly been reminded that the RAF still possessed the power to strike.

All of this activity was not completed without loss. Casualties amongst experienced crews were mounting, and during October 1940 in an effort to give newly formed crews some much needed experience, Leeming Operation Orders began to list "Operations" and "Nursery Operations". The latter, later known as "Fresher Ops", were raids against less heavily defended or more accessible targets and were intended to give operational experience to inexperienced crews. However, this inexperience, when allied to the inherent difficulties of navigation, not to mention the intervention of the Germans, meant that the operations were not always a soft option, with at least three such unseasoned crews from 10 Sqn crashing while flying on Nursery missions. One of these came down in Wales, some two-and-a-half hours outbound to Lorient in France, another crashed

into high ground in the fells of Westmorland when returning from Le Havre, and the third, returning with its bombs after failing to find Dunkirk, crashed into a house at the edge of Leeming airfield after avoiding a collision with another aircraft. A total of three crew members were killed in these wrecks and another seven were injured, but with the many faults inherent to the Whitley considering the nature of the crashes, all of the survivors must have blessed the fact that its structural strength was a major factor in their survival.

The dangers of wartime flying were also brought home to the people of Leeming village during that first winter of operations from the new base which was literally just over the fence from their dwellings. A Whitley, taking off on a training flight a few days before Christmas 1940, hit a house in Greengate Lane, and Barbara Huggins, the five year old daughter of the household, was killed by falling masonry. Also killed was one of the crew, but the parents of the little girl escaped with only slight injuries when they were flung into the garden by the force of the crash. Naturally, they were severely shocked by the disaster which had befallen them and moved away from the area soon afterwards.

Before the end of 1940, 10 Sqn had taken part in some of the *Propaganda* raids on Berlin that stemmed from an attack on London, later to be discovered as accidental. The error had occurred on the night of 24/25 August 1940 when bombs were dropped for the first time on the British Capital, arousing in the War Cabinet an immediate demand for a retaliatory raid on Berlin, particularly in the face of Goering's promise that no bombs would ever fall on that city. Thus, on the very next night, the first bombing raid on Berlin took place, and although little material damage was done the psychological effect was immediate and several more raids of this sort were made in the ensuing weeks. The first major raid on Berlin was then launched on 30 September 1940 with the primary objective of disrupting civilian life as much as possible by the destruction of some of the city's power supplies. A total of 42 aircraft took part, including 12 Whitleys from 10 Sqn, with the Squadron mission report recording that two aircraft attacked the Reich Air Ministry, another, the Potsdam Power Station, and two more, the West Power Station; the remainder bombed the marshalling yards at Scharenburg or the BMW aero engine factory. In carrying out this raid the crews from Leeming had anything but an easy time of it; one Whitley had to return early when the rear turret became unserviceable, one landed at Pembrey in S Wales, one at Abingdon near Oxford, six landed in Norfolk, (five at Watton and one at Marham), with only one managing to return to base direct from the operation. What was worse was the loss of two aircraft, T4130 crashed in Germany,[4] and another N1483, became lost, eventually coming down in the Irish Sea.[5]

Losses were beginning to mount during the autumn of 1940, and on 14 November, the Squadron lost one of its most experienced crews when Sqn Ldr Ferguson's aircraft went missing. It was a particularly heavy blow, because not only was he the senior Flight Commander but he appeared to have a charmed life. He, along with Sgts Rogers and Fraser who were lost with him, had been rescued some two months earlier after the ditching of their aircraft in the North Sea. This had quickly been followed by another lucky escape when they were forced to parachute from their stricken bomber when it ran out of fuel over Northumberland after an operation which had lasted for more than 11 hours. Unfortunately there was to be no good news in the days that followed, and with no trace of the aircraft ever being found, its crew, like many to follow, have no known grave. Since suffering its first loss after arriving at Leeming, 10 Sqn had lost at that stage a total of 17 aircraft, and the incidence of aircraft failing to return had reached a point where the Squadron was losing an aircraft for every 17 sorties mounted. This toll would be far exceeded in the future, but with most of the crews knowing each other well, some since pre-war days, each loss was

made that much more painful. The loss of Ferguson's crew would have hit hard, as would the loss of Flt Lt Phillips and his crew who failed to return from a mission to Stuttgart on the night of 21/22 October 1940. He was very experienced, had been awarded the DFC and had only recently returned to operations following serious injuries sustained in a crash in June. The Whitley, still carrying its bombs, crashed in open country near the medieval town of Schwabisch Hall and exploded on impact, killing the crew of five. The loss was later found to have given rise to an unusually chivalrous gesture by the Germans, as the crew was buried with full military honours in the presence of officers and a ceremonial party from the local airfield headquarters.

Following the formation of a Photographic Reconnaissance Flight equipped with Spitfires on 16 November 1940, it soon became evident that the accuracy of night bombing was considerably less than had been supposed. Priority had already been given to the development of navigational and bomb aiming equipment, but before those aids became available, the Government's "Area Bombing Directive" was instituted. This was the term used to describe an operation where a concentration of a large number of aircraft would all bomb a comparatively easily identifiable target. Bomber Command was therefore instructed to find and bomb targets in a selection of industrial centres where, even if a stick of bombs missed the primary target, they might still inflict damage on other worthwhile objectives in the vicinity. The bombing of Coventry in November 1940 had removed the restriction of avoiding the enemy's populated areas, but there was still no official intention of indulging in indiscriminate bombing. Notwithstanding this fact, more and more people were beginning to harbour the feeling that a more ruthless approach towards the bombing of Germany was imminent, and this idea could perhaps have been seen at Leeming. Gp Capt Staton was known to pin photographs of bombed English cities, such as London and

Coventry, to the walls in the briefing room while exhorting the crews to return the destruction with interest.

Mannheim was selected as the target for the first of these raids, and on the night of 11 December 1940, the largest number of aircraft sent out thus far by Bomber Command left their bases in England. The total of 134 aircraft, which included 33 Whitleys, three of which were from Leeming, carried out an attack on the city. The aircraft from Leeming returned safely, but the original optimism shown by the crews, and accepted by their Commanders, was somewhat dampened by the photo-reconnaissance photographs which showed that many of the incendiaries used as markers had been dropped outside the target area, with a high proportion of the bomb loads being aimed at these.

By the end of 1940, 10 Sqn had produced 94 Operation Orders for bombing missions of which about 23 had been cancelled, mainly because of bad weather. In fact, this, the first winter of Leeming's operational life, produced some of the worst weather of which the Vale of York is capable: snow, sleet and many days of continuous rain. As a consequence, when it was all added to the high water table of the Station, the airfield was turned into a quagmire, producing an increasing incidence of aircraft being bogged down to their axles in mud when being refuelled, loaded with bombs, or even when taxiing. In these circumstances, a caterpillar tractor had to be used to rescue the aircraft, and the winter was such that it was kept in regular use. The whole perimeter around which the aircraft were dispersed became churned up by the servicing vehicles, and unless the ground was actually frozen, then prior to a raid aircraft again had to be flown off, usually to Linton-on-Ouse, for fuel and bombs. All of these problems caused a slowing down of the rate of operations, so, bearing in mind the fact that the crews usually wished to complete their obligatory thirty operations as soon as possible, and knowing that the whole performance would probably have

to be repeated the following day, a decision to "scrub" an operation because of the weather was never very popular. Life was certainly made very difficult for all concerned, and in order to keep the aircraft serviceable the groundcrews worked exhaustingly long hours in the foulest of conditions with little protection from the elements. Their Group Commander, Air Vice-Marshal A "Mary" Coningham, (later to achieve great distinction while commanding the Desert Air Force and then the 2nd TAF from D-Day to the end of the war in Europe), was one individual who made no secret of his appreciation of their work, as can be seen from his reaction to a suggestion put forward in October 1940 by the head of Bomber Command. This was to the effect that aircrew should be further recognised by the award of operational chevrons, but far from agreeing with the idea Coningham considered that it would in fact only add to what he saw as the trend towards the glamorising of aircrews. Within the Service, they already received a great deal of preferential treatment and certainly were given the almost undivided attention of the press, but "Mary" felt that with the bombing of airfields also putting the groundcrew at risk, any further discrimination between the two groups would possibly alienate the people on whom his aircrew depended so much. His opposition to the idea was mirrored by other group commanders, and the proposal was dropped, but a counter-proposal put forward by him, stating that the efforts of all including the airwomen, who operated from an operational base should be acknowledged with a similar award of chevrons, was in itself not taken up by the Air Ministry. It was also at this time that he made the proposal that the aircraft on the strength of his squadrons should be increased from 16 to 24 aircraft, with a corresponding increase in crew numbers. His reasoning, perhaps still valid in the post cold-war RAF, stemmed from criticism from Churchill relating to the financial cost of operating the airfields, and was a way in which he saw that the personnel on each base could be used more effectively. It would also have saved the use of airfields and base stations, as well as giving more authority to junior commanders, but history shows that the Air Ministry did not follow this line of argument, but instead increased the number of available squadrons.

Prior to the onset of the bad weather, the airfield had withstood some fairly heavy punishment from aircraft movements, and apart from the first attack on British railway systems which caused damage to the track at Northallerton five days after the Station opened, plus a brief visit from enemy raiders on their way somewhere else in November, RAF Leeming had thus far been free from air-raids. So, notwithstanding the threats from Lord Haw-Haw, it was partially as a result of this lack of attention from the Germans that Leeming had been recognised as a logical locale for the training of newly forming squadrons or even for those converting to a different aircraft type.

The first of these temporary visitors was No.7 Squadron, which when re-formed at Leeming on 1 August 1940, became the first squadron in the Second World War to be equipped and operate with a four-engined bomber. To these ends it received its first Stirling Mk1 in September, and there followed a great deal of work-up flying to find out what this new bomber could do, as well as to prepare the aircraft and crews for operations. One of these aircraft (N3640), captained by Fg Off T Bradley DFC, did not return from a cross-country navigational flight, coming down at Hodge Branding in Lancashire on 29 September 1940. The Stirling had been hit and severely damaged by anti-aircraft fire whilst over the Isle of Man, just making it back to the mainland. The aircraft, which could not maintain altitude, crash-landed and was wrecked after ploughing through a stone wall. Soon after this crash, in October 1940, the Squadron began its move to its operational base at Oakington, and from there on the night of 10/11 February 1941, the Stirlings made their first bombing attack against the enemy on oil storage tanks at Rotterdam.

From Driffield, No.102 Squadron, equipped with the Whitley Mk V, alighted briefly at RAF Leeming during August and early September 1940 while en route to its new base at Prestwick for a short term loan to Coastal Command. Whilst at Leeming, the Squadron only flew on training missions but still had fatalities when it lost one aircraft which crashed on the moors near Keighley in Yorkshire. The burial of Sgt Harrison, the observer of that aircraft, in the Leeming village churchyard of St John the Baptist was to be the first of many such military funerals that Leeming personnel carried out in the area. The graves, marked during the war years with a simple wooden cross, were adopted in the Leeming churchyard by local children who, in addition to tending the graves, often helped ease the pain of loss by writing to the relatives of the dead. A small gesture perhaps, but in some cases it went further developing into regular correspondence where for many years to come all manner of anniversaries were remembered.

In October 1940 the Blenheims of 219 Sqn left Leeming to return to Catterick, but it was not to be long before another squadron took its place. The task however of No.35 Squadron was not to be one of hunting German raiders. Although it had been used as a training squadron at the beginning of the war, when it arrived at Leeming on 20 November 1940 it was for the express purpose of introducing to the RAF the second of the new four-engined bombers, namely the Handley Page Halifax. Again the stay was not to be a long one, because after some necessary conversion training and flying, the Squadron, now at full strength, moved to its operational base at Linton-on-Ouse on 5 December 1940.

There was at this time, and throughout the war, occasional cryptic mention of Army units at the Station, such as in September 1940, 697 Coy RE. This is possibly related to the fact that at the beginning of the war, the Army had taken over Newton House, later to be known as Northern Command Technical School. In addition, from the outset until the early part of 1942, the Station used army personnel in various static defence posts, including that of anti-aircraft protection. However, even after the RCAF had taken over, there were always Army personnel on the established strength of Leeming.

All in all for those who operated from Leeming when the airfield was closed in January 1941 it was not before time. It was not the best time of the year for construction but contractors worked for the next three months in laying concrete to build three runways, along with dispersal areas around the perimeter. During this period, 10 Sqn aircraft still continued on operations, but flew to Linton-on-Ouse, Topcliffe, or Dishforth, for bombing-up purposes. Consequently, empty beds and table places in the Messes continued to be salutary reminders that the war was still affecting Leeming. The need to return "home" after an operation was in itself still a hazardous undertaking, as the crew of T4231 would have confirmed in February of that year. They had returned with a full bomb load from an abortive raid on Boulogne, then had to land on a snow covered airfield! The upshot was that the rough landing caused the undercarriage to collapse, and although the crew were not hurt in the subsequent toboggan ride the aircraft was badly damaged. However, routine still held sway in many areas; experts came and went, giving briefings on such matters as escaping, actions and tactics for use against enemy fighters, searchlights or flak, with even someone to lecture them on the importance of their raids against oil targets. Even Trenchard himself came to talk to the crews who gave him a great reception when they were gathered in a large group to meet the great man outside one of the hangars.

Through the spring and summer of 1941, the Squadron's Whitleys continued to take part in Bomber Command's strategic and tactical offensive against Germany. Raids were made on the Ruhr industrial area, or "Happy Valley" as it was known; to Berlin and Mannheim, but the disastrous losses of merchant ships in the "Battle of the Atlantic" led to a concentration on U-boat bases, naval installations and shipyards. Operation Orders began to sound quite colourful with the introduction of code names for the various targets, eg "Salmon" (Bremen), "Kipper" (Wilhelmshaven), "Minnow" (Kiel), "Whitebait" (Berlin), and with some feeling, "Toads" (the Battle Cruisers at Brest). The destinations however, were not at all as pleasant as they sounded and 10 Sqn had a long and bloody summer. In the period June through August 1941, 10 Sqn flew 280 sorties on 36 operations and lost 20 aircraft with 84 men killed or missing. From that figure only 16 had been taken prisoner, but of these two would later be shot by German police after escaping. In addition, there would have been further casualties in those aircraft that returned with battle damage, with the subsequent visual effect adding to the impact that the losses were having on morale. Bomber Command had a system that required aircrew to fly on a tour of 30 operations, followed by a break and a second tour of 20 raids, at which point an individual could request a posting from the Command. It could be seen from the total of crews involved, that if the aircraft loss rate went above four per cent, the mathematical chances were such that the level of experience could decrease to a level where there would be an inadequate number of crews surviving their first tour of operations to provide the *backbone* for the rapidly increasing number of freshly trained reinforcements. The losses sustained by 10 Sqn during that summer exceeded 7.1 per cent!

The Germans themselves had not been idle over North Yorkshire during the spring of that year, with RAF Leeming being attacked by enemy aircraft on 1 April 1941, when approximately 15 bombs were dropped; damage was confined to the MT Section, and it was considered that the Station had got off lightly. A decoy sight situated at Maunby Demesne on the east bank of the Swale between the villages of Gatenby and Maunby assisted in this "escape" when one raider mistook its lights for those of Leeming and unloaded a stick of bombs into the open fields. A further raid two days later saw eight bombs come down on the area of the landing ground, but these too caused little damage and the new runways were relatively unscathed. It was also in April that Wg Cdr Bufton had moved on from 10 Sqn to become Commanding Officer of No.76 Squadron, then at West Raynham but shortly to move to Linton-on-Ouse. He was replaced as the CO of 10 Sqn by Wg Cdr V B Bennett, and by September 1941 the Squadron had received its 200th Operation Order, having had little or no respite since its arrival at Leeming some 15 months before. However, many were hoping that this situation was about to be improved, if only slightly, because on 5 September 1941 No.77 Squadron, coded "KN", arrived at Leeming.

No.77 Squadron

The Squadron had been formed at Edinburgh on 1 October 1916, and had spent the remainder of the war in Scotland as a "Home Defence"

Squadron, until its disbandment in 1919. It was reformed at Finningley in June 1937, but when the war began the Squadron was flying the Whitley bomber and operating out of Driffield. Much of its early role was in the dropping of propaganda leaflets and it was not until the spring of 1940 that it began bombing in earnest.

The new arrival, like 10 Sqn, had considerable experience over enemy territory with No.4 Group Bomber Command, and the crews from 77 Sqn wasted no time in getting into action with their first operational sorties taking place on the night of 6/7 September, when they accompanied 10 Sqn on what was originally planned as a raid on Berlin. In the event of a problem with the primary target there were at the time other choices, some of which included those that went under the broad headings: "Self Evident Military Objective" – SEMO, "Military Objective Previously Attacked" – MOPA, "Any Military Objective" – AMO, and "Any Invasion Port" – AIP. On this particular night the town of Huls, a centre for synthetic rubber, received the bombs, but with five Whitleys failing to return it was a disaster for Leeming and a harsh introduction to the Station for 77 Sqn. It suffered the loss of three of the missing aircraft, although five crewmen survived from one of them crash landing in England.

In truth, the tasking placed on two squadrons did not usually mean much of a reduction in the number of operations that were placed on one. Typically it only meant that twice the number of aircraft were involved, but at least the load was seen to be shared. It was not surprising though, that the arrival of a second squadron meant that the station became overcrowded and really began to *burst at the seams*. To help alleviate this problem, aircrew SNCOs had been moved into the terraced married quarters, which was a method of billeting that continued throughout the tenure of the RCAF. Each crew shared a house, each house being basically the same; a parlour in front, a kitchen-come-scullery in the back and two small bedrooms and a bathroom upstairs. The parlour was also used as a bedroom, with each room usually being shared by two members of the same crew. The houses were gloomy and cold with none of the comforts of home. Although there were small fireplaces where fires could be lit to provide heat, wood was practically non-existent, and coal rationed to one galvanised wash-tub-full per week – officially that is!

Notwithstanding the reality of the situation, the arrival of 77 Sqn should have meant that 10 Sqn could have hoped to gain at least some relief from operations while it embarked upon the conversion of its crews to the Halifax BII under yet another Commanding Officer. Wg Cdr Bennett was promoted to Group Captain on 3 September 1941, and posted to command Dishforth, with his place being taken by Wg Cdr J A H Tuck. He arrived with the instruction that the conversion was to be completed by December 1941, and despite the demands that the training placed on everyone, he made sure that 10 Sqn remained operational throughout the period continuing to work in conjunction with 77 Sqn. The Squadrons settled down to the almost routine missions to familiar targets: Rostock, Berlin, Kiel, Cherbourg, Le Havre, to name but a few. Their conversion to the Halifax completed, the first and second sorties planned for the crews of 10 Sqn on 8 and 11 December 1941 were cancelled because of weather conditions, but eventually on 18 December 1941, on an operation codenamed "Veracity", six Halifaxes left Leeming to join a force that was to attack the German Battlecruisers lying in Brest. Not the luckiest of COs, Wg Cdr Tuck, flying in an aircraft sporting his *Friar Tuck* motif had to jettison his bombs in Filey Bay after hydraulic faults caused the undercarriage to stick down. That was to be the only problem for 10 Sqn that day because the remaining aircraft reached their target and returned safely for a landing at Boscombe Down. Operation "Veracity II" soon followed, but out of the six aircraft prepared by 10 Sqn, one became unserviceable before take-off, and a second had to abort following a coolant leak

from an engine. A total of 14 aircraft took part in the raid, but this time they found that the Germans were ready with their smoke screens and were also putting a great deal of flak into the air during the bombing runs. One of the aircraft from Leeming, R9374, lost an engine from this fire before an attack from a German fighter killed the rear gunner and put a further two engines out of action. The Halifax gradually lost height and was finally ditched by the pilot, Flt Sgt Whyte, some 80 miles from the Cornish coast, with the surviving crew being rescued some hours later. The Luftwaffe were out in strength that day, and with most of the small attacking force returning with varying degrees of damage, it was fortunate that the raid was escorted by Spitfires. The bombers themselves were not totally defenceless, and Sergeant Porritt, the rear gunner of R9370, proved himself to be a real sting in the tail of his aircraft by shooting down one Me109. Although slightly wounded he later drove off attacks made by another two fighters while the escort disposed of yet two more. He was later awarded the DFM.

Attacks on these targets, the Scharnhorst and Gneisenau, continued during the next two months until finally on 12 February 1942, a maximum effort, codenamed "Operation Fuller", was mounted with 242 aircraft attacking in three waves. The raid was massively hampered by bad weather, and of the seven Halifaxes from 10 Sqn that took part, only one was able to attack the ships. This ratio was reflected over the whole attacking force, and as a consequence little harm was done to the enemy, apart from making it obvious to them that their ships were extremely vulnerable. This meant that within a matter of days orders to sail were given, and under cover of sea mist the two great ships, along with their escorts, escaped almost undetected through the Straits of Dover to a more secure haven in Germany. The move did not mean that the RAF would give up in its attempts to sink or damage the German capital ships, but the distances involved meant that attacks had to be made at night, and without fighter cover. Attacks by aircraft from Bomber Command were carried out frequently, and late in February in one of the operations against the port of Wilhelmshaven, 77 Sqn lost three of its aircraft with only one survivor from the 15 crew members lost. In years to come the loss of these aircraft was to achieve an element of prominence when there was a very emotional postscript to the death of one of those brave men. In 1986 a young man named Carl Field, was engaged in examining the loss of a Whitley bomber, Z9280, and while visiting the site of the crash he found a crushed cigarette lighter, a coin, along with a gold wedding ring. Inquiries into the origin of these items discovered that the ring was the wedding band of Sgt Wilfrid Whittham, the WOP/AG of the Whitley. Further investigation found that the wife had since died, but his daughter, born just after Sgt Whittham had been killed, was traced and invited to the Netherlands to collect the ring.

The fact that there was often as much danger in training as there was in actual operations was once again brought starkly home on 29 December 1941, when a Halifax taking off on a night training exercise chose the wrong runway and collided with a second being flown by Wg Cdr Tuck, who was taking-off on an air test. Both aircraft were destroyed, with two of the crew killed in the first bomber and a total of five others injured. The collision blocked the runway, which meant that the operation planned for 77 Sqn had to be cancelled. This accident was then followed at the beginning of 1942 with a reminder that danger did not only lurk in the skies, when Plt Off MacMillan of 77 Sqn walked into a spinning airscrew which caused severe injuries to his left arm.

A further German warship that figured large in No 10 Squadron's Operation Orders was the Tirpitz, an extremely powerful and fast battleship, which presented a real and deadly threat to British shipping in the North Atlantic and especially to the convoys to Russia. Consequently, in January 1942 a detachment of Halifaxes and Stirlings was sent north to Lossiemouth for a highly secret operation against the target lying in Aasen Fjord near Trondheim, in Norway. The initial attack failed to trouble the Tirpitz, but during the next three months, varying numbers of Halifaxes from 10 Sqn were amongst those detached for a few days of "Special Operations" at what was termed "an advanced base", with the battleship as their objective. In the spring of 1942, there had been a change of Squadron Commanders at Leeming, with an Australian, Wg Cdr D C T Bennett who had taken over 77 Sqn only in December, being told in April to take over at 10 Sqn. Whilst commanding 77 Sqn, Bennett had led several raids himself, including one from Wattisham on 12 April to attack Genoa and Turin, from which all 14 aircraft returned safely. Thus it was he who led the 10 Sqn detachment of 11 aircraft which left Leeming for Lossiemouth on 23 April for another *crack* at the Tirpitz. It had been estimated that with the ship anchored about 15 yards from the shore it would be possible to roll some special mines down the sloping sides of the fjord and into the water beneath it; fitted with hydrostatic fuses the mines should then go off underneath the Tirpitz and rupture the relatively vulnerable lower hull. To enable this form of attack to meet with some degree of success, the Halifaxes, starting at an altitude of 2000ft then had to descend on a timed run so that they reached the dropping point at a height of 200ft. Each aircraft was loaded with four of these special 1000lb mines, which, as they would not quite fit into the bomb bay caused the Halifaxes to fly with the bomb doors partly open, with the induced drag causing a reduction in the speed and range of the aircraft. In March, Bomber Command had already lost six Halifaxes, including two from 10 Sqn, and the ORB shows that the raid that took place on 27/28 April 1942, caused a further two losses to the Leeming Squadron. It also shows that on 3 May, and without explanation, Wg Cdr J B Tait was appointed as the Commanding Officer of 10 Squadron vice Wg Cdr Bennett. This was the only indication that one of the aircraft shot down (W1041) had contained the CO of the Squadron and that he was missing. However, the appointment turned out to be somewhat premature. It was soon discovered that the Tirpitz had been sheltered by a thick smoke screen, and was extremely difficult to identify, never mind hit. In addition this sort of raid against a single target in the confines of a fjord was not an ideal role for a heavy bomber. Consequently, in an attempt to spot the ship, Bennett had taken his Halifax down to about 200 feet and had been repeatedly hit by the intense barrage of flak. With his starboard wing burning fiercely, and with no chance of dropping his bombs, the only hope for his crew was for him to get back as much height as he could to allow everyone to bale out. This he succeeded in doing, so when the aircraft finally crashed, all of the crew had escaped by parachute. Three, including the badly wounded tail gunner, were captured, but the Wing Commander had encountered Sgt Forbes, his wireless operator, and the two of them had struggled for three days through thick snow before eventually arriving in Sweden, where in the internment camp they found another two members of their crew. Although neither the Swedish authorities nor the British representative in Stockholm seemed in much of a hurry to arrange repatriation, Bennett made such a nuisance of himself that he was flown back to England. The flight was in broad daylight at low level in a Lockheed Electra piloted by a Norwegian pilot, and it was an experience that the Wing Commander admitted as being one of the most nerve wracking trips he had ever made. He was back at RAF Leeming within five weeks of the day he had left, but two months later he was appointed to direct his energies towards the formation of the Pathfinder Force which he continued to command until the end of the war.

One of the "gadgets" to be used by the Pathfinder Force had been introduced into squadron service in March 1942. Codenamed "GEE", it used synchronised radio pulses sent out from three radio stations about 100 miles apart,

and a receiver in the bomber allowed a navigator to see the time differences in the reception of each. The results were plotted on a GEE Map and the point where the lines intersected was the position of the aircraft. Range was about 200 miles and though GEE was an excellent new aid to navigation, it could also be used as a means of bombing blind through cloud or of homing to base; the latter attribute it was hoped would decrease the number of crashes caused by navigational errors on the way home. However, it was not the bombing aid for specific targets that people had hoped for. (An aid was sorely needed, as was shown in September 1941, when photographic interpretation indicated that only one in three crews claiming to have scored hits had bombed within five miles of the target, but the bombers had much longer to wait for the more sophisticated "H2S"[6] and "OBOE" devices.)

This, the first of the much needed radar navigation aids had reached the aircraft of 10 Sqn in limited numbers, but since there was only a small number of aircraft fitted with GEE, a bombing technique called "Shaker" was instituted which involved three waves to each attack. The first wave, equipped with GEE to determine the lead-in route and pinpoint with incendiaries, the second, also with the aid, to follow the patch blazed by the first and pinpoint the target itself with incendiaries, and the third without GEE, would then drop their bomb loads on this concentrated area of fire. On 3/4 March 1942, eight Halifaxes from 10 Sqn took part in a full scale operational trial of this method to find out whether the use of flares would light up the target for long enough to enable the following crews to identify it visually. The target selected was the Renault Factory at Billancourt near Paris, and the raid, which lasted for one hour and fifty minutes, was highly successful. There was an average concentration of 121 aircraft per hour over the target; 59 aircraft attacked the factory in one 10 minute period alone. Almost every building in the factory was destroyed or severely damaged and some 40 per cent of Renault machine tools were destroyed. All the Halifaxes from Leeming returned safely to base. At long last it seemed as if the odds in favour of the bombers' effectiveness were improving.

Further raids were carried out on the same principle. On 13/14 March both 10 and 77 Sqn took part in the third of these raids on Cologne which was reasonably successful. Lübeck was the target on 28/29 March and finally, for four consecutive nights 24-27 April 1942, Rostock was raided. RAF Leeming was represented by aircraft from 77 Sqn on all four raids to Rostock and were joined on the last night by aircraft from 10 Sqn. Records show that 77 lost an aircraft on the first and the last of these operations, and uncommonly, that each Whitley had dispensed with the need for a second pilot, operating with only four crew members.

The local population continued to be aware of the almost constant aerial activity at Leeming, but were reminded of the real proximity of the airfield to their homes when an aircraft from 77 Sqn returning from a Fresher operation to Boulogne crashed into Grimescar House, which was close to the eastern end of the East/West runway. The impact tore the roof from the house and caused the deaths of all five in the crew, but miraculously the members of the Hunter family, who were asleep in the house, were unhurt. When the wreckage had been cleared the roof was repaired by the RAF with the use of a tarpaulin, then by fitting asbestos panels, but the fact that the house was directly in the flight path and close to the end of the runway meant that its days were numbered, so when the Canadians took over the family living there was rehoused, and the house demolished.

The level of support needed to keep bomber stations such as Leeming in operation, especially during these periods of maximum effort, was staggering. The work load necessary for the preparation and repair of aircraft, meant that the dispersals and hangars at Leeming were a constant hive of activity, irrespective of the weather and at all times of the day. The distances involved meant that a bicycle was a necessity, and once at

the *frying pan* type dispersals the groundcrew often remained with only the most meagre of facilities. Hours were often long and hard, with breaks few and far between, with shelter often non-existent, or at best a tent or a shed, usually home-made. The airfield would have been a pleasant place to be when the weather was warm, but these shelters would have been more than welcome at those times when the groundcrew were soaked to the skin or blue with cold. To meet the task, fitters topped up oil tanks and removed cowlings, adjusted, tuned, and finally ran up the giant Merlin engines; riggers inspected the aircraft structure, checked out control runs and topped up hydraulic systems; electricians, instrument tradesmen and radio mechanics ran up their equipment, searching for faults. Petrol bowsers, usually the Matador which held 2,500 gallons, moved constantly between the fuel dump and the aircraft, where airmen waited to manhandle the refuelling hose onto the wings before pumping hundreds of gallons of 100-octane into the aircraft tanks. Armourers prepared the aircraft bomb bays and double-checked the release circuits, while in the bomb dump convoys of trolleys were loaded with bombs, incendiaries or mines, then towed, often by WAAF drivers, to the fusing sheds from whence they were taken to the bombers as they became serviceable. There the trolleys were manoeuvred by hand under the open bomb doors and the load carefully winched and crutched into place. The armament groundcrew worked particularly hard, working all hours, day in day out, whatever the weather. In normal circumstances they prepared and fused the bombs, loaded the aircraft, serviced the bomb carriage equipment, as well as the turrets with their machine guns, not to mention the replenishment of bomb dump stocks and the loading of tens of thousands of cartridges into ammunition belts. If things went to plan the preparation and loading of bombs weighing a total of 150 tons per day was not unusual, but when targets were changed, often at short notice, the load often had to be changed too. The armourers while trying to work against the clock, often in a tired, cold and wet condition, could without doubt say that their life could be particularly grim and often dangerous. In reality, life for everyone had its hazards, as one groundcrew team at Leeming in 1942 found to the cost for one of their number. They had just finished servicing a Halifax when the rear gunner inadvertently fired a burst from his four Browning machine-guns and seriously wounded one of the airmen. In preparing for a raid, the pressure was always on the groundcrew to complete their task quickly, irrespective of the weather or time of day. The process of loading the aircraft with its armament had its own dangers, with the bomb and incendiaries, as well as the photoflash flares, all spelling danger to the careless or unwary. One of the groundcrew with 10 Sqn at this time was Leading Aircraftsman M Griffin, a fitter of the Royal Australian Air Force who had been awarded the Distinguished Flying Medal, a decoration only very rarely awarded to non-aircrew personnel. In fact, the display of a ribbon for this decoration on the uniform of an LAC along with the lack of an aircrew brevet, would have almost certainly invited comment from those who were not aware that he was entitled to wear the ribbon![7]

Keeping his eye on all of the servicing activities was the ever present Flight Sergeant who like all of the groundcrew would look on a particular aircraft as his own. The aircrew knew this, and as a means of showing their gratitude for the way the team serviced their bomber, many of the crews would take *Chiefy* and his "gang" down to the village for a drink at the "Black Ox", the "Willow Tree" or the "Crown", or perhaps even to "Jock's Cafe" which was opposite the Willow Tree, but this time for "something" and chips. Recreation however, was not confined to visits to the pub, but with the lack of transport preventing regular trips to the surrounding area, a night out on the town in Northallerton meant hitch-hiking there and hopefully, the early milk train back. There was a great

deal of entertainment on the Station itself with for example, a *self-help show* such as "Dusty Miller's Concert Party starring The Leeming Lovelies", who were a group of WAAF girls as the chorus line. Needless to say they were very popular after they first appeared in April 1942.

In March of the same year, an entry had appeared in Station Routine Orders which must have seemed like the answer to many people's dreams. The order was to the effect that all personnel who had engineering experience could apply for demobilisation, which would then enable them to work for certain engineering companies as a civilian. Almost all of 77 Sqn applied; 50 were recommended from Leeming and 25 were accepted. LAC Bill Hird was one of those accepted and after being recalled from leave to be given the glad tidings, he cleared from the Station on 1 April and found he was to work for Westool at Dunstable, a firm that manufactured items of electrical equipment such as the gun firing solenoid for the rear turret of the Halifax. He also recollects that towards the end of 1943, he was recalled to the RAF and rejoined 77 Sqn as an LAC, where he found some of his old mates had long since been promoted to Sergeant!

Also in March 1942, Leeming was honoured by a visit from the King and Queen and it can be said that their stay, though a brief one, must have been quite memorable. On the morning of the 28th, which was the day of the visit, a pupil of No.10 Sqn Halifax Conversion Flight was flying solo and had to divert into Croft. It was considered prudent that a more experienced pilot should return with the aircraft so Flt Lt Stanley Wright set out to collect his pupil and fly back the Halifax. However, after he had set out on the short drive north, Murphy's Law began to rear its head when an experimental mine fell from an aircraft, delaying the Royal visit until the mine could be defused and moved. It finally meant that the whole programme was put back for more than an hour, but Wright, unaware of this, was flying back from Croft under the misapprehension that the visit was over. He had decided to arrive both low and fast and was coming in over the hangars when he saw a parade. Of course it was THE parade, with the King and Queen carrying out their inspection accompanied by an entourage of senior officers! It can be guessed what their reaction was and of course the following morning a chastened and somewhat apprehensive pilot was carpeted by the station commander, Gp Capt Graham, who summarily informed the young man that he was to be posted that very day.

The stage was now set for Air Marshal Harris's master stroke – an operation, soon to be termed the "Thousand Bomber Raid", where a massive and concentrated attack would be made on one target. However, before it took place 77 Sqn left Leeming for RAF Chivenor on 6 May 1942, leaving 10 Squadron as the Station's only operational squadron. The big raid was ordered for the night of 30 May; the target was Cologne; the code name "Millennium". Every available aircraft from every possible source was mustered, producing 1016 for the main raid and 50 for diversionary attacks. Security everywhere was very tight, with everyone confined to camp and even the telephone box by the guardroom at Leeming was sealed and secured with a large strap and a padlock. The Station provided 22 Halifaxes for the raid, of which 16 reached the target, four had aborted because of technical trouble, one bombed a diversionary target and one was reported missing. This was shot down by a night-fighter and though four of the crew escaped, the pilot and the two gunners were killed. In the aircraft flown by Sqn Ldr Ennis, one of the 10 Sqn flight commanders, the rear gunner, Sgt Groves, was wounded when the aircraft was hit by flak while it was coned in searchlights. While his pilot fought to evade the lights Groves sustained a severe leg wound as well as being blinded in one eye, but he continued to fire at the enemy positions. It was not until they were clear that the severity of his injuries became apparent, along with the fact that he was trapped in his turret. With a seriously wounded crewman

on board Ennis knew he would have to get the badly damaged Halifax back to a safe landing, which he finally did at Manston, Kent. Groves was quickly admitted to hospital, but though he survived his wounds he was not to fly on operations again.

The raid itself was considered by the planning staff to have been entirely successful and caused as much damage and devastation as all previous raids on German cities added together. What might have been of greater comfort to the Leeming crews, though to what degree is debateable, was the fact that their single loss that night amounted to 3.8 per cent of the attacking force as opposed to the 4.6 per cent they had averaged up to that time!

It was also during this raid on Cologne that by one of those ironies of fate, Flt Lt Wright, the pilot who had recently *buzzed* their Majesties and as a result had been posted to Marston Moor, was one of those who was shot down. If he had remained with the Conversion Flight at Leeming it is probable that he would not have gone on the raid – but who knows what would then have been in store for him? As it was, the error that put him in the aircraft that night was not to be a fatal one, as he parachuted to safety, was captured and sat out the rest of the war as a POW.

For the second Thousand Bomber Raid on Essen on 1 June 1942, Leeming contributed 18 aircraft of which three from 10 Sqn were posted missing, but because of cloud obscuring the target this attack was not considered successful. Smaller groups of aircraft, including some from 10 Sqn, followed up with raids on Essen on the nights of 2, 3, 5, 8 and 16 June, but the third Thousand Bomber Raid on 25 June saw 15 aircraft from Leeming take part in a raid on Bremen. It was noted that German night-fighters appeared for the first time and overall losses had climbed to 4.9 per cent, although 10 Sqn incurred no losses. Notwithstanding the success of these massive raids, since the strength of Bomber Command was still not increasing in proportion to its losses and with the transfer of some squadrons to other

Commands, this third raid was the last of what were termed the Thousand Bomber Raids for almost two years.

In a non-operational sense, the Station had already had an eventful year in the months leading up to June 1942, starting on 19 January with the arrival of a new Station Commander, Gp Capt Strang Graham whose personal history seemed to come from a "Boys Own" tale.[8] His arrival was followed by a series of VIP visits, with the most notable visitors being the King and Queen, who arrived on 28 March. Viscount Trenchard made a return visit on 10 May followed within a few days by the Prime Minister, Winston Churchill, accompanied by the Deputy Prime Minister, Clement Attlee. The Station was also honoured in April, though in a different and more permanent way, when King George VI conferred his authority on the use of the Station Badge, previously proffered for his approval. The Badge with the motto, "Straight and True", related to the description of a sword erect, the point uppermost and represented the fighting instincts of the squadrons stationed there.

In early 1942 the number of personnel on the Station had been increasing at an alarming rate, with the April strength figures of "Units whose

sick are being treated", giving some idea of the numbers (*see* Table 1)

When No 77 Squadron departed in May[9], the situation was eased somewhat, but from July 1942 there began a series of major moves that were to leave the Station in a state of turbulence for almost

Table 1

	COMMISSIONED	OTHER RANKS
SHQ RAF Leeming	37	727
2718(D) Squadron	5	322
WAAF	5	68
10 Squadron	3 + 31 aircrew	577 + 139 aircrew
77 Squadron	2 + 22 aircrew	526 + 111 aircrew
10 Conversion Flight	2	94
6 Works Flight Detach	–	71
Army	1	72
	55 + 53 aircrew	2457 + 250 aircrew

a year. On 2 July, 10 Sqn flew its last mission as a squadron from Leeming, losing one aircraft on a raid to Bremen and then prepared for a move to the Middle East for attachment to No.205 Group. The detachment of 16 aircraft and crews from Leeming, along with a similar transfer for 76 Sqn, was in reaction to the loss of Tobruk in North Africa: the surrender of which gave Rommel a major port through which he could supply his Africa Corps with the petrol and ammunition necessary to threaten Cairo and the Suez Canal. The order to move was at very short notice and it found Wg Cdr Bennett already tasked by Air Chief Marshal Harris with the setting up of a Pathfinder Force, so when the Squadron left on 5 and 6 July, it was with a new Commanding Officer, Wg Cdr Seymour-Price. Within days of the move, those who remained at Leeming quickly realised that the detachment was not to be a rest cure as word came back that one aircraft had been lost en route, with a second loss occurring very soon after getting there. In fact the detachment soon ceased to be two independent squadrons, first becoming No.249 Wing and later still being amalgamated into a single Squadron, finishing the war operating from Italy.

With the advent of the Royal Air Force Regiment, the anti-aircraft defence of Leeming had been given over to a unit initially identified as 2718(D), but on 17 July 1942, the task was officially handed over to No.2878 Sqn RAF Regt. The Station itself was beginning to "run-down" in importance, but crews of the few aircraft still remaining continued to make token contributions, with two or three aircraft occasionally being supplied to assist with operations over Germany. Yet again these had to be flown from another station, this time Topcliffe. The need for repairs to the main runway and its extension to the edge of Gatenby Lane had meant that work had to be started at the beginning of July, with the airfield becoming completely unserviceable by 11 August. The repair aspect of the work was long overdue, with crews and aircraft being increasingly put at risk by the condition of the landing surface. One instance in early April, had seen one of the Conversion Flight's aircraft touch down and hit a pothole in the runway, causing a tyre to burst, quickly followed by the collapse of the undercarriage. The aircrew were unhurt, but with the airfield in such a terrible state, the CO of 10 Sqn decided that enough was enough. He subsequently wrote an official complaint about the condition of the runway and insisted that work on it must be commenced at the earliest possible opportunity. It would have been interesting to have seen his reaction when he was informed by his opposite number in Station Headquarters that repair work was ongoing and had been for weeks!

THE EARLY CANADIANS

During the early summer of 1942, the rear party of 10 Sqn received word that they would be reinforced but at another station, and personnel soon began to move to their new base at Melbourne, a satellite of Pocklington near York. The move was completed by 18 August 1942, and their Conversion Flight joined them a week later, hopefully to a serviceable runway. Meanwhile, a new satellite airfield to Leeming had been opened at Skipton-on-Swale, but with the buildings not yet completed and with the arrival of the Canadians who were to operate from Leeming until May 1946, daily travel between the two stations was necessary. It took nearly a year before the Canadian Squadrons settled down into permanent homes and until then, there was a considerable amount of moving about between the stations in North Yorkshire and South Durham.

The first new arrival was No.420 (Snowy Owl) Squadron RCAF which had been formed at Waddington in December 1941 and though based at the satellite at Skipton-on-Swale, it did fly from Leeming on some operations. The advance party arrived at Skipton on 4 August 1942, and the main party equipped with the Vickers Wellington

Mk III arrived two days later. Following the re-opening of its runways, the Squadron's first operational sortie was from Leeming on 5 October 1942, when nine aircraft participated in an attack on Aachen. The following night the same number successfully raided Osnabrück, but their third mission on 13 October, this time to Kiel, had a very different outcome. Of the 10 aircraft that took off, two collided over enemy territory but managed to return without injury to the crew, two had to turn back with technical trouble, and of those that reached the target, one crashed in Norfolk on return with no injuries to the crew, but another hit a house on landing and the crew of five were killed. That operation to Kiel was notable, if only for the fact that it was the last to be carried out by aircraft from Leeming until the Canadians took over formal control of the Station at the beginning of 1943, and within 2 days of the raid 420 Sqn had been moved from Skipton, and was operating from its new base at Middleton St George.

A second batch of new arrivals to turn up at Leeming in August 1942 belonged to No.419 (Moose) Squadron RCAF, and when they began to arrive from Mildenhall where the Squadron had been formed in December 1941, its personnel were not to know that their stay would be an even briefer one than the Snowy Owls. It too, was equipped with the Wellington Mk III, but as the runways at Leeming were still out of commission when the Squadron appeared on the twelfth, it was moved to Topcliffe on 19 August, although remaining under the administrative control of Leeming until 20 September. That month also saw the arrival of a third RCAF Squadron, No.408 (Goose), with its advance party appearing on the 14th closely followed by the remaining personnel who arrived within the week.

No.408 Squadron RCAF

This Squadron formed in June 1941 at Lindholme, had come from Balderton, Notts where it had been

operating for 14 months in No.5 Group with the Hampden I. During this time it had sustained some heavy losses, including four that failed to return from an operation just days before the planned move, with the Squadron Commander amongst those who were killed that night. In tandem with the move, 408 was in the process of converting to the Halifax B.V and so aircrew were immediately detached to the Halifax Conversion Flight at Marston Moor, while small parties of ground crew were sent to Pocklington, Melbourne, or Marston Moor, to gain experience on the new aircraft. However, on 29 September when the runways at Leeming became serviceable once more, all personnel returned to Leeming to continue with their training. The need for instructing new crews on the "heavies" had already been recognised as being one of great importance, and the first unit in No.6 Group with this as its primary task was No.1659 Heavy Conversion Unit, formed at Leeming on 6 October 1942. It absorbed 408 Sqn Conversion Flight and on 28 October when 405 Sqn Conversion Unit arrived from Topcliffe, it too was absorbed. The significance of this training could not have been overstated, yet at that juncture of the war its importance was not matched by the quality of the training aircraft. It was an unfortunate necessity brought about by the need to carry the war to Germany, but as replacement aircraft were built they were always sorely needed by the front line squadrons. As a consequence conversion units of all types had to make do with aircraft that were almost always aged or repaired. They were at times even dangerous to fly as a direct result from their long hours in the air. The servicing of such aircraft with worn out engines, components and systems, was a never-ending problem for the groundcrews. The situation at that time often dictated that many aircraft were allowed to fly in what could at best be described as an uncertain condition. If that was not enough, the Halifax was initially plagued with a major problem with its rudders, which when used to keep the aircraft straight at low speeds could cause it to veer abruptly and stall. It doesn't take much imagination to see what could happen on take-off, or when flying at very low altitudes if this occurred; even with plenty of height it could flip onto its back and go into an uncontrollable spin. Added to this was the unreliability of the Merlin engines and if one failed, then the loss of power would accentuate the problem of control. Many remedies were tried and though some worked they were always a temporary *fix*. It was not until a Halifax engaged in a study of the problem was lost, that the real remedy was found. A re-design increased the size of the rudder, altering the shape of the fin to a rectangle, and the aircraft could at last be controlled. However, while this idea was still in the future, training flights in the early Marks of Halifax, usually by inexperienced pilots, frequently in atrocious weather conditions, were all too often brought to a sudden and unplanned finish. There were numerous accidents with a consequent high number of fatalities and injuries, so it was of little wonder that some thought that training was more dangerous than flying on operations.

With all of these problems to contend with, 408 Sqn trained throughout the autumn and early winter of 1942 and became operational on 1 January 1943, a date, however, that was of considerable significance to the history of Leeming for a totally different reason.

CHAPTER TWO

ROYAL CANADIAN AIR FORCE LEEMING
January 1943 to May 1946

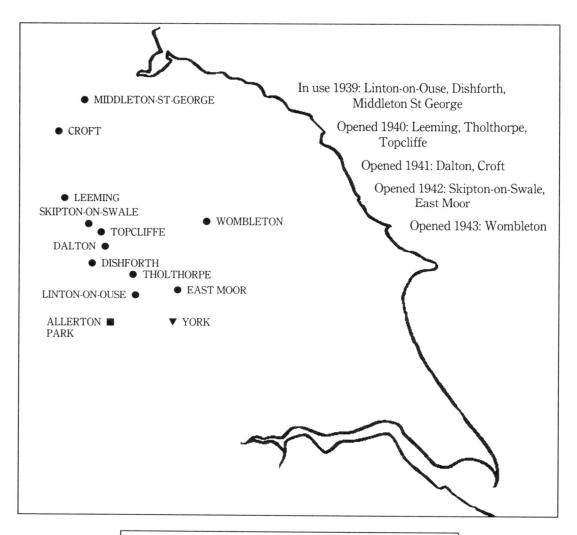

In use 1939: Linton-on-Ouse, Dishforth, Middleton St George

Opened 1940: Leeming, Tholthorpe, Topcliffe

Opened 1941: Dalton, Croft

Opened 1942: Skipton-on-Swale, East Moor

Opened 1943: Wombleton

No 6 (RCAF) GROUP AIRFIELDS 1943–45

On 1 January 1943, Leeming, along with its satellite Station at Skipton, was handed over by No.4 Group (RAF) to the new No.6 Group (RCAF) within Bomber Command. There were no handover ceremonies.

Unique in the annals of Bomber Command by virtue of its overseas nationality, No.6 Group (RCAF) Bomber Command was formed in and operated from Yorkshire and South Durham during the second half of the war. The financial cost, with the single exception of the pay and allowances of attached RAF and other non RCAF personnel, was borne by the Canadian Government; full upkeep of the operational squadrons, including the cost of fuel and ammunition, was defrayed from Canadian taxes and domestic loans. The headquarters of the Group was at Allerton Park, east of Knaresborough, previously the home of Lord Mowbray.

For administration purposes as well as the conduct of operations the seven operational stations that made up the group were organised into three bases. The "parent" stations served as a sub-department of the Headquarters at Allerton, with the 4 satellites operating as sub-stations. All of the Squadrons had been formed and had moved into their final "homes" by August 1943, with the exception of No.415 Squadron, which joined a year later after being on loan to Coastal Command.

The final disposition was:

62 Base   Headquarters *LINTON-ON-OUSE*
          408 (Goose) Squadron
          426 (Thunderbird) Squadron
    Sub-station *EAST MOOR*
          415 (Swordfish) Squadron
          432 (Leaside) Squadron
    Sub-station *THOLTHORPE*
          420 (Snowy Owl) Squadron
          425 (Alouette) Squadron

63 Base   Headquarters *LEEMING*
          427 (Lion) Squadron
          429 (Bison) Squadron

    Sub-station *SKIPTON*
          424 (Tiger) Squadron
          433 (Porcupine) Squadron

64 Base   Headquarters *MIDDLETON ST GEORGE*
          419 (Moose) Squadron
          428 (Ghost) Squadron
    Sub-station *CROFT*
          431 (Iroquois) Squadron
          434 (Bluenose) Squadron

The Canadians were responsible for their own conversion training, with the four stations that made up the Canadian Training Base originally forming part of No.6 (RCAF) Group as No.61 Base. At a later date in the autumn of 1944 it was linked with the RAF Training Group and renamed as No.76 Base. This was for administrative reasons only and it retained its Canadian personnel and close association with 6 Group until the end of the war.

Training Base Headquarters: *TOPCLIFFE*
          1659 Heavy Conversion Unit
    Sub-station: *WOMBLETON*
          1666 Heavy Conversion Unit
    Sub-station: *DISHFORTH*
          Various, mostly 1664 HCU
    Sub-station: *DALTON*
          Housed aircrew ground training
          school, fighter affiliation flights
          and other miscellaneous
          formations.

This then was the organisation of which Leeming became a part at the beginning of 1943. As previously indicated there was a mixture of personnel, with the RCAF providing the majority of the aircrews and the RAF the administration and support, although this division was never rigid. In fact the majority of the flight engineers in the RCAF Squadrons were originally from the RAF, and RCAF Postal Clerks started to man the Station Post Office very soon after the

Canadians had taken over. Then somewhat later, on 15 October 1943, to be precise, urgent requests were sent to 6 Group asking for Canadian catering staff to be posted in to solve what was diplomatically described as... "dietary points of difficulty". However, their arrival did not prevent later complaints about the standards of the food, on items as varied as the taste of the Coca Cola to the quality of the dried beans!

It is worthy of note that throughout the wartime regime of the RAF at Leeming, and later that of the RCAF, it was possible to see the shoulder flashes of many parts of the Commonwealth and occasionally even the USA. For instance in 1943, 37 per cent of Bomber Command pilots came from Canada, Australia, or New Zealand, and by 1945 this figure had risen to 46 per cent. However, the RAF continued to provide a large number of aircrew for RCAF Leeming, with figures in February 1944 showing that out of 200 aircrew on the Station's strength 75 were from the RAF.

In 1943 Bomber Command was entering a new phase of offensive action, with better aircraft equipped at last with OBOE and H2S along with an increasing degree of accuracy in bombing aided by the efforts of the Pathfinder Force. On 21 January 1943, the Casablanca Directive gave the British and US Bomber Commands in the UK the primary objective of:

> ...The progressive destruction and disloca-
> tion of the German military, industrial and
> economic system, and the undermining of
> the morale of the German people to a point
> where their capacity for armed resistance is
> fatally weakened.

The sole squadron at Leeming at that time was No.408 Sqn, coded "EQ", which began to play its part in achieving this aim on 9/10 January 1943, when eight aircraft dropped mines in area "Nectarine", which was the area around the Frisian Islands. Mining operations were codenamed "Gardening", and the mines as "Vegetables" which were laid in areas given individual codenames derived from plants, trees, fruit and fish. For instance, "Lettuce" for the Kiel Canal, "Silverthorn" for the Kattegat and "Jellyfish" indicating the approaches to the harbour at Brest; in all, some 80 locations were given such names. The necessity for flying at a very low altitude in order to lay the mines and the heavy volumes of flak thrown up from shore and ship defences made Gardening an extremely hazardous business and a substantial number of aircraft were lost, often with all of the crew. However, the results obtained from the Bomber Command mining operations were seen after the war to have been very impressive indeed, with records showing that almost 500 warships and 450 merchant vessels had been sunk or damaged by its mines.

This first operation was soon followed by others, and before January was out the submarine pens and dock installations at Lorient had received four visits from 408. The Squadron lost its first Halifax on one of these raids when it crash landed near Newark during its return. Despite Pathfinder Force assistance the weather sometimes negated the efforts of the bomber crews and the attack on Lorient that took place on 29 January is described by the Leeming crews as taking place:

> . . . under impossible weather conditions.
> Severe icing, 10/10 cloud, rain, electrical
> storms and zero visibility militated against
> success so that the raid was largely
> abortive. Bombing was done almost entirely
> on ETA and no observation of results
> was possible. Flak was intense and accu-
> rate....several enemy night fighters were in
> the air.

Perhaps it is against this sort of background that after they had the variation of a raid against Turin at the beginning of February the same crews commented:

... The defences were more numerous than in December but they were handled with little skill and in the opinion of the crews were not up to the German standard.

The experiences of individual crews highlights the dangers being faced at this time. During the first two months of 1943 408 Sqn lost one aircraft in Nottinghamshire while still outbound, with three others failing to return from operations. Two others went down in England during their return: the aforementioned emergency landing at Ossington near Newark, and when almost home another crashed at Kirby Wiske while on its way back from Cologne at the beginning of the so-called "Battle of the Ruhr". The Halifax, piloted by Flt Lt Boosey, bombed the target successfully but on the return journey the navigator's intercom and the rear gun turret ceased to function. Then, as they were down to 300 ft and making their approach to Leeming the port outer engine caught fire, and the port inner stopped. Somehow Boosey succeeded in coaxing the aircraft to climb before ordering his crew to abandon the aircraft, which they did before he made a successful crash landing from which he was able to walk away. He was awarded the DFC for his actions, but sadly the rear gunner, Fg Off Parker, a US citizen, was killed when his parachute failed to function fully before he had hit the ground.

The fact that danger was seen to be almost commonplace can be gleaned from the condensed nature of the reports, but sometimes such brevity actually highlights the drama of returning from an operation in a damaged aircraft. One such report from a crew that returned from a raid on the Bosch Engineering Works at Stuttgart in March 1943 ends with:

... was attacked by a Me110 causing the port inner and the starboard outer engines to cut. All excess equipment was jettisoned over the Channel. Just before landing, the port outer engine began to surge, but a successful wheels up landing was made, none of the crew being injured.

It appears that it is not only the British who are prone to understatement!

Leeming crews at this time were more and more frequently noting in their reports the apparent resurgence of the German defences, particularly the increase in activity by night-fighters. Even the more exuberant reports of highly successful raids were tempered by respectful mention of the opposition. After one such attack on Berlin on 1 March, in which nine Halifaxes from 408 Sqn had taken part, the report from Leeming reads:

... The attackers were favoured by a cloud-less sky and excellent visibility enabling the crews to identify their exact position by reference to such landmarks as the River Spree and Berlin's famous lakes. The early arrivals did their work so well that crews scheduled to arrive later were guided to their targets for 20 minutes before they reached Berlin, by the brilliant glare of the huge fires which could still be seen over Hannover and Bremen on the way home. Columns of smoke rose so thickly that large areas of the city were blotted out .... Crews reported that timing was perfect, enabling them so to concentrate their attack as to give the defences little chance to aim at individual aircraft and preventing the fire services from functioning while the attack continued ... The most powerful defences were encountered on the outskirts of the city ... bombers there, were met with heavy gunfire and cones of searchlights, but having penetrated this ring the crews found the flak by no means as intense as had been expected. On the route, especially on the way back, night fighters were up in great numbers and there were several encounters.

The ability of the German defences that night can be gauged from the fact that 17 aircraft were lost from the force, with two of them failing to return to 408 Sqn.

Between January and March 1943, 408 Sqn had been the only operational unit at Leeming, although the training carried out by No.1659 Heavy Conversion Unit meant that the airspace over the local area was often in use. However, on 14 March 1943, the HCU removed to Topcliffe after having rather an unhappy time in its three months at Leeming, with a number of accidents that included the loss of five aircraft to crashes.[10] This move did not leave 408 on its own, because the previous day had seen the arrival of No.405 (Vancouver) RCAF Squadron from Topcliffe, equipped with the Halifax BII, and coded "LQ".

No.405 Squadron RCAF

This Squadron had been the first Canadian squadron to be formed in Bomber Command, and while at Leeming its crews flew on 12 operations,

all in the company of 408 Sqn. The first one was to St Nazaire on 22 March 1943, when a force of 15 Halifaxes from 408 and 10 from 405 went out and returned without loss. This good fortune was not to last. In barely three weeks from 26 March to 14 April 1943, the period covered by the remaining joint operations, 408 Sqn lost eight aircraft and 405 lost another five. The menace of the German defences was always the major danger, but the weather at this time often lent the enemy a hand; a claim borne out when 11 aircraft from each Squadron flew through almost continuous cloud when they attacked Berlin on 27 March. One aircraft was lost but later it was found to have come down in neutral Sweden after flak over the target had holed its fuel tanks. Two nights later with the same target to attack aircraft flew through:

... the worst weather for weeks. Ice laden clouds were banked up over the North Sea to such a height that the aircraft had to climb almost all the way to get over them. As the raiders crossed the enemy coast they flew out of the worst of the cloud but only one reached the target, the rest aborted because of icing or engine trouble.

A mission to Duisburg on 8 April fared no better with the freezing conditions:

... Ice laden clouds extended to a height of 20,000 ft for almost the whole distance ... Some of the aircraft became so heavy with ice that the pilots had great difficulty in controlling them. Flak along the whole of the Ruhr Valley was as vicious as ever and night-fighters tried to intercept. Plt Off C Stovel of 408 Sqn, reached the target in 10/10 cloud with one engine unserviceable. The aircraft was then caught in heavy flak and because of icing went into a spin after violent evasive action. The remaining three engines cut, and the captain warned the crew to stand by to bale out. Apparently misunderstanding instructions, the second pilot, flight engineer, and both gunners did so. However, the pilot regained control of the aircraft, with three of the engines starting up again. On the return journey, the engines cut again and the aircraft went into another spin which was corrected at 6000ft. The four remaining members of the crew reached home safely after a very shaky trip.

The pilot of the aircraft, Plt Off C Stovel, was awarded the DFC for his actions that night, but his luck was not to last and while on a raid to Hamburg on 27/28 July 1943 his aircraft was shot down, killing him and four of his crew.

On a more light hearted note, the Met Officers whose job it was (more often than not) to deliver bad tidings to the aircrew had been commissioned in the RAFVR on 9 April, and presumably totally unrelated to that fact, it was said that the weather did show some slight improvement towards the end of the month![12]

On 17 April 1943, 405 Sqn left Leeming for Gransden Lodge, Bedfordshire for training with No.8 PFF Group, where it remained with the distinction of being the only RCAF squadron on Pathfinder duties. At the same time in view of the pending move of 424 Sqn from Topcliffe to the Middle East, and in order to allow more room for the expansion of 1659 HCU at their new base at Topcliffe, 424 Sqn personnel and aircraft were dispersed to other Stations in the Group, with a number arriving at Leeming for billeting and messing purposes. The Squadron was non-operational at this time and the lodgers did not stay long, moving out within a month.

Domestically, RCAF Leeming had settled down sufficiently well by this time to be able to cope with this and subsequent upheavals. Canada was taking a great interest in its overseas Squadrons: during the first four months, the Mayor of Ottawa, the Archbishop of Toronto, and correspondents from the "Toronto Daily Star", and from the

Canadian Press Association, had called in to see how things were going. Even enemy aircraft had appeared in the vicinity on 2 February but no bombs were dropped. There was much more excitement recorded on 21 April over the arrival of a Canadian Nursing Sister for the Station Hospital which was sited in, what was and is, the Station Commander's Residence. A weekly ENSA show had been organised and much energy was expended at the end of March 1943 in organising various functions in aid of the Red Cross Prisoner of War Fund. These functions took the form of dances: a show entitled "Hellzapoppin", a concert by the Station Concert Party from RAF Catterick, a fun fair, and a boxing exhibition featuring the ex-heavyweight champion, Jack London, and sparring partner. The entertainment was extremely popular and raised £540 for the Fund.

Between 16 April and 11 June, 408 Sqn was once more on its own at Leeming. It carried on with a steady programme of bombing missions on a variety of targets, the first of which on 16 April representing something of a feat of endurance. The target was the Skoda Works at Pilsen in Czechoslovakia and involved a round trip of about 1800 miles, roughly 1200 of them over strongly defended enemy territory. Total losses were the most serious thus far suffered by Bomber Command from one raid and of those lost, four were from Leeming. In other words they all came from 408 Sqn, and with no survivors from the 29 crewmen, the majority of whom were Canadian, it was a tragic day for both the RCAF and the Station. The month of April also saw large numbers of bombers being concentrated on mine laying operations, with the objective of helping the Russians by impeding the movement of German materiel, which was being shipped in preparation for a possible spring offensive on the Eastern Front. An example of the degree of effort spent on mining operations could be seen from the night of 28 April when the number of aircraft sent out was comparable to the force employed in a major bombing raid, and in that one night Bomber

Command laid as many mines as it had in a month in the previous year. Unfortunately, losses to the attacking force turned out to be the heaviest suffered whilst engaged on minelaying operations, and a total of 23 aircraft failed to return, with only four survivors from the 149 men who made up the crews. Leeming played its part that night by supplying 11 aircraft for a mission to the Kattegat, but luck was with those crews that night and all returned safely.

When attention swung back to the Ruhr in May, this kind of increase in the number of aircraft involved was equally in evidence. There was also a corresponding increase in the number of bombs dropped, and during a raid on Dortmund on 4 May, in which 14 Leeming aircraft took part, 4000lb "Blockbuster" bombs were dropped at the rate of four every minute. Then later in the month, the same target was attacked by a bomber force that numbered 826, with 408 Sqn providing 12 of the total.

It was at this time at the beginning of May 1943 that 408 received some support, and there arrived at Leeming the first of the two Squadrons that were to remain resident at the Station until after the end of the war.

No.427 Squadron RCAF

No.427 (RCAF) Squadron, formed at Croft on 7 November 1942 was the eighth squadron out of a final total of 50 formed by Canada. It was equipped with the Wellington Mk III and used experienced crews, borrowed from 419 Sqn, to enable it to be ready by 1 December 1942, for No.4 Bomber Group operations against the Frisian Islands. Transferred to No.6 Bomber Group when it was formed, the Squadron was then re-equipped with the Halifax Mk V, coded "ZL", for its move to Leeming on 4 May 1943. The RCAF squadrons were all individually named, many after Canadian cities, wild birds or animals, and 427 was "Lion" Squadron. The adoption of a squadron was seen

by many as a way of showing support for the war effort and much of the work for the adoption of 427 had already been carried out prior to the move to Leeming. As a result of this preparation, on Monday 24 May 1943, 427 Sqn was formally adopted by the Metro-Goldwyn-Mayer (MGM) Film Company of Hollywood, which also had the emblem of a lion. The day began with all personnel, dressed in their best uniform, being paraded outside of No.2 Hangar around the front of a Halifax named "London's Revenge", which sported a motif of a winged lion carrying a very large bomb. At the ceremony, Samuel Eckman Jr, managing director of MGM (UK), presented the Squadron with a bronze Lion – 18th century design – with an inscription commemorating the occasion, along with a crate of whisky and free tickets to the company's theatre in London! This gesture was subsequently extended, and members of the squadron were given a special Lion medal that entitled them to two free seats at any cinema showing an MGM film, and under-

standably that courtesy was very popular. Following the presentation, pilots drew from a hat the name of the particular star who was to be "foster mother" or "foster father" of their aircraft and crew. The 17 names had already been selected from a vote taken from all members of the Squadron, and included stars such as Lana Turner, Joan Crawford, Hedy Lamarr, Greer Garson, Spencer Tracy, and Robert Donat. Winston Churchill got into the act at a later date when he was asked if one of the cubs fathered at London Zoo by his lion, "Rota", could be adopted by the Squadron. He agreed, but at the presentation ceremony at the Zoo on 3 November 1943, when "Mareth" shared centre stage with a large contingent from Leeming, it was noted with disappointment that no one was present to represent the Prime Minister. However, the BBC, along with several film companies were in attendance and the proceedings received widespread coverage for the Lion Squadron. The Squadron did not always get good publicity by having the lion as its emblem, as could be seen when *The Lion* was stolen from the portico of the "Golden Lion Hotel" in Northallerton, and the local constabulary was brought in to solve the "crime". It did not take the local police chief, Superintendent A E Clark, very long to realise that the culprits were probably from Leeming, and he was soon hot on the trail. Common sense prevailed at this point, and in coming to an arrangement with the Adjutant, he agreed that the incident would be considered closed if the figure was returned the next day. It was duly returned, but a tale persisted at Leeming, intimating that *The Lion* was taken on an operation by a 427 Sqn aircraft on the night before it resumed its perch at the Hotel. The story is perhaps apocryphal, but is the kind of legend that not only holds the flavour of the times, but also sits easily on the imagination.

The first operation from Leeming for 427 Sqn took place on 29 May 1943, when 13 of its aircraft were prepared to join 12 from 408 Sqn for an operation to Wuppertal. All aircraft returned safely,

but the new arrivals at Leeming had four of their aircraft severely damaged by flak. Throughout June and July, both Squadrons then proceeded to combine in the non-stop bombing offensive against the Third Reich. Individual crew stories continued to add to the Leeming saga. One Halifax, piloted by Fg Off Bennett of 408 Sqn, while returning from a raid on Gelsenkirchen on 9 July:

> ... was hit by incendiaries which entered the fuselage, started a fire and rendered useless much equipment including the hydraulic system. Some of the bombs landed on the navigator's table, others on the port wing, and others on the starboard side of the aircraft and remained there. The wireless operator, Sgt A Rodgers, helped by the bomb aimer and the flight engineer got the fire inside under control in approximately 12 minutes. Meanwhile the pilot put the aircraft into a dive and the force of the wind extinguished the flames on the fabric. The aircraft was then flown safely back to base.

Bennett was later awarded the DFC, and Rodgers the DFM.

With the two Squadrons operating from Leeming the number of aircraft involved increased and perhaps inevitably, the number of casualties went up as well. The operational statistics for June 1943 give some indication of these facts (*see* Table 2 on page 32) with a total of 15 aircraft lost in under three weeks. During the same period, 427 Sqn had a further two aircraft written off, one following a training accident and a second after it had sustained severe battle damage.

Domestic life on the Station continued smoothly with the Canadian High Commissioner, Vince Massey and his wife, visiting on 18 June with still more reporters making an appearance. The CO, Gp Capt Carscallan, who as a Wing Commander had taken over from Gp Capt Dunlap in April 1943, made a recording about the

Table 2 Operational statistics for June 1943

DATE	TARGET	AC OUT		AC MISSING	
		408	427	408	427
11/12	Düsseldorf	18	17	1	–
12/13	Bochum	12	12	1	1
19/20	Le Creusot	13	17	1	–
21/22	Krefeld	13	14	2	–
22/23	Mulheim	8	14	–	4
24/25	Wuppertal	9	11	–	2[11]
25/26	Gelsenkirchen	8	9	1	1
28/29	Cologne	10	9	–	1

efforts of the RCAF, which was later broadcast throughout Canada.

In July the Station was able to report the successful inspection of the Pigeon Loft, presumably housing those birds carried from time to time by the bombers. It is reassuring to know that in the midst of total war someone, somewhere, was concerned with such detail in such matters! A Wing Commander from the Air Ministry made a general check of the pigeon policy, visited the loft, inspected the birds and interviewed all pigeon keepers – or was that the other way round? Much attention was also given to training for the Ripon Sport Meet on 16 July which Leeming won. This led to representation in the White City Sports Meet on 24 July, where the Station again distinguished itself by gaining five firsts and two seconds. A minor hazard at the beginning of September was the first of the predatory visits from the Blood Transfusion Team, which took contributions from 303 personnel to supply the RAF Hospital in Northallerton (now the civilian Friarage Hospital). Accommodation remained a major problem and to help ease the situation large Nissen huts had been erected on a new Communal Site near the Married Quarter buildings, with the WAAFs similarly being provided for on their own site. This last accommodation later housed seven Land Girls

who had been hired to help run a Station Farm, which was to amount to about 160 acres, with swine and cattle as the main livestock. Where this farm was to be situated was unspecified, but reports show that things soon got underway. However, even though the venture lasted until well after the war, there were continual problems with it, not least of which was when the proposed size of the farm was reduced to 90 acres in October 1943 because of the difficulties involved in regaining some of the land previously leased to a local farmer!

Not all the hazards had to be faced over Germany. At 2244 hrs on 9 July 1943, JB959 of 408 Squadron, while carrying a full bomb load, crashed when its undercarriage collapsed during a take-off from Leeming. Fortunately the aircraft did not explode and Flt Sgt Sanderson of the Station Armoury was called in – to remove the bombs. One was a 1000lb medium capacity type, which he removed to a trolley by means of a crane before moving it to a gully about 300 yards northeast of the bomb dump, where it was left until it could be demolished. Hardly had he started breathing again, when another 1000lb bomb dropped through the bomb doors of a Halifax which had just landed after returning from an aborted operation. Now the *expert*, Sanderson was again called upon and he carried out a repeat performance, though this time the bomb was found to be in a condition that allowed its return to the bomb dump. The initial bomb had been armed with a long delay fuse and as it was considered unwise to attempt to defuse it, the bomb was detonated by the Station Armament Officer on 11 July, not surprisingly leaving a large crater.

It must be noted that this saga began on the day after the ORB entry for 8 July had tempted fate by briefly stating that nothing of interest had occurred that day. Flt Sgt Sanderson was clearly a man to have on your side when there were unexploded bombs around, and his fame had obviously spread by April 1944 when 604 Bomb Disposal Flight at Snaith specifically requested his presence at an incident near Goole.

In the air, the war continued with as much intensity as ever. After the "Battle of the Ruhr", came the "Battle of Hamburg", which began on the night of 24 July. This particular raid was notable in that *Window* (metallised strips, dropped in bundles from aircraft to confuse the enemy RDF early warning systems) was used for the first time that night, but only after the Prime Minister had given his authority. Bomber Command embarked upon an attack, which in the course of six major operations and the space of nine nights, produced catastrophic devastation in Hamburg: the heaviest blow yet struck against Essen, and a lighter, though highly effective thrust against Remscheid. As always, Leeming was well represented and on four nights in July/August, upwards of 25 aircraft flew each night from the Station to attack Hamburg. In addition on 25 July, 26 aircraft from 408 and 427 attacked Essen without loss. On this raid all crews reported:

... a huge column of thick smoke rising to a height of 20,000 ft. Another smaller column mushroomed up from a violent explosion. Two other violent explosions occurred during the attack. As the aircraft left the

target, fires were seen to have got a good hold and became more concentrated. The glow of these was seen by most aircraft from as far as the Dutch coast.

After the raid on Hamburg on 27/28 July 1943, in which 30 aircraft of the two squadrons took part, a somewhat more emotional view was expressed by James Stuart, Air Correspondent of the Evening Standard who wrote:

... As darkness fell, I watched the Halifaxes of the RCAF "Lion" and "Goose" Squadrons roar off on their way to Hamburg with mighty loads of high explosives and incendiaries . . . As the returning crews, Canadians, Americans, British and Australians got out of their bombers, they were all emphatic that Hamburg was blazing more furiously than on Saturday night. Some of the crews found the opposition a bit heavier but others over the target later, found that the defences of the battered port had been completely swamped by the terrific weight of the attack. Few of the men of these squadrons encountered enemy fighters and the biggest danger, they told me, was the risk of collisions with other bombers as they swept over Hamburg in waves.

Just as the "Battle of Hamburg" was warming up, RCAF Leeming had to cope with yet another change of Squadron location, although this was to be the last till the end of the war. At the end of August 1943, 408 Sqn moved to what was to be its permanent base at Linton-on-Ouse, and was replaced by No.429 (Bison) Squadron, which had already arrived at Leeming on 11/12 August from East Moor where it had been formed in November 1942.

No.429 Squadron RCAF

The Squadron was in the process of converting from the Wellington to the Halifax Mk II, coded "AL", and initially was occupied with flying training in the new aircraft, taking part in a number of *Bullseye* bombing exercises during August and September. It was commanded by Wg Cdr J D Pattison, a short, bristly character who was variously described as peppery, eccentric, and a martinet. On one occasion in February 1944, when Leeming was a blanket of white and bitterly cold, he took all aircrew personnel on a route march/run around the perimeter track; and at another time after being upset whilst on a parade, had the Squadron aircrew drilling until most were nigh on exhausted. However, he was at the same time known as a popular and well respected leader to those on 429 and whatever the truth of his character, he was certainly the driving force behind the squadron.

Thus, RCAF Leeming in August 1943 housed the two squadrons, No.427 (Lion) Squadron and No.429 (Bison) Squadron, which were to remain there for the best part of the next three years.

Nearby, on the satellite station at Skipton-on-Swale, No.433 (Porcupine) Squadron was formed on 25 September 1943, as the first of the Station's two resident squadrons, with 11 of its pilots flying with 427 to gain operational experience. The second squadron arrived in November 1943 when No 424 (Tiger) Squadron returned there from operations in the Middle East. Both Squadrons flew the Halifax B.III until January 1945 when they were given the Lancaster B.I, which they flew until they were disbanded from Skipton in October 1945.

Meanwhile, while 429 Sqn crews were concentrating on their conversion flying, the period of August and early September saw 427 Sqn carry out a number of operations on its own. Apart from what had become fairly routine raids (in choice if not in execution) on targets such as Mannheim, Nuremberg, Berlin and Munich, nine Halifaxes carried out a single operation to Milan on 12 August. One aircraft was reported missing from that raid, and the story behind the apparent loss was told some weeks later when it returned to Leeming, via a slightly circuitous route, with a bomb bay full of fruit. The aircraft had one of its engines put out of action making it impossible for the pilot to gain sufficient height to cross the Alps, and rather than bale out over enemy territory, a rough course was set for the North African coast where a safe landing was made. After some diplomatic difficulties, the details of which can only be wondered at, the Halifax turned up in Gibraltar and Flt Sgt Countess and crew finally returned home to Leeming on 15 September after an operation lasting almost seven weeks!

While the Flight Sergeant and his crew were on their extended holiday, 12 aircraft from 427 took part in a rather special raid on 17 August. This was a precision attack on Peenemünde, classified in the orders as a "Radio Location Research Station", but of course later revealed as the main centre for the development of the V-2 Rocket. Because the aim was to destroy a number of specific buildings, the *area bombing tactics* could not be used and for the first time a *Master Bomber* was employed. This was a technique where a specially selected and usually very experienced pilot directed by radio the force of aircraft on to the target. The raid met with only limited success and losses were high among the 597 aircraft taking part; 40 aircraft did not return, but only one was from 427 Sqn. Diversionary actions had been arranged and *Window* was used to deny close control of the German night-fighter crews, who had to rely upon a general running commentary by ground controllers. Before the true destination was discovered, they were heard to give the target successively as Kiel, Berlin, Rostock, Swinemünde or Stettin. However, the deception was not to last and it was when the bombers were on their way home in conditions of clear visibility, that many were shot down.

The dangers of wartime flying were generally only seen at second-hand by the groundcrew, but towards the end of August one incident brought the fact home to the groundcrews at Leeming in a singularly tragic and more personal manner. Following the diversion to Ford (near Arundel in the South of England), of a Halifax from 427 Sqn which was returning from a raid on Nuremberg, an attempt was made to get it repaired as quickly as possible. An Airspeed Oxford, used as Leeming's airborne taxi, took off in weather conditions that were described as being rather unfavourable for flying to ferry a party of three ground crew who were to carry out engine repairs on the Halifax. No more was heard from them and later in the day the Oxford was declared missing. A search was instituted but it was not until the following day that the burnt out wreckage was found north east of Kirkby Lonsdale, some 50 miles west of Leeming, with no survivors from the four personnel on board. It transpired that the pilot was inexperienced as a navigator and was not sure of his position, and this fact allied to the poor weather along the route prompted him to turn back. He took that decision without having a flight plan for the return journey, a precise course was not steered and he flew his aircraft into the high ground above Dentdale.

However successful in devastating German cities Bomber Command had become, once again losses showed that the German night-fighters seemed to have taken on a new lease of life. After a raid on Mönchen Gladbach on 30 August, 427 Sqn crews reported:

> . . . many combats with German night fighters out in full force. Search lights co-operated with the fighters by silhouetting bombers against the convenient clouds, thus making them easier targets.

Many crews at this time reported contact with fighters, with records showing that some found themselves defending against five or six attacks during a single raid. It was a relatively common occurrence for bombers to return to Leeming with wounded or dead on board and even on occasions with missing crew members; some of whom may have risked the uncertainty of baling out rather than face further operations with Bomber Command!

On 15 September 1943, 429 Sqn was ready for action and eight of its new Halifaxes joined 13 from 427 Sqn on a raid on Montluçon. This was the first of 28 bombing operations, along with three mine laying taskings that were carried out jointly by the Squadrons before the end of February 1944. However, the upheaval that affected Leeming over the summer months had not ended with the transfer of squadrons on a so-called permanent basis. After carrying out their first two operations together from Leeming, and dating from 21 September 1943, the aircraft of 427 and 429 Squadrons plus approximately 450 personnel had to crowd into Skipton-on-Swale for operational purposes, although most were still billeted at Leeming. The temporary move had been brought about because the airfield at Leeming had withstood a great deal of heavy use during the preceding months, and bad weather and aircraft crashes on the field had left the surface of the runways bordering on the hazardous. Teams brought in by contractors were needed to re-concrete the runways and cover them with a carpet of asphalt as quickly as possible. The original plan, which proposed that operational flying would continue whilst the work was in progress, was never very feasible so perhaps delays were inevitable. Understandably, the flying, and the enforced delays that resulted from it, did not go down well with the Contractors or their civilian workforce, and the net result was the removal of operational activity to Skipton. However, further delays occurred even after the move and work would still have to be suspended at Leeming to allow the RCAF to fly in any aircraft requiring major repairs. At that time there were approximately 240 workmen engaged in the work on the runways, but even that number was inadequate for the work involved. Many of them were from Eire and the tax free rates of pay they were receiving meant that they were extremely well-off financially, both in England and on return home to Ireland. As a consequence they were a difficult gang to manage, a fact borne out when, with the job still not finished and with only two days to the agreed return date for the aircraft, 60 of them failed to turn up for work on 9 October 1943. Following their pay-day on the 8th they had obviously decided to enjoy themselves before the end of the contract and rather than go to work they chose to attend a race meeting on the Saturday! In addition, having worked on the previous two Sundays they had also decided not to work on the one that fell on the 10th, and it took some high level intervention, with no doubt some veiled threats and possibly some favours recalled, to ensure that the work continued. However, the success of all of the work behind the scenes could be seen from the return of 427 and 429 to RAF Leeming on 11 October 1943.

During the latter part of 1943, the need for increased engine power for the Halifax had become more and more apparent and because of the rising losses in Bomber Command, Leeming's aircraft were supposedly restricted to less hazardous targets. Notwithstanding this decision, losses from 427 and 429 were frequent, and in the period from October 1943 to the end of March 1944, the two squadrons lost a total of 56 aircraft from operations and a further five whilst on training exercises. The losses were particularly heavy on the first raid following the return of the squadrons from Skipton, when on 22 October 1943, 28 aircraft from Leeming took part in what turned out to be a disastrous mission to Kassel. Seven of Leeming's aircraft failed to attack the target and five were posted as missing, along with a sixth, which had crashed south of York whilst outbound, killing all of the crew. In addition, there were others that returned with dead and wounded aboard as well as with battle damage of varying degrees of severity, so all in all, it was a bad day for the Station. One of those that returned safely that night carried the Station Commander, Gp Capt Plant, who had flown as second pilot to Sqn Ldr Earthrowl, who was completing his 50th trip and in doing so concluding his second tour of operations. The force as a whole lost 48 aircraft that night, but notwithstanding the losses sustained, the raid itself was considered as a success, even without the knowledge that there had been a more far reaching strategic effect resulting from the scale of damage sustained by the city. The majority of the major factories and power stations in Kassel had been hard hit, the transport system was wrecked, and there were many casualties among the work force. The hidden consequence of all of this death and destruction was that it became a factor that conspired to affect the production of flying bombs at the Feisler factory in the adjacent town of Rothwesten. The subsequent delay this caused to the V-1 offensive was, therefore, possibly one of the most important contributions made by Bomber Command in the battle against Hitler's secret weapons.

The heavy casualties cast an air of gloom on the Station, but on the day following the raid the

Station received a signal advising of the award of the Conspicuous Gallantry Medal (CGM)(Flying) to a SNCO from 427 Sqn. During the Second World War, the powers that be had realised that the award of the DFM did not always sufficiently reflect the level of gallantry shown by non-commissioned ranks and as a consequence, the CGM as awarded to the Royal Navy, was authorised for the Royal Air Force. However, notwithstanding the vastly enlarged size of the RAF at that time, the fact that only 103 of these medals were awarded to RAF personnel in the period from its inception in 1943 until the end of the war, indicates just how sparingly the decoration was bestowed. Sergeant W H Cardy RCAF, had been the flight engineer in one of the aircraft hit hard by German night-fighters on a raid, by coincidence also on Kassel, on 3 October. The aircraft was severely damaged, the wireless operator, and the rear gunner had been killed, and Cardy was badly wounded in one arm and an eye. Notwithstanding these wounds, he refused to leave his post and carried out his normal duties until he fainted from loss of blood. Later, when he recovered consciousness he did all he could to assist the pilot in the homeward flight to Leeming, where it was found that the undercarriage would not come down. Cardy then instructed others in the crew to sever one of the hydraulic pipelines, the wheels were finally locked down and a safe landing was made. In addition, the pilot, Flt Lt Laird, received the DFC for his skill and courage in getting the bomber home. The news of the award of these medals, in particular the CGM which by its rarity was considered by many as being a close second to the Victoria Cross, was a real boost to morale and of course, was of sufficient note to require some form of celebration. Therefore that very night, in what was considered to be one of the rowdiest mess parties ever experienced by those attending, the awards as well as Sqn Ldr Earthrowl's screening, were celebrated. The evening also saw the institution of the recently arrived "Winco" as the "Grand Lion" in the Royal Order of Leo's. The initiation ceremony required all potential Lions to *osculate the rectum of Leo* (in official terms), which of course was the statuette previously presented by MGM! (This particular CO, Wg Cdr Turnbull, had a rather spectacular record of promotion, having moved from the rank of Sergeant to that of Wing Commander in the 11 months from December 1941 to November 1942. Before he was repatriated to Canada in June 1944 after completing his second tour of operations, he had been decorated with the DFC, AFC, and the DFM.)

On numerous occasions throughout the war, the dangers associated with flying were to be seen on Leeming's own doorstep and all too often, aircraft barely got into the air before they were in trouble. Examples abound, such as when the month of November 1943 saw one Leeming aircraft crash-land near Burneston minutes after take-off, the "choice" of which area by happy chance happened to be the decoy site built for Leeming back in 1939. Both of the aircraft's port engines had failed, but fortunately the landing was sufficiently smooth, the bomb load remained safe, and no injuries were reported. Then on 2 January 1944, another Halifax crashed soon after take-off, this time into the playing fields at the rear of the married quarters after a port engine had caught fire in the air and its hydraulics failed. Although no serious injuries were sustained by the crew, it took 25 minutes and 2700 gallons of foam for the firecrew to extinguish the flames! These were but two of many, not all from Leeming, but from wheresoever they came, the Leeming Crash-Crew would respond, which meant that the team received plenty of practice. Aircraft from many other bases came to grief within sight of the airfield, and two such crashes where Leeming became closely involved occurred almost 12 months apart, but both had the all too often tragic outcome. On the afternoon of 1 March 1943, a Wellington from Middleton St George, crashed beside the airfield after its port wing had become detached from the fuselage.

There was little the firemen and medics could do but attend, as they again did on 11 February 1944, when a Halifax from Topcliffe crashed near Maunby. Dense fog covered the region that night and the aircraft, unable to find its home base, came down while it was attempting to land at Leeming. Three of the crew were killed, but there were four survivors, thanks mainly to the efforts of a local farmer who pulled three of them from the wreckage. The remaining survivor was the rear gunner who had been thrown free when the aircraft broke up on impact. The report made after the crash showed that even with four survivors a sense of frustration was felt by those involved.

> . . . One of the survivors took off from the scene of the crash, walking. Auxiliary Fire Service (AFS), Home Guard and Station Crash Crew instituted a search without success. The airman was eventually picked up on the Northallerton Road and brought to Leeming by an officer in his car. The survivor was suffering from concussion. Special note: Mr M B Raine, Rush Farm, Maunby, Thirsk, proceeded to the crash site and, in the face of a heavy petrol fire, removed three of the crew from a very dangerous position and but for his assistance at the time, two would undoubtedly have lost their lives.[13] It was noted that lack of bridges across the Swale hampered access to the crash site.

It had taken the crash-crew 27 minutes to reach the wreck and though they later estimated that if adequately sited bridges had been in place this could have been cut to six, that statement was made **with** the benefit of hindsight, and aircraft have always been in the habit of coming down in inaccessible places! Crashes were frequent, with the area immediately around Leeming littered with accident sites from a wide variety of different aircraft types. In addition to the crashes of aircraft operating from the airfield itself, an assortment, including a Mosquito, a Mustang and even a Northrop P61A, a specialised USAAF night fighter known as the "Black Widow",[14] all came to grief in the immediate vicinity. The immediate reaction from those at Leeming would have been the same, irrespective of the type of aircraft that had crashed, but perhaps the pilot who received the most solicitous of welcomes would have been Section Officer Davies of the Air Transport Auxiliary who, in early June 1944, was unhurt when the Swordfish she was delivering elsewhere came down in a field near the runway. No doubt she was well looked after in the Mess before being allowed on her way. Similar stories relating to crashes (though not to that one) are legion, and indeed, the impression could be gained that it was almost as dangerous to be on the ground in Yorkshire as it was in Germany! However, the skies over the British Isles and Europe continued to hold sway in the danger stakes, and not only from the night-fighters and flak. Aircraft from Leeming had their share of occasions where they were hit by bombs from other aircraft, and one such incident was encountered by a 427 Sqn crew while raiding Berlin on the night of 29 December 1943. The crew had just released their bombs when they were showered with incendiaries from a Halifax above them. The bombs crashed through the tailplane as well as the starboard wing, and with the aileron buckled, the aircraft went into a spin. The pilot regained control, but being unable to take evasive action he soon found his aircraft hit by flak, with shrapnel penetrating the aircraft in several places. The flight home found the aircraft continually listing to starboard, and with the fuel state made critical by strong head winds, the first airfield sighted in England was a welcome haven to a very relieved crew. The weather also continued to play its part in creating problems and on an operation to Kassel, Halifax JD384 flown by Flt Sgt Bowly, had to contend with ice many inches thick on the leading edges of the wings and even more on the airscrew spinners. Even with the engines on full power the aircraft continued to lose height before rain began to clear the ice. This allowed the pilot to regain full control so he continued with the operation, completed it and got the aircraft back safely. Bowly, an Australian, was not so fortunate on an operation in March 1944. Then, as a Pilot Officer and still with 429 Sqn, he was shot down by a night-fighter over Nuremberg and as a result spent the remainder of the war as a POW. In the very same raid, Fg Off Jim Moffat, the rear gunner of LV923 of 427 Sqn, was one of only two survivors of a mid-air collision with a Lancaster of 622 Sqn. His pilot, who was killed, had been Sqn Ldr G Laird who was awarded the DFC for the courage and skill displayed in the return of the crippled Halifax where Sgt Cardy gained his CGM. After parachuting to relative safety Moffat evaded capture and was able to make contact with the resistance group in Etalle, Belgium, where along with Sgt W Jones, another evader, he was sheltered in the house of Albert and Cecile Paul. Albert was a gendarme, as well as being the leader of the local resistance, so he was well aware of the dangers of sheltering the Allies, but notwithstanding his official position, he still had no inkling of a raid when the Gestapo made their move on his house. He was taken, as was the air gunner from No.158 Sqn who was shot in the leg, but Moffat escaped and after further time with the Belgian Resistance and then the French, he was liberated by the Americans in September 1944. Jones spent the rest of the war as a POW, but Albert Paul paid the ultimate penalty for his courage when he was executed by firing squad in Liège on 15 August.

The variety of names of the RCAF squadrons in 6 Group gave their personnel an identity and though 429 was already known as *Bison* Squadron, its personnel received further recognition of this name when, on 7 January 1944, Mr Clews, who was the European Manager of Canadian National Railways, presented a Bison emblem to the Squadron. There is no mention of

any *extras* similar to those received by *Lion*, not even a free train ticket, so on that occasion "Bison" certainly came off second best.

In February 1944 a new commander took over at Allerton Hall, the grim Victorian mansion built near Knaresborough for Lord Mowbray of Stourton, which by this time as 6 Group HQ was also known by the Canadians as *Castle Dismal*, allegedly because of the operation orders that stemmed from the place. Air Vice Marshal C M McEwen, a First World War fighter ace, soon to be named *Black Mike* by his crews, was known as a stern disciplinarian, and at the outset, he instigated a crew training programme and insisted that they smartened up. The Group had a very difficult first year, with its rapid expansion and a run of very heavy losses keeping it constantly short of experienced flight and squadron commanders. Morale had been very low, but as 1943 wore on things had improved and many of the problems were being sorted out. Following the arrival of McEwen, TIME MAGAZINE reported that:

... The Canadians scorn casual attire, keep the wire in their caps, always look as if they were ready for a Dress Parade and consider themselves the cream of the RCAF who felt that they had no need to wear the "costume" of combat veterans. They knew they had carried their share of the fight.

The month of February 1944 was also a month that brought salutary reminders to those at Leeming that bombs intended for Axis targets were still a danger if not handled with care. On the afternoon of the 4th, a train load of bombs, mostly incendiaries, were being offloaded into trucks in the sidings of Catterick Bridge railway station, prior to being taken to the area bomb storage depot at 224 MU. Some form of mishap caused an explosion which rapidly became a chain reaction that was first heard and then seen at Leeming. At the scene of the disaster a local hotel ceased to exist and the station and other buildings suffered severe damage from the blast and flames. In all, twelve people were killed and over a hundred injured.

A reminder that the danger could come even closer to home then occurred towards the end of the month, when following an accident immediately prior to a raid, 429 Sqn lost its CO, Wg Cdr Pattison. A total of 32 aircraft from both squadrons at Leeming were ready to go, and just at the time when all were lined up around the perimeter track, an incendiary container fell from one of the bombers. Pattison and the Station Warrant Officer were able to reach the burning incendiaries and kick them clear from the aircraft, which probably averted a disaster. Unfortunately, one 4lb incendiary bomb exploded and both men were hospitalised with serious injuries, with the Wing Commander subsequently being invalided back to Canada.

Problems with the bomb-loads were not as uncommon as would have been liked and the Station was again unlucky when it lost MZ866 from 427 Sqn on 28 October 1944, after incendiaries had dropped out while the Halifax was being refuelled. The incident would have been much worse but for the immediate action of Cpls Hall and Chapman, who showed great presence of mind and a complete disregard for their own safety, when they shut off the fuel and drove the vehicle to safety. The same night saw another incident when a high explosive bomb and some 4lb incendiaries were dropped, but the crash-crew was able to extinguish the flames before they "cooked off" the HE bomb.

By March 1944, both squadrons had been re-equipped with the improved Halifax Mark III and during the month, raids continued on the familiar targets in Germany. Some of the new aircraft carried a mid-under gun emplacement fitted to take a single .5 inch machine gun, but its addition did not seem to bring much good fortune. The month of March was a black one for both squadrons, when in only five of the raids, 427 lost

a total of 11 aircraft, with seven going down from 429.

An account written by one of the crew members of a 429 Halifax after the attack on the Krupps works at Essen on 26 March 1944, in which there were no aircraft losses, could be mistaken as a basis for a film script, but it also gives some indication of the danger and frenzied activity experienced by the crews:

... As zero hour approached, there was still no sign of the target indicators. Finally they appeared – way off the port wing. What now? The only solution was a circuit to port and make another run up. While coming out of a cloud and heading into the stream, the bomb aimer and the pilot observed another ac coming head on. Both pilots banked their ac to the right and luckily avoided each other. After a proper run up and bombs away, we found the bomb doors wouldn't close, making the Halifax stagger. The flight engineer resorted to emergency procedure to finally close them. A short while later the rear gunner hollered "fighter, fighter" – the pilot shouted back, "which side"? The rear gunner said, "doesn't matter, there's 3 of them." From then on the ac was under attack for a period of 30 minutes. It seemed like an hour and thirty. We corkscrewed to the right and to the left with the machine guns going all the time. After a long burst by the rear gunner, a fire started in one of the night fighters, forcing the pilot to bale out and the enemy ac went down in flames. Another enemy ac came in from the port side. The Halifax banked into him. As he went over, the mid-upper gunner was able to get in some telling shots. The enemy ac caught fire but continued to curve around after our ac. By now the rear gunner had joined in but still the enemy ac, although on fire, kept coming. The Halifax continued on its violent corkscrewing with the rear gunner saying, "He's getting closer. Why doesn't he bale out?" Finally the enemy ac exploded. No one baled out of that one. Shortly afterwards, the UK coast arrived and what welcome information that was from the navigator. Suddenly the Halifax was bracketed by heavy flak. Even though the IFF was turned on something was wrong. More violent manoeuvring to get out of this. Finally base. How many more do we have to do?

March also saw the Leeming crews involved in the Nuremberg raid on the night of the 30th. The Squadrons at Leeming were warned of freezing rain before take-off and to help counter it, their aircraft were sprayed with anti-freeze every hour. There was little for the aircrew to do at this time; many tried to sleep or take their mind off the coming raid with billiards, cards or chess. When the time came for the crews to board their aircraft they were taken to the dispersals where many of them took time for the last cigarette, as well as the traditional pre-operational custom of urinating with their comrades against the tail wheel! The raid itself turned out to be a disaster, with Bomber Command suffering its heaviest loss of the war, and five aircraft failed to return to Leeming.

From April 1944, the attacks in which 427 and 429 took part were very much concerned with the build up to "Operation Overlord", the invasion of Europe. New names began to appear in orders: marshalling yards, railways, construction works, supply depots, coastal gun positions, airfields; in fact anything that would dislocate transport and communications and hamper the German capacity for resistance. On 4 June, as part of the deception plan as to where the invasion would fall, Leeming crews attacked one of the heavy gun batteries at Calais. Then on the night of 5/6 June they assisted in a raid on what was thought to be a particularly important target, the concrete gun emplacements at Merville in Normandy which overlooked Sword Beach where part of the British

landings would take place. The whole area was heavily cratered, but unfortunately the battery remained in action and had to be taken by airborne forces during the morning of the sixth.

After D-Day, the Squadrons continued their raids behind the enemy lines in France in the face of very heavy flak and still meeting with fairly intensive enemy fighter activity, particularly near the coast. On such a raid on the night of 7 June, Halifax LW128 of 429 Sqn was hit by flak while en route to the railway marshalling yards at Acheres, and the pilot, Sqn Ldr Anderson DFC, was badly wounded. He ordered the crew to bale out before lapsing into unconsciousness and the aircraft went out of control. Three of the crew left the stricken aircraft, but the flight engineer, Sergeant C E J Steere RAF, refused and took over the controls. He began the careful return to English soil while the two air gunners, who also remained, gave what aid they could to the pilot. The bombs were jettisoned, but realising that a crash landing would certainly kill their skipper, and in a last ditch attempt to prevent this, the gunners attached him to a static line and all four parachuted from the stricken aircraft. The Halifax crashed near Benson in Oxfordshire, but sadly the pilot did not survive his ordeal. The actions of the three men were later recognised when each gunner was awarded the DFM, and Sgt Steere received the CGM (Flying). Two of the crew who had baled out were captured, but the navigator was able to evade the Germans and return to the UK some weeks later. The decoration awarded to Steere was the second CGM awarded to Leeming aircrew, both of them flight engineers in an RCAF squadron. The position of flight engineer was a relatively new one which had come about with the advent of the four-engined heavy bomber, and along with it, the decision was taken to dispense with a second pilot. It was considered though that the workload for a pilot of these bombers would be too much at times for one man, so to assist him the post of Flight Engineer was introduced. The crews themselves were not overjoyed with the loss of the second pilot, because uppermost in their minds was their probable fate if the pilot was incapacitated and as a consequence, many flight engineers, whose crew position was close behind the pilot's shoulder, were often given some rudimentary flying experience. This training was, of course, unofficial and was primarily intended to enable the flight engineer keep control of the aircraft while the remainder of the crew could bale out. On a significant number of occasions these men did much more and like Sgt Steere, often brought their badly damaged aircraft back home.

The understated and seemingly casual nature of many of the reports written immediately following an operation, however *hairy* it had been, can also be seen in the summaries given later by those who had been shot down, and either evaded capture, or spent the rest of the war as POWs. However, it takes little imagination when reading these accounts to be able to picture some of the drama, and all too often the tragedies, that preceded the loss. One such aircraft failed to return from a raid on the railway marshalling yards at Metz in June 1944, but having had more than their fair share of drama, all of the crew survived. The report was written by the rear gunner but in such a matter of fact way that he may just have been an observer:

... Outbound – fighter followed by fire. A/C slow and would not climb well: Monica found to be u/s. Crossed enemy coast at 14,000', pilot saw an e/a. 15 mins later, Nav. took gee fix & found they were about 20m off track: change made & two minutes later a/c was suddenly attacked by Ju 88 from dark part of sky. Just before the attack pilot saw S/L come to s/board & saw fighter planes on track to port & s/board. Fighter fired first from port quarter & 500' below – first shots went under a/c but some hit the bomb bay & set IB's on fire. R/G opened fire almost simultaneously with e/a. Pilot turned to port & dived & R/G continued firing. E/a

broke away up wash & to s/board at about 100 yds & R/G hit its belly and cockpit – e/a rolled over & went down in spin. 2nd Ju 88 attacked about 20 secs later & hit Halifax. Pilot stalled & dived. Third attack by Ju 88 from s/board quarter & level. R/G operated one gun manually – e/a dived away underneath. First attack damaged the hydraulics, fired IB's and controls made sluggish. Second attack – whole bomb bay burning furiously, bombs jettisoned: MUG badly burnt coming forward. Crew ordered to bale out. 2nd attack – hit in rear turret, R/G wounded in face. Nav, W/op, FE & MUG baled out before 3rd attack. R/G, BA & pilot left after 3rd attack. R/G landed N. of Diest at about 0040 hrs & pilot landed 2 or 3 miles from him.

On 16 June 1944, a total of 35 Halifaxes from 427 and 429 were prepared to participate in what was RCAF Leeming's first daylight raid, an attack on a flying-bomb site in the area of the Pas de Calais. In the event, for whatever reason, an inordinately high figure of 9 aircraft from 427 developed faults and did not take part, but daylight raids were to remain the norm for Leeming crews for much of the remainder of the war. One notable operation took place on 18 July and saw them in the force of almost 1,000 Halifaxes and Lancasters in support of "Operation Goodwood", where their massed bombing was designed to smash ways through the German lines near Caen. Each squadron lost an aircraft in this operation, LW127 from 429 in particularly tragic circumstances, when it crashed after being hit by bombs from another Halifax. There were only four survivors from the seven man crew who baled out but then drifted into the target area. The aerial operation also caused some casualties among the Allied ground troops, but with two German divisions suffering heavy losses, the raid was considered a success, even though the battle for Caen was still to grind on until 15 August. On the day before Caen fell, the fourth major operation carried out in support of the ground forces in Normandy took place. Leeming aircraft were taking part again, and as Canadian troops were among those in the front-line, it must have given the crews a great deal of satisfaction to know that they were actively supporting their own troops. The bad weather that had dogged the previous close support operations had cleared with visibility excellent. The bombing of German strong points, all very close to the Canadian positions, was reported as being extremely accurate:

> . . . ours was one of several aiming points clustered about the Caen/Falaise highway just ahead of British and Canadian troops straddling the road ready to surge ahead as soon as the bombardment ceased.

However, the results were not as they seemed, some of the bombs falling short, causing many casualties among the assault forces. The Canadians later stated that the bombing had a real effect on the morale of their troops and was a major factor in reducing their determination in the battle that followed. Notwithstanding the losses, the attack still went ahead and after some heavy fighting, Falaise was cleared of Germans by nightfall on 17 August. The cause of the accident will never be totally confirmed, but with the Canadian 1st Army troops using their usual yellow identifying smoke and Bomber Command using yellow target indicators on that day, a tragedy was there waiting to happen. The troops claimed that the bombs came before they lit their flares, although the crews reported that the smoke was showing before the first bombs were dropped in the area!

Other targets at that time included the Flying Bomb sites at La Breteque, Le Hey and Bois St Remy. These operations required precision bombing, as did those on another site situated in a quarry at Wizernes, and one north of Paris where the Germans had a Flying Bomb store in the mushroom caves at St Leu d'Esserant on the River Oise. The sites were heavily defended and casualties were often heavy among the attacking force, with the weight of bombs dropped seldom matching the damage caused. There were other specific precision targets such as on 15 August, when the attack on Soersterberg aerodrome was part of a major operation, mounted with the objective of cratering airfield runways to a degree sufficient to keep the Luftwaffe on the ground. Then through August and into September the coastal gun batteries and defences of Brest, St Malo, Le Havre, and Calais, all received some attention from the Leeming squadrons. The raid on 31 August on the coastal gun batteries on Île de Cézembre, a small island just outside the port of St Malo in Brittany, was described with some enthusiasm and a dash of humour by one airman, although he was talking about someone else:

> . . . No. 429D (MZ377) bomb aimer, because of mechanical trouble with release mechanisms, released his load on "safe". Ac directly behind saw 1000lb bombs bouncing around merrily on the rocks below.

This operation was the last of 24 different operations carried out by the Leeming squadrons during the month of August, along with a substantial number of training sorties, and it was with some pride that the ORB for August reported that during that month all records had been surpassed:

427	429
264 operational sorties	274 operational sorties
Two aircraft missing	Three aircraft missing
Two early returns	Four early returns
1337.20 hrs. op.	1320.20 hrs. op.
269.50 hrs. non op.	299.30 hrs. non op.

In addition, throughout August there had been no aircraft accidents, and in having the least number of operational failures due to technical faults, the ground crews received the serviceability honours for No.6 Group. These ground crews had overcome many difficulties in achieving this accolade. Not least of which was the fact that the normal routine maintenance task had been aggravated by the necessity of converting from the B.II Halifax to the B.V and finally in March 1944, to the B.III. The latter requiring retooling for the Hercules engine which replaced the Merlin. Minor alterations, such as the installation of modified cupolas in the rear turrets, gave little trouble, but others were less routine. For example, also in April 1944, nine new aircraft were received with a modification that allowed the petrol tanks to be pressurised with nitrogen, based on a theory that this would provide protection against petrol fires. In practice, however, the theory never did work properly and simply provided more headaches for the technical staff until its use was suspended by an instruction from Group in June. Another source of much work for the groundcrews came from the wish to lighten the Halifax, to give it more speed and altitude. It was considered that these improvements could be achieved by the removal of the mid-upper gun turret, and the fairing over of the subsequent hole. Wg Cdr Pattison, the CO of 429, had been a keen advocate of this modification, in part because he believed (correctly) that bombers were being shot down by fighters attacking from below. As a consequence, his Squadron's aircraft were soon flying with a redundant gunner lying on a mattress in the belly, keeping a look-out from a newly installed perspex blister! The fitting of *Gee* and eventually *H2S* systems in all 427 and 429 aircraft, required the acquisition of new skills and techniques for the *sparkies*, but in all cases the majority of the work was carried out on an opportunity basis, with the operational requirement always applying the most severe pressure to get the aircraft prepared. Even when bad weather intervened and stopped the flying, the groundcrew did not stop; for them as the Canadians put it, it was "make and mend". At such times many of the minor faults, which had

been noted and then deferred to a more opportune moment, were dealt with.

Alongside all of this routine work were, the unfortunately all too common, battle damage repair requirements. These repairs varied from the frequent patching of holes, to quite major recovery tasks such as the one presented to the groundcrew at Leeming after a collision between LV987 and LV985, while they were on a raid to Le Bourget on 18 April 1944. Both aircraft got back home safely and with the former it was possible, by changing an engine and propeller as well as carrying out some skin repairs, to get it back in service in two days. However, LV985 took somewhat longer as it had lost seven feet from its starboard wing, which necessitated the fit of a new outer mainplane, a job which took considerably longer. Repairs of even greater magnitude were often successfully undertaken, such as the work carried out on MZ819 of 427 during the winter of 44/45. The Halifax swung on landing, hit and demolished a concrete blockhouse (fortunately empty), the undercarriage collapsed and the port outer engine caught fire. Yet it was repaired and flew on until it was struck off charge in December 1946.

Away from direct aircraft work, the maintenance of Direction Finding and Wireless Telegraphy equipment was also a continuous task. This increased with the arrival of more powerful equipment, such as the receiver/transmitter for the new medium power High Frequency Transmitter installed at the Theakston Grange Transmitter Site in September 1944, and ultimately the VHF equipment in February 1945. Structural alterations to the Signals Section which commenced in October 1943, brought about the change-over to a new open switchboard system in January 1944. The Armament Section too, had its problems and despite some major improvements, their work remained physically hard and hazardous. Incredible as it may sound, at one stage in April 1944 they had to cope with a shortage of 1000lb bombs at the depot, and consequently, had to borrow from Dishforth. It was nearly a month before new supplies started arriving at Leeming Bar Railway Station, and no doubt to keep the books straight, the loan would have been repaid!

The period of time immediately prior to and following the landings at Normandy, was a time of intensive effort for those at Leeming. At the end of the month, the Chief Technical Officer could be excused for boasting about the efforts of the groundcrews. For example on 5 June, the Station Armament Officer received an instruction from 6 Group to the effect, that sufficient bombs to complete three sorties were to be placed at each dispersal, with the aircraft to be bombed-up immediately they returned from the first sortie. At the same time, the Base was tasked to send all available transport from Leeming and Skipton, to collect 37,000 bomb tails from 28 MSU for the Group to use on 6 June, in a maximum effort operation against a major road junction at Condé sur Noireau in France. As a result of these orders, on 5 June a total of 36 aircraft were loaded and after their return, the total made ready rose to 37, which at that time was the total Station strength. They all took part in the operation to Condé and were then prepared again, when the refuelling, rearming and repair of all *snags* was undertaken in roughly three hours. An example, which can be used to gauge the amount of pure physical effort that was put into the bombing-up of a large number of aircraft, can be found in the preparation which began when 39 aircraft were loaded at Leeming on 20/21 June. This work was completed by 0100 hours, but within the hour, as the ground-crew were probably trying to get some much needed rest, the operation was cancelled and the order given for the load to be changed. The aircraft were therefore unloaded and then re-armed with full loads of 500lb bombs by noon. This operation was then carried out, but bad weather meant that most of the aircraft returned with their bombs, which then had to be removed. All within 24 hours. In April 1944, an additional responsibility

had been added to the long list held by the armourers, when a new bombing range at Snape opened. But it was probably not until 13 June, that the Station Armament Officer realised a less obvious aspect of what had become somewhat of a liability, when he had to conduct an inquiry about the accidental dropping of a practice bomb on a farm building close to the range. He was no doubt pleased that it was only a practice bomb, but probably not as pleased as the farmer!

However, particularly in the first half of 1944, things were not always going well at Leeming. Mysterious fires were started, such as on 27 April, when one flared up on the west side of the bomb dump and before it was extinguished, had burnt or badly charred a tarpaulin and several ammunition boxes, fortunately empty. Two days later, an aircraft wheel cover was found burning on one of the dispersals, but again no culprit was found, nor was there after other fires were discovered under equally suspicious circumstances. Problems also existed in some areas of the civilian workforce on the Station, and in June, the Administrative Officer had occasion to gather together and admonish the 28 civilian batmen, following complaints about their standards of work and behaviour. In fact, at this point things had obviously reached a head, because four of the offenders were discharged from employment on 5 June 1944.

For a little while in 1944 the prize possession of 427 Sqn was Halifax LW163, U for Uncle, which on 3 August 1944, when piloted by Fg Off Murphy, had been taking part in a raid against the construction works for a V-1 storage site at Forêt de Nieppe near St Omer in France. The operation was a success, but unfortunately, this particular aircraft found itself below one of the bomber streams. As a consequence the aircraft was hit, not from flak, but from above from whence came three 500lb bombs: one passed through the port wing, one through the middle of the fuselage and a third through the starboard fin. Miraculously the control rods were not hit, although the Elsan (chemical toilet) was wrecked! The pilot decided to continue and after pressing home his attack he managed to get the severely damaged aircraft and his crew safely back to Leeming, no doubt wondering whose side they were on. The Halifax was subsequently shown off to the King and Queen, who along with HRH The Princess Elizabeth, visited the base on 11 August 1944. The crew were paraded in front of the aircraft and after the King had discussed the incident with the pilot they were all greeted by the Royal Party. The King was primarily at Leeming to decorate 29 aircrew, and a full blown parade had been organised, with a red carpet and all. Unfortunately, the wind was not in on the organisation and as it was rather strong that day the carpet was constantly being flapped about and rolled up behind him. As a consequence the Station Adjutant was tasked with preventing this distraction, which he did by standing on the carpet behind His Majesty. However, the wind veered and then began to roll the front portion of the carpet, this time onto the feet of the King who smilingly turned to Flt Lt Bell and suggested that it be removed as it was serving little purpose. It is not recorded if the Adjutant held up the ceremony in order to comply with the King's suggestion, or for that matter who rolled the carpet up! Following the departure of the Royal Party the Station "threw" a dance in the Airmen's Mess in honour of those decorated. No doubt it was a success but 427 Sqn felt that a bouquet of thorns should have been presented to the girls from the Canadian Women's Division (WDs or Wob Dobs) based at Group HQ, who had attended the parade but refused to stay for the dance!

Throughout the remainder of 1944 and until May 1945, 427 and 429 Squadrons continued their attacks on enemy targets. As the Front moved eastward into Europe, so by mid-October familiar names like Dortmund, Duisburg, Essen, Cologne, and Düsseldorf, reappeared. The war may have been coming to a close but the winter of 1944 saw no let up in the ferocity of the Luftwaffe's attacks, and flak was as heavy as ever. Losses continued

to occur, but occasionally Leeming's squadrons were able to turn the tables on their airborne opponents. There was no question that the efficacy of the nose armament of the Halifax, which was a solitary hand operated Vickers K gun, known as the VGO (Vickers Gas Operated), was doubted by many. However, following an operation to Oberhausen on 1 November 1944, the bomb aimer in MZ474 of 429 Sqn would have had few reservations remaining after he shot down a FW190 during a head-on engagement. Crews from 427 Sqn were also successful that night when they came under attack from the relatively new threat from German jet fighters. Conditions were not ideal for the bombers, with clear skies over dense cloud illuminated by a full moon, which meant that they were silhouetted against the clouds and were clearly visible to the Luftwaffe crews. Nevertheless, this apparent advantage could in fact be a double-edged sword, as they too could sometimes be seen. In this raid the results showed that even the fastest of the German night-fighters could come off second best. The action began when the rear gunner of Halifax LV945 spotted a jet fighter in the distance, but as he lost it he spotted another which attacked them. The air gunner, who was all the while giving instructions to the pilot, opened fire as the fighter got closer, and the bomber attempted to escape by turning and diving towards the clouds. However, before they reached this temporary sanctuary, the enemy aircraft was hit, burst into flames and fell away to crash. At the same time, but some miles distant the flight engineer of LW130 also spotted a jet fighter, off and above their port wing. The pilot of his Halifax also dived towards the clouds, corkscrewing the aircraft as he did so in an attempt to lose their opponent. The enemy aircraft followed and opened fire, but in turn came under fire from long bursts from the mid-upper and rear gunners who each manned turrets armed with four machine guns. The fighter got very close, and its pilot was still pressing home the attack, when his aircraft was hit and fell away in flames. This particular fighter was positively identified as a rocket propelled Me163, and if so was a very rarely recorded occasion of this type being used as a night-fighter.

Aircraft continued to be lost or damaged in a variety of ways, sometimes the crews were saved, sometimes not. Returning from a raid on Chantilly on 8 August 1944, LW132 of 429 went down in flames after an engine fire. It exploded at 5000 ft and fell into the sea near Littlehampton in Sussex – almost home, but only the navigator survived after being blown clear with his parachute. On 12 September 1944, the crew of MZ864, also of 429, was more fortunate after being hit by flak while mining off Oslo. The pilot succeeded in ditching the aircraft in the North Sea, and the crew were picked up by an Air Sea Rescue Launch directed to the position by another Halifax from their Squadron. Danger, as ever, was always present, even in the relative haven of another RAF airfield. On one such occasion after a successful operation on 1 November 1944, 429 Sqn lost four aircraft in a few minutes. The aircraft had previously been diverted to Spilsby, but were caught and wrecked in the fire and explosion that followed the crash of a fully laden Lancaster. This bomber was in the process of taking-off when it spun into one of the Halifaxes and caught fire. The resultant blast and burning debris also caused a second Halifax to catch fire, and it too, was completely destroyed. Two others sustained damage that later caused them to be written off. Fortunately at the time of the crash the Leeming crews were not in their aircraft, and though a number of the Squadron's groundcrew were working on them, they escaped injury. However, when the crash occurred, one of 429s flight engineers, Plt Off Platt, had run to Halifax MZ824 and attempted to start the engines to move it from the rapidly increasing conflagration. The Chief Technical Officer at Spilsby also entered the Halifax to assist him and they succeeded in starting one engine, which resulted in the aircraft swinging round to face the burning wreckage. Unfortunately, it was then that the

explosion occurred, blowing in the nose of the Halifax and fatally injuring the flight engineer, who died while being rushed to hospital.

Later the same month, a Halifax from 420 Sqn at Tholthorpe hit a tree just prior to landing at Leeming, with the resultant crash killing one, and injuring another four from the crew. The majority of the crew from that aircraft, along with many others involved in similar crashes, frequently had cause to be thankful for the inherent strength of the Halifax. A claim borne out only a few days previously, when a 427 Sqn aircraft swung on landing. First of all MZ819 demolished a concrete blockhouse, then the undercarriage collapsed, and as the aircraft scraped to a halt the port outer engine caught fire. The crew escaped relatively unscathed, and fortunately, as the blockhouse was empty at the time, there were no casualties amongst the guards. The aircraft itself was severely damaged but flew again after it was repaired, and was not struck off charge until December 1946. Similar calamities continued during the winter of 1944/45, with one such occurrence on 27 December when MZ291 of 427 Sqn was seen to have flames coming from its underside while it was on its take-off run. A tyre burst, the aircraft wobbled, swung, and finally crashed before bursting into flames in the scrap dump some 150 feet from the end of the runway. Fortunately, the crew was safe and quickly exited from the wreck and its immediate vicinity, no doubt hastened by the knowledge that the bombs were still on board. The area was cleared, the village of Leeming Bar evacuated, all roads in the vicinity were blocked and a warning tannoyed for everyone to take cover. The danger presented by the bombs meant that the aircraft was left to burn, but almost half an hour had elapsed from the time of the crash before there was an explosion. A further 30 minutes elapsed before there was a second detonation, but good fortune continued to smile and there were no casualties from either blast.

Nevertheless, this was not always the case. On

23 February 1945, with the war almost won, LW139 of 429 Sqn, being flown by a crew from 427, had two engines fail on take-off causing it to crash-land in a field SW of the airfield. The pilot was killed, and of the remaining six crew, three died later in hospital. Then, some four days later, the Station had more tragedy on its doorstep, with 427 Sqn losing its last Halifax of the war when RG347 blew a tyre on take-off, crashed on one wing and exploded, killing all but the rear gunner.

The air gunners in Bomber Command had a particularly lonely and dangerous task in protecting their aircraft with very little in the way of recognition, and it was no different for the squadrons based at Leeming. Only very occasionally did they come out on top in battles against the German fighters, but the month of February 1945 saw one such occasion for 427 Sqn. They had a particularly successful night while returning from an operation to Goch, when the air gunners from three separate aircraft entered claims for German fighters destroyed. The claims were for a FW190, a jet fighter and a flying wing (possibly the Me163), with all three being seen to explode on hitting the ground. The gunners, then in Lancasters, were again heavily involved in March when they drove off a number of attacks, but on that occasion only one claim, albeit for a Me262 jet, was made.

In the last six months of the war Leeming base itself still had a few more hair-raising experiences to endure. If the hazards of war were in themselves not enough, one odd report that came in from the Watch Office made people sit up and take notice. It stated that the building had shaken violently at 0240 hrs on 30 December 1944, and being the middle of the festive season they were no doubt reassured to discover that the cause was only an earth tremor! Then a month later on 31 January 1945, the base had to deal with the largest diversion in the history of No.6 Group. In the incredible time of 45 minutes, 62 USAAF B24 Liberators, one Barracuda and one Halifax were diverted to, and

landed safely on, the airfield. The sheer numbers of aircraft involved meant that almost 600 personnel arrived, all requiring food and sleeping accommodation, which was allocated wherever it could be found. The following day must have been another busy one for the Station, particularly for Air Traffic Control, when most of the visitors departed, leaving the Station to return to what was to be a relatively quiet and non-operational couple of weeks.

The tide of war was by then in full flow for the Allies, and returning aircrew had long ago got used to returning to well-lit airfields. On reaching the English coast the crews would see ring after ring of Drem lights, and adjacent to each airfield a red light flashing its identification code. In addition, Leeming, like many other bases, switched on two searchlights to form a "V" in the sky. With the Luftwaffe still operating the obvious danger of this procedure had been weighed against that of trying to get up to 40 returning bombers in safely to blacked-out airfields, but nonetheless a risk still remained. The fact that a hazard existed was brought sharply into focus for those at Leeming on 4 March 1945, when a report came in that the Luftwaffe had intruders in the shapes of the Ju88 and Ju188 in that night's returning bomber stream. Leeming was not on operations that night, which could only be described as being a filthy one with icing conditions prevalent, but the base was already on alert to receive diverted aircraft from No.4 Group. Emergency precautions with the runway lights were put into operation and in due course 12 aircraft, guided in by flares and colours of the day, managed to land while avoiding the AA fire put up by the gunners of the RAF Regiment. One enemy raider found Leeming and strafed the airfield with cannon fire while the bombers were landing, then flew very low over Hangars 4 and 5, firing onto Runway Three Zero and the perimeter track near the bomb dump. A number of bombers were lost elsewhere that night but no great damage was done at Leeming, although one eye witness related that while it lasted it had been like watching a mad firework display.

In the air on 2 March 1945, Flt Lt J E Creeper flew a sortie to Cologne that was number 3000 for 429 Sqn. Also in March, 427 Sqn won the Bristol Bombing Trophy for the greatest accuracy in practice bombing. This had probably been gained with the Halifax, but by the middle of the month the Squadron had been re-equipped with the long awaited Lancaster BI, closely followed by similar provision for its sister squadron. Soon afterwards on 12 April 1945, 429 Sqn finally received its official badge, when Air Marshal G O Johnson, AOC-in-C RCAF Overseas, arrived to carry out the presentation to Wg Cdr Evans, who had taken over command of the Squadron a mere two days before.

By that stage of the war bomber losses had plummeted, and from Leeming's point of view there was to be only one more aircraft, a Lancaster, that would fail to return from operations. Consequently, casualties amongst the crews were minimal, although enemy fighters were reported to be still active up to two months before the end of the war, and there was the ever present danger from ground fire.

Throughout much of the war aircrew losses stemming from enemy action or aircraft accidents remained terribly high, but even on the ground there were dangers, and in 1945 two aircrew from 427 Sqn were killed in separate road accidents on the Base itself. Then at the time when there were to be no more war-time losses for the Station, the accidental death of a civilian just a month before the end of hostilities, was perhaps a reminder to everyone that fate was indeed fickle. A Lancaster from 429 Sqn, after landing with no brakes, overran the runway into Gatenby Lane, fatally injuring Mr James Thomson, a batman, who was walking home from his job in the Officers' Mess. This accident highlighted the possible dangers to any sort of traffic in the lane, and within days of the accident a set of traffic lights operated from air traffic control was installed in the road.

Finally, came the last operation to be tasked on the two RCAF Squadrons from Leeming and appropriately enough, it was to be the same as the first carried out way back in January 1943 – a mine laying sortie to the Dutch Islands. The 18 Lancasters took-off on 3 May 1945, but the aircraft were in fact recalled and at long last the war in Europe was almost over.

During five years of the war, aircraft from Leeming had carried the war to a Europe dominated by the regimes of Nazi Germany and Fascist Italy. It is a sobering thought that during this time, in excess of 300 aircraft allotted to Leeming were lost from one cause or another, along with numerous others damaged, and that while training for operations, as well as in their execution, many hundreds of the Station's aircrew died, were injured, or became prisoners of war. The value of their sacrifice should never be underestimated, a sentiment borne out from the words of the German Minister for Armaments, Albert Speer:

> . . . The real importance of the air war consisted in the fact that it opened a second front long before the invasion of Europe. That front was the skies over Germany . . . every square metre of territory we controlled was a kind of a front line. Defence against air attacks required the production of thousands of anti-aircraft guns, the stockpiling of tremendous quantities of ammunition all over the country and holding in readiness hundreds of thousands of soldiers, who in addition had to stay in position by their guns, often totally inactive, for months at a time.

The reference to anti-aircraft guns relates to a figure estimated as being close on 20,000, and it must be remembered that guns such as the 88mm Flak was arguably the most potent anti-tank gun of the war. Their use would have certainly made a difference to the anti-tank defences on the Eastern Front!

The losses sustained by Bomber Command were heavy, as were those of Leeming. It could be said that No.6 Group has been the forgotten group, and even though at the end of the war Bomber Harris paid particular tribute to its achievements as being surpassed by none, when compared with No.5 Group, it has been largely ignored. Leeming has had similar treatment, with its part being underplayed or disregarded, but its crews, whether from 4 Gp or 6 Gp, consistently played a large part in the Victory in Europe and paid a high price to achieve it.

The events of Tuesday 8 May 1945, brought scenes of celebration throughout the country, and none more so than at Leeming. That afternoon at 1500 hrs Prime Minister Churchill broadcast the announcement of Germany's unconditional surrender, a message heard by all personnel over the Station tannoy system. To celebrate the occasion free beer was available to all, and during the evening a Victory Dance was held in the NAAFI with music supplied by the Station Band for more than 800 personnel who were in attendance.

The war in Europe was over, but not everyone was able to enjoy the free beer, though in view of the mission that was being prepared for, it is probable that those involved were happy to postpone the festivity. With remarkable speed the Lancasters had been stripped of guns, ammunition, and all unnecessary gear, so on the very same day that victory was announced, 13 Lancasters from each Squadron were able to take off for Brussels to carry out "Operation Exodus". This operation was laid on specifically to return newly released prisoners of war to the UK. During the three days they were involved, the Leeming Squadrons carried almost 1900 personnel to the two main reception centres at Wing and Westcott.

Although Japan was still in the fight, to all intents and purposes the war was over for RCAF Leeming. On the Sunday following VE day, after the victory celebration Church Parade had been held in No 3 Hangar, came the problem of what to do with the multitude of RCAF personnel whose main thought was how soon they would be repatriated.

Taking a step backwards from those thoughts of repatriation to the early days of RCAF Leeming can give some idea of the size of the problem that awaited No.6 Group at the end of the war. The initial build-up of personnel had presented the administration staff with problems in the provision of accommodation and catering that never really went away. By the end of November 1943 it had become clear that the accommodation situation was acute, in the main because of the increase in the number of aircrew. In the Officers' Mess for example 12 beds were placed in the Games Room, 22 single rooms each received three beds, others received two, and the Padre's suite was vacated to produce another nine bed spaces. In December, an additional Sergeants' Mess was opened in a Nissen Hut on the Communal Site, and though the idea of having two such Messes was regretted, it was considered necessary because of the large number of SNCOs on the Unit. The Communal Site, where a number of large Nissen Huts had been erected, was on land leased temporarily from a local farmer, and its position is alluded to in an entry in the ORB on 9 December 1943:

. . . The piece of land situated between our Communal Site and the existing Station Boundaries, namely Airmens' Married Quarters, has now been acquired following our requisitioning in August 1943. This piece of land is to be used as a Sports Field since the existing fields are muddy and swampy. It is the intention of the Station to build a road across one end of the field in order to join up the Communal Site with the parent Station thereby closing the entrance to the Communal Site and doing away with another Picket Post. Road will be built by Station labour.

On 18 January 1944, a new Dining Mess for aircrew personnel was also opened on the Communal Site, because at this stage of the war aircrew were still being given augmented rations and it was not considered wise to display the different standards in the same mess. A medical report presented on 18 November 1943, had already recognised a further complication in this area, other than that of morale, when it pointed out the underlying problems that could stem from poor nutrition, stating:

> . . . the supplemented diet of aircrew gave much healthier state of teeth, gums, eyes etc. Attention to post war results of diet of other personnel necessary.

Clearly it was felt that problems were being stored away, but at the time there was a war to be won! The report also estimated that the methods used in the preparation of vegetables indicated that they would cause a loss of approximately 85 per cent of what it termed as "the scurvy preventing factor", and that problems relating to this deficiency would not appear until about ten years hence. To counter the loss of these vitamins, the report recommended that diets would have to be supplemented with synthetic forms of ascorbic acid! It is difficult to say if anything came of this particular suggestion, but a more popular addition to the diet did actually come on the scene in November 1944, when a mobile dairy was set up at Leeming. Its success can be seen from the fact that it was soon able to supply ten ounces of milk per day for each and every person at Leeming, and that was a positive step forward. Perhaps surprisingly, the general state of health of the Canadians in 1943/44 was often a cause for concern, with repeated reference to large numbers of personnel suffering from "upper respiratory problems". Undoubtedly the Vale of York took some getting used to after the wide open spaces of Canada. Scabies was rife on the Station in late 1943, but with the changing of 36,000 blankets the incidence

had dropped to nil by the end of November. Perhaps not surprisingly the medical reports consistently indicated that VD was a major, and ongoing problem. For example, in July 1944 attendance was made compulsory for everyone to attend one of the three screenings of the anti-VD film "The Three Cadets". Each showing of the film was followed by a lecture from the Unit Medical Officer, but the incidence of the disease remained high until well into September.

The authority for the combining of RCAF Leeming with RCAF Skipton-on-Swale to produce No.63 Base had been given by No.6 Group on 1 May 1944, and the first Base Commander was Air Commodore Bryans, who was promoted from his position as CO of Leeming. Within the week his previous position as Station Commander was filled by another officer from Leeming, acting Gp Capt Newson, who was promoted directly from the rank of Squadron Leader! Also in May, combined messing, and presumably equal rationing, began in the Sergeants' Mess, when 132 SNCOs moved from No 1 Mess to No 2 on the Communal Site, which meant a total of 413 were now messing together. At the same time a barrack block was released for airmen's accommodation when the WAAF Officers were moved into the Officers' Mess where they could also be fed, and the Base Commander moved into Gatenby House. This had originally been designated as the Station Commander's Residence, but was only made available for use by moving the Hospital, which had so far been housed there, into the annex next to Station Sick Quarters. Notwithstanding all of these moves, accommodation remained a major problem until the end of the war, and as far as the quality of food was concerned even after Leeming had won the No.6 Group Dining Room Competition in September 1944, complaints about the state of catering, real or imagined, remained fairly high on the agenda.

These, therefore, were the type of administrative problems that still could be seen at Leeming when the war ended. The priority had always been to win the war which often meant that the need for many improvements had been met with little in the way of urgency. It was almost paradoxical therefore, that as victory approached it became equally understandable that little would be done to change this state of affairs. Consequently, it was not until July 1945 that the accommodation situation started to ease when the first drafts for repatriation to Canada, via Torquay, began to come through. Also at this time, but only for those remaining for a while in North Yorkshire, plans were laid to organise improved liberty runs, entertainment, sport and education. Indeed, from that time until the RCAF closed the Station, it is easy to get the impression that the hardest worked individuals on the base were the officers who were in charge of the recreational facilities.

Throughout their stay at Leeming, the Canadians had ranged far and wide over the Yorkshire countryside. The local hostelries did well out of their stay, particularly the "Black Ox", "The Crown", and the "Willow Tree" (of which only the latter remains), with many airmen making friends with the local people; enduring friendships at that. The establishment known as "Jock's Café" was always popular, and Nellie Hunter who at the age of 13 worked there, remembers the Canadians in particular for the quantity of "Spam, egg and chips" consumed, even at the price of half a crown, which was a considerable sum in those days. The aircrew were allowed two eggs, groundcrew only one, but the source of the large tins of Spam can only be a matter of speculation. In spite of that, the café's owner moved to Canada after the war, and the profit he made may have had something to do with his decision! Balancing the high spirits and occasional escapade, the generosity with which the *goodies* from Canada were shared is remembered especially by those who were children during the war. Albeit, at the beginning of their "peacetime" residence at Leeming, the Station Commander, before authorising the extended liberty runs, felt it expe-

dient to deliver a directive to show that he expected:

> . . . attention to be paid to dress and behaviour in the local towns and villages, in order to leave behind a good impression.

Entertainment facilities had been fairly well organised during the war: dances, concerts, ENSA shows, cinema shows, numerous activities in aid of the Red Cross, Canadian Victory Loans, and on one occasion, a "Salute the Soldier" week sponsored by – the WAAFs! Dances became an almost nightly event, though not surprisingly with their frequency, less well supported than before. The old favourite, "Bingo", was always there with 20 cigarettes and two shillings and sixpence the usual prize for a "House". The popularity of the type of entertainment on offer can be seen by the size of the audiences at three functions held on 25 January 1945. An ENSA show in the NAAFI attracted 500 personnel, a film shown in the YMCA had a further 500 in the audience, and the Officers' Mess seated an additional 240 at a film show. Even allowing for a certain degree of rounding-up of the totals the numbers are still impressive, but at the same time they also help to highlight the relative isolation of the Base.

Sport had flourished consistently throughout the war, with weekly trips to Ripon Spa Baths; Canadian track and field meets were held, mostly at Topcliffe, and tennis courts were marked out on the Parade Square. One of the hangars which had been marked out with badminton courts in 1944, was later opened for roller skating for up to 200 people a time. Soft Ball was always popular, as was Ice Hockey which was played at Durham City Ice Rink. The ice rink had been built by a local businessman in 1939 and although the skating surface was not ideal (the roof was supported by a number of pillars, some of which rose from the ice), all Canadian units in the area put together squads of players to form a total of ten teams that competed in the Northern Ice Hockey League. The sport was extremely popular with the Canadians, and with a number of players who had played back home, as well as professionally in the USA, the standard of play was very high. Obviously operational commitments took their toll, but on most days of the week there was either a match or practice taking place on the ice rink.

A newspaper, "By Leeming personnel for Leeming personnel, price two pence", appeared in the early part of March 1945, and though originally called "Leeming Lines" opinions for a new name had been sought. Before the third copy appeared, the title of "Pundit" was agreed upon, but like many other such endeavours it gradually faded into obscurity as repatriation became the goal. The apparent immediacy of returning home to Canada was the catalyst for many to think of their future, and with most people's thoughts centred on civilian jobs, business for the Education Section increased dramatically with the coming of peace. With the disbandment of No.63 Base in August 1945, Leeming was left as an independent unit with Skipton as a sub-station. Station Headquarters personnel moved into the old base HQ beside the main entrance to the Station. Into the top floor moved the education staff, who even managed to put together a Chemistry Lab for classes. The Canadians had planned for peace, and as early as September 1943, the Deputy Minister of Pensions and National Health in the Canadian Government had visited Leeming to discuss the rehabilitation of Canadian personnel at the end of the war. Even at that early stage there followed lectures on post war Canada, along with classes designed to encourage study for civilian careers, so naturally, at the end of the war these activities were stepped up.

An activity of a different sort, but one that still involved the entire Station, took place at Leeming a few weeks after the end of the war in Europe. This was a brand new venture, where on 16 June, after years of war when the Station was "off-limits" to most civilians, RCAF Leeming threw open its doors to the general public. Amongst the

events laid on that day was a track and field meet, with soft ball and football games also being played. A buffet tea was served in No.2 Hangar, with the distribution of chocolate and gum to all of the children a very popular way to conclude the day. The day itself was considered a huge success by everyone concerned, with an estimated 4000 civilians receiving the hospitality of the Station.

On various occasions in the weeks following VE day, special flights, under the codename, "Spasm", had been laid on from Leeming to take the groundcrew on trips to Berlin to view the effects of the bombing. They had been very popular, but perhaps a more personal "thank you" was arranged for 25 July 1945, when the Commanding Officer made an address to all WAAF personnel:

> ... I extend to you "The Keys of the Station" for this day, with our most hearty thanks for your splendid efforts in the past.

The WAAF personnel were given the day off from work and trips in Lancasters were available for those who wanted them. The SNCOs were entertained to a Cocktail Party in the Officers' Mess, and in the evening all WAAFs were served a steak dinner by the senior officers. They were also presented with packs of cigarettes from the Canadian YMCA, plus copies of a photograph taken with all of the girls in front of a Lancaster.

While much of this was going on, and particularly as the RCAF had not been involved against the Japanese, Japan's surrender on 15 August must almost have been seen as an anti-climax – but not quite. As the ORB records:

> ... News of the Japanese surrender was received over the radio at 0015 hrs this morning, and from then on the remainder of the night was very lively and a good time was had by all personnel. There was a large bonfire and lots of singing. Pyrotechnics

illuminated the celebrations which lasted for most of the hours of darkness. Discipline and behaviour of all personnel for the night was very commendable under the circumstances.

However, in the midst of all this festivity the sound of aircraft engines could still be heard over Leeming, although the local inhabitants were no longer kept awake by the sound of waves of bombers overhead in the early hours. The Station, when part of No.63 Base, had been tasked with the disposal of all unserviceable incendiaries from within the Group. Throughout July and into August two or three trips were being made every day to dispose of the munitions at sea, and in addition, the aircraft were kept busy ferrying bombs and ammunition back to central collecting points.

A further celebration in the shape of the first "Battle of Britain Day" to be held at Leeming took place on 15 September 1945, producing an air display, children's sports, ice cream for all, plus an invitation to see over most of the sections on the Unit. More than 3000 locals attended, but the reduction in numbers since the open day in June perhaps reflected that they too wanted to put the memories of the war behind them.

When no munition disposal missions were scheduled, training continued, although it was not very popular. It was on one such training flight on 5 November 1945, that Leeming's Canadian aircrew suffered their final casualties. The tragedy occurred when a Lancaster from 429 Sqn, piloted by Plt Off Conley, crashed into a hill while breaking cloud at Pallan's Farm on Beamsley Moor near Ilkley. Of the crew, four were killed and four injured:

. . . WO2 Belenger played a highly commendable part after the accident. Although injured and suffering from shock, he was able to remove several of the crew away from the burning aircraft, after which

he set out for help. He located a Farm House from where he phoned the local police who organised assistance.

A more satisfying reason for flying than taking part in training sorties over the UK was on-going at the time of this crash. Understandably, the crews were delighted when the Lancasters from both Squadrons had started a series of flights to and from Italy, under the codename, "Operation Dodge". These flights were for the transportation of British Army personnel back to the UK, and it is clear that the trips were not considered as being "all work", because the crews were never in too much of a hurry to return to England. One crew even felt inclined to report that the food and accommodation provided for them in Italy was "quite satisfactory". It was not to remain such a popular operation though, because by the time it ceased in April 1946, more than half of the non-squadron personnel at Leeming had already been repatriated to Canada. This was a fact obviously noted by those belonging to the Squadrons because Operation Dodge had meant that very few of their people had been included in that number! However, as the operation wound down and the aircraft themselves were ferried back to Maintenance Units, more and more Canadians were released for the trip home. By 16 May 1946, all personnel, except the Rear Party,[15] were posted to Topcliffe prior to their repatriation on 20 May 1946. The final entry in the records of RCAF Leeming reads:

. . . Today is the last day of existence for 427 and 429 Squadrons. This means that this Station will be disbanded wef 30 June 1946. Both Squadrons closed down on schedule thanks to the co-operation of everyone.

The entry was wrong on two counts. Firstly, 427 and 429 were to exist again within the RCAF, and secondly, the Station was not to be disbanded but was about to take on a new role.

CHAPTER THREE

No. 228 O C U
June 1946 to September 1961

The dust from the departing Canadians had not even begun to settle before the advance party of the new inhabitants came through the main gates of what was once again to be RAF Leeming. They were followed by the main body of approximately 700 men and 288 women from No.54 OTU, RAF East Moor, who arrived by road and air on 28 June 1946. The problems that were soon to be all too apparent were already surfacing by then, and Gp Capt Ryan, the newly appointed Commanding Officer, must have wondered what he had let himself in for. A few days earlier, on the 21st, the first few aircraft were ferried in, and as and when they came ready from a routine inspection, others followed. The total included variants of the Mosquito, the Wellington T 10, the Martinet, the Master, and the Oxford, all of which were to be used in the training of night-fighter crews.

In the first situation report at the end of June no great enthusiasm was expressed about the state of affairs with which the airmen of the day found themselves having to contend. The post-war climate of austerity meant that RAF Leeming was only one of many stations that would suffer from parsimonious funding and the disincentives it engendered. A plight brought about by a mix of the country's near bankruptcy and exhaustion from a long and bitter war, along with the usual peacetime apathy of government towards the Fighting Services. It was noted that:

... Officers' and Airmens' Married Quarters (MQs) are in such a state of disrepair that few are fit for occupation . . . General shortage of personnel, particularly SNCOs in Cook, Fitter and Rigger trades is being keenly felt....Airmen of Servicing Wing have been accommodated in Barrack Blocks 35 and 36; SHQ airmen in 37 and 37A; WAAF in 33 and 34 on main camp and the old WAAF Dispersed Site is now only used for Course pupils but none of the Barrack Blocks can be considered up to standard.

On the recreational side, a puzzling comment was made:

... As a result of the Station being in occupation by the RCAF for nearly four years, sports fields are almost non-existent.

Whether that statement implied that the Canadians were not interested enough in sports, or that the fields had suffered from excessive use, is unclear. It possibly came from the cancellation of the Sports Day planned for August 1946, which had to be abandoned because its site, the field at the side of the airfield, became waterlogged. However, in an attempt to remedy this problem along with some of the other deficiencies at RAF Leeming, a plan of action was instituted immediately.

Work started at once on refurbishing the married quarters, but with the majority of personnel in single accommodation, and morale at a low ebb, a diversion of the workmen in October

1946 to repaint the barrack blocks meant that the original task on the houses was not completed till March 1947. In addition during the autumn and winter accommodation problems were aggravated by two further factors. First of all, in October the main water supply for the Station was found to be unfit for drinking purposes, with installation of an independent chlorination plant an urgent requirement. Then as winter drew on it was discovered that there was a shortage of heating fuel, a deficiency which coincided with particularly severe weather conditions. As it happened, in February 1947 what fuel there was ran out, and it became necessary to despatch personnel on ten days "accommodation leave". Then as winter slowly retreated, possibly in an attempt to give encouragement to those at Leeming, a demonstration vehicle arrived in April to display plans for future accommodation layouts. At the same time, in an attempt to counterbalance the poor living conditions, strenuous efforts were already under way to improve the welfare and recreation facilities on the Station. In January 1947, in some unused Nissen hut crew rooms, a Recreation Centre had been opened to house table tennis and darts facilities as well as a miniature rifle range. By way of alternatives, Boxing, Riding, and Clay Pigeon Shooting Clubs, were formed, and in contrast, a Music Circle and Dramatic Society. A Club for families was opened in the annex to Station Sick Quarters, and the NAAFI was refurbished. Volunteers re-opened the cinema, weekly dances were started, a bus service to Leeming Village was arranged, and a civilian 32 seat bus was made available for recreation runs. Nevertheless, the type of recreation had to be seen to be wholesome, because it was considered necessary to publish in Routine Orders a list of several local addresses that were to be considered "out of bounds" to all personnel!

Thus the problems, arising from poor accommodation and few amenities, appeared, at least, to be capable of being alleviated. Unfortunately, the main difficulties at work, caused by a lack of trained personnel and inadequate equipment, continued to present a less hopeful outlook. The problem had been recognised as early as July 1946 when the Station Commander gave the despairing comment:

> . . . Misemployment has reached its zenith and it now becomes a question of the blind leading the blind.

A local Establishment Committee was formed, with the task of allocating personnel where they were most needed, but it was found that the difficulties involved in moving people around did not justify the benefits so the idea was abandoned. Ironically, some of the most useful help came from the German POWs, moved in from East Moor in July 1946. They were accommodated in the old Communal Site, and were employed as gardeners and cleaners as well as in sundry other unskilled positions. In December of the same year, their numbers were increased from 17 to 77, and they remained invaluable to the Station until their departure, prior to repatriation in August 1947.

Certainly the long-term problems remained, not really capable of local solution but part of the Service-wide difficulty of transition to a peacetime force. In fact, the reintroduction of pre-war routine and discipline were two of only a few things that could be achieved without outside help or funding. Examples of how things could be done in these areas first became apparent in September when the flagpole was re-erected on the Parade Square, daily working and monthly Station parades were ordered, and all airmen marched to and from work. In reality, considering all of the problems that were not being addressed at the time, using the word "achieved" would definitely not have been the one that would have immediately sprung to the minds of many of the airmen!

Despite this background of trials and tribulation, at the beginning of July 1946 a start had actually been made with flying-training. All sections had been established, and were functioning as well as could be expected, although Servicing Wing remained extremely short of skilled personnel. The flying at Leeming commenced at a time when the whole Training Policy for the RAF was under review. In August, as a temporary measure, Fighter Command had given instructions that the night-fighter course was to be reduced to nine aircraft with a target of 48 hours flying per pupil. Although providing some respite to Leeming, even this reduced programme was difficult to maintain once winter weather set in. This element may or may not have been a contributory factor in the two crashes that occurred in November, when in a space of two days the Unit lost two Mosquitos, and four men with them. The shortage of proficient tradesmen may also have had an effect, because one of the aircraft, which had a known history of engine defects, crashed while on an air test a few miles from Leeming, killing the pilot and a fitter who was on the flight to assist in diagnosing the problems. However, though there were still to be other accidents to contend with during the following year, none could be considered as major. Initially, following the two tragedies the winter helped curtail the flying, particularly following the blizzard which hit the Unit on 26 February 1947. The snow was not completely cleared until 22 March, but, never at a loss to find something to do, the RAF took the opportunity to carry out experiments to test the feasibility of flying off from snow. One would hope that the students were not involved in this, but rather obviously the conclusions that were reached indicated that it was possible to take off from packed dry snow up to a depth of approximately one foot, but once it started to thaw it was not possible to fly!

As part of the re-organisation of flying training in the Royal Air Force, it was decided that No.54 OTU would be joined on 1 May 1947 by No.13 OTU, a unit responsible for light-bomber training. The amalgamation resulted in the formation of No.228 OCU. As a newly formed unit, the OCU was not entitled to receive the official sign of recognition that came in the form of a "badge". It was not until 1972, long after the Unit's departure from Leeming, that approval from the Sovereign for such a badge was finally obtained. Initially, when it was formed, it was obvious that new equipment and facilities were both required and long overdue. Furthermore, the Unit remained short of a large number of technical personnel, in the main due to a sudden flurry of postings. One of the first areas to be re-equipped was the Signals Maintenance Section, which was moved into a building near ATC; special equipment from Middleton St George was installed, and to give the transmitters mobility, suitable additions to MT stock were received. A new Morse Room was prepared, a new Central Signals Workshop was produced, along with signals installations at Helmsley Bombing Range, and R/T facilities at Acklington Firing Range. The aircrew were not forgotten, and in May 1947 Harwell Trainers, and an airborne demonstration room were tested and taken over. Later, in August, while a receiver room was being installed in the SHQ building, the mobile transmitters were moved to a permanent home in their own Transmitting Station. So, as could be expected, the vehicles were returned to MT for disposal.

Life at Leeming during the early months of the existence of the OCU, appears to have continued in the same rather grim and austere vein as had been the norm since the end of the war. Accommodation and general leisure facilities were still problems affecting morale, and in May and June there was an outbreak of petty larceny. This included one case where the Clothing Store was broken into, with clothes to the value of £20-£30 stolen; "a well planned raid", was how the CO described it. The "mini crime wave" caused the Service Police to institute a series of searches and checks on all personnel leaving the Station, with the almost predictably negative results. Roving patrols were set up in the technical site, and later in the year, when various items were stolen in the burglary of nine married quarters, the patrols were extended to cover the domestic area. No arrests were made, but with the incidence of such crime dropping to almost nil, presumably most of those responsible were posted or moved away.

Many sections were undermanned, none more so than MT which was down to 50 per cent of its established strength. This clearly meant longer working hours for those personnel available, and delays in the repair of vehicles became the norm. A new cinema was opened in the summer of 1947, but even in that distinctly pleasant event, there was a reflection of the problems of life at that time. The cinema was genuinely welcomed, even though its final structure had its seating capacity reduced by about one third from the original plans. This was because it had been recognised that the prevalence of Infantile Paralysis amongst the dependants at Leeming meant that children with leg irons, sometimes in wheel chairs, would need extra room between the rows!

Even in the area of Education, things did not bode well for the future.

This claim could be seen to be borne out at Leeming in July 1947, when 20 RAF and WAAF personnel sat an examination up to the standard of the War Educational Certificate in Maths and English. Only two airmen gained sufficient marks to obtain a "pass"!

A period of annual leave in the summer months has long been of prime importance to the majority of those serving in the RAF. So, it was probably with a feeling of relief to most people, that the Station closed down for 14 days at the beginning of August for what was described as the "summer recess". However, the CO was later moved to comment that the system was not practicable, and that if such a scheme was contemplated again, it should only apply to Training and Servicing Wings and not to SHQ! Just what his reasoning was behind this statement can only be guessed at.

Notwithstanding this background of problems the Station as a whole was still required to settle into a routine, and by September 1947 a reasonably clear picture of the training task for 228 OCU

had begun to emerge. There were two main taskings on the OCU: to train the crews for night-fighter or light-bomber operations. To achieve these aims there were three internal training units, each with its own specialisation:

Airborne Intercept Nav/Radar Course

This course flew with the Wellington T.10 and Martinets for approximately 14 weeks, and then proceeded to 204 Advanced Flying School at Cottesmore for training with their pilots for three months, before returning to RAF Leeming for night-fighter crew training.

Night-Fighter Crew Training

A 5-6 weeks course on the Mosquito Mk XXX.

Light-Bomber Crew training

Approximate 10 week course on the Mosquito Mk VI.

It becomes clear however, that notwithstanding this apparent clarity of task, during the next few years changes were made in practically every aspect of the courses. Their size, duration, as well as aircraft type, all saw change. Even the course titles were modified several times, and the confused way in which the alterations are recorded in the Operations Record Book may well reflect the difficulty experienced in keeping up with them. In October 1947 the first signs of Planned Maintenance appeared with the formation of a separate Repair and Inspection (R&I) Squadron in Servicing Wing, and on 1 December 1947, the Three Wing System was introduced:

Flying Wing: with the three self-contained Sqns.

Technical Wing.

Administration Wing.

Gp Capt Lowe the new CO, who assumed command on 9 January 1948, voiced some doubts about the new ideas:

. . . I am not yet satisfied that Planned Maintenance and Planned Flying are working in proper harmony and producing all that the organisation should. Flying Wing has suffered much from a very unstable "Staff" position. Its efficiency cannot be fairly gauged unless its principal staff posts are manned quantitatively and qualitatively iaw establishment. Aircrew category substitutes for officer staff posts and excessive aircrew supernumerary staff, militates against development of Wing spirit and efficiency . . . no amount of flying training and aircrew production will be of avail, unless supported by ground staff of equal calibre....higher planning and intensity of effort towards the training of aircrew, will not help if tending to leave too little time and opportunity to ensure the all round development of others.

A prophet indeed!

A few months before Gp Capt Lowe made this statement, a formal trade structure for airmen had been introduced. This was certainly a step in the right direction in an attempt to improve the calibre of the groundcrew, and in fact it had resulted in numerous applications for remustering. Unfortunately at Leeming, in only one case was the applicant recommended as being educationally suitable, which was again a reflection on the general decline of educational standards of service intakes. The shortages of trained man-power in the technical trades was an obvious and major problem, but the best way to use what little expertise was available was recognised at Leeming, and in March 1948 the CO took steps to change things:

. . . . in such a unit as the OCU the three pronged organisation should not attempt to create independent Training Squadrons. The best interests of students and ground personnel will be served by centralizing the latter within Technical Wing and by allowing Flying Wing staff to single-mindedly devote their attention to students' training, discipline and welfare. On the principle that Technical Wing provides, maintains and sustains the Flying Wing in all technical aspects, this would improve the quantity and quality of Flying Training.

As it happened, at a Fighter Command Conference the following month, the CO obtained agreement that his policy for the centralisation of ground crews in Technical Wing could be implemented locally. (Over the years this idea has been resurrected on a number of occasions and with the reduction in size of the RAF in the "nineties", perhaps will be one that will have to be revisited.) Clearly, the CO had some very radical ideas for that time and was not averse to voicing them. It is conceivable that the loss of an aircraft in each of his first two months in command had an effect on his views, but when he laid much of the blame for the general state of things at the door of the National Serviceman, he showed that even he could be a little too blinkered in his approach:

. . . the apathetic and disinterested (sic) influence of the non-regular element.[16]

Perhaps he should have looked more carefully at matters a little closer to home to find the cause of so much apathy. It is possible that he would then have seen that in addition to the externally generated problems that beset the Station as a whole, the treatment of the airman of the day certainly appeared to leave a lot to be desired. A case in point, where a thoughtless approach did little more than have an adverse effect on the attitude of the junior ranks, stemmed from the fact that the Station had its own farm. Notwithstanding the apparent advantages in the years of austerity that followed the war, the "ownership" of this farm in October 1947 was seen more as a threat than a benefit, especially to the free time of those involved. A scheme, perhaps more notable for its lack of common sense than its aid to rations or morale, was introduced to assist in producing sufficient green vegetables to make the Station self-sufficient. This required all personnel, other than commissioned officers, to put in 10 hours of gardening per month, either in their own time or during working hours when they could be spared. Personnel were issued with a card on which they were obliged to obtain a signature from the NCO in charge of the farm to confirm the time worked, and this was then to be taken into account by Section Commanders when considering the granting of leave!

Notwithstanding the difficulties experienced by the personnel at Leeming, the flying effort continued apace. Replacement aircraft were beginning to arrive, and by September 1947 five of the new NF.36 Mosquitos had made an appearance, although in November they had to be ferried to Colerne to have the necessary American radar installed. This was not the only problem relating to the programme; originally intended to replace the MK XXX, shortages in the supply of the NF.36 did in fact mean that the earlier model had later to be reintroduced! The changes in the marks of training aircraft did not help matters, but it was only one of the problems affecting the training schedule, and in fact, by the end of 1947 yet another obstacle had presented itself to those who were trying to train the new crews for the RAF. This obstacle stemmed from the constant unserviceability of the radar in the Wellingtons, although the lack of trained radar mechanics in the Service at that time only exacerbated the problem. Consequently the rectification of faults often took up a great deal of time, and courses, particularly those of the navigators, were having to be extended. Additionally in 1947, there had been a spate of minor flying accidents of various types and causes, fortunately with no casualties, but all of which created additional work, adding to the problems affecting the Station. The good fortune associated with this chapter of accidents was however soon to end, because in January 1948 a Mosquito had complete electrical failure while in flight. The crew managed to bale out, but the pilot left it too late and he was killed when his parachute failed to open in time. This then was followed within a few weeks with another major accident. Fortunately, on that occasion the crew escaped unhurt after engine trouble had forced the pilot into a crash landing, severely damaging the Mosquito.

In December 1947 and January 1948, the personnel strength figures surged upwards from 700 to a figure in excess of 900. Unfortunately, this increase was not going to be the solution to the Station's manning problems because it was soon to drop again. In accordance with Air Ministry Policy, the Station was instructed that all WAAF personnel were to be posted away from the Unit during February 1948, with replacements to come from RAF personnel. The CO again had comments to make, stating that the decision was one that was:

> . . . universally regretted. The comparative isolation of the Station offers no hope of compensation to social welfare. There was also regret in losing . . . the stimulant of friendly competition, and the breaking of continuity in those duties that have of so long and so skilfully been undertaken by WAAF personnel.

As a consequence by the close of March 1948, after a farewell dance the WAAFs were all posted away and the Station was back to a strength of 712 . . . with no more weekly Station dances![17]

Notwithstanding these problems the Station had in many ways continued to function as a unit. The normal institutions such as Battle of Britain and Remembrance Day Parades became routine. The OCU had survived visits from the AOC in July 1947, the AOC-in-C who flew in with the World Speed Record breaking Meteor F.4 in

August of the same year, and the Inspector General of the RAF who came in May 1948. In May 1947 Middleton St George had become a satellite of Leeming, No.12 Group's Gliding Club was in operation, with gliding taking place evenings and weekends throughout the summer months, and a Boy Scout Troop had been formed in October. The Boxing Team fared well as runners-up in the Lord Wakefield Competition, a Station Tug-of-War Team competed in the Royal Tournament, and eventually a successful Sports Day on the new field (the present one) had been achieved.

In the first few years after the war there was only one thing that the people stationed at Leeming could be sure of, and that was that everything was constantly changing. One of the changes that appeared to be for the better came about in June 1948, when a new intake policy for the Nav/Radar Course was introduced. Selected navigators from Advanced Navigation School would then go to the Advanced Training School before their radar training course at 228 OCU, which meant that they could proceed directly to the night-fighter course with their pilots. This procedure was much more popular with the aircrew, and several French, and two Belgian crews were included in this "Straight Through" programme. From time to time external influences have had their effect on training policy, and the clashes in Palestine in 1948 meant that for a while priority had to be given to the training of reinforcement crews for the Middle East. This meant the curtailment of the Mosquito light-bomber courses in August of that year, and the introduction of the Brigand B1 conversion courses for 5, 39, 45, and 84 Squadrons. This programme had no better luck than the others, with the last of these conversion courses finishing well behind schedule in November 1949, mainly because of frequent aircraft unserviceability. At that juncture, the Station reverted to Mosquito "light bomber" courses, which was a tasking that continued into the early fifties. Flexibility was

certainly the key word at Leeming in those days, with 228 OCU receiving the additional responsibility during 1949 of converting the crews of 34 Sqn to the Beaufighter. Then, in November of that year, the staff pilots had a chance to gain some experience in jets, when two Meteor Mk.7s were loaned for a period of three weeks. This kind of adaptability had gone even further at the beginning of 1949, when the CO, Gp Capt Lowe, took off on 25 January from Manston in Kent to ferry a Spitfire to Greece. Just what a Station Commander, from a base in North Yorkshire with no Spitfires on strength, was doing flying a single engined aircraft to the Mediterranean is lost in the mists of time. Perhaps the truth lies in the fact that the way of life in the RAF was different then!

More importantly in 1949 things had not gone well for the Station, and it had a particularly bad year with regard to reportable aircraft accidents. The month of December 1948 had seen out that year in a tragic manner when a Mosquito had crashed and killed both of the crew. The year that followed was actually free from fatalities, but that was the only good news as there were 33 aircraft accidents of varying causes and severity! Some were the result of technical problems, especially with the engines, still more came from servicing errors, and others, such as the occasion when a Brigand struck the perimeter fence with its propellers and wheels, were attributable to pilot error. In many ways it was clear that the Service was still suffering from many of the problems that bedevilled training operations throughout the war. Improved levels of training for both aircrew and groundcrew, as well as stricter servicing standards, were coming into the Service, but really noticeable improvements in all of these areas and the subsequent reduction in accident figures were still ten years and more away. In fact, things would get worse before they would get better.

By January 1950 aircraft recorded at RAF Leeming were: the Mosquito T.3, VI, and 36, the Wellington T.10, Martinet, Brigand B.1,

Buckmaster, Oxford and Tiger Moth. Nevertheless, by February a decision had already been taken to replace the new Mosquito NF.36 with a modified version of the older Mk XXX, a task that not surprisingly necessitated the ferrying of each aircraft to the manufacturer for two weeks of work. Then in July of that year, came a sequence of apparently unrelated events that led to a major change in the training role at Leeming. It began when the last Mosquito light-bomber course finished and 3 Sqn was re-equipped with Brigands and Buckmasters; their Mosquitos being transferred within the unit to 2 Sqn (NF) now mainly equipped with the Mosquito NF.36. In August, with their new aircraft from the Bristol Company, 3 Sqn (LB) restarted the bomber courses, each lasting 10 weeks, but it was not to be for long and in April 1951 the Squadron was disbanded entirely. As there was to be a role for its aircraft, they too remained on the Station to undergo a conversion programme which would enable them to join with the purpose built, and newly arrived, Brigand T.4 trainer – of which only nine had been built. The conversion meant that a radar scanner had to be fitted in the nose of the B.I, and provision made for the blacking out of the rear cockpit, made necessary by using the type for the initial instruction of those radar navigators destined for night-fighter duties. In fact, this series of moves was only the beginning, and for the next two years there was a general shuffling about of aircraft into, out of, and within Leeming. This culminated in the transference of most of the training to jet aircraft, at the outset in the shape of the Meteor.

It was at the beginning of all of this reorganization that a change in Station Commander took place, and Gp Capt Clouston took over control. Gp Capt Lowe, who so enjoyed "going into print", was posted to one of the many outposts that still remained in that era, one that went under the name of RAF Khartoum.

The new Station Commander arrived in plenty of time to be involved in Exercise "Winter Trek", which took place towards the end of March 1950,

but his involvement with the Station was only to be a short one, as he was on his way by July. The exercise was really an escape and evasion drill designed to give aircrew some experience of the type of problems they might meet after coming down behind enemy lines. There was no indication as to whether the new CO was one of the 60 aircrew who as "escapers from a prison camp" had to make it across the "frontier" of the Great North Road between the bridges at Catterick and Sinderby. The security forces consisted of men from the North Yorkshire Police and the RAF Regiment from Catterick, who were aided by personnel from RAF Leeming. The final "score" indicated that 33 escapers got across the road to safety, 26 were caught, and one was still at large at the end of the exercise. Unfortunately there is no further mention of this young man, so it is to be hoped that he did finally turn up!

The period covered by the late forties and early fifties at Leeming, saw continuing problems with the unserviceability of aircraft and accidents almost became commonplace. In November 1950, 3 Sqn had said goodbye to the Mosquito Mk VI, though with mixed feelings it must be said, and in the early fifties were entirely equipped with aircraft built by the Bristol Company. The workload placed on some trades was almost routinely excessive and at one stage in March 1949 there was so much work for the engine tradesmen, that there was a backlog of 13 aircraft with engine defects. The Brigands and Buckmasters were constantly having trouble with their engines; so much so that in April 1949, two of the latter had to carry out single engine landings at Leeming following engine failure on the delivery flights from the Bristol company. If it was not the power plants it was something else, and at one stage in 1951, following a spate of faults where the undercarriage became unlocked when the engines were shut down, the Brigands were grounded until the cause could be discovered. However, problems were not only to be found on these aircraft. In the latter part of 1951 a further series of engine incidents, particularly on the Mosquito NF.36, were instrumental in creating a drop in the morale of the student crews. It was an awkward time, and the situation was only improved following another period of intensive work by the engine tradesmen. In truth, it is easy to conclude from the accident statistics that the attitude of the crews must have been at best ambivalent. The year 1949 had seen the Station deal with more than 30 reportable aircraft accidents and the two year period to the beginning of 1951 saw ten aircraft written off. In December 1950 in one such accident a Mosquito had its undercarriage collapse on landing, after the emergency system had been used to lower it. The crew were unhurt and the aircraft was not destroyed, but it was discovered that the undercarriage control valve had been assembled incorrectly. Furthermore, there had been no retraction test carried out before the aircraft was cleared as serviceable! Examples were to be made, so after the board of inquiry the AOC stated that disciplinary action was to be taken against the NCO i/c, as well as the engineering officer involved. This case brought matters to a head, and in January 1951, because of the lack of SNCOs for technical supervision, all resources were pooled into the Central Rectification Flight. Unfortunately, despite this attempt to solve the problems of poor engineering practice, scarcely a month went by without two or more flying accidents; with engine failures, undercarriages failing to lock down, and loss of coolant, just some of the numerous engineering causes given. It appears though, that the official attitude towards this catalogue of disasters and near disasters can be viewed as being complacent, with the ORB occasionally taking a rather detached view of the proceedings when there were no casualties. When one pupil overshot and damaged the aircraft, it was attributed to inexperience and when another had an engine fail, the comment was that the accident had been unavoidable – no questions about the training syllabus or if the engine failure was due to error.

In another case when one of the groundcrew was responsible for damaging an aircraft the statement was made:

> . . . The increase in flying and the desire to become airborne at every possible opportunity was carried too far when the propeller tips of a Martinet were damaged during a ground run (a case of a Cpl remustering to u/t pilot).

A further example of this type of almost whimsical reporting could be seen from the report of the crash of a Wellington near Carthorpe in which the pilot received minor injuries:

> . . . Incident allowed a member of the medical profession, taking time off from the local hunt, to render first aid.

This accident had been caused by an airman who had failed to ensure that the spinner was securely fastened, and was the first of three Wellingtons lost in 1951; two crashed and the third (ND109) caught fire in No.3 Hangar on 26 April. In this case a tradesman had washed down the oil stained port engine with petrol (a not uncommon practice at the time). Of course as Murphy's Law dictates, there was another tradesman who re-connected some electrical leads while power was on. This action created a spark which caused the engine to burst into flames, and damage was considered severe enough to require the airframe to be scrapped. Disciplinary action was taken against the electrical trade NCO, but a solicitor was hired (a National Service hand in this – maybe?), paid for from a collection by other NCOs and was instrumental in the Corporal being cleared. In the air some accidents were of course caused by student error, so as early as April 1950 a conference had been held to consider the selection and qualities of the students received at 228 OCU, matters that were causing real concern. The root of the problems that beset Leeming at that time may well have stemmed from poor funding, but in many cases it appears that the attitude was very much a case of "muddling through", or "it must be right, we have always done it this way".

The accidents, as always, ranged from the comic to the tragic. Of the former variety was the occasion on 3 May 1951, when a driver, with a lorry-load of cheese, was proceeding peacefully down the Great North Road and found himself in collision with an aircraft; specifically a Mosquito NF.36 (RK984), which while carrying out an asymmetric landing, overshot the runway and ran across the road. When the aircraft was dragged off the lorry there was cheese scattered everywhere, including some inside the aircraft's nose-cone. Fortunately, the most serious injury was the pupil in the aircraft who suffered a fractured foot, but no doubt there were also some severely shocked fellow participants, particularly in the lorry. However, the other extreme was only too apparent on August 13 of the same year, when one of

Leeming's most disastrous accidents occurred. A mid-air collision between a Wellington and a Martinet during an airborne intercept exercise resulted in eight deaths. The only survivor was a 16 year old air cadet, Derek Coates, of 1869 Squadron (Middlesbrough) Air Training Corps, who was among a party of cadets on the annual summer camp at the station. The disaster occurred shortly after both aircraft had taken off from Leeming, when they collided near Richmond, North Yorkshire, where the force of the impact caused both aircraft to break up. Cadet Coates was bundled into a parachute and consequently saved by Flt Lt John Quinton DFC, who was a navigator undergoing instruction on 119 AI course. Unfortunately, he was killed along with the other five members of the crew, as also was the pilot of the Martinet and his passenger, another cadet. Perhaps the citation for the award of the George Cross to Flight Lieutenant Quinton can best describe both the horror and the heroism of the situation.

CITATION FOR THE AWARD OF THE GEORGE CROSS

On August the 13th 1951, Flight Lieutenant Quinton was a Navigator under instruction in a Wellington aircraft which was involved in a mid-air collision. The sole survivor from the crash was an Air Training Corps Cadet who was a passenger in the aircraft, and he has established the fact that his life was saved by a supreme act of gallantry by Flight Lieutenant Quinton, who in consequence sacrificed his own life. Both Flight Lieutenant Quinton and the cadet were in the rear compartment of the aircraft when the collision occurred. The force of the impact caused the aircraft to break up and as it was plunging out of control towards the earth, Flight Lieutenant Quinton picked up the only parachute within reach and clipped it onto the cadet's harness. He pointed to the rip cord and a gaping hole in the aircraft, therefore indicating that the cadet should jump. At that moment a further portion of the aircraft was torn away and the cadet was flung through the side of the aircraft clutching his rip cord, which he subsequently pulled and landed safely. Flight Lieutenant Quinton acted with superhuman speed, displaying the most commendable courage and self sacrifice, as he well knew that in giving up the only parachute within reach he was forfeiting any chance of saving his own life. Such an act of heroism and humanity ranks with the very highest traditions of the Royal Air Force, besides establishing him as a very gallant and courageous officer, who by his act, displayed the most conspicuous heroism.

Despite the disbandment of the LB Squadron, flying commitments started to increase. The size of the remaining NF Courses had reached a stage when there were 16 crews per course (as opposed to five), and in August 1951 officer cadets were being received, whose training involved extra personnel and additions to the syllabus. As could be expected, this further influx of personnel drastically affected the accommodation situation, particularly in the Officers' Mess, and by September 1951, a total of 60 Officers had to be housed at Topcliffe.

Solutions to these problems however, were only to be forthcoming at the end of the next major upheaval to hit the Station – the conversion to jet training mentioned earlier. As far back as September 1950, the airfield had been inspected to discover what needed to be done to make it suitable for jets, and the plans made then were about to come to fruition. The installation of emergency VHF in the ATC Tower for use with jets had already been completed and permanent buildings erected to house VHF Remote Control. The changeover to jet aircraft was not scheduled to occur until 1952, but well in advance of that, in April 1951, a Meteor T7 had been borrowed from 611 Squadron to begin the conversion of Staff pilots. This aircraft crashed in May, killing the Staff pupil and fatally injuring the CO of 2 Sqn, but not withstanding the loss, the Station quickly obtained a replacement and the conversion training continued. However, even this newly acquired Meteor added its name to the list of incidents and accidents, when in August it lost its canopy while flying at 30,000 feet. As the canopy ripped away from the aircraft it caused some damage to the starboard mainplane and the rear fuselage, but fortunately, the aircraft was landed safely and was flying again soon afterwards.

On the ground, the winter of 1951/52 was to be one of total disruption for RAF Leeming. Contractors moved in during the late summer of 1951 with the task of extending runway 17/35 (as it was then) over and south of Gatenby Lane, and

with laying down accessible aircraft servicing platforms and new perimeter tracks. This major project necessitated the closure of the access road from the A1 through Londonderry and the joining up of a new access road through the village of Gatenby. In addition to all of this work, contracts had been laid for the building of married quarters for officers and airmen, and there was also a plan to build a new Officers' Mess, using SECO huts. Unbelievably, as if this were not enough, at the same time as all this was happening the Station was also to change over to jet aircraft and the Meteor T7 and NF.11, were scheduled to begin operating in the early part of 1952. However, by December 1951, it became obvious that all of this and flying training too could not go on at the same time and place. Consequently, Fighter Command agreed to re-deploy the night-fighter training to Coltishall until the new 2500 yard runway was ready for operational use. No 1 Squadron (AI Training) was to remain but only because it was to move anyway to its new base at Colerne by May 1952.

The move to Coltishall in early January was planned with great care and attention to detail, but the chaos of the actual move through circumstances mainly beyond anyone's control, must have seemed like the last straw to the hard-pressed Leeming personnel. The two Valetta aircraft from Transport Command were delayed by snow and were 24 hrs late in arriving at Leeming, and the Dakota from 12 Group was delayed for the same reason. Three airlifts were made, but the Dakota burst a tyre landing at Coltishall, and rapid deterioration in visibility caused one Valetta to divert to Marham. On the following day, this Valetta reached Coltishall, but on the return journey was diverted to Leuchars where it became unserviceable and took no further part in the move. Meanwhile, the second Valetta developed an oil leak at Leeming and had to return to Abingdon, and the Dakota only managed one more trip before it had to return to its base. By means not specified, the move was completed, but not before the beginning of February 1952!

Once most of the training aircraft were out of the way, the first Meteor NF.11 arrived on 23 January 1952. Technical Wing became involved with receiving the night-fighters, carrying out acceptance checks, fitting the radar equipment and sending them off to Coltishall. The Station found that the recent introduction of a new system of servicing, which dealt progressively with work previously carried out with the aircraft grounded for a number of days, enabled aircraft availability to improve. The process was also a boon to Aircraft Servicing Flight, which in addition had to deal with the disposal of the remaining Mosquitos while still being hampered by the seemingly perennial problems caused by the continuing shortage of NCOs. This was particularly noticeable in the work areas of those who were then known as belonging to the Advanced Trades (airframe, propulsion and electrical). At Coltishall, the detachment had further problems including the non-availability of ground equipment to re-arm the Squadrons, but the visit of the AOC and Staff Officers from 81 Group in April 1952 soon changed that. Predictably, their interest in the matter resulted in equipment being allocated from the Fighter Command pool, and the situation was partially alleviated before the return home.

The winter and spring of 1951/1952 appeared to have been a particularly difficult one for many at Leeming, but in particular the CO had a stressful time of it. Gp Capt McIntyre had been extremely lucky on 7 January 1952, when he escaped unhurt from what was reported as a ground loop in a Mosquito, which resulted in the aircraft being very severely damaged. The accident appears to have been his fault but as he was considered to be inexperienced on type no further action was taken! Apart from the distraction of the transfer of the Station from 12 Group to 81 Group on 22 February 1952, and the move of the night-fighter training, the CO also had to worry about the progress of the construction work on his airfield. Reports vary from the optimistic state-ment that work was proceeding well in February 1952, to the desperate comment in March:

> . . . Because of the vast building projects being undertaken on the airfield, the contractors' lorries running through camp and digging of trenches for draining and cable laying, the Station resembles an open-cast coal mining site.

(The firm of contractors responsible for the work was "Mowlems", which at the time of writing, was again at Leeming, this time with the responsibility of "Facilities Management". To the uninitiated, this means that the firm carries out the work previously carried out by AMWD, MPBW and PSA).

Incredibly, despite the situation at Leeming, the Station won the Group Sports Cup in May, followed by the Group Competition for the best dining hall. It was in this area that it went on to win at command level in June, then in July it became the first Fighter Command Station to win the Jolliffe Trophy after being adjudged as the best dining hall in the RAF.

Although the construction work had not been completed at that time, the detachment from 228 OCU moved back to Leeming from Coltishall between 3 June and 1 July 1952. This time, with the benefit of hard won experience, personnel came back by rail, with equipment and spares loaded into 10 ton Matador lorries. The jet aircraft strength, including 24 flown in from Coltishall, then amounted to 36 Meteor NF.11 and six Meteor T7. It was at about this time that there was a major change in the type of fuel used in jet aircraft, and the substitution from AVTUR to AVTAG was made. This was a change that was instrumental in creating a great deal of additional work as the new fuel caused numerous problems with the aircraft fuel pumps and transfer systems. The flying rate at the time was so high, there being such a large number of aircraft on the flight-line, that a Refuelling Flight was formed and tasked to operate six refuelling vehicles on the apron with at least three to be immediately available at all times. Initial trials to confirm the viability of the operation produced a time of 11 minutes for refuelling an aircraft, with a total turn round time of 20 minutes. However, the Meteors flew day and night, normally 0800 till 0500, but occasionally right through to the following day shift. Such an intensive flying programme meant that fuel was used and needed so quickly that aircraft were sometimes grounded awaiting a bowser. An indication of the quantity of fuel that could be used can be seen from the day when issues peaked, 18 July 1952, when 50,441 gallons of aviation fuel were issued to aircraft at Leeming. It was soon apparent though, that with the requirement for newly delivered fuel to stand in the bulk tanks for a minimum of 24 hours (to separate it from any water or other contaminants), the rate of use would far exceed the rate of deliveries, so naturally a brake was put on the flying.

The return from Coltishall meant the reconstitution of Meteor training, at first into two Squadrons. The initial training course completed entirely at Leeming ended in September 1952, and thereafter, the courses continued reasonably smoothly. Pilot training was never really problem-free though and incidents continued to arise, with one in particular that would have taken some living down. This occurred when a student flying solo in an NF11, having left the landing lights on, thought his aircraft was on fire when he flew through cloud, and following a rapid descent damaged the aircraft with rather a heavy landing. He was obviously a fortunate young man because the subsequent Board of Inquiry had this theory checked out and agreed it could have happened that way! As could be expected, good fortune was not always the order of the day and accidents were not always that forgiving, so funerals continued to be a depressingly regular occurrence. The period immediately following the return to Leeming was a particularly bad one, with the loss of four Meteor's in a period of a month, and the deaths of six of the eight aircrew involved. When there was to be a funeral where full military honours would be bestowed, it was customary to use the coal lorry for the cortege, which would be taken from its primary task to allow for its repainting. Consequently, at this time the Leeming vehicle must have been one of the smartest in the Service. The funeral services were held in St Michael's, the Station Church, which was situated in a Nissen hut that dated back to the war when it was used as a briefing room for crews of the RCAF. At the funerals the bearer party had then to be aware of a particular problem with the church, as it was known that its entrance was not high enough to allow for a coffin to be carried through on the shoulders of the pallbearers. It is said that practice makes perfect, and over the years no doubt the various Station Warrant Officers found this to be very true in this case and had the procedure off to a fine art!

On a more cheerful note, the Polish Chief Flying Instructor on 3 Sqn had novel means of increasing Sqn funds: any mistake by the trainee pilots was to be reported to him and a fine was levied – any argument and it was doubled. One amusing tale relates how a trainee pilot who overran his chocks was fined 10 shillings, and after indignantly claiming that he had not run over the chocks only crept up them, he was grandly informed that creeping was not allowed in the RAF and the fine was increased to £1! As he was the CFI, this individual could also ensure that the fines were paid before he allowed pilots to clear from the Station.

The Station's aspect had taken on a new appearance following completion of the construction work which had actually come about in stages. The runway and perimeter tracks were completed in October 1952, and this meant that the method of access to the Station from the A1 through Londonderry via the old Gatenby Lane public highway was lost. Traffic was diverted through Gatenby Village on the new road being constructed by the North Riding County Council along Saddlers Lane. This way now led to the main entrance, but at first was a typical country lane without any tarmac covering, and the bus company which provided the only means of transport for many of the Station's personnel soon decided that it was too muddy to use. Consequently the old access road was re-opened, although, because it now crossed the runway, traffic had to be controlled by the use of lights operated by ATC. However, it was in the nature of things, and for various reasons, that the lights were often left on red and the bus company soon became tired of the delays to their timetable and refused to include the Station on their route; a decision that temporarily accentuated the isolation of the Station. A major improvement for family life came when the new married quarters were completed in 1952 and then occupied successively until all were in use by 1953. The new Officers' Mess was to take longer and it was not until October 1953 that it was finally taken over. To be known as No.2 Mess it was occupied by student officers previously housed in a wing of the Sergeants' Mess.

All around the Station improvements were beginning to take effect, but problems in the flying training were still to be found, and in May 1953 there had been so many overshoots that it appeared to be only a matter of time before a major accident occurred. Therefore in order to decrease the risk to the aircraft and crews, a request was made to the AMWD (Air Ministry Works Department) to replace the existing concrete posts and wire fencing with weaker structures in the vicinity of the ends of the runways. This presumably did nothing to reduce the incidence rate for overshoots but at least it would have been less dangerous to hit a wooden fence post than a concrete one! It was also in 1953, on the first day of October to be precise, that a rather spectacular flying accident occurred when a Meteor NF.11 caught fire after a belly landing with its external tanks still fitted. Fortunately the fire-crew was equal to the emergency and though the aircraft was in a sorry state the blaze was extinguished with no injuries to the crew. The aircraft was provisionally evaluated as being Category 5, which meant it was to be scrapped, but WM265 was in fact repaired. Though this task took almost a year, it was flown again and soon afterwards finally written off charge from the RAF by being sold to France!

The responsibility for training crews for the new or enlarged all-weather squadrons for the RAF, was almost solely that of 228 OCU. Probably the two most difficult skills for aircrew to master were night and "weather" flying, when a pilot had to be able to out-manoeuvre his enemy while flying solely on instruments and being directed by the orders of his navigator/radio operator. It was to the OCU that pilots and navigators came as individuals, were trained together and departed as two-man teams. To do this, they had in the early 1950s, an aircraft well equipped for the role and though the Meteors NF.11, NF.12 and T.14 were not as fast as they would have liked, they were considered a delight to fly. They were well-built, reliable, and most important, as instrument-flying aircraft, they had a stability that was very necessary for the "weather" flying. These all-weather Meteors were equipped with airborne intercept radar which enabled the crew to approach another aircraft up to visual range at night, but also was capable of being used for map reading as an aid to navigation. The main navigational aid however, remained the GEE Mk 3. Pilots would come to the OCU having completed their initial flying training at a Flying Training School and having become proficient in jet flying at an Advanced Flying School. (This policy would soon change though, and pilots would first have to complete a tour in an operational day squadron). The navigators on the other hand, having started at an Advanced Navigation School where they learned their basic navigation, had also graduated from the Airborne Intercept OCU at Colerne, where during a ten-week course, they grasped the intricacies of the airborne radar equipment and the Gee navigational aid. As well as the normal

Royal Air Force commitment, there was often a percentage of students on each course from the Royal Navy and from Commonwealth and NATO Air Forces. The station at that time had the normal administrative and technical wings but the flying wing was split into seven areas – three operational training squadrons, one handling and gunnery squadron, a ground control-intercept squadron, a ground school and an air traffic section. At the ground school over a period of ten days the pilots learned about local weather conditions, the aircraft with its cockpit layout and special equipment, AI techniques, search and rescue, including emergency procedures as they applied to the NF Meteor, as well as other subjects such as the defence organisation of the UK. They then proceeded to the handling and gunnery flight where they were given dual handling and instrument flying checks in the Meteor 7, before being divided among the Station's three operational squadrons where they would each complete one trip with a staff navigator. Meanwhile, at the time when the pilots were making their initial handling flights, an equivalent number of student navigators preceded them to the operational squadrons where they carried out seven exercises with staff pilots. On those flights they practised the various types of contacts they were likely to meet as well as being shown the standard and speeds which would be expected of them. Each of the three operational squadrons took three courses of six crews (the numbers of crews sometimes varied) at a time, with each course at a different stage of progression. A free choice was given to the students to select whoever they would like to crew up with, but their Squadron Commander always reserved the right to alter individual pairings. Crew training continued until about two weeks before the end of the course, by which time the students should have completed all of the airborne intercept exercises, a cross country exercise, a height climb and seven ranging and tracking exercises using the "cine" gun. They then transferred to the Gunnery and Handling Squadron, where, after the

pilot had been given a demonstration in a Vampire T.II, he and his navigator made six air-to-air firing sorties in a Meteor NF.11. A third of all the AI exercises were at night and the night flying programmes were as a consequence, busy ones, with aircraft taking off in pairs every few minutes. They operated in pairs to enable one to act as target, the other as the interceptor, and then to alternate during the exercise. Students were normally assessed throughout the course by a staff navigator who sat alongside the GCI controller, watching the intercept on the "tube" and listening in on the student navigator's instructions to his pilot. On the final night exercise an assessment was made in the air by an experienced staff crew, flying in line astern formation on the students who were acting as interceptors. The target aircraft, of course, displayed no lights but the student's fighter operated with its navigation lights on to enable the assessing crew to keep formation at about 1500-3000 feet range. The staff navigator followed both aircraft on his AI, which enabled him to assess the interception, while the staff pilot judged the student pilot's reaction to orders as well as his standard of instrument flying. The visual trailing of the student by the staff pilot was always dependent on the student pilot's instrument flying to keep them both the right way up, so it can be imagined that the staff crews occasionally found themselves in some strange attitudes!

In the late forties and throughout the fifties, the RAF went through a difficult period, but "Service humour" was still firmly in place. In 1953 for instance, the SWO, Warrant Officer Hamilton, got himself into a discussion with some Sergeant pilots over the merits of their jobs. He considered that flying was easy, but as they considered he could not even strap himself in, they invited him to show them otherwise. Unbeknown to him, when he appeared on the flight line to prove them wrong, one of the pilots was already prepared in the cockpit of the Meteor and to the SWOs initial surprise and dismay as soon as he was strapped in, the aircraft was off, up and away, for a very eventful flight. For those involved it is to be hoped that the SWO had the sense of humour they are not normally renowned for! In another case, a particular RAF Police Sergeant, who was the scourge of the airmen at that time, also received his comeuppance. On one occasion on a night when a dance was being held, in the hope of catching some airman breaking some rule or other, he hid in a large bin behind the NAAFI. He was, however, seen and the airmen saw their chance, tied on the lid and rolled and kicked the bin around the yard, before leaving a very disorientated "snoop" to be rescued.

New aircraft types and marks kept appearing, especially in 1954. The Vampire T.II was first recorded in April when five were accepted; the ubiquitous Chipmunk arrived in June, followed by the Prentice and finally the Meteor NF.12. A total of nine of these latest marks of night-fighter came in October 1954, although around August 1955 some of these were re-deployed for a time to North Luffenham for continuation of training in the new AI 21 equipment. Indeed, during the following year, between April 1956 and December 1956, all of the night-fighter/all- weather training for 3 Sqn was moved to North Luffenham, which enabled the contractors to appear yet again. At Leeming, 2 Sqn retained a dozen or so aircraft for staff continuation training, and eight Meteor NF11 remained at Leeming in "unit storage" to be recovered at 48 hours' notice, a decision that effectively put 1 Sqn in "suspended animation". As had become usual when the contractors arrived, there were several projects: resurfacing the runway, adding a new wing to and altering the existing buildings of the Officers' Mess, more married quarters, new central and general radio workshops, a ground control-intercept station and a permanent ground studies training centre. Extensive overhaul of the aerial towers at the transmitter and receiver stations was also in hand. Consequently it was to be January 1957 before training recommenced, although throughout it was still possible to carry

out a degree of flying from Leeming, albeit of a restricted nature which included no night flying.

Between 1952 and 1956, various other changes on the non-flying side had been taking place. For example, a series of exercises had been held but their objectives were changing from the old "escape and evasion" type to the then more current anti-sabotage, ground and nuclear defence scenario. Possibly the last of the old type of exercise to be held at Leeming took place in February 1954, when at very short notice the aircrew were taken out in flying kit and left some ten miles from the Station with instructions to make their way back while evading the search parties of Station personnel. The weather during the evening and night was a mixture of sleet and snow with freezing temperatures and mention should be made that a number of pupils swam the River Swale in these conditions! The following year sees the report that:

> . . . In September 1955 during Exercise "Beware", a major UK Air Defence Exercise, the Unit operated as 228 OCU Sqn with 16 Meteor NF11 in the night all-weather role: 89 ops were flown and 79 "enemy" aircraft probably destroyed was claimed; control was by Northern Sector. At the same time an anti-sabotage phase, Exercise "Creep", was introduced to test the defences of the Station. The saboteurs, 15 of whom were captured, had few successes and were unable to interfere with the operational efficiency of the station.

This level of expertise, both on the ground and in the air must have helped scare off (sic) many a possible enemy, but at the same time it is apparent that the objectivity of this sort of official pronouncement does leave something to be desired; especially as this exercise came three months after an instruction from HQ Fighter Command, which ordered a reduction in flying by the OCU to 70 per cent of the previous levels. This had been a precaution against the possible break down in fuel supplies due to rail strikes, but the claims of enemy aircraft "destroyed" show that it had no adverse effect on the operational efficiency of the night-fighters, or was it a case of the "opposition" having their flying reduced even further?

Later in October 1955, the IRA threat reared its head for the first time at Leeming, requiring diversion of manpower for sentry duty. A detachment from No.48 Field Squadron RAF Regiment was requested to help cope with this, but there is no indication that the request was granted, and to counter the threat, Leeming had to mount up to 210 guards and pickets each week. Unfortunately this requirement has seldom gone away for long, and over the years many thousands of hours have been expended in the cause of securing the Station against the terrorist menace.

By way of achievement, the Fire and Rescue Section had won the 81 Group Inter-Station Competition in May 1954. This section as well as others on the Station had at last begun to receive new and more efficient equipment. This had undoubtedly helped the firemen when they then went on to win the Fighter Command Competition the following year, as well as when they made up the majority of the Command team that won the RAF Competition in July 1955. In January 1956 a successful demonstration in extinguishing an aircraft fire with foam was given using the new Mk 5A tender, which, with its greatly improved level of performance over the previous vehicle used by the Station, was a real step forward in the field of "Flight Safety", as well as being a genuine confidence booster for the aircrew, both pupils and instructors. Other improvements for the Station in 1954/55 saw the installation of a new airfield lighting system and the introduction of the Weather Information Computer in the Met office. No doubt the older aircraft tradesmen would have cast disparaging remarks about the fortitude of the "modern airman" when heating was installed in the hangar that housed Aircraft Servicing Flight. New signals equipment of all kinds also

became available and a new Wing Operations Room was established in July 1956. Good news for the families came in the form of the opening of the Leeming RAF County Primary School, adjacent to the married quarters, in August of the same year. In 1955 it was clear that a determined effort was made to increase the number of officers and airmen playing organised games, and the venture resulted in an average of 600 personnel being involved in sport on a Wednesday afternoon. The variety of sports along with the number of teams involved is quite staggering to those who came later. There was station football or cricket during the week and at weekends, inter-section football and cricket, teams involved in athletics, weight-lifting, cycling, basket-ball, badminton, table tennis, and swimming. In itself, the inter-section cricket league involved 17 teams. This was also the time when sportsmen of top class ability were spread throughout the RAF while doing their National Service and one example at Leeming was LAC Platt, an armourer, who as a pace bowler played cricket for Yorkshire's 1st XI.

This period also saw a considerable decrease in the number of aircraft accidents and many of those that occurred were caused by bursting tyres when the Meteors landed. In spite of this, there were too many that were more serious, with occasional fatalities still being recorded. Notwithstanding these accidents, evidence that the OCU was building up a reputation could be gleaned from the number of visitors from other air forces, including the RCAF, who came to study methods of training and maintenance. The visit of an officer from the Royal Naval Air Station at Yeovilton in March 1955 heralded the inclusion of RN students in the training courses, as well as the subsequent appointment of a Naval Officer to the OCU Staff. The Unit's reputation was certainly in the ascendancy, but the reaction of two RAF pupils to the methods of training in November 1955 would probably have been kept from the ears of the visitors. Not surprisingly. It does seem a little too far down the training road for an OCU to be the place to discover that a pilot would have to be suspended because he was too short to handle a Meteor NF.11, and in the same week a navigator, because he was too tall!!

After the break caused by the reconstruction in 1956, training re-commenced on 1 January 1957, with the flying re-organised in two wings: Flying/Basic Wing equipped with the Valetta and Advanced Wing to be equipped with the Javelin FAW 5. Although the Javelins did not actually replace the Meteors until June 1957, in November 1956 a Javelin Cockpit Trainer had been installed in the new Airmanship Hall, which was then a part of the new Ground School, and the Javelin Mobile Conversion Unit had started converting Staff Navigators to the AI Mark 17. The first Javelin to arrive landed on 04/22 runway, which meant that immediately prior to touch down it had to cross the Great North Road at Londonderry. On this occasion, and of course on many others in the future, one of the tasks given to the firemen was to climb over the boundary wall and stop the traffic by placing a stop sign for each direction into sockets previously prepared on the footpaths. To ensure maximum use of this runway, the Javelins had to cross the road and clear the wall and hedge by a mere six or seven feet and it is not difficult to imagine the stir these proceedings caused amongst those held up in the traffic queues. During the next two years, the Javelin Mks 5 and T.3 and the Canberra T.4 and T.11 were fed into the training machine until by December 1960 the final shape of 228 OCU had stabilised. At that date there were 54 jet powered training aircraft on the Unit, a total made up of Canberras, Meteors, and Javelins. Flying Wing (ex Basic Wing), used the Canberras and Meteors, with No 1 Squadron responsible for the ten weeks' basic training of the navigators. The Squadron could also operate some of the Meteors to tow targets for gunnery exercises, where the Javelin T.3 was normally employed. This type was a dual-control trainer with no radar fitted but with the armament retained, and the instructor in the rear seat oper-

ating with a horizontal periscope as a gun-sight. Only 22 of this version were built and most of them operated from 228 OCU at Leeming.

After a navigator had completed his basic training, he had a week's leave, then moved on to Advanced Wing to join up with his pilot for a further 15 weeks. This Wing consisted of four Squadrons: 2, 3, 4 (Handling), and 5, with a Wing Commander responsible for all crew training. After a little over two weeks' concentrated ground training, which pilots and navigators did together, the pilots went on to dual trips in a Javelin T.3 before going solo on the FAW 5. At the same time, the navigator was given six trips with an instructor to become familiar with the standard AI equipment and the techniques of interception.

There was also a "Wing Commander Flying", who was responsible for the supervision of all flying and supporting services such as ATC, GCA, GCI, Ground Training and crash services. The GCA, two mounted caravans on a turntable for quick change of direction, had three facilities – search, precision and communication. This gave them control of an aircraft up to 40 miles away, pictures of its glidepath in both azimuth and elevation, and transmission and reception by both VHF and UHF radios. (All Javelins had UHF, Canberras and Meteors had VHF). This type of close control produced an enviable record of no accidents attributable to pilot error.

While the training carried out by the OCU was developing to this high standard, the Station was involved in a number of subsidiary activities. The Javelin Major Conversion Unit (JMCU) moved in, and while using the Station as its home base it carried out its training at various locales around the country. Leeming has often played the "host" to squadrons operating away from their home bases, and the latter years of 228 OCU's stay at Leeming were no exception. In September 1957, No.264 Squadron was detached from Middleton St George while the runways were being length-ened there, but was immediately disbanded and reformed as No.33 Squadron for conversion to the

Javelin – a task carried out by the JMCU. This newly designated squadron remained at Leeming for a little over a year before moving on in September 1958 with the Javelin Mk 7. While at Leeming it was honoured with the presentation of the Queen's Standard, and then in July some time was spent "on state" after being called to readiness for possible deployment to the Middle East during the Suez crisis. Then No.60 (FEAF) Squadron arrived with additional Meteors for a somewhat extended stay from June until August 1959 to carry out an intensive training programme for relief crews. While they were in residence, Leeming achieved one noteworthy record, but one that won no prizes, when the fuel issues in July totalling 729,123 gallons of AVTAG were the highest ever recorded to that date by any unit in the Royal Air Force. The Javelins of No.72 Squadron, normally based at Leconfield, came for a while in 1961, as did No.33 Squadron, which returned just before the closing of the OCU.

Throughout the years at Leeming there have been many problems relating to accommodation, whether it is for people or planes, and the extended stay of 33 Sqn, which necessitated the tenancy of a hangar, meant problems for some. In particular, the Cleveland Gliding Club had to be moved to Topcliffe, but this was only a small inconvenience compared to problems that followed a major fire in number 2 Hangar in 1958. A battery driven mechanical handler, designed to tow aircraft, had collided with a Meteor and the resultant spillage from a punctured fuel tank was ignited by the handler's hot exhaust pipe. Fireman Tony Eaton who, when in the RAF, was involved in fighting the blaze recollects:

> . . . I was on duty that day in our tin hut on the Londonderry side of the airfield, when I heard a loud explosion and saw a ball of flame through the hangar windows. We jumped into our tenders, myself in Crash 1, and sped across the runway. I ran into the hangar, wearing my tin hat and carrying a

10lb CO_2 fire extinguisher, which, when confronted by blazing aircraft and the hangar roof going well too, quickly achieved a degree of irrelevance. It took quite a while to get the fire under control, even with the help of the local fire service and the ground-crew in the hangar who remained and fought the fire with us. When it was over, three aircraft were badly damaged and the roof had been destroyed.

The "tin hut" mentioned was in use at the time as the fire/crash bay, and was known as an ALTENT. These were metal versions of the conical roofed huts commonly seen in Africa, and had been built for the then defunct Groundnut Scheme of 1946/47. The RAF found uses for them of course, and the one at Leeming had a coke stove in the centre and duck boards for the floor. However, with no sanitary facilities it was not the ideal place to spend the long hours while night flying was in progress.

More satisfying for those undergoing training, was the completion of a new vertically split ATC Tower in October 1959 and the installation of the Mk 6 Arrestor Barriers on runway 34/16 in April 1960. Also in 1960, the staff crews of Advanced Wing were formed into No.137 (Reserve) Squadron and that year took part in the major air defence operation "Exercise Yeoman". Aircraft at Leeming at that time were Meteor NF.14, Meteor T.7, Javelin FAW 5, Javelin T.3, Canberra T.4, Canberra T.11 and an Anson. The Canberra T.11, used for the training of AI radar operators, was easily recognisable from its extended radar nose of the type fitted to the Javelin. The frequency with which flying accidents occurred at Leeming had been much reduced at this time, though the servicing of the Canberra T11s was causing concern and the Javelin was prone to undercarriage faults. On two occasions in 1960, aircraft had to make a landing with the starboard leg locked in the "up" position, and in both cases great skill must have been shown because neither aircraft received more than slight damage. Away from work, another attempt was made at producing a Station Magazine, and "Leeming Life" appeared on the scene in September 1959. The Station also had at this time a radio station, named the "Leeming Forces Network", which broadcast to sections, messes and barracks on a Redifusion channel. Some years later, one of its volunteer "DJs", Junior Technician Pete Jackson achieved an entry into the record book by playing 3,000 singles (LPs not permitted) in a marathon 144 hours of "air" time. During his time on the air he was not allowed to sleep, and to help him break the solo disc jockey marathon record he drank 120 cups of coffee. There is no record of the answer to the obvious question about his capacity, but he did raise £150 for charity, and received a bottle of Champagne for himself from the CO. On the sports front in April 1960, as an addition to the usual station facilities, three golf tees and greens were sited on one of the internal fields and AMWD prepared them for use. Gp Capt Smales hit the obligatory opening drive, but apart from the remains of a few hazards there is little to show where these *holes* were once sited, and the chance to play golf on the Station has long since disappeared. A study made in 1994/95 showed that it was entirely feasible to resurrect the idea, but

unfortunately the climate of cut-backs was against the notion of the Station developing its own nine hole golf course.

By February 1961, changing policies in training had begun to catch up with 228 OCU. The intake to Basic/Flying Wing ceased at that time and the training task began to run down by processing the final courses through Advanced Wing. For the period up to September 1961, the remaining aircraft were occupied in various ways, such as when the OCU was tasked with supplying the Canberras and Meteors to fly as targets for Lightnings and Bloodhound Squadrons. Then as No.137 Reserve Squadron, which was made up of aircrew instructors, they were engaged in Exercise Matador with Vulcans from 44 Squadron. In July, 1 Sqn moved to West Raynham to form a Target Facility Squadron and 137 Reserve Squadron was disbanded. In August the GCI was dismantled after being made non-operational, and by the end of the month all aircraft had been allotted elsewhere and flown out prior to the disbandment of 228 OCU on 14 September 1961. This, however, was not the end for the Station as the very next day saw RAF Leeming become the home of the reformed No.3 Flying Training School, under the control of 23 Group Flying Training Command.

CHAPTER FOUR

No. 3 FLYING TRAINING SCHOOL
September 1961 to September 1984

The rebirth of No.3 FTS at RAF Leeming on 15 September 1961 was in fact only the continuation of a long training history. Originally formed at Grantham on 2 April 1928, the School's first course trained on the dual control version of the Armstrong Whitworth Atlas, and passed out on 25 March 1929. By 16 August 1939, when 3 FTS moved to South Cerney, 618 pilots had been trained on such aircraft as the Avro Tutor, Armstrong Whitworth Siskin, Bristol Bulldog and the Hawker Hart, Audax, and Tomtit. Although the majority of the pilots had been trained for the Royal Air Force, the FTS also trained pilots from countries as varied as China, Iraq and Estonia.

In 1938, in order to carry out more advanced instruction, the School was also equipped with the Airspeed Oxford, but even with war clouds on the horizon the peacetime regime of training continued until the outbreak of hostilities in 1939 when the war training syllabus was introduced. The most dramatic aspect of this change was the drastically reduced period of training, and skills that had taken 12 months to obtain then had to be gained in eight to twelve weeks! In 1942 the Unit changed its name to No.3(P) Advanced Flying Unit (AFU) and devoted the major part of the war years to giving advanced flying instruction to RAF pilots on refresher courses, as well as to a number from Australia, Belgium, Canada, France, Holland, New Zealand, Norway, Poland and Yugoslavia. The AFU operated until December 1945 when it reverted, in both name and role, to No.3 Flying Training School. The following year saw the FTS move to Feltwell, where it trained pilots for the RAF and RN, initially with the Tiger Moth and Harvard, but soon afterwards in 1948 Tiger Moth training ceased and the Prentice was introduced. However, in 1954 when the Piston Provost made its appearance the Prentice was phased out, and when the Harvard training ceased in March 1955 the Provost became the sole training type. This work continued until 1 June 1958, when No.3 FTS was disbanded, to reform again three years later at Leeming with the task of starting the new concept of "all through jet training" for the RAF.

The Jet Provost trainer had been chosen to provide the next logical step from the Piston Provost to Vampire sequence of training previously used, and came into service for ab initio training at No.2 FTS Syerston in late 1959. By early 1960 Syerston had been completely re-equipped, but the change-over at other 23 Group Schools was delayed until the RAF College at Cranwell had received its aircraft; so by the end of September 1961, Leeming had received only 9 of the Mk.3 version of the new jet trainer. Needless to say, it was still expected that the first course would start on schedule, and notwithstanding the small number of aircraft, the 15 students began their training on 4 October 1961. The course was initially designed to last 36 weeks, with ground instruction taking up the first two weeks. At the end of the course, having been allowed 120 hours flying time, the student would proceed to an Advanced Training School where he would receive his "Wings" after a further period of 36 weeks. By the time the fourth course started in March 1962 the structure had been amended, and under the new scheme the student was required to complete a 160 hour Course lasting for 48 weeks, covering basic training on the Mk.3 and advanced flying on the more powerful Mk.4 aircraft. On completion of this he now received his "Wings" before starting advanced training as a qualified pilot.

The Station moved smoothly into its new role, and adapted to the various changes that were found to be necessary. To cope with the increase in the number of aircraft and the possible overlap of courses, a second Training Squadron was formed in January 1962, and still a third in January 1968. The courses were initially a mix of commissioned and non-commissioned trainees, many with acting rank, but following policy changes the days of the NCO pilot were soon to be numbered, and the final such recipient at Leeming, Acting Sergeant Gardiner of No 9 Course, graduated on 3 April 1964. The "Wings" were presented at formal ceremonies, when, in the presence of the families and friends of those graduating, the Parade would be reviewed by a serving or retired senior officer, usually from the RAF itself. There were excep-

tions, such as when Her Royal Highness Princess Marina, Duchess of Kent reviewed the sixth course on 24 July 1963, and much later in August 1971, when Major-General A C Hull DFC of the Canadian Armed Forces was the Reviewing Officer. He was no stranger to the area, and had in fact returned to the Station where as a Group Captain in the RCAF he had been Station Commander during April-May of 1945. Included amongst the pilots graduating that day were four Canadian Air Force students, who were being watched by a number of friends and relatives who had chartered a plane to Leeming especially for the ceremony.

Whilst the primary task facing each student was to qualify as a pilot, there was competition within each course for the award of individual trophies. Originally there were four of these honours, to be awarded to students for showing outstanding achievement in specific areas of their training, but this total later rose to six after two former Station Commanders of RAF Leeming presented further trophies.

DETAILS OF TROPHIES

The Sword of Merit
The Sword of Merit was presented by Lieutenant Colonel R W Bradley, DSO 24th Regiment South Wales Borderers, to symbolise the spirit of co-operation that exists between the fighting Services. To be awarded to the best all-round student of the graduating course.

The "Glen" Trophy
Presented by Group Captain J G Glen, OBE, to be awarded to the student who showed the greatest proficiency in general flying.

The "Broughton" Trophy
This Trophy, presented by Group Captain C Broughton, CBE, to be awarded to the student who obtained the highest marks in the final examination in ground subjects.

The "Delwyn" Trophy

This Trophy was presented by Mrs M L Brown, in memory of her son, Flight Sergeant D V Brown, who lost his life on flying duty on 5 April 1954. The Trophy was awarded to the student who showed the greatest proficiency in aerobatics.

The "Radley" Trophy

This Trophy, presented by Group Captain R S Radley, DFC, AFC, to be awarded to the student who obtained the highest marks in officer qualities in the graduating course.

The "Silver Spurs" Trophy

This Trophy, presented by Air Commodore J W Allan, DSO, DFC, AFC, to be awarded to the student who showed the greatest all-round improvement in professional and personal development during the Basic Flying Training Course.

In 1968 from 26 Course, the winner of The Sword of Merit and The "Broughton" Trophy was a certain Flt Lt A D Steadman, later to achieve notoriety and a jail sentence for selling V Bomber secrets to the Soviet Union. In earlier days Plt Off D T J Collinson, who graduated with 9 Course in 1964, also achieved recognition, but in his case it was of an honourable nature. He went on to win an immediate DFC for gallantry and exceptional flying skills during helicopter operations in Borneo, just eleven months after graduating from Leeming.

Throughout its existence at Leeming, 3 FTS built up an enviable reputation in training pilots from all over the world. A total of 65 courses were trained at Leeming, with 930 students graduating between 15 September 1961 and 11 October 1974 at a success rate of almost 74 per cent. More to the point, this high success rate was achieved with only three training fatalities. (The first three courses with a total of 53 students, had passed out from Leeming to advanced flying training schools to continue their training, and from there they received their "Wings".)

It was not all work for the instructors though, and from the outset, though originally only from No.1 Squadron, a formation aerobatic team was formed by the Staff pilots of 3 FTS. They had started their training ready for the new season in 1962 and for a number of years, The Gemini as they were called, were in demand for displays in all parts of the country.

It was also in the early sixties that the Equipment Section at Leeming took the giant first step into the computer age. On 16 July 1962, Leeming became one of the first six Units in the RAF to operate with the new procedures that followed the completion of the installation of the Automatic Data Processing (ADP) system. The control of spares for the Jet Provost was further improved in January 1966 when records were transferred to the RAF Supply Control Centre Computer at Hendon; a move designed to give greater speed of reaction to priority demands than the previous manual system. It was also around this time that the name of the Equipment Branch was changed, with "Main Stores" becoming "Supply Squadron". With the image of the "storeman" being akin to that of a hoarder, it was almost inevitable that they were exhorted "to stop storing and start supplying"!

Major construction work particularly on the airfield continued, and the sight of workmen carrying out maintenance on the runway surfaces became almost a routine occurrence. New additions to the airfield operating area were added in 1962 when the Operational Readiness Platform and a concrete taxi loop to runway 34 were completed. This provided permanent facilities for the dispersal of two V Bombers although for a number of years previously Leeming had been the appointed dispersal airfield for up to four Vulcans from No.83 Sqn involved with Exercise Kinsman. Once the readiness platforms were completed deployment instructions relating to the dispersal of Bomber Command aircraft were revalidated and kept under constant review, thus emphasising the wider range of the Station's responsibilities beyond training. Increasingly, in conjunction with the other military services, Leeming was establishing its place in the various NATO plans for both offence and defence, and at the same time was co-operating with the Civil Defence organisations. A number of war appointments connected with civil defence were allocated to Station personnel and operating instructions from the Northern Civil Defence organisation were issued to the Unit. One exercise held in June 1962 even found Jet Provosts acting in the ground attack role in support of Army units deployed at Kirkby Stephen, and is but another example of the scope of involvement from Leeming.

A particular formation having increasing mention at this time was the Mountain Rescue Team, which after transferring from RAF Topcliffe, re-formed at Leeming on 6 July 1959. It began operations with only three full-time and two part-time members, so their primary task after arrival was to recruit enough new members to form a viable operational team. Seventeen volunteers attended the first meeting and many of them were well on the way to being fully trained when they were first "called out" on 13 September 1959. With three or four full-time members and upwards of 20 volunteers, the team's first duty was the rescue of personnel from crashed aircraft, from an area covering central Yorkshire to Dunbar, including the Lake District, Cheviot Hills, and North Yorkshire Moors. However, team members were always taking part in regular exercises with their civilian counterparts, to assist in making them ready for "call out" at any time, day or night. Additionally, in those early days at Leeming several of its members took part in a number of expeditions to many parts of the world, including places as far apart as Greenland and North Africa.

The Station has played host on a number of occasions to members of the Royal Family, and the Queen who carried out the Royal Review of the RAF Regiment at RAF Catterick in April 1962 travelled to that Unit via RAF Leeming. It was to be the first of many subsequent opportunities for the Station to act as host to VIP air travellers who were in transit to engagements in the area. Some years later, the Station was further involved with a Royal Review when the 50th Anniversary of the formation of the Royal Air Force was celebrated in such a fashion. This took place at RAF Abingdon on 14 June 1968, when the Review was opened by a fly-past of 31 Jet Provost aircraft depicting the Royal Cypher E II R, with all aircraft drawn from the Basic Flying Schools including No.3 FTS RAF Leeming. Somewhat later in June 1971 came the York Centenary Celebrations, with Leeming contributing personnel for the Cathedral Service as well as staging a fly-past during the Queen Mother's visit.

The use of its aircraft at such times has always been recognised by the RAF as being good for public relations, but the Station has always taken pride in the fact that it has consistently worked for the establishment of good relations with the surrounding neighbourhood. This effort has taken many forms, and in the sixties these varied from the opening of the Sports Centre to civilian organisations, to visits to local authorities and societies to explain the work being carried out at Leeming. This being said, arguably the most popular public relations exercise since the formation of the Service has been the holding of an Open Day. The first "Good Neighbours Day", as it was then called at Leeming, took place in September 1964 when an invitation to "come and see" was accepted by more than 8000 visitors. Since that date an invitation to visit has been given many times in a variety of different ways, culminating in the Air Fairs of the nineties when tens of thousands of members of the general public took the opportunity to call. The Station was also busy in other ways, especially when playing host to other Service Units such as to the TA by providing them with parachute training facilities, but also to RAF Regiment Squadrons and the Royal Observer Corps. On occasions, it even provided this assistance to non-military organisations, and for a time in 1964 the Detached Wing of No.2 District Police Training Centre was located on the Station before it moved

1. (left) Londonderry Airfield in 1937 with a DH Puss Moth and a Miles Hawk on display. The Puss Moth, a 3-seat high-wing cabin monoplane, is of the type that made the first landing at Londonderry in 1930.

Charles E Penty

2. (left) Leeming airfield on 4 May 1940, taken from a Whitley bomber of 78 Sqn from Linton-on-Ouse.

RAF Leeming archives

3. (below) The domestic and technical sites in May 1940. The Station Commander's house is in the centre foreground, with those for his senior offices paraded to the front and right. The terraced buildings on the extreme right were the airmen's married quarters. *RAF Leeming archives*

4. (above) 'Bombing-up'. A
Whitley V from 10 Sqn
(Z8342) being prepared for an
operation from Leeming in
1940.   *RAF Leeming archives*

5. (right) A Whitley V from 10
Sqn (T4230), taken in 1940.
Note the figure in the rear
hatch position; he is probably
being photographed from the
same position in the other aircraft. The aircraft, coded
ZA-R, was lost in the North
Sea with Sqn Ldr Ferguson
and his crew on the night of
13/14 November 1940.
    RAF Leeming archives

6. (right) Military funeral of
the crew of T4152. This official
German photograph of the ceremony at Schwabisch Hall
Cemetery was received by the
Air Ministry in January 1941,
and from it the size of the
Ceremonial Party can be clearly gauged. Each of the five
coffins was draped with the
Union Flag and a wreath.
    RAF Leeming archives

7. Looking towards Leeming village during the early summer of 1941. The structure in the centre foreground housed the main stores for the Station, and a Whitley V from 10 Sqn is about to be towed into No.3 Hangar. Still more of the Squadron's aircraft can be seen at the various dispersals at the far side of the newly constructed runway. The fir trees planted around the buildings for camouflage and blast protection were not to last – they were used for firewood during the following winter. *RAF Leeming archives*

8. Operations room, 6 August 1941. The CO, Gp Capt W E Staton (with pipe), is apparently discussing with Wg Cdr V B Bennett the previous night's raid on Frankfurt. The board indicates that 'G' had not returned to base by 0845 hrs, however, as 10 Sqn did not lose an aircraft on that raid it is possible that the aircraft landed elsewhere and the crew had failed to report in.

RAF Leeming archives

9. (right) One of the Halifax
B.IIs from No.10 Sqn that took
part in the operations against
the *Tirpitz* in 1942. This aircraft, R9376, was lost in an
accident following the move of
the Squadron to Melbourne
RAF Leeming archives

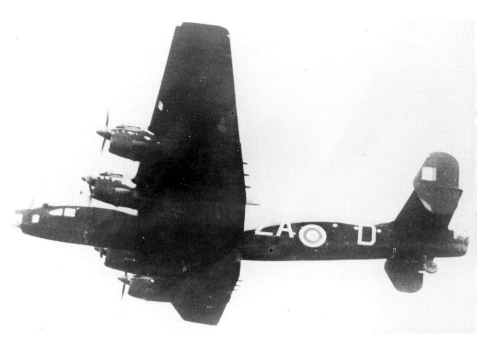

10. The mix of nationalities at RAF Leeming in 1940/41. In addition to the British in the uni-
forms of the RAF and RAFVR, they came from Argentina, Australia, Canada, Newfoundland,
New Zealand, South Africa and the USA.   *RAF Leeming archives*

11. (below) Flt Sgt Sanderson surveys his own 'hole' in the ground as he stands in the crater left by the controlled detonation a 1000 lb bomb. He had previously supervised the removal of the bomb from the wreck of a crashed Halifax. *RAF Leeming archives*

12. (above) His Majesty the King in August 1944, inspecting some of the damage inflicted by three 'friendly' bombs on U-Uncle of 427 Sqn. The figure half masked by the King and still looking bemused by his escape is the pilot, Fg Off Murphy, with the Base Commander, Air Commodore Bryans, making up the trio. The piece of aircraft structure suspended by the hangar door is the piece of tailplane which had its fin removed by another of the bombs. *Charles A Appleton RCAF*

13. The second prototype of the Miles Martinet (LR244), which was the first aircraft type specifically designed for the RAF as a target-tug. The winch, normally installed in the side of the centre fuselage, had not been fitted to this aircraft. The Martinet operated at Leeming from 1946 to 1952. *Crown copyright MOD*

14. The Bristol Buckmaster, for its time, was one of the fastest training aircraft used by the RAF. It carried a crew of three, had a top speed of 350 mph and was used at Leeming between 1948 and 1951 for training aircrew destined for Brigand B1 operations. *Crown copyright MOD*

15. (below) A Bristol Brigand B1 of the type used by 228 OCU from 1947 to 1951 for training crews in the light bombing role for squadrons stationed in the Middle East and Far East. *Crown copyright MOD*

16. (above) The flight-line at night in 1952, with a Meteor NF11 of 228 OCU being 'turned round' by the ground-crew. *Crown copyright MOD*

17. (left) Javelin flypast in 1959. The formation from 228 OCU is made up of three FAW5s with a T3 bringing up the rear. The tail badge is that of 137 (Reserve) Sqn. *Crown copyright MOD*

18. (below) The flight-line at Leeming in 1961, with 29 Javelins of 228 OCU sporting the badge of No.137 (Reserve) Sqn on their fins just prior to the closure of the OCU and dis-bandment of the Squadron. *Crown copyright MOD*

19. (above) The Gemini Pair flying the Jet Provost Mk4 in the area of Sutton Bank, North Yorkshire, in 1968. The famous white horse can be seen clearly, a good enough reason for it to be concealed during the war. The 'top' aircraft in the formation was flown by Flt Lt Raynor, and his 'mirror' was Fg Off Pook. In 1982 Pook was rescued from the South Atlantic after ejecting from his Harrier GR3 which had taken hits from ground fire over the Falkland Islands. *Crown copyright MOD*

20. (left) The Leeming Sword as represented by No.3 FTS before the fuel crisis of 1973. *Crown copyright MOD*

21. (below) The Leeming Sword as represented by the pilots of No.3 FTS during the fuel crisis! *Crown copyright MOD*

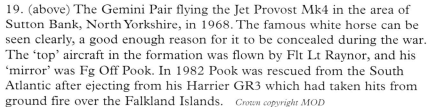

down the road to Dishforth. Individual visitors came too, often to study training and maintenance methods on behalf of their own Air Forces. The Station saw personnel come from Sweden in 1964, India, then Turkey in 1965, Burma in 1966, Belgium, Italy in 1969, and finally, from Ecuador in 1972. Furthermore, this degree of international liaison could also be found reflected in the numerous nationalities present as students. Over the years this figure included pupils from Australia, Burma, Iraq, Jordan, Lebanon, Malaysia, Oman, Saudi Arabia, Siam, Singapore and Sudan, as well as, of course, those from Britain.

However, even these training responsibilities were beginning to expand, with one example that started in April 1964 for VR(T) officers in the Air Training Corps. Held in the Ground School and lasting one week, these courses were concerned with preparing officers for the instruction of ATC Cadets, particularly in the "Theory of Flight", and initially ten courses per year were planned. In December of the same year, Refresher Flight was formed in HQ Squadron, its purpose being to provide refresher flying for pilots with whom the School at Manby was unable to cope. The Flight operated intermittently until the School itself moved to RAF Leeming in December 1973, to form No.3 (School of Refresher Flying) Squadron. Later, as RFS operating with Jet Provosts, its aims were to restore the flying skills and procedures of pilots returning to the air environment from ground appointments. Courses, seven strong, arrived every fortnight and the students, ranging in rank from Pilot Officer to Air Marshal, spent some six weeks at RAF Leeming, although the actual length of the course was flexible depending on the ability of the individual. Then for a brief spell beginning in 1966 the Vampire Unit moved from Church Fenton to Leeming to continue the Vampire Training Courses. In fact, the end of the Vampire T.II in the pilot training role with the RAF was marked at Leeming on 29 November 1967 when the AOC led a display and flypast.

On the cultural side, the Station Magazine still known then as "Leeming Life", was again in publication by 1964, and the Station Dramatic Society flourished. The entry of a team from Leeming in the Royal Tournament of 1967 would in itself be of only passing interest, but details of the organization for the event brings to light another milestone. This, although it had actually occurred back in 1966, was the return of servicewomen to the strength of RAF Leeming after an absence of 18 years. It had not appeared to be of sufficient importance to appear in the ORB of 1966, but at last the WRAF, as they had been called since 1949, could return to those unnamed duties that the CO in 1948 had thought were undertaken so skilfully by WAAF personnel. Perhaps the oversight can be laid at the door of the World Cup win, but in the same year one of the most exacting of commitments ever to come to Leeming was officially accepted by the Station on 1 December 1966. The work-up to the assumption of this demanding responsibility had gone on for some months, but after gaining the mantle of a Master Diversion Airfield (MDA), Leeming was required to keep the airfield open on a 24 hour basis. Its personnel had to be ready to receive any aircraft diverted from any landing ground in the North of England, civil as well as military, at whatever time and for whatever reason. To assist the Station to be ready for any situation however catastrophic that might have developed from such a diversion, a Special Safety Team was formed in January 1967. The Station was kept very busy with routine arrivals, and a not insubstantial number of diversions, along with an occasional emergency. The team responded to many incidents, but fortunately no disasters, and other than for some general assistance following emergencies their expertise was fortunately never needed at Leeming. The extent of the commitment maintained throughout 1969 can be seen from the statistics relating to visiting aircraft, planned and unplanned. There were 68 different types of aircraft making 7,655 visits carrying 18,624 passengers (mainly trooping) and

3,744,880lbs of freight, with 924 aircraft logged in July which was the busiest month.

With this volume of traffic, constant attention had to be paid to improve the techniques of controlling aircraft in the air, and in the early days Leeming was the scene of a number of trials for methods that were later to be adopted, or in some cases improved upon. As early as July 1965 a trial of Centralised Approach Control had been implemented, where aircraft taking off under aerodrome control were handed over to what was known as Area Radar Control Recovery Visual (ARCRV). In Leeming's case this was Humber Radar at Lindholme in Lincolnshire for climb under control, in-flight surveillance if required, and recovery to destination aerodrome approach radar. The trial was considered a partial success in that it suggested that the system could work for airfields involved with flying training.

The quality of instruction of student pilots, the flying characteristics of their aircraft, along with the improved training of those who serviced them, had come a long way since the attrition of the forties and fifties. Unfortunately No.3 FTS still had its accidents, although during its stay at Leeming they were relatively few and far between, with 1965 as their worst year by far. A mid-air collision between two Jet Provost T3s left one student dead and two aircraft written off, and later in the year a fire warning which turned out to have been spurious, led to a successful double ejection, but of course the loss of another aircraft.

The improvements in training methods were followed in the early seventies with Station facilities and buildings once more receiving attention. On the occupational side, the building of a new Fire Section was begun in 1971 and after some delays was completed in 1972. The allocation of master diversion responsibilities to the Station back in 1966 had meant a large increase in the workload for the firemen, so these improved facilities, as well as improvements in their equipment, were long overdue. An important enhancement to their skills was assuredly the ability to lay a foam

strip on the runway. This reduced the risk of fire from an aircraft having to land without all, or even part of its undercarriage, and on 9 December 1971, an Argosy with a suspect nose undercarriage defect allowed the Station its first operational use. On the aircraft, the system used to show the position of its undercarriage indicated that though the two main legs of the four engined transport were down and locked, the nose-leg was down but in an unlocked condition. The possible consequence of this kind of problem would be the collapse of the unlocked undercarriage, with potentially catastrophic results if this failure occurred on landing. In the kind of situation faced by this crew, all a pilot can do is to land on the main wheels and keep the nose wheels from the ground for as long as possible, thereby reducing the speed at which any forces are initially placed on the nose-leg. This, the pilot of the Argosy did, and the aircraft was carefully brought down for a safe though spectacular landing through the foam. As it happened, though no one was aware of the fact till later, the defect was actually an indication fault, and the undercarriage was in a "locked down" condition for the whole of the emergency. As a consequence, the only assistance required from the fire-crew was from the use of their hoses in the clearing of the foam from the aircraft and then the runway.

In September 1972, a more welcome event, at least from the point of view of the many people who lived at Leeming, was the positioning by Royal Engineers of a bridge over Bedale Beck at the north-east corner of the airfield giving access to a lane leading to the road connecting Leeming Village and Northallerton. Although limited in its use by the flying programme and its unsuitability for heavy vehicles, it provided a much needed short-cut to the railhead at Northallerton, and in addition, saved those exiting from RAF Leeming from the problems of the very risky means of access to the north bound lane of the busy A1 trunkroad. Six years later, in October 1978 when, as part of the NATO commitment, Leeming was assigned for use by Allied Air Forces, attempts were made to have the lane widened for use by heavy vehicles. Negotiations with the North Yorkshire Council came to naught because of disagreement about the source of the £20,000 that was needed, and access to Leeming still remained poor until 1992 when the flyover was constructed.

This period however, did see other improvements throughout the Station and the domestic side was not ignored, with the new extension to the NAAFI Shop being opened on 13 June 1972. This was followed by the conversion of the airmens' NAAFI into a Social Club, which after completion was formally opened by the Commanding Officer and named the "JP Club" in February 1974. Work was also started on converting single airmen accommodation to a flatlet standard, a task which because of successive defence economies, was never completed.

On the recreational scene, the Physical Fitness Section, which having moved back into a new Sports Centre in No. 1 Hangar in July 1963, continued to remain a popular venue, supporting numerous sporting fixtures. The hangar had undergone a major conversion programme after the Nuffield Trust had provided a grant to cover the major portion of the costs, helping it become one of the best equipped centres in the RAF. It is always problematical when comparing costs from bygone days, but the Station must have felt that for the sum of £6,314 it had a bargain in the sports arena, with the following facilities available:

4-lane Running Track.
Tennis Court.
Indoor Cricket Pitch.
Three Badminton Courts.
Indoor Pits with run-ups.
Two Table Tennis areas.
60-yard Spring Strip.
Fencing Piste.
Basket Ball Court.
Boarded 5-a-side Football Pitch.

In addition, there was a trampoline, synthetic parachute training equipment, a weight training bay, as well as volley ball and gymnasium equipment. As an AAA standard arena it certainly gained the interest of local athletic clubs and competitive fixtures were soon being organised.

In a noisier environment Leeming had been represented in the Isle of Man TT Races of 1968, and in 1970 the Fencing Team won the RAF Inter-Unit Competition. The Soccer Team won the Yorkshire Services League in 1971 and the Faville Trophy in 1973, with the Angling Team coming first in its section of the latter competition in the same year. In addition, throughout those years, a wide variety of other activities were being enjoyed at Leeming and several successes were seen to be gained. The Theatre Club, then performing under the name of "The Leeming Lights" was extremely popular, regularly playing to full houses for their productions of plays such as "Boeing Boeing", "Say Who You Are", and even "The Imaginary Invalid" by Molière, the 17th century French playwright. In 1971, after their performance of "Billy Liar" in the RAF Training Command Drama Festival, they were placed first and in 1972 when they again took part the players had their efforts rewarded with a creditable third place. Teams competed in the Nijmegen Marches and in 1974, the extremely gruelling "Three Peaks" Race. This required that entrants in any given 24 hour period should climb the three mountains: Snowdon (3,560ft), Scafell (3,210ft) and Ben Nevis (4406ft). The five man team from Supply Squadron at Leeming, aided by a number of colleagues, three cars and a Landrover, completed the course, although the last man made it with only 12 seconds to spare! The walkers had each covered over 30 miles and climbed over 11,000 feet while each vehicle logged more than 1100 miles, so the night spent under canvas at Fort William on completion of the walk, will undoubtedly have been preceded by some celebration.

Operationally by the end of 1973, pressure on the Station started to build up once more. In October, the CO of Leeming also assumed command of the Relief Landing Ground at

Topcliffe, and in the following May, responsibility was assumed for parenting Ouston prior to its handover to the Army in August 1975. This change of ownership meant that two units based there would have to move and in September 1974 they came to Leeming: the Northumbrian Universities Air Squadron and No.11 Air Experience Flight.

NUAS

Northumbrian Universities Air Squadron was established in 1963, from Durham UAS which had originally been formed in 1941. The name was changed when Newcastle University was founded; students were also accepted from Newcastle and Sunderland Polytechnics, and those selected were required to join the RAFVR for two years, from where they would be given 65 hours flying tuition. During college term, a student would normally visit Leeming once each week and again at weekends, with more intense flying taking place during the Christmas and Easter vacations. In the summer recess, the Squadron would spend four to five weeks at another RAF station on "Summer Camp" where the student would be expected to be present for at least two weeks. Although it was always hoped that a UAS would produce some of the future pilots for the RAF, their formation was also a medium for public relations to provide interest in and knowledge of the Service both at Universities and among the graduates.

The other new arrival, No.11 Air Experience Flight was one of 13 such flights in the UK and its task was to provide air experience to just over 2000 ATC Cadets located in Cumbria, Northumberland and Durham. Once a year each cadet would be given a 25 minute trip, consisting of local flying, basic handling of controls and aerobatics in one of the Chipmunk T10/11. Approximately 40 cadets would be flown each weekend, mainly by VR pilots who gave of their spare time and skills to provide this unpaid service. First line servicing of the aircraft was originally provided by RAF personnel working as NUAS groundcrew with second line support supplied by the Station's establishment. The arrival of 11 AEF was not Leeming's introduction to ATC Cadets, as local Squadrons had been visiting the Station for air experience flights since the inception of the Corps, and instruction sessions were frequently given by Leeming officers and NCOs at the headquarters of each of those Squadrons.

No sooner had these new units settled in at Leeming when the Station found that it was having to prepare for the next influx, but this time it was not so much an addition as an exchange. The last Basic Training Course, No.65, had graduated on 11 October 1974, so bringing to an end a period of training, where, from the end of the war to that date the School had trained 1,749 pilots to "Wings" standard.

Taking the place of the Basic Training Courses within 3 FTS came the Royal Navy in the shape of the Royal Naval Elementary Flying Training

Squadron, (RNEFTS). This squadron, although run on RAF lines, was commanded by a Naval Officer and staffed by both RAF and RN Instructors. Its function was to instill into the RN students the principles and skills of fixed-wing flying using Bulldog aircraft, in order to permit the student to progress successfully to RN Helicopter Training at RNAS Culdrose. There were five courses of 20 weeks per year with a combined annual input of 75 students. As could be expected when the Royal Navy made its first official appearance at the Station they arrived in style, and the 16 Bulldog aircraft of RNEFTS flew in on 29 November 1974. They were met by Miss Tyne Tees and two large bulldogs borrowed from a local villager; champagne flowed freely to the accompaniment of clicking press cameras and the first RN course at Leeming started soon after-wards . . . but definitely not on that day!

Thus, by the end of 1974, Leeming was beginning to accumulate a varied selection of units:

RNEFTS	– Bulldog
Refresher Flying Squadron	– Jet Provost
NUAS	– Bulldog
No 11 AEF	– Chipmunk

Additionally, because of the forecasted increase in the volume of flying from the Station, in November it had taken over responsibility for Dishforth, which would become a second relief landing ground available for use by the students.

Local events came and went. The almost obligatory annual fête was held at Leeming in March of 1974, and visitors to the hangar in which the fete was held found themselves a few yards from history in the re-making. This took the form of the remains of a Fairey Battle which in 1940 had to crash-land in the interior of Iceland. The pilot and his passenger survived and had to walk about 40 miles to safety, but the aircraft was declared as beyond repair and left to the mercy of the elements. Strangely enough, the wreck remained relatively corrosion free and the sand laden winds

had caused less damage than the original recovery party. Consequently, it was considered a viable operation to recover it and the wreckage was salvaged in August 1972 by a team of 12 engineers from Leeming. They collected some parts that were scattered around the crash site and dismantled what was left of the aircraft, before transporting everything to Keflavik for a flight back to Leeming in an RAF transport aircraft. By the time the fête came round, volunteers had restored the Merlin engine almost to its original condition, and had carried out a great deal of work on the structure of the Battle. The purpose of the project was to present to the RAF Museum at Hendon a restored version of what would be the last of its type, at least in all Europe.

Once again, this time in May 1975, the MT Section won the "Rosebowl" for the section with the safest driving record in Flying Training Command. In the same year a new Community Centre was opened on the Station, RAF Leeming contributed to Leeming Village Primary School Centenary Celebrations, and the Scout Troop had a new standard dedicated in the Station Church. An interesting echo from the past was then heard in 1976 when a film unit of the Canadian Broadcasting System visited RAF Leeming on 30 March to record details of the association of 427 Squadron RCAF with the Station during the war years. This was to form part of a documentary commissioned to help celebrate a Squadron Anniversary in May 1976 on the occasion of the receipt of its new Standard.

Flying training had proceeded fairly normally throughout 1975 and into 1976, but on 13 February, the inherent dangers of flying were brought home once again when engine failure caused a Jet Provost to crash about a half mile north of the airfield perimeter. The crew ejected but unfortunately the senior instructor, in ensuring that the aircraft would miss a house, left the aircraft at a very low altitude and received very serious injuries which caused him to be invalided out of the Service.

In April 1976, yet another new arrival was added to Leeming's complement. As a result of the 1975 Defence Cuts it had been decided to close Little Rissington, the home of the Central Flying School, and its units were dispersed. Leeming received the CFS Bulldog Squadron, which was responsible for training the flying instructors for units operating that aircraft type. This course was planned to last for six months and included amongst the students were RN pilots, as well as members of overseas Air Arms equipped with the Bulldog. With the arrival of the Bulldog Squadron, the Station acquired a second aerobatic team to join the "Swords". The "Synchronised Pair", as they were named, were quickly cleared for public display and soon joined the display circuit. The Jet Provost team, known as the "Swords" had already been formed in April 1974 from the Instructors of the Refresher Flying Squadron, and equipped with four JP Mk5 aircraft. They had opened their season on 1 July of that year and the Managing Director of Wilkinson Sword took the opportunity to present one of their swords to Leeming. This particular "blade" has since been used in the ceremonial hand-over of command between outgoing and incoming Station Commanders.

The final production Bulldog of the RAF purchase of 120, was collected from Scottish Aviation at Prestwick on 21 June 1976, and delivered to Leeming, where all of the aircraft were being serviced and allocated on a common user basis. The large number of aircraft operating from the Station at that time ensured that the airfield was a very busy place, and because of this, the Air Traffic Control section acquired its second closed circuit TV system which was set up to give the controllers an ability to keep an eye on all corners of the airfield.

However, before the end of 1976, news was received of another type of aircraft scheduled to appear at Leeming. This was the Scottish Aviation Jetstream which, though acquired some 18 months before, had been put in "moth balls" after the 1974 Defence Cuts had meant the pruning of the Transport Fleet, with the subsequent reduction in the number of pilots to be qualified on multi-engine aircraft. Now plans had been changed, and the Jetstream was to be brought out of storage to train pilots for such aircraft as the Vulcan, Hercules, and Nimrod. As with any new aircraft, manuals for operating procedures and various kinds of engineering data were required. Consequently, from November 1976 a three man team was engaged in producing these books, using the layout of instructions from the likes of the Jet Provost as their guidelines. Eventually, the Multi Engine Training Squadron (METS) was formed with one Squadron Commander, 12 Instructors, and two Standards Officers. A Jetstream Simulator from Locking was installed in March 1977 and courses were started in May of that year. Students, when coming direct from basic training after completing approximately 100 hours on the Jet Provost, took a 20 week course, or if they were already pilots with experience on multi-engine aircraft, they flew on a refresher course of seven weeks. At the outset the aircraft suffered from a large number of engine defects, but even when they had been overcome the engines still continued to present a problem to the Leeming groundcrew. The high pitched whine, particularly in the arc forward of the engines, was so penetrating that without ear protection damage to the hearing was a distinct possibility, and orders were promulgated restricting the time allowed in the vicinity of aircraft with engines running. However, the Jetstream was still a popular aircraft, which as a consequence of having been built as a mini airliner, had all the navigation and instrument systems of a full scale passenger carrier, and the kind of flights carried out by that type of aircraft were actually included in the training. A flight to Berlin was a popular part of the advanced stage of the course, with the diversion airfield at Hannover, but when done in shirt-sleeves was somewhat different from those raids carried out on the capital of Germany by the Whitleys,

Halifaxes and Lancasters of the Leeming of yesteryear.

Naturally enough, one side-effect of the influx of aircraft at Leeming was to be a shortage of hangar space, which in 1977 resulted in No.1 Hangar being taken over from the Sports Centre. Yet again Leeming was without indoor sports facilities, this time for a period of three years, when a reduction in aircraft numbers enabled the Sports Centre to be re-established in the Hangar. In the past, sport had always played a large part in Service life, so with facilities at their poorest it was perhaps just as well that an outdoor sport grabbed the limelight when the Sports Centre closed. The cricket team had a season of unprecedented success, sweeping all before it and winning all four competitions they entered: The RAF "A" Cup, The Faville Trophy, the Yorkshire Services' League, and the Yorkshire Services' Knockout Cup.

The year of 1977 will be remembered by many in Britain as the year of the Queen's Silver Jubilee, and in July of that year Leeming acted as a mounting base for the Royal Review at Finningley. Some weeks prior to this event, by way of preparation, 30 aircraft made a simultaneous start followed by a stream take-off and flypast in front of the Air Officer Commanding. He liked what he saw, gave his authority for the display, and on the 29th a flypast of six Hawks, five Hunters, five Gnats, five Jetstreams and nine Dominies, along with their airborne whip in the shape of a Jet Provost, took off from Leeming to take part in this memorable occasion. The following day saw Leeming and Finningley go through the whole process again, and the formation display was repeated for the delight of the general public.

The interest in the Queen's Jubilee Appeal in 1977 had resulted in a great many ideas being put into operation with the sole idea of raising funds for the Jubilee Appeal. One such idea, and one that was truly unique, though nonetheless profitable, stemmed from the Commanding Officer at

Leeming at that time. Gp Capt Vangucci approached a number of his peers with the idea that they should participate in a sponsored walk over a 17 mile length of the Pennine Way, from Hardrow near Hawes, via Thwaite to Tan Hill (which co-incidently has the highest public house in England). In all, 19 Station Commanders, two wives and a dog completed the trek, and no doubt all of them were extremely pleased about the situation of the "finishing post". It was to all accounts an exceedingly hot day and though there are no records as to their condition on reaching Tan Hill (or perhaps, on leaving the Inn), reach it they did to be presented with a Pennine Way Perambulation Certificate signed by Prince Charles, and better still, raised approximately £6,000 for the Appeal.

The problem of industrial relations in 1977 affected the people at Leeming in much the same way as everyone in the UK, but in November of that year a non-military operation which went under the name of "Operation Burberry", had a direct effect on the Station's personnel. This was the code-name for the operation where military personnel were to act as replacements for civilian firemen who were on strike. Leeming's personnel played their part, with four officers, 16 NCOs and 87 airmen deployed, between November and January 1978, to 21 centres in Lancashire and Cumberland. Those winter months saw them carry out a great deal of valuable work and deservedly receive the gratitude of those who had been in need. Their efforts were also recognised by local authorities and a number of letters of appreciation were received. When the Strike was finally over, there is no doubt that the return to Leeming was welcomed by their colleagues, who had played their part in no small way by coping with the additional work and duties. One of the surrogate firemen, Sgt W J Mcleod, was later to be awarded an Immediate Commendation from the Air Officer Commanding in Chief, in respect of his courage and determination in December when he attempted to rescue an elderly civilian from a burning house. Though the involvement in the "firemen's strike" received a great deal of good publicity for the fighting services, it was not the only involvement with industrial relations that came Leeming's way. In February 1978, soon after the cessation of this strike, the threat of further industrial action resulted in the positioning of fuel bowsers on the Station in case a requirement arose to ferry fuel about the country.

However, after the period known as the "Winter of Discontent", a much happier event took place on 23 April 1978, when the town of Northallerton ceremonially presented an "Illuminated Address" to Royal Air Force Leeming. This was similar to the awarding of the freedom of the town and conferred the right to march once a year through Northallerton with bayonets fixed, a privilege which has been claimed on a number of occasions since. By way of return, the Station, in the company of an estimated 10,000 civilian visitors, held an "Open Day" on the day following the parade, marking the 60th anniversary of the founding of the RAF and the 50th birthday of No.3 FTS, as well as, a little prematurely, the 40th birthday of the Station.

The flying displays of that day were somewhat eclipsed a few weeks later, when on 18 May 1978, some really spectacular flying took place at Leeming. The reason for such a claim lies in the fact that the Wright Jubilee and Brabyn Aerobatics Competition was held there for the first time that year and in fact, continued to be held at Leeming until 1983. The competition brought together some of the most accomplished "aero" pilots in the Service and needless to say, the contest held in 1979 brought the most satisfaction to the host Station, when one of the winners was Flt Lt Stevenson from CFS Bulldog Squadron.

Yet another impressive display of flying was witnessed at RAF Leeming in June 1978 when 11 different types of RAF training aircraft took part in a special display over Yorkshire. Piloted by CFS Instructors for the benefit of members of NATO and other foreign air forces who were represented at a convention on training techniques. The types used were the Jetstream, Bulldog, Chipmunk, Gazelle, Dominie, Gnat, Hunter, Hawk, and Jet Provost with a special appearance of the "Vintage Pair" – a Vampire and a Meteor.

The standards of aircraft handling at Leeming were perhaps even more apparent a few weeks later when on 4 August a splendid piece of flying of a different sort unfolded before the Station's personnel. A Jet Provost Mk.3A had been carrying out "roller"[18] landings at nearby RAF Dishforth when, after getting airborne after one such landing, the crew received what must have been a rather unsettling call from air traffic control, informing them that a main wheel had been seen to fall from their aircraft. It was soon confirmed to be the one from the port leg and then, because of doubts about the integrity of that piece of structure, the decision was made to leave the undercarriage down and the aircraft recovered to Leeming airspace where it circled until a foam carpet was laid on the runway. Almost all of the Station was outside awaiting the outcome but the pilot brought the JP in smoothly, keeping it on the starboard wheel until the final moments when he allowed the nosewheel then the port brake unit to touch, although the aircraft had barely slid off course before the aircraft came to a halt. The ORBs report of the landing was as succinct as could be wished, – the landing was executed well with minimum damage – but said all that was needed to be said. In point of fact when the results of the landing were being assessed, it was already considered that there had been probably as much damage suffered by another Jet Provost back on the ground at Dishforth. The wheel, as can be imagined, took some time to come to rest and before it did it struck and damaged the rear fuselage of a Mk5A which was taxi-ing prior to take-off. Fortunately there was no injury to either the occupants or to any groundcrew.

Some months later on 22 May 1979, a Gnat in the process of paying a visit to Leeming, and also carrying out a "roller" landing, was not so favoured. The pilot of XP539 lost control and though the aircraft crashed beside the airfield at Gatenby Grange Farm, "Lady Luck" was not totally against the two occupants and they both ejected and escaped with slight injuries. This crash brought further reaction from Richmond MP, Sir Timothy Kitson, who in 1978 had called for the grounding of all training aircraft flown by the RAF. On this occasion he wondered if the cutbacks in RAF training were responsible for what he saw as a succession of crashes, where there seemed to be an element of human failure in the accidents.

The "Vintage Pair", which flew in the special display back in June, were in the charge of Leeming's newest incumbent, the Central Flying School. Previously, with the dispersal of the CFS Units, a move that brought the Bulldog Squadron to Leeming in April 1976, the CFS HQ Unit, Examining Wing, JP Squadron and Training Squadron had been moved to Cranwell. It did not take long to find though that this arrangement was not proving to be a satisfactory one and in November 1977, these units also moved to Leeming.

The Central Flying School had been established at Upavon in 1912 with a complement of ten Staff Officers and 80 students, whose flying instructional course lasted 16 weeks. The Unit moved from Upavon to Wittering in 1926, where it stayed for eight years before returning to its "birthplace" until 1942 when it moved again, this time to Hullavington which became its base for the next four years. In 1946, the School finally arrived at Little Rissington, where it was to remain until 1976. In 1962 CFS celebrated its 50th Anniversary, an event which established its position as the oldest flying training establishment in the world, and on 26 June 1969, the Queen presented the Unit with its Queen's Colours.

The objectives of CFS, commanded at that time by an Air Commodore, were to develop and maintain the highest possible standards of flying instruction on both fixed and rotary wing aircraft

throughout the RAF and by virtue of its high reputation when it came to Leeming, its advice was sought after by many other air forces.

On the move to RAF Leeming, CFS HQ took over the Education Centre which was a converted barrack block, and the "displaced" staff moved to temporary accommodation in one of the SECO huts of No 2 Officers' Mess until a new Education Centre, built on to the Ground School, was ready for occupation in June 1980. Besides control of its units at Leeming, CFS HQ also supervised the Hawk Squadron at Valley, the Helicopter Squadron at Shawbury and the famous "Red Arrows" Aerobatic Team.

CFS Examining Wing, staffed by experienced instructors, checked standards of professional ability and flying instruction within Support Command as well as supervising the appointments of CFS Agents. Visits, on request, were made to the Royal Navy and the Army, as well as to Commonwealth and other foreign air forces, to carry out duties such as that of the recategorisation of instructors.

CFS Training Squadron, which included Jet Provost Squadron, and once again the Bulldog Squadron, was established to train selected RAF, RN and foreign pilots to become flying instructors. It also had a commitment to provide conversion and refresher courses for qualified instructors who had been on other types of aircraft or away on ground tours.

With the arrival of CFS, RAF Leeming was by 1978 yet again "bursting at the seams". This problem with accommodation seems to have been a perennial one at Leeming, but on this occasion the work of Engineering Wing, bedevilled by the twin shortages of skilled manpower and of space, had almost reached crisis point; the necessity for stringent economy measures seemed to aggravate the problems. However, to most people's relief, another move was soon to occur and with the transfer of METS Squadron to Finningley on 30 April 1979, when all ten aircraft were started and flown out together, the subsequent all round reduction in the numbers of aircraft and personnel went some way towards alleviating the pressures to more manageable proportions.

It was also in 1979 that a rather unique request came out of Leeming when the Royal Naval Elementary Flying Training Squadron petitioned the Ministry of Defence for official recognition within the Royal Air Force, by the award of a Unit Badge. There appeared to be a good case put forward, and the Squadron was advised by the relevant department (F11(Air)) that notwithstanding the establishment of a RN Lieutenant Commander as the Officer Commanding, because ten of the QFIs were from the RAF and only six from the Royal Navy, then the officer element could be allowed the title of an RAF Squadron. Unfortunately, the reply went on to say, that owing to the fact that no groundcrew were established within the Squadron, and as a consequence all necessary engineering support was given by Engineering Wing RAF Leeming, it was doubted that the circumstances matched the criteria for the grant of a Unit Badge to an RAF Squadron!

Between 1978 and 1981, as and when financial restrictions allowed, more improvements were made to the infrastructure of Leeming. A new concrete apron on the airfield side of No 1 and 2 Hangars was completed in August 1978, and RFS moved into new operations and crew rooms in October of the same year. The runway lights were replaced during the following February, a new NUAS SECO building was opened in July 1980, and the Station C of E Church was at last refurbished and re-consecrated in September 1981.

The Station itself has often been in the forefront of change, whether it has been from within or from the seemingly endless list of new arrivals. Even with this varied background it was however, a new and unusual concept for Leeming, when in September 1978 it was tasked with providing a landing ground for "Her Majesty's Mail". This, one of the numerous "odd jobs" which can come a station's way, lasted for a total of three months and came about when engineering works on the

railway caused closure of the lines between London and the North. A chartered aircraft of British Island Airways Ltd was used to carry the mail northwards, leaving Gatwick at 1320 hours and reaching Leeming some 90 minutes later, where the mail was unloaded by Post Office staff for delivery to towns in Cleveland, Yorkshire and North Humberside.

One of the happiest visits to come Leeming's way was the visit on 4 July 1980 of Her Majesty The Queen Mother as Commandant-in-Chief of the Central Flying School, her second visit to the Station in that capacity. A special programme was laid on, partially to celebrate the Golden Jubilee of the CFS, but also in view were the forthcoming celebrations for her 80th birthday. One individual, Flight Lieutenant Frederick, the Pelican mascot of the School, was very much in evidence and enjoyed the attention. The children of Leeming RAF Primary School presented the Royal visitor with the large birthday card they had produced, and both the Red Arrows and the Vintage Pair flew special displays in her honour. The occasion was made particularly memorable by the presence of HRH Prince Andrew who had joined No.93 RNEFTS Course on 27 May 1980, (codenamed the "Golden Eagle" project), and was there to greet his grandmother on her arrival. As a surprise follow-up to the Queen Mother's visit, CFS aircraft were given special permission to fly in an "E" formation over London on 4 August 1980, the day of her birthday.

The arrival of Prince Andrew had been covered very comprehensibly by the Press; so much so, that it appeared that everyone, including the Pelican, had been interviewed about the forthcoming five month course. From his flying instructor to his batwoman, his CO to a local publican, all were questioned on HRH in the hope of a careless quote. The RAF had previously been at pains to stress that within the bounds of security he would be treated like any other student pilot. This consideration meant that there was a specific aircraft, with a reserve, both prepared and serviced by selected groundcrew. His personal detective was accommodated in the adjoining room, but otherwise the Prince passed or failed on his own efforts. His stay received very little further coverage from the press, other than a mention of his first solo flight, and of course, a paragraph about him leaving Leeming in October after completing his course successfully.

A visitor of a different sort arrived on the Station on 3 November 1981, when a Meteor NF 11, WD790, made its final landing after a flight from RAE Bedford. This aircraft, built by Armstrong Whitworth with its characteristic "greenhouse" canopy and oddly pointed nose, had enjoyed a particularly distinctive career as the airframe used in the testing of the radars for such aircraft as the TSR 2 and the Buccaneer. Squadron Leader "Budgie" Burges, an F3 navigator, remembers his early days in the Service when he flew a few times in this aircraft while it was on trials and development at Pershore, near Worcester. His recollections show mixed feelings of that time as he remembers colleagues testing the terrain following radar (TFR) which was to be fitted to the Tornado GR1. They had to fly at low level, sometimes at night, sometimes "hands off", and the aircraft did not have ejection seats! Sadly the aircraft is no more, because the purpose of the final flight to Leeming was only to enable the cockpit section to be removed and presented to 405 Sqn ATC (Darlington).

Another very special guest, this time in the person of His Holiness Pope John Paul II, arrived at RAF Leeming on 31 May 1982. Having departed in a helicopter from Knavesmire, York, he needed somewhere to transfer to a larger aircraft prior to his journey to Scotland, and the ever open runway at Leeming enabled the Station to receive the honour. The day was fine and bright, and to the delight of the families who had assembled hopefully at the airfield, the Pope devoted approximately half an hour to meeting almost everybody making it a memorable day for everyone on the Station.

Other visitors in 1982 included the personnel of the 131st Tactical Fighter Wing of the US Air National Guard whose aircrew flew 12 Phantom F.4Cs non-stop across the Atlantic from their home base in St Louis Missouri, to conduct a two week exercise while based at Leeming. The advance party had already impressed the Station by the speed with which they transformed No 1 Hangar into a "plywood palace" with four man cubicles to accommodate over 200 personnel; it also boasted a 75 seat cinema and three colour TV rooms! The main party and their equipment arrived on Saturday 26 June, giving Leeming a particularly international look with a stream of USAF C130s and C141s arriving throughout the day. The official purpose of the exercise was to indulge in some operational flying, but away from work, efforts to teach soccer and cricket to the Americans were probably no more successful than their attempts to teach us the rudiments of baseball and softball. With "welly whanging" and "schooner races" also very much in evidence, "Exercise Coronet Cactus" was considered by all to be a resounding success, and a particularly good example of Anglo/US friendship.

Another innovative and popular event that occurred in 1982 arose out of the Station's response to a low-flying complaint from a local member of the public. The RAF has always attempted to foster good community relations and in an effort to explain the function of a busy station a group of people were invited to visit RAF Leeming. During their stay it transpired that one member of the party was a member of the Board of Racing in Yorkshire and as a consequence, the Station received an invite to sponsor an evening race meeting at Catterick Race Course. This event duly took place on 12 August 1982, and was reputedly the best supported meeting at Catterick for some time. The races were appropriately named, with "The Jet Provost Stakes" just one example, with senior officers, including the Commander-in-Chief, Air Marshal Sir Michael Beavis and officials of the RAFA, presenting commemorative plaques to the winning owners.

Bands played, the Mountain Rescue Team climbed down the Approximate Odds board, the Meteor from the "Vintage Pair" flew past, and a fine time was had by all. Such a good time in fact, that the whole exercise was repeated in 1983 on which occasion the "Falcons" Parachute Display Team jumped onto the Race Course. The closure of Leeming led to the cessation of this event but recent years have seen its revival, though with references to the Tornado F3 and its squadrons as the race sponsors.

It was unclear when the rumours about the future of RAF Leeming first began to circulate, but certainly by the middle of 1982 most of North Yorkshire knew that Leeming was being considered for development as a base for the F2 Air Defence Variant Tornado. Speculation became fact on 3 August 1982, when the following announcement was made by the Station Commander, Gp Capt Batt:

> . . . I am able today to tell you of proposals which will affect the future of RAF Leeming. Firstly, it is proposed to move the Central Flying School from RAF Leeming to RAF Scampton at the end of 1983 or early 1984. Consideration is also being given to re-deploying No.3 Flying Training School within the same timescale. Thereafter, the Station will be kept open but on a reduced level, to support the University Air Squadron and No 11 Air Experience Flight, pending the deployment of three Tornado F2 Squadrons to RAF Leeming before the end of the decade. The plans are obviously at a very early stage at present, and we can expect a busy year ahead as things take shape. Rest assured that I shall keep you all informed of developments as they happen.

From that moment on, planning began in earnest for the estimated £90m project which was to transform RAF Leeming into the most advanced fighter station in the United Kingdom.

However it was still a case of "business as usual" for those at Leeming, with the training of pilots still their reason for being there. The work was generally routine, but there was still to be one more aircraft that 3 FTS would lose, their last while stationed at Leeming. A JP Mk3A sustained a multiple birdstrike at midday on 21 November 1983, while flying over the Pennines. The engine flamed-out, leaving the crew with no choice but to eject, which they did safely, and the aircraft crashed at Deer Bank, a remote area of moorland near the Settle to Carlisle railway line. The crew were quickly rescued but the crash site had to be cleared and guarded in the meantime, so for the next six days and nights there were a lot of very cold airmen on those moors (the temperature dropped as low as -4.5 C on the 24th).

Uneasiness in the local community about the possibility of increased noise went hand in hand with the knowledge that there would probably be a lean interim period for their economy in the years before 1987. However, this was matched by an awareness that the re-build of RAF Leeming would present a considerable boost to that economy, as well as providing additional jobs for the area. In any case, the Station had for a long time enjoyed a most cordial and much valued relationship with the people of the area, a fact previously borne out in 1978 by the presentation of the Illuminated Address from the town of Northallerton. It was therefore, on 28 April 1984, a poignant ceremony for those involved when Councillor D Walkland, who was Mayor in 1978, once again presided over what was felt to be the last substantial Freedom Parade in Northallerton for a number of years to come.

Despite delays to the programme originally announced during August 1982, the Refresher Flying Squadron departed for RAF Church Fenton on 29 March 1984, and the departure of RNEFTS to RAF Linton-on-Ouse on 26 April 1984 signified the demise of No 3 Flying Training School. The Navy, of course, were returning to whence they came some 15 years before. With the loss of No.3 FTS also went the responsibility of the relief landing grounds at Topcliffe, (the responsibility for Dishforth had passed to Linton-on-Ouse during July 1983). Thus Leeming entered its final chapter as a Support Command flying training station bereft of RLGs, and with its remaining major units comprising the Jet Provost and Bulldog fixed wing elements of the Central Flying School. In addition, the "Vintage Pair", Vampire XH304 and Meteor WF791, were still at Leeming and were much in demand, appearing for example at 56 displays throughout 1982. Flown and maintained by volunteers, they kept up this effort and during the first half of September 1984 appeared at 11 different venues, from Leuchars to the Channel Islands and St Athan to Scarborough, before returning to Leeming. They were, however, soon to be away again as it was from there on 19 September 1984, that the Commandant of the Central Flying School, Air Commodore Kemball, flying the Vampire from the "Pair", led a formation of two Meteors, 16 Jet Provosts and nine Bulldogs away from Leeming and onwards to their new home at Scampton.

CHAPTER FIVE

ROYAL AIR FORCE LEEMING OCTOBER 1984 – ONWARDS

The cessation of Leeming's role within Support Command was made official on 1 October 1984, when, with a strength of 156 Service personnel and 89 civilians, it was transferred to Strike Command. The future meant that for the second time in its history it was to become a fighter station, and on 5 October Gp Capt Curry handed over the Leeming Sword to the new CO, Wg Cdr Bates. Initially, NUAS and No 11 Air Experience Flight remained, and with the station retaining its commitment as a master diversion airfield it played its part in October 1984, albeit with visiting aircraft and personnel, in Exercise Priory 84-1. This exercise was designed to test the ability of the RAF to defend Britain against air attack, with elements of both "sides" operating from the station: six Hawks for the "friendly" forces and three Canberras for the "enemy". These aircraft played their part in an exercise that mounted over 1100 sorties in offensive or defensive operations involving airfields, missile sites and radar stations throughout the United Kingdom.

It was known at this time that following an upgrade of the facilities on the station a number of Tornado F2 interceptors were to be based at Leeming, and with the RAF taking delivery of its first F2 in November 1984, local newspapers, with editorials and letters from the public, were voicing their concern over the effects the aircraft would have on the community. Most of the anxiety was centred around the noise problem, from the frightening of livestock to the more obscure claim of compensation for the cost of phone calls, which

because of the noise, would have to take longer! The fact that the RAF takes the noise problem seriously could be seen from the trial which took place at Leeming in April 1985. Two Tornado F2s from Coningsby were detached to fly set patterns on both runways in order to redefine the precise positions of the Tornado noise contours, with noise levels being monitored at various sites including the runway approaches, Little Fencote and Scruton. Teams from the RAF Institute of Community Medicine, the National Physical Laboratory, Southampton University and the Hambleton District Council Environmental Health Office, carried out the checks and a briefing was given to councillors and officials from the surrounding parishes and districts, as well as to reporters from the Press, the BBC, Yorkshire TV and Tyne Tees TV.

Preparatory work for the conversion of the airfield began in 1985, but notwithstanding all of the necessary planning, normal life continued at Leeming. Occurrences as varied as the annual summer camp for the Royal Observer Corps, with 450 of their number completing courses in 1985, to the return of HRH Prince Andrew in September of that year. He stayed overnight after piloting the Lynx helicopter which took the Captain of HMS Brazen to an official reception in the coastal town of Seaham in County Durham. The airfield remained busy with frequent VIP movements, and the list of aircraft types that used it either as planned or as an emergency diversion, reads like "Jane's". From the Andover to the

Wessex, Pembrokes, Pumas, F111s, Mirages, Falcons, Phantoms, Nimrods and once in a while, a Jolly Green Giant. On one notable occasion there was even a DC8 to uplift 4 Para (TA) to the USA. In addition, the fact that a significant number of Tornado aircraft, albeit the GR1, had begun to "call in", was no doubt in the minds of the local councillors when in November they attended the presentation of the results of the April noise test. Also in November the station was used as the forward mounting base for exercise "Purple Victory", where up to 15 Hercules aircraft were involved in the considerable number of aircraft movements required for the deployment of a large body of troops and their equipment. The importance of this exercise can be gauged by looking closely at a visit by an HS125, or to be more precise, by who was actually in that aircraft. The party was a group of nine very senior British officers (their combined rank totalled no less than 30 stars) who had come to view one of the day's proceedings. No doubt there were a few fingers crossed that day while they were airborne!!

The year 1986 saw a long standing inhabitant of RAF Leeming leave for pastures new which it was hoped would give it a new lease of life. As one of the "Guardians" of the Station, Spitfire TE356 had given eight years faithful service, but a decision had been made to transfer it to the Warbirds Museum at Bitteswell. So in April it was dismantled and transported to its new home where it was hoped to restore it to flying condition. The Mk XVI-E had originally been restored at Kemble in 1970 and erected first at Little Rissington, but then it was moved to Cranwell in 1976. It arrived at Leeming in February of 1978 and had since been displayed on a plinth outside a building housing the HQ CFS. In exchange for the Spitfire the Museum was giving a Thunderbolt fighter from World War II, which in turn was to be loaned to the RAF Museum at Hendon.

The airfield was to close at the end of 1986, but taskings on the Station continued right to the end. October was extremely busy with three major but separate exercises, that saw the arrival of Chinooks and Pumas, then Hawks, and finally Phantoms and Harriers, with F18 Hornets from the Canadian Armed Forces, all coming with their respective support personnel and equipment. This was followed at the end of the year by the hosting of two pilot training courses from RAF Cranwell, one of which was attended by Prince Faisal of Jordan, followed by the official closure of the airfield on 31 December 1986. The responsibility of maintaining a MEDA commitment went with it, and with NUAS and 11 AEF already operating on a temporary basis from Teesside Airport, those personnel left at the Station could concentrate on the future.

It had been as far back as July when work on the major construction projects actually commenced, and as a consequence when the Station closed at the end of the year it was already in somewhat of a mess. The plans had included the construction of sufficient hardened aircraft shelters for three Tornado squadrons, their associated command and control buildings, with suitable shelters for personnel and critical items of equipment. In the event with the requirement for one of the squadrons to operate as an out-of-area force, the plans for building the third HAS site in the SE corner of the airfield were soon cancelled. With so much building going on this did not make that much difference to the appearance of Leeming, because at the same time as the concrete buildings were being constructed, a start was made on the building of new living accommodation. This meant the modernisation of existing barrack blocks and the building of others to house the single personnel, as well as the demolition and rebuild of almost all of the Airmen's Married Quarters. The total construction project was also to include the levelling and resurfacing of the runway along with the realignment of some of the taxiways, with the programme to be sufficiently complete by mid 1988 to permit the first squadron to commence its work-up training.

By January 1987 after the runway was closed,

the number of Service personnel had been reduced to 120, with RAF Leeming resembling a vast building site – probably at 40 acres the largest in Europe and possibly the most expensive at an estimated cost of £148,000,000.

While the Station was undergoing this period of massive change, ex-servicemen from Canada still continued to show an interest in their old base. For instance, in May 1987 three former members of the RCAF, Frank Brazier, Harry Wilson and Victor Garland, presented a Maple tree to the Station and dedicated it to the memory of the former air and groundcrew of 427 and 429 Squadrons. The tree still thrives with its plaque acting as a reminder of a time easily forgotten. Within four months of this dedication Leeming again played the host when on 25 September a reception was held for approximately 200 guests, many of them Canadians, who had been present at the unveiling ceremonies of the nearby Croft RCAF memorial. Included among the guests was Brigadier W F M Newson DFC CAF, who had been CO of Leeming from June until October 1944.

In the final few months of 1987 personnel began arriving to form the Tornado Engineering Planning Team (TEPT), whose task was to prepare the way for the arrival of No.XI Squadron. The team's workplace was a set of huts built in the dim and distant past at the rear of the Officers' Mess; huts that continue to be used for a variety of purposes that range from a sportsman's bar to a ceramics club. From these basic surroundings they gradually became organised, then began to place the orders for all of the engineering support equipment needed to maintain three squadrons of the Tornado. At this time each new arrival was issued with a pair of wellington boots, and because of the very muddy "building site" conditions that existed throughout the Station, authority was given to wear the footwear as part of the normal working uniform. The conditions, far from creating problems, actually helped that small group of people to bond into an extremely capable and well motivated company who in later

years would all refer to those times with a great deal of nostalgic pride. It was not all work though, and personnel continued to involve themselves in a wide variety of interests such, as for example, when a team from Leeming entered a marathon wheelchair push held at Church Fenton. Thirty five teams took part in the event, sponsored by Wilkinson Sword in conjunction with the British Sports Association for the Disabled, and the Leeming team finished in first place. The three team members took it in turn to push a wheelchair for a total of 2 hours and 51 minutes, which was the time they took to complete the "Marathon" distance of 26 miles 385 yards. It was apt for the Station that their trophy was a genuine Wilkinson Sword which takes pride of place on display in the Office Suite of the Station Commander.

Notwithstanding the wet winter of 1987/88 the work continued apace, although there was some slippage of target dates. In November for instance, the AR1 radar was put out of action by a "Plant" operator who damaged the power cables while digging on the airfield. The damage was considered to be severe with the cost of recovery excessive, so until a replacement system could be put in place the airfield received a tactical mobile radar which was quickly sited, calibrated, and then licensed for use by ATC. The radar only provided a raw picture of the area with no map display or direction finder, but it was to be adequate until the new "Watchman" radar was fully operational.

The main runway of Royal Air Force Leeming finally reopened on 11 January 1988, when a pair of Tornado F3s from 229 OCU RAF Coningsby touched down, and Leeming's Station Commander, Wg Cdr D C Smith, who had recently completed the F3 conversion course was the first person to alight. The Station was not due to revert to its MEDA role until the end of the month, but within two days of the opening of the airfield its proximity to an emergency meant that it received its first visitor, a USAF F-111 which arrived with fuel transfer problems.

In the early part of the year a lack of adequate working accommodation, allied to the wet and muddy condition of the Station, helped make Leeming a truly inhospitable place to be. At one stage consideration was given to the idea of transporting the workforce to Dishforth and using the hangars there for office accommodation. Be that as it may, an environment that was purely a building site may have seemed like a home from home to the next new arrivals, because on 1 April the HQ element of 234 Field Sqn (Airfield Damage Repair) (V) Royal Engineers, arrived from its previous base at Waterbeach. This specialist RE Squadron of the Territorial Army came with the primary role of airfield repair and maintenance in wartime, but also with an earthworks and general combat engineer capability. The HQ was made up of a cadre of Regular Army personnel augmented by Territorials on weekend and annual camp training, but in times of conflict the Squadron would be required to fulfil its role on a 24 hour basis for an indefinite period. It was declared as operational in September 1989, but in common with all TA units recruiting and retention forms a major challenge, so full operational readiness remained a problem.

The month of April also saw the reintroduction of the more traditional RAF command structure at Leeming, with Operations, Engineering and Administration Wings forming on 8 April when Gp Capt Rooum assumed command. Soon afterwards on 11 May 1988, ZE161, the first Tornado F3 allotted to Leeming arrived to join No.XI Squadron which had been designated as the lead squadron in the build-up. Initially this aircraft had a mundane, though nonetheless important existence for the ground training of Leeming's aircraft tradesmen, but others with a different future were soon to follow.

No.XI Squadron

No.XI Squadron has had an illustrious history that dates back to its formation at Netheravon on 14 February 1915 as the first unit of the RFC specifically tasked with fighter duties. The Squadron deployed to France in July of that year with the Vickers "Gunbus" and began operations almost immediately. Many combats followed and after one of these, a Squadron pilot, Lt S M Insall, was awarded the Victoria Cross. It was re-equipped with the Bristol Fighter in early 1917 and was engaged in intensive air fighting until the Armistice. Then in 1919 like many other squadrons it was disbanded, reforming on 13 January 1923 operating mainly in the bombing role until 29 December 1928 when it embarked for India. Once there, it spent almost 12 years carrying out army co-operation duties against tribesmen in the North-West Frontier region before deploying to Aden in 1940. The next two years saw XI serve in Egypt, Greece, Crete, Palestine, Iraq and then to Ceylon, to help defend the Island against a Japanese carrier force. In September 1943 the Squadron returned to India and with its Hurricanes supported the fight for Burma. In 1945 after the end of the war the Squadron was re-equipped with Vampires, continuing over the next 20 years with fighter operations until disbanding in January 1966. During this time the Squadron flew Venoms, Meteors and Javelins, but it was with the Lightning at Leuchars that it reformed on 1 April 1966, this time as one of the air defence squadrons in the UK. In March 1972 it moved to Binbrook where it continued its long association with the Lightning, ending up as the last squadron to operate that aircraft type in the RAF. Its move to the Tornado F3 meant a return to its original role as a two seat fighter squadron, symbolised by the two eagles which form the Squadron Badge.

On 9 May 1988 at RAF Binbrook, XI Squadron (Tornado), accepted the Squadron Standard from XI Squadron (Lightning), and as a reminder of the Squadron's recent past a Lightning F6, XR753, was flown to Leeming on 24 May in completing its final flight. At that time neither of the hardened aircraft shelter sites were ready for use and consequently, XI was to operate from No.4 Hangar and its adjoining aircraft servicing platform until the first site was completed. (Ultimately XI Sqn remained in place, and was declared to SACLANT as the out-of-area squadron, with 23 Sqn and XXV Sqn operating from the shelters and declared to SACEUR.) Work-up training for the first crews did not commence until after 1 July, a date marked by a formal "arrival" flypast of four Tornado F3s marked by heavy media coverage. By the end of the month the station strength had risen to over 1200 personnel, and soon afterwards the first of many station exercises was called at 0430 on 18 August. These exercises were to practise the response to a recall where personnel were to report for duty immediately without stopping to wash, shave, or eat. In addition, it was to test the speed and ability of the Station to generate the required number of serviceable, armed aircraft to meet the requirements of SACEUR.

On 10 September 1988, the station received formal recognition as an air defence main operating base, when the Chief of Air Staff, Air Chief Marshal Sir David Craig, carried out an official unveiling ceremony. (The use of the term "Air Defence of Great Britain" was not a new one, though its first use in 1944 to describe Fighter Command was never popular and consequently was soon dropped.) With a guard of honour formed from personnel from RAF Leeming and music provided by the RAF Catterick band, Sir David put the official stamp of approval on the base when he unveiled a plaque mounted on a slab of limestone mined from Black Quarry near Leyburn, North Yorkshire. There followed an air display where a Spitfire and a Hurricane, from the RAF Battle of Britain Memorial Flight, performed in stark contrast to a Phantom and of course, the Tornados from XI Sqn. Security and operational needs prevented the base from being opened to the public, so apart from RAF personnel and their families, the celebrations were attended by only 200 invited guests. However, notwithstanding the foul weather, many hundreds of enthusiasts were scattered around the perimeter fence hoping for a sight of the display; one man even turned up from Cornwall and though he appealed to be let in had to be turned away. The celebrations continued on the following day when the Illuminated Address, given to the station in 1976 by the people of Northallerton, was again paraded through the town.

The rebuilding of RAF Leeming was still ongoing at this time with 16 of the 400 new Airmen's Married Quarters accepted during October 1988, with the first being handed over to Cpl and Mrs Morgan on the 28th of that month. Many more houses were still needed though for the large number of personnel being posted to the Station. House prices in the area had rocketed with estate agents advertising for houses to sell, and stories of airman gazumping airman became commonplace. At the same time, concern was still being voiced about the level of noise generated by the Tornado and after a meeting with the National

Farmers Union, Mr Leon Brittan, the then MP for Richmond, wrote to the Armed Forces Minister about its possible effect on farm animals and farm workers. Quite separately, grants for noise insulation were made to approximately 1000 residents, and up to 20 houses in the noisiest areas were purchased by the MOD. In addition, a local community liaison group was formed to meet with senior officers on the station to discuss the practical effects of the build-up, and to press the claims for double glazing to be fitted to certain local primary schools.

Elements of the second Tornado Squadron were also arriving before XI Sqn was declared as fully operational and assigned to SACLANT on 1 November 1988, but it was on that day that the advance party of No.23 Squadron received their Standard at a ceremony in the Officers' Mess.

No.23 Squadron

Gosport was the birthplace of No.23 Squadron which was formed on 1 September 1915, and FE2Bs were issued when the Squadron left for France in March 1916. Originally the crews undertook a great deal of offensive patrol work, but when the French Spad arrived in early 1917 the Squadron operated in the ground strafing role in support of the Army. A switch to the Sopwith Dolphin occurred in March 1918, but low-level ground-attack flying remained as their role. Disbanded in 1919 and re-formed at Henlow on 1 July 1925, it operated with Snipes, then Gamecocks when the Squadron moved to Kenley where it stayed flying Bulldogs and then Harts. In 1935 after a brief detachment to Malta it took up residence at Northolt. The Demon turret fighters were issued in May 1937, but the fighter version of the Blenheim I became the Squadron's equipment at Wittering in December 1938, and it was with this aircraft that the Squadron went to war in 1939. Beaufighters and Bostons joined the unit in late 1940 carrying out night intruder sorties over France; a role that continued into 1942 with the Havoc and then the Mosquito. At the end of 1942 the Squadron was moved to Malta to initiate this type of action over Sicily and Italy until the Axis forces had retreated out of range. This meant a transfer to Little Snoring in Norfolk in May 1944 to provide night escorts for Bomber Command. At the end of the war the Squadron was disbanded but re-constituted in September 1946 as a night-fighter unit flying the Mosquito. Equipped with the Vampire in 1951 while at Coltishall the Squadron then flew Venoms, which in turn were replaced by Javelins after a move to Horsham St Faith. A transfer to Leuchars saw the Lightning taken on charge in 1964, which the Squadron flew until it disbanded on 31 October 1975, to immediately re-form with the Phantom at Coningsby before moving to Wattisham. In 1983 the Squadron was tasked with a deployment to the Falkland Islands where it operated from Stanley, then at the newly constructed airfield at Mount Pleasant. The new chapter in the history of 23 Sqn which began with the presentation of a Standard, also saw the restoration of the familiar Red Eagle to the fins of its aircraft with the red and blue "fighter bars" repositioned in a dart shape either side of the nose roundel.

However, 1988 was to end on a sombre note, when as a result of a terrorist bomb planted in the baggage hold, a Pan Am Boeing 747 aircraft exploded in flight at 1918 hours on 21 December. The wreckage decimated the town of Lockerbie and Leeming was immediately alerted to provide assistance. A local recall was initiated and the Station Mountain Rescue Team departed by road at 2015, with further personnel following in a Chinook helicopter, plus two road convoys at 2245. Additional manpower was dispatched over the next two days, but as there were no survivors their main task was to search for wreckage, personal effects, and of course, the dead. This necessary, though highly traumatic operation for those who took part, lasted for Leeming personnel until the afternoon of 23 December when they were stood down to return to the station for a subdued Christmas holiday.

The Mountain Rescue Team had only just come back to Leeming after five years of operating from Linton-on-Ouse, and the call to attend at Lockerbie was only their second since the return. In keeping with their motto of "Whensoever" the team remain on immediate readiness. Over the years they have attended all manner of emergencies, from lost hill walkers to fallen climbers, trapped potholers to stranded motorists, not to mention aircraft crashes. In fact, within four months of the Lockerbie disaster they attended the crash of the British Midland 737 on the M1 near the East Midlands Airport, as well as three crashes involving aircraft from the RAF. Whenever possible the team has carried out training exercises and while on one of these in the Lake district in December 1990 their expertise was called upon by Cumbria Police to assist in a genuine emergency. The weather had been extremely bad with blizzard-like conditions, and many cars were stuck in the snow that blanketed the A66 trans-Pennine road. Working with the aid of their Landrover, as well as on foot, the team searched for stranded vehicles and rescued 22 people of all ages, some of whom were suffering from mild hypothermia. On confirming that their section of road was clear the team was then asked to search another stretch of the Pennine route, although because of the worsening conditions this task had to be done on foot. No stranded travellers were found, but four of the team still managed to get themselves cut-off overnight at the Bowes Moor Hotel! Whilst all of their training and equipment are geared towards rescue, to become an accepted member of the MRT an individual has to undergo a great deal of training. This is carried out mainly in the hills, but as it is usually in their own time at weekends, members have to be a dedicated crew. There are times though that many of their skills are channelled in another direction, that of fund raising for charity. This often takes the form of training those people who wish to abseil as a means of fund raising and in this capacity in 1995 for example, the team assisted in the raising of £54,000 for Cancer Research.

The start of the new year in 1989 saw No.23 Squadron crews commence their work-up flying, and the number of personnel on the Station continued to grow until by the end of the month there were close on 1500 people working at Leeming. Additional aircraft continued to arrive, and for the first time since conversion to air defence duties, the Station took over the Northern Quick Reaction Alert (QRA) commitment, albeit only for the last two weeks in July. However, it turned out to be one of the quiet periods with no "visitors" to intercept and consequently there were no live scrambles for the crews of XI Sqn.

Meanwhile, the training of 23 Sqn continued, though not without incident. In June 1989 while the Squadron was at RAF Akrotiri in Cyprus carrying out air firing practice, one of its aircraft (ZE834), was involved in what could be described as a very heavy landing, suffering a collapsed nose undercarriage leg, as well as severe damage to the fuselage. When the aircraft struck the ground its crew had ejected and although they escaped with only minor bruises, they did not avoid being held responsible at the subsequent inquiry into the accident. The aircraft, though badly damaged, was still considered repairable, so after being dismantled and enduring a protracted journey by sea and road, it came home to Leeming. At first, there it sat, gathering dust along with comments from many who thought it would never fly again, but after approximately three years the repairs were eventually begun. This in itself was another marathon effort, and it took another two-and-a-half years to reach the point in September 1995 where aircrew were again to sit in the aircraft. Things did not go immediately to plan, but all things considered the problems encountered were relatively minor ones. After a few adjustments, the aircraft was test flown, given a clean bill of health and finally handed over to XXV Sqn as an almost new Tornado with only 144 hours on the clock. To those who doubted the viability of the repair, it was later estimated that the cost of rebuilding the aircraft was less than half of the cost of a replacement F3!

That, however, was all in the future when 23 Sqn suffered an even greater disaster in July 1989 when one of its aircraft (ZE833) crashed into the North Sea off Newcastle and although the navigator ejected safely, the pilot Flt Lt Moir, was found to be dead in the water when picked up by the rescue helicopter. The loss shocked and saddened the Station, but despite it, life had to go on and the Squadron continued with its training programme before being declared as fully operational on 1 August.

The third Tornado Squadron allotted to Leeming began its work-up flying on 3 August and after an absence of 26 years, the Squadron recommenced duties in fixed wing aircraft with a "four ship" formation. It had already been rumoured that the third and final squadron at Leeming was to be No.XXV but it was actually disbanded at that time. Consequently, the title could not be assumed until 28 September 1989, when the Standard was transferred from West Raynham, with the Squadron officially reforming on 1 October.

No. XXV Squadron

In a manner similar to the other two Leeming Squadrons, No.XXV had been formed in 1915 and came onto the strength of the RFC on 25 September of that year. It was at Thetford in Norfolk where its crews began their training on the FE2B, the "scout" aircraft it was to fight with after its move to France on 20 February 1916. These were replaced in December 1917 by the DH4 and the role of the Squadron was altered to that of long range photo-reconnaissance and high altitude bombing. A short stay in Germany after the war preceded the disbandment of the Squadron at Scopwick on 20 January 1920, reforming the next day at Hawkinge with Snipes to become the only home-based fighter squadron in the UK. For the next 18 years the Squadron flew a variety of aircraft: Grebes, Siskins, Furies, Demons, and Gladiators, but commenced the war with Blenheims in the night-fighter role. Beaufighters replaced the Blenheims in October 1940 and exactly two years later these in turn were replaced by Mosquitoes. At this stage the Squadron took on trial the Whirlwind and the Havoc and in February 1943 it commenced night intruder missions and bomber escort. Various marks of Mosquito stayed with the Squadron after the war and it was not until 1951, that the jets in the shape of the Vampire arrived to establish the Squadron as the first to operate jet aircraft in the night-fighter role. These were replaced by Meteors in 1954, but the Squadron was disbanded on 23 June 1958, although it was only a week before it was reformed at Waterbeach when 153 Sqn became XXV Sqn with its crews continuing to fly in the Meteor. The Javelin was soon to take over and in March 1959 it became the last manned aircraft to be flown by the Squadron for some years, when it was again disbanded on 20 November 1962. The Squadron was then resurrected at North Coates to become the first to operate with the Bloodhound Surface-to-Air Missile, responsible for the defence of the V bomber bases and the training of all operating personnel. A move to RAF Germany was commenced in April 1970 and Flights were established at Bruggen, Laarbruch and Wildenrath. In March 1983 the Squadron left Germany to occupy Barkston Heath, Wattisham and Wyton, before being disbanded again, this time on 2 July 1989.

Throughout the whole of 1989 Leeming was a hive of activity and not only from the viewpoint of flying. The final major hardened buildings were being completed and handed over to the RAF, but many other types of construction were still in the process of completion. Amenities had not been forgotten, although it was in this area where there was a characteristic example of what some people would describe as "democracy – Service style". In true populist style, Station personnel had been canvassed for their opinion about the choice of a major amenity that would be constructed at Leeming – a swimming pool or a bowling alley.

The pool received the popular vote and a four lane bowling alley was opened on 20 July 1989!

The early part of 1989 saw another type of aircraft "move" at Leeming, although initially it was only an internal transfer for the "Gate Guardian". The Meteor NF(T)14, which in 1986 had replaced the Spitfire, was itself to be replaced. The aircraft, with the original identity of WS788 and painted in the markings of No.68 Sqn, had come to Leeming from Patrington in 1974. It was later restored and repainted in 1982, this time as WS844 and coded JCF, which was one of the aircraft of No.264 Sqn, temporarily based at Leeming in 1957 before it was disbanded to become No.33 Sqn, and the initials were those of Wg Cdr J C Forbes, its CO at the time. The aircraft was to be disposed of by tender and was at first moved from its mounting outside Station Headquarters and left on the far side of the airfield whilst it awaited the highest bidder. There it languished until in April 1992 when it was moved to its new home at the Yorkshire Air Museum at Elvington, but only after it had received more refurbishment and a further repaint to restore it to its initial identity.

While the Station was being rebuilt there was another non-flying aircraft on display at Leeming. This was a Javelin FAW Mk.4, coded XA634, which had sat for some years by the entrance road to the Officers' Mess before it was decreed that it was to be the Station's new "Guardian". The project to renovate it was commenced in November 1988 and after the tailplanes, fin, engines and other heavy equipment were removed, the Javelin was relocated. This was carried out with the help of a Chinook from Odiham, with its final short flight to the hangar where Aircraft Maintenance Flight was domiciled. At the completion of the refurbishment programme, much of it carried out by airmen in their spare time, the "as new" Javelin resplendent in the livery of No.137 Squadron was towed to its new home close to the original main gate on 1 December 1989. The number of this squadron was in fact the "shadow squadron" allotment given to 228 OCU, but purists will realise that neither 228 OCU nor any other unit at Leeming operated with the FAW4. Furthermore, this particular aircraft never saw operational service, although it is interesting to note that after receiving a special trial fit of a refuelling probe in the port wing the aircraft was used for air-to-air refuelling trials. However, the results of these trials were far from satisfactory, so when a fuselage/nose mounted refuelling probe was adopted for later marks of Javelin, XA634 was transferred to ground instructional use, less than four years after coming into service.

At the same time as the tradesmen in AMF were working on the Javelin, their Flight was carrying out the initial acceptance of the first aircraft for Leeming's third squadron. However, when it was rolled out for its "flight test" the identity of this squadron had not been announced, so a compromise had been reached as to how the aircraft could easily be identified. All of the XI Sqn aircraft had two letter fin codes, with "D" as the first letter and 23 Sqn used the same system with "C" as the prefix. When the third squadron arrived a decision was made on which letters it would use, but until then the large white question mark painted on the fin of ZE858 certainly made it easily recognisable!

The MEDA commitment continued to keep people busy with diversions, both emergency and otherwise, arriving on almost a daily basis. Examples of the types of emergency could be seen first on 20 March when a Mirage 2000 overran the runway before finally coming to rest 30 yards past the threshold. Then on 25 May an F-111 made an emergency landing when hydraulic failure caused the nose undercarriage to stick in the retracted position. The soft ground prevented the easy removal of the Mirage and recovery was made with help from a servicing team from France, but the US bomber was cleared from the runway by Leeming personnel in less than three hours.

Exercises and deployments were commonplace

at this time, with code names such as "Tornado Leap", "Typhoon Delta", "Whisky Troll", "Open Gate" and "Speedy Spirit", to name but a few, (and someone, somewhere does just that!). Aircraft types such as the Mirage 2000, Mirage F1 and the F-16, as well as the Phantom, Hawk and Tornado GR1, along with air and groundcrews from Belgium, Denmark, France, Norway and the United States, arrived and renewed old friendships and rivalries formed around Europe and Scandinavia. In addition, from October 1989 the Station took on the commitment of Northern QRA(I), and personnel on standby were kept busy with an occasional launch of a Tornado on a "live" scramble. One such launch on 10 November 1989, saw a 23 Sqn aircraft carry out the first Leeming intercept of the Soviet Bear D type aircraft. Later in the month, the Under Secretary of State for the Armed Forces, The Earl of Arran, was present when a tasking to intercept two Soviet Backfire bombers came through. Aircraft from XI Sqn were scrambled but before they could intercept the targets turned away from the UK Air Defence Region, and a chance to photograph these elusive aircraft was lost.

The obvious vulnerability of a Main Operating Base to a counterstrike from an enemy such as the Backfire bombers was a problem which in part could be met by the point defence of the airfield against attack by low flying aircraft. This responsibility was tasked to the RAF Regiment and on 1 October 1989 the advance elements of No.54 Sqn RAF Regt, which was to be equipped with Rapier short range surface-to-air missiles, began to arrive at Leeming. On 27 July of the following year 54 Sqn received the Standard of No.15 Sqn RAF Regt and on 1 August assumed its title, before being declared fully operational in October 1991.

No.15 Squadron RAF Regiment

No.15 Squadron RAF Regiment was originally formed at Netherton on 1 June 1946, as No.2700 Light Anti-Aircraft Squadron, before being re-numbered as No.15 LAA Sqn. Based variously at Watchet, Netheravon, Pembrey and Innsworth, before the "troubles" in Northern Ireland in 1957 triggered its deployment to protect RAF personnel and installations there. In October 1958 the Sqn was renamed as No.15 (Field) Sqn, and for the next 24 years carried out deployments to many "trouble spots", including the Far East with Labuan, Malaysia, Singapore and Hong Kong, the Middle East with Salalah and Muharraq, the Near East with Malta and Cyprus, and closer to home, repeatedly to Northern Ireland. Equipped with light armoured vehicles in March 1982 the Sqn was declared operational in September with the title of a Light Armoured Squadron, and after retraining in the Internal Security role returned to Northern Ireland for duties. In the period following its move to Hullavington in 1983, No.15

Sqn continued with its detachments, including the one where it carried out the exercise defence of Bruggen immediately before the official disbandment of the Sqn on 1 April 1990.

Along with the "Regiment" the Station itself was working up towards being declared to NATO as an operational main base. In the latter part of 1989 exercises were frequently generated by a team of Station personnel who monitored the various scenarios designed to test the Station's performance under wartime conditions. Operating from the concrete shelters required a change of procedures for many personnel, from the basic problems of aircraft handling to that of command and control, but as the winter passed people learned. Externally the three aircraft squadrons combined in October to take part in the UK air defence exercise, "Elder Joust", even though at that time XXV Sqn was not "combat ready". The Squadron had to receive special dispensation from 11 Group HQ to enable it to be involved, although it was soon to become operational when it received that recognition on 1 January 1990. Finally, the effort put in during all of these exercises was at last seen to pay dividends during the early part of 1990, when a NATO team conducted two tactical evaluations on the operational capability of the Station, with tests to confirm its readiness as well as its ability to sustain operations in a hostile environment. That they were considered a success could be seen after their completion when RAF Leeming was declared as fully operational, for in a period of 21 months a muddy building site had become a fighter base.

Leeming moved into the nineties secure in the belief that its tasking for the air defence of the UK and its ability to meet that task were there for the foreseeable future. However, things were about to change, and events in the Arabian Gulf in 1990 were to have a significant effect on the life and future of everyone at Leeming. On 2 August Iraq invaded the neighbouring state of Kuwait, deposed the ruling family and annexed the country as one of its territories. After the

United Nations passed a resolution that Iraq should withdraw from Kuwait, various member countries of the UN started to deploy forces to the Gulf to counter any further aggression by Iraq. To this end Her Majesty's Government announced on 8 August that British warships and aircraft would be deployed to the area to form part of a joint force to reinforce Saudi forces already in position on the borders of Iraq and Kuwait. All of the preparation and training at Leeming had been intended to make ready the Station to fight in a conflict in a European theatre of operations, but this invasion of Kuwait was to put elements of this capability to the test in a totally different environment. By one of those coincidences that do occasionally occur, a number of personnel from Leeming had not been back for long from the Middle East, and though the area was not in the immediate region of the invasion it was a great deal closer than North Yorkshire. The experience stemmed from an operation in April of that year when XI Sqn had been involved in Exercise Nile 90, which as the name implies, took place in the skies above Egypt. A total of eight F3s flew from an XI Sqn detachment in Cyprus to take part in simulated combat sorties against the F-16, Mirage III and MiG-21, of the Egyptian Air Force. Therefore, on 9 August 1990, when the Station Commander, Gp Capt Rick Peacock-Edwards, was notified that he would be the detachment commander for the RAF element of the military forces forming in the region he knew that there had already been an element of regional training for some of his crews. His orders were to fly out to the Gulf that very night, so having quickly handed over the Station he was soon on his way to Strike Command HQ at High Wycombe for a briefing on his role and from there on to Lyneham, where a Hercules awaited his arrival. The briefing caused a slight delay, but Peacock-Edwards and the advance party of some 120 men who held all manner of specialisations finally left during the early part of the following morning. It was a jour-

ney that took them first to Cyprus, where a force of 12 Tornado F3s was being held and then on to Dhahran, which, considering the "comfort factor" of the Hercules would have been a very welcome sight for the majority of those men on the four aircraft. The F3s they had seen at Akrotiri belonged to No.5 and No.29 Sqns from Coningsby in Cyprus for an air firing exercise, and notwithstanding the fact that XI Sqn was the designated "out-of-area" squadron for the RAF, these aircraft would be the first to go to the Gulf. Consequently, this small force commanded by Wg Cdr Euan Black, OC 5 Sqn, followed the four Hercules to Dhahran, although XI Sqn supplied four of its own crews to augment those from Coningsby. A reserve force of combat-ready crews from Leeming, led by Wg Cdr David Hamilton, OC XI Sqn, was not far behind, and this group was first used at Akrotiri to utilise the six Tornado F3 aircraft left there following the initial move into Saudi Arabia. At this time the shortcomings of the F3 when used on the type of operations envisaged had already been recognised, and at a very early stage the MOD had decided that the initial 12 aircraft "in theatre" would be replaced by the same number of substantially modified airframes, to be known as the Stage 1+ (one plus). This programme although named after the enhanced radar fit also included work on other avionic equipment, the provision of night vision goggles, an anti-missile flare and chaff system, and the addition of radar absorbent material in the engine intakes. Consequently the aircraft in Cyprus were needed back in the UK, so were soon to return to join the production line set up at Leeming for this programme of improvements. The requirements for the exchange with Dhahran left little margin for delay as the first six aircraft and crews trained on them were to be ready to leave the UK on 29 August. The size of the task necessitated the efforts of additional tradesmen and in a short space of time the production line in Hangars 3 and 4 had more than 500 personnel, including 200 from other stations, operating on

12 hour shifts to enable continuous coverage of the work. Combat ready aircrew were selected from the Leeming Wing to provide the required number of experienced crews and as soon as there were modified aircraft available, a training programme for these crews was started. At this stage the whole station was involved, for along with the modification task was a flying programme that ran for seven days a week, and a ground training schedule for those who were to be deployed. All of this meant that difficulties and frustrations were frequent, but they were solved by a Station that knew that it had a job to do. One of the complications that caused more than a little stress to those involved was "The Mother of All Storms", which hit the immediate area on 24 August. What in effect was a Tropical thunder storm raged over the airfield for about one hour, and with over an inch-and-a-half of rain adding its volume to the normally high water table of Leeming, the flooding of hangars, workshops, and offices, was unavoidable. Drains overflowed, water rushed under doors, manhole covers were lifted by the sheer weight of the water, and the under-floor hydraulic and electrical power supplies of Nos. 3 and 4 Hangars were inundated and ceased to function. Almost inevitably, the flying programme was disrupted, with communications both on and off the Station being interrupted for several hours. It really was a case of "all hands to the pumps", but the additional efforts of those involved meant that the delays did not prevent the Station from deploying the first of its ground support party, along with the eight aircraft, on 29 August. The aircraft flew first to Cyprus and from there the following day, six flew on to Dhahran with the two reserves returning to Leeming. Meanwhile, work continued apace at Leeming to ensure that the second batch of modified aircraft along with the groundcrew were ready to go within a week, and the final six, closely followed by the remaining aircrew and groundcrew, departed for Dhahran on 16 September. All but one Tornado F3 arrived on

schedule. This aircraft suffered an engine failure some seven hours after take-off when a fuel shutoff valve developed a fault and did what it was designed to do – albeit at the wrong time. As a result, the crew were forced to divert to the airport close to the remote and Holy City of Medina where they were welcomed by the airport manager who wasted no time in informing them that he had carried out all of his air traffic control training at Teesside Airport! In retrospect Medina was perhaps a good place for a diversion because the sensitivity of the situation required the Saudi Arabian Air Force to immediately provide a C130 to transport a party of six tradesmen led by an engineering officer, and a spare engine to the stranded jet. They arrived after midnight and set to work to replace the engine on the F3 which was parked in the nether regions of the vast desert airfield. The task, including the ground run to confirm the serviceability of the new engine, was complete by four in the morning and the F3 departed for Dhahran as dawn broke, closely followed by the weary groundcrew in the C130. It later caused them no little amusement, albeit of a wry variety, when they discovered that the efficiency and speed with which they had completed the engine change had caused the HQ at Riyadh to doubt that an engine had ever failed!

With the arrival in Saudi Arabia of the first Stage 1+ aircraft and their support personnel from Leeming, the task, previously covered by the squadrons from Coningsby, devolved to XI Sqn led by Wg Cdr David Hamilton. He had requested that his force, initially made up of crews from various F3 squadrons, come up with a name by which they could be identified. A number of ideas were put forward, some tongue in cheek, before the "Desert Eagles" was finally agreed upon. By 22 September the F3 force at Dharan consisted of 18 aircraft, 27 crews, and 336 groundcrew, which was a composite body made up of personnel from all parts of Leeming. This total was to increase, and in October the Station strength, which on paper was in excess of 2,000 personnel, was reduced by over 400 servicemen and women who had been detached to the Gulf. The aircrew formed into three flights, with A Flight from XI Sqn, B Flight from 23 Sqn and C Flight from XXV Sqn. The necessity to supply 24 hour engineering coverage meant that the groundcrew were divided into three shifts that were alternated to give everyone a fair share of the different duty times. The Squadron was tasked with flying combat air patrols in defence of Saudi airspace, while under the control of US or Saudi AWAC aircraft. These sorties were lengthy affairs, and by using air-to-air refuelling from VC10 tankers from the RAF their duration was often in the region of four hours. The aircraft were flown fully armed, and the F3's excellent navigation systems and good loiter capability made it well suited for this type of mission.

A mammoth engineering effort under difficult conditions for both personnel and equipment ensured that there was always a high level of air-craft availability, but not without a number of hiccups. One persistent problem that created a great deal of work for the groundcrew for much of early September stemmed from the fitment of radar absorbent tiles to the intake area of the aircraft. These tiles, or at least parts of them, were occasionally being ingested by the engines, an occurrence that sometimes caused enough dam-age to require an engine change. As would be expected the question of adhesion was addressed as a matter of urgency and not surprisingly the problem was finally solved by some of the trades-men involved. At that stage of "Operation Granby", the UK codename within "Operation Desert Shield", all personnel were particularly conscious of any drills relating to the use of res-pirators and protective clothing against the threatened use of chemical agents, which meant that they were never very far from their kit. With the benefit of hindsight it is easy to forget that in the first two months of the operation the coalition was still in its embryo stage with little in the way of heavy equipment. It was faced by one of the

largest military forces in the world, possessing an enormous and varied armoury of weapons and led by an utterly ruthless individual. The per-ceived danger at that time made the deployment to Saudi Arabia anything but a straightforward exercise to a hot country. Although the shooting war had not begun at the end of November when the first large scale replacement of Leeming per-sonnel occurred, the safe return of the airmen in an RAF Tristar to Teesside airport on 26 November was met with a feeling of relief from all concerned. It was, as it happened, the first such return from the Gulf and a substantial contingent of reporters and cameramen were also on hand to carry out interviews of airmen and their families. Over the next few weeks more groups of Leeming personnel returned, with the final Tristar arriving on 21 December leaving only 16 unfortunate souls from the Station in the Gulf area for Christmas and the early part of the new year. However, Leeming's involvement was still not over, and during December eight aircraft and their crews were placed on standby under 24 hours notice to move, with a further four on 48 hours notice. The new year arrived at Leeming with the technicians still employed in modifying aircraft to prepare for the first of the scheduled replacement of four of the airframes in Dhahran, a substitution duly made on 11 and 12 January when Leeming crews using air-to-air refuelling carried out the exchange.

The missions that heralded the commencement of "Operation Desert Storm" on 16 January also had some effect back at Leeming. The Station was tasked with placing four aircraft and their crews on 12 hours standby with four more on each of 24 and 48 hours of notice to move. In addition, 15 Sqn RAF Regiment was tasked to provide manpower for counter-terrorism duties by placing half of its personnel on a 12 hour standby rota with the remainder to be available within 24 hours of a call. The concern over the high number of casualties that might have been expected in the Gulf stemmed from the assessments made of the fighting ability of Iraq's armed forces, conclusions that to the public were reinforced by the number of "experts" who had been given a great deal of exposure by the media to enable them to put forward their estimates. Consequently, as in many other places, preparation was made at Leeming for the receipt of the wounded; freight and passenger handling facilities were extended, and additional sleeping accommodation was prepared in one of the hardened personnel shelters. All in all, Leeming had a very committed and integral part to play in the whole operation, so notwithstanding the absence of the majority of its personnel from the theatre of operations when the declaration of a cease fire was made on 28 February, a feeling of relief that the pressure was off was felt by everyone. The pressure was not however to be totally removed, and maintenance of a standby force by XI Sqn continued until the formal ratification of the treaty between Iraq and the Multi-National Coalition of Forces on 7 March. This meant that the rotation plan could be cancelled and the aircraft began to return as the RAF reduced its air defence task in the region. However, with the return of the aircraft and equipment, Leeming had yet more tasks to perform. It was in March that it began to receive a further 15 aircraft and to reassign a total of 24 between the squadrons at Coningsby and Leuchars. The receipt of the F3 equipment used in the Gulf was in itself a huge undertaking and with over 13,000 items to receive, unpack and repack, before forwarding on, the personnel of Supply Squadron were kept busy for some months following the end of the war.

Leeming spent a considerable amount of time in the spring and summer of 1991 in getting back to a normal footing in all parts of the Station, and in one area a decision was implemented that should have lightened some of the load. On 1 March it relinquished its commitment as a MEDA, a responsibility that had brought a few extra personnel to the establishment, but also many a visiting aircraft. In reality, the situation meant that there was little in the way of change to those involved, mainly because there was no tangible reduction in the number of aircraft needing to use Leeming in an emergency. The truth of the matter was that in the area where most of the operational and flying training of the RAF and the USAF took place, there was no comparable, large, well equipped military airfield between Finningley in Yorkshire and Leuchars in Fife. However, the additional staffing previously supplied for MEDA purposes did not return.

The year 1991 saw the beginning of Leeming's involvement with a major policy decision from the MOD, which went under the title of "The New Management Strategy". This in effect meant that from 1 April the station was to be responsible for its own financial budget, and to this end received £41,072,385 for use in the payment of the many and varied bills incurred in the running of an air base; expenses as diverse as aircraft fuel costs and official telephone bills.

During the month of April the personnel of 15 Sqn RAF Regiment carried on with their work-up towards operational status when they were deployed to the Royal Artillery range in the Hebrides. They took with them their Rapier missile systems to this practice camp, where live missiles were fired by the fire unit teams. A period of evaluation followed their return to Leeming, culminating with the "Operational" declaration being made on 1 October 1991.

The year also saw No.XXV Sqn supply the F3 team to represent the RAF at public events such as military or civil flying displays. From early spring, Flight Lieutenants Neil and Brown worked hard to perfect their programme, but before they could appear in public they were first required to perform the proposed display under the eyes of the AOC. Their efforts met with his approval, and the pair commenced their season at North Weald on 17 May. They flew a specially liveried aircraft, ZE167 and with their groundcrew from the Squadron, performed at many venues throughout the summer, usually at the weekends.

Additionally in May, as if to remind the West that the Soviets had not really gone away while the Gulf war was in progress, the last week of the month saw an intensive period of Soviet out-of-area flying, mainly with Blackjacks and Bears. As a direct consequence, the QRA crews and their groundcrew at Leeming were kept very busy with scrambles. How busy can be seen from the records which show three of Leeming's aircraft, usually with the necessity of air-to-air refuelling, spending a total of almost 30 hours in shadowing the Soviets.

While the recovery of aircraft and spares was ongoing, Leeming received word that HRH The Princess Margaret was to visit the Station and on 26 June 1991, she duly arrived. The visit was looked on to be a great success, with HRH visiting many areas of the Station and meeting many of its personnel and families. She marked the visit with the planting of a Maple tree in the grounds of the Officers' Mess before departing later in the day in an aircraft of the Queen's Flight. Her departure was followed by the opening of the £1,500 worth of beer donated by British Aerospace in recognition of the efforts of Leeming's personnel during Operation Granby. Two stories from behind the scenes however, show that even with the best of plans there is always the human element waiting to foul things up. First of all, at the moment the Princess alighted from the aircraft a phone call was to be made to the Guardroom to indicate the precise time for the Royal Standard to be raised on the Station flagpole. The first part of that plan went off well, but the Standard was upside down when it was connected to the cords! Consequently, it had been fluttering proudly for a few minutes before the fault was noted and rectified. Then later in the day two young officers had a fire practice on the recently planted tree. The tree was not badly damaged but when the incident came to light they had to face the Station Commander and no doubt will long remember their fall from grace. As is usual in trying circumstances in the RAF, humour was found in the incident. Comments such as, "I gather that the maple is now an ash", not to mention, "The CO wanted to call in the Special Branch but he twigged who did it", were but two that did the rounds.

The requirements of the Gulf operations had kept the Station at full stretch since the previous August, but it still had to find time during the late summer months of 1991 to prepare for and undergo another NATO evaluation on its ability to survive and operate under simulated war-time conditions. A Tactical Evaluation carried out by a team from the Allied Air Forces Northwestern Europe, with all of the long hours and discomfort that accompanies it, has usually been seen as a necessary evil and an examination to be passed. This one in early September was no exception, and, notwithstanding the fact that many of those who operated in the Gulf had carried out these tasks for real, everyone got on with the job and good results were obtained. Exercises still continued for the flying squadrons, one of which may have brought back memories of what occurred following the last such trip of XI Sqn to Egypt in 1990. "Exercise Nile 91", in October of that year, saw eight aircraft deploy to Cyprus and from there three flew to the Egyptian Air Force Base at El Barraged for briefings and dissimilar air combat against the F-16 and Mirage V, but on this occasion the MiG-27 did not take part.

After all of these exercise scenarios and the fuss and excitement of the previous 18 months, the year actually drifted towards 1992 with a very welcome two week break for most of its personnel at Christmas. However, before that on 2 December, the Quinton Memorial Room was dedicated to the memory of Flt Lt Quinton GC DFC, who in 1951 at the cost of his own life had saved that of an Air Training Corps cadet. At the dedication was his widow and son along with members of his family, including two of his brothers. Unfortunately, Mr Derek Coates, the sole survivor of the crash, then lived in Australia and was unable to attend.

On 16 July 1992, four of the Station's aircrew had very lucky escapes, when ZE158 from XI Sqn and ZE159 from 23 Sqn were involved in a head-on, mid-air collision in the Low-Level Overland Training Area, in Northumberland. It was described as a "grazing" collision, and occurred when the top of one aircraft's fin and the port side lower fuselage of the other met in the same airspace. Fortunately, control was not lost and both crews were able to recover their aircraft to Newcastle Airport with no injuries sustained. One, ZE159, sustained damage to the top of the fin, which received a temporary repair at the airport to enable a recovery back to Leeming, where it was found necessary to replace the fin. The other, ZE158, was obviously much more severely damaged; damage that necessitated the major task of dismantling much of the airframe to allow for road transportation back to Leeming, where the repair work could be carried out. It could be seen from the condition of the two airframes just how near the crews were to total disaster, and the comment was made later that each of the four aircrew involved should now celebrate two birthdays – their own and that day in July. As a postscript, the superstitious may ponder on the fact that the tail letters of ZE159 were EC, which had also been those of ZE833 lost from 23 Sqn in 1989. So, after this accident and the subsequent fin change, the aircraft was re-painted as EG; the Squadron was clearly not going to tempt fate again![19]

The development of Leeming as an interceptor base always required the Station to continually practice its skills. As a means to this end in the early part of the nineties, squadron detachments were both frequent and wide ranging, with Andoya, Cyprus, Decimomannu and Goose Bay, just four of many locations used. Even further afield was the destination of 23 Sqn in September 1992, when in an endeavour to "sell" the F3, Malaysia was the goal, and again in 1994, although on that occasion, XXV Sqn carried out the sales tour. However, not all detachments could be as pleasant. For instance from October 1992 to January 1993, 15 Sqn RAF Regiment carried out

its second tour of duty in the Falklands and in March 1994, XI Sqn deployed to Stornoway. This latter detachment was designed to enable a NATO team to conduct a tactical evaluation on the Squadron's ability to operate in their "Out-of-Area" role. The weather was as unkind as can be imagined for that part of the UK in March, with gale force winds, sleet and low temperatures throughout, but notwithstanding the elements, the Squadron acquitted itself well. Its personnel were able to relax somewhat and get away on some well deserved leave during May which saw the remainder of the Station evaluated in turn on its readiness and ability to continue operations during a simulated war. The results gleaned from both exercises showed that both XI Sqn in isolation, and then RAF Leeming itself, had this ability and excellent gradings were achieved in many areas of the evaluations.

The demise of the Warsaw Pact raised many questions about the doctrines of NATO and presented new settings within which the role of air power could be assessed. The fighting in what was Yugoslavia presented one such chance and the hope that Leeming remained in the forefront of RAF operations was initially borne out on 19 April 1993. Thus, in support of "Operation Deny Flight", six Tornados were deployed from Leeming to Gioia del Colle, an Italian Air Force base near Bari. The Station Commander, Gp Capt Phil Roser, was placed in command of a force centred on No.XI Sqn, with the majority of personnel being airlifted to Italy over the weekend of 17/18 April. A great deal of work went into the preparation for this deployment, and though the detachment received considerable support from the Italian Air Force, the work load remained high in the weeks that followed. The success due to this effort was in fact soon apparent, with fully armed aircraft being flown on their first assimilation flights within 4 hours of arrival at Gioia. This was followed on 26 April, when four aircraft carried out the first operational mission for the RAF in enforcing a no-fly zone over Bosnia Hercegovina.

The NATO tasking for the F3 required the Squadron to operate its aircraft in pairs on Combat Air Patrols for periods of approximately four hours, with necessary air-to-air refuelling over the Adriatic. However, especially with the F3's ability to fly at night and in bad weather, the only constant to this tasking was the way in which the times of the patrols varied; everyone was kept extremely busy with their primary duties, with "time off" at a premium. At the outset the ground-crew prepared the area allocated to the RAF, put up tents to operate from and with each entrance festooned with a very individual "home-made" engineering trade symbol, they were soon showing their own brand of parochialism.

There are many problems with working with aircraft at a detached site, especially if it was also an operational base of another country. At Gioia space was at a premium and originally the aircraft were usually parked in the open, with covered areas only available for certain levels of engineering work. To enable the aircraft spares and tools to be stored in a secure area the supply branch had the "luxury" of one of the two available hardened aircraft shelters, but even they would have had trouble in explaining the loss of one particular spare part. The small item in question had just arrived by air and was lying with other recently arrived equipment on the floor of the HAS when a wild dog (and there were many such animals on the Base), snatched it up and made off across the flight-line. The chase, carried out with great amusement by the Italian liaison NCO who had seen the "theft", was fortunately successful and the carton was returned to the supply staff who had hopefully learned something about secure storage! The detachment soon settled in and within the first week a volleyball net was in place, with football soon making an appearance in the corner of the flight-line, and later matches were played against the Base team on their grassless pitch. What the Italians thought of it all is anyone's guess, but in the early days the media was there in force with the tent symbols achieving a

great deal more video time than the aircraft. The size of the deployment was increased by a further two aircraft in May and by November all three of Leeming's Squadrons, plus many support personnel, had been deployed from the Station and during this time on no occasion was there a case of a tasking not being met. The crews from Leeming spent many hours over the "No-Fly" zone, and though many of their reports related to the sightings of shell-fire, there were frequent helicopter violations. However, the rules of engagement for the NATO air forces were extremely rigid and it did not take long for this fact to alter the reactions of those in the helicopters. Their response to the radio contact warning them of the violation became bolder and replies varying from, "we will be continuing anyway", to, "this is helicopter **, we have women and children on board", all added to the frustration of the Leeming crews. The operation continued for almost three years, with personnel from Coningsby and Leuchars sharing the deployed task. However, throughout all of that time Leeming carried on in the support role, with the preparation and rotation of suitably modified aircraft continuing as a vital and oft repeated task.

During the second world war, many lasting relationships developed between the Canadians and the people of North Yorkshire. Throughout the years RCAF veterans have frequently returned, in groups or as individuals, to re-acquaint themselves with the area and of course to remember their comrades who did not return. Obviously, age will finally curtail this particular kind of pilgrimage so it was particularly satisfying to many that the RCAF effort at Leeming was given public acknowledgment on 19 June 1993, when a permanent memorial was unveiled in the village of Leeming. The block of Yorkshire sandstone bears a carving of the Maple Leaf of Canada and the Yorkshire Rose, and carries a plaque which commemorates those who were based at RAF Leeming, stating:

**This memorial is dedicated to those men and
women who served at RAF Leeming during World
War II, including those from the Royal Canadian
Air Force Squadrons, whose members came from
all parts of the Commonwealth from 1942 to 1945;**

**405 (Vancouver) 408 (Goose) 419 (Moose)
427 (Lion) 429 (Bison)**

**also to the many Civilians who supported them
during their term of duty in North Yorkshire.
We remember too the RAF Squadrons who preceded
the Canadians from 1940 to 1942;**

7 – 10 – 35 – 77 – 102 – 219

**TO THOSE WHO PAID THE SUPREME SACRIFICE
WE WILL REMEMBER THEM**

Dedicated June 19, 1993

The service of dedication and remembrance was held in the presence of serving personnel from the Station, as well as from the Canadian Armed Forces, and many members of the general public, but pride of place naturally went to the party of approximately 100 veterans who had flown over from Canada for the occasion. The memorial was unveiled by representatives from three of the squadrons, 408, 427 and 429, with the ceremony being closed by a flypast from a Spitfire from the Battle of Britain Memorial Flight and a Tornado F3 from Leeming.

Also in 1993, while 23 Sqn was carrying out its share of the "Deny Flight" missions over Bosnia Hercegovina, Leeming received notice that as part of the "Options for Change" package the Squadron would be disbanded on 30 April 1994. The information was passed on to the CO of 23 Sqn, Wing Commander Lambert, who had the unenviable task of informing his Squadron of the decision. The Squadron returned to Leeming soon afterwards and continued in its normal role of UK air defence until the early part of 1994, when on 17 January the Station received word that the disbandment was to be brought forward to the last day of February. A parade, reviewed by the Chief of the Air Staff, Marshal of the Royal Air Force Sir Keith Williamson, himself an ex CO of 23 Sqn, was held at RAF Leeming on 26 February. Included on the guest list were various Squadron veterans, who, following a luncheon at the HAS site, had the opportunity to view a number of F3 aircraft and

22. The Leeming Swords in July 1974. Flying the Jet Provost T.5s were Flt Lts Thompson, Aldington, Fox, and Thomas. *Crown copyright MOD*

23. RAF Leeming in 1975. In the upper left, buildings belonging to the wartime communal site can still be seen alongside the old married quarters. The short grass in the foreground gives an interesting variation to the current belief that longer grass tends to deter birds from settling, and from there becoming a flight safety hazard. *Crown copyright MOD*

24. Aircraft (including reserves) lined up at Leeming before taking part in the Royal Review at Finningley, 29 July 1977. The photograph shows 12 Dominies, 6 Gnats, 6 Hunters and 8 Hawks. Note the scorched grass behind the low slung Gnats   *Crown copyright MOD*

25. Meteor T.7 (WF791) and Vampire T.11 (XH304) that made up the Vintage Pair, pictured following their arrival at Leeming in 1977.   *Crown copyright MOD*

26. (above) The final landing of Meteor WD790 on 3 November 1981 pictured against a backdrop of Jet Provosts of No.3 FTS.

Crown copyright MOD

27. (left) Prince Andrew with the CO of Leeming, Gp Capt J Curry, and the Golden Eagle of the RNEFTS. This was taken in May 1980, prior to the commencement of flying training for the Prince. *Crown copyright MOD*

28. (below) An unusual array of visitors in December 1984. The three Tornado GR1s in the foreground are from the Tornado Weapons Conversion Unit at Honington and carry the badge of No.45 Squadron's winged camel, their designated shadow squadron. Then comes two Phantom FGR2s from No.56 Squadron at Wattisham, and one of the ubiquitous Hercules or 'Fat Alberts' from Lyneham.

Crown copyright MOD

29. Tornado F3 'EZ' of No.23 Sqn fitted with a dummy missile load and displaying its new livery just prior to the squadron reforming in October 1988.   *Crown copyright MOD*

30. The first outing of FK of ? Sqn, soon to become XXV Sqn. The tailfins of a number of XI Sqn aircraft can be seen in the background, including the distinctive and 'personal' aircraft of the squadron CO, Wg Cdr David Hamilton. Hence the letters DH!   *Crown copyright MOD*

31. (above) Farewell to another Gate Guardian. Meteor NF(T)14 WS788 after its refurbishment by volunteers prior to its move to the Air Museum at Elvington. *Crown copyright MOD*

32. (left) The final 'flight' of Javelin XA634, 21 January 1989.
Crown copyright MOD

33. (left) Work continues on ZE161, on loan from 43 Sqn, during the violent storm on 24 August 1990. The photograph was taken the instant that the lightening bolt struck the ground, and is not a composite.
Flt Lt I C Black RAF

34. (left) The situation in No.4 Hangar following the storm. The aircraft ZE206, mirrored in the lake of water created on the hangar floor, carries a Phimat pod on the left hand wing pylon. The pod, for dispensing 'chaff', was a new addition, and along with a new flare system gave the F3 some additional defensive measures.
Flt Lt I C Black RAF

35. (right) Not a new tip tank, but a Skyhawk from the exiled Kuwait Air Force keeping station with a Leeming F3 over the deserts of Saudi Arabia.
Flt Lt I C Black RAF

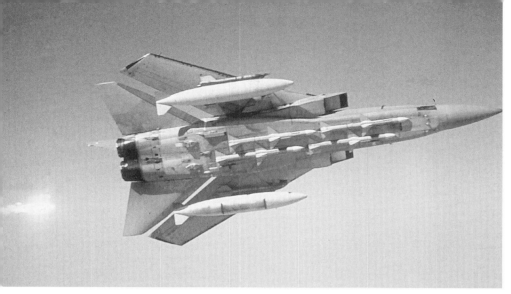

36. (left) A Tornado ejects a flare while on a training sortie from Dhahran. The flare magazines are fitted to the engine doors, and can be seen to the rear of the Skyflash missiles. While in the Gulf the F3 flew on all sorties, including training, with a live missile load.
Flt Lt I C Black RAF

37. (left) The post Gulf War formation flown from Leeming 16 May 1991, comprising of the four combat types that operated from the war zone.
Flt Lt I C Black RAF

38. (below) The shape of things to come? A prototype Eurofighter 2000 (Development Aircraft 2) on the flight-line at Leeming, 24 May 1995.
Crown copyright MOD

39. (left) Arrival flypast of No.100 Sqn at Leeming 21 September 1995 framed by a Tornado from XXV Sqn.
Crown copyright MOD

40. (below) Hawk from 100 Sqn over the NE coast of Lincolnshire. The distinctive badge used by JFACTSU is that of the Joint Warfare Staff. The gloss black finish, the new livery for fast training aircraft, is to improve visibility in an air to air situation.
Crown copyright MOD

41. (left) Diamond nine flown by Tornados from Leeming over Elvington Air Museum 13 September 1996 to commemorate the official 'towing out' of Halifax, FRIDAY THE 13TH.
Crown copyright MOD

associated weaponry displayed in the hardened aircraft shelters. However, the weather was particularly unpleasant, requiring the parade to be held under the cover of No.4 Hangar and with the planned flypast cancelled, the disbandment was something of a sad anti-climax for those involved.

The winter months of 93/94 saw the gradual construction of what was to be the new ecumenical church for the Station, and on Sunday 10 April a service of dedication was held in the new church which was to be named St Bedes. It marked the replacement of St Michael's, which was situated in a Nissen hut and though a "temporary" choice, had been in use since the end of the war. However, the move did not mean that the old church would be forgotten, because in January the Memorial Altar had been moved and re-sited in its new home, where it resides in the Blessed Sacrament, a small side chapel intended for use for private worship. The altar, a piece of marble-topped Yorkshire stone weighing nearly four tons had been donated by Royal Canadian Air Force veterans in memory of their comrades who died while serving at Leeming, and its abiding presence will continue to remind people of that sacrifice.

In addition to the disbandment of No.23 Sqn, 1994 brought other "peace dividends" to the RAF and of course to Leeming. Initially disclosed in July, the Defence Costs Study (DCS) planned for the reduction of the Service from 72,000 to approximately 52,000 by 1 April 1999. The details of the study and its possible effect on the Air Force at large were then published in a special bulletin for distribution to all rank levels, but though these facts helped understanding there was still some natural anxiety at what the future might hold. Notwithstanding this concern, the Station still had a job to do and was being kept very busy in various areas, not least of which was its continuing involvement with Operation Deny Flight. The workload on many of the Station's personnel remained high, although it was accepted that in some areas strength figures slightly exceeded that

established. On 8 August, Gp Capt E J Black arrived to take over command of the Station, but he was soon to realise that this extra "assistance" was not to last. A Manpower and Vehicle Audit (MAVA) had already been programmed in for Leeming, and by October its findings recommended that in most areas of the Station there should be a 9 to 12 per cent reduction in the establishment.

In the latter part of 1994, there were a few wry smiles at Leeming at one aspect of that "peace dividend"; in particular in the way that though some things change, others never seem to. The Station still held the commitment for QRA in October, and was required to react on two occasions with a "live" launch against "tracks" approaching the UK Air Defence Region from the area that used to go under the name of the Soviet Union. No contact was made before the "tracks" turned back, so the sorties could be seen as just two more training flights. However, in the same month Leeming received an official visit from a party of senior officers from the Russian Air Force, one of whom, a Colonel, was flown in an F3, although it was not a QRA launch! A sign that times were changing in other areas then followed in December, when Flt Lt (W) Taylor was posted to Leeming to join XXV Sqn as a navigator. Her arrival made her the first female aircrew to serve on a Leeming squadron, achieving her combat ready status in June 1995.

With the limited number of F3 squadrons in the RAF, the task of flying over the area that once was Yugoslavia was one that came round relatively quickly for the squadrons and in November 1994 it was the turn of XI Sqn again. At the beginning of the month, the advance party arrived in Italy and it was not long after the Squadron had commenced operations on what was the second tour for many of its personnel, that the flying became more dangerous. This was as a direct consequence of NATOs decision to bomb the airfield at Udbina and Jaguars from the RAF, also based at Gioia, took part in the bombing on the

21st of the month. The F3s of XI Sqn were not involved in protecting that raid, but a week later two of its aircraft were engaged by a SAM missile. It actually missed by a considerable margin when the F3s carried out their defensive manoeuvres, but in recognition of the threat, the decision was made that for a short while all aircraft carrying out combat air patrols would operate from over the Adriatic. Generally speaking though, the deployment remained routine, although the importance placed on the patrols meant that the periods of relative inactivity were often the busiest time for the ground crews, who worked long hours to ensure that sufficient aircraft were always available. The Christmas and New Year holidays were spent in Italy before XI Sqn was relieved by XXV Sqn at the end of January 1995. This type of deployment of aircraft and personnel has become accepted as commonplace in recent years. With detachments in the years following the Gulf War becoming an even greater part of squadron life, most of the personnel could expect to be away from home for something like four to six months each year. No argument would have come from the RAF Regiment either, with 15 Sqn detached to Belize for seven weeks of jungle warfare training in 1995, followed in October by another four month tour of duty in the Falkland Islands. The Squadron had been down declared from NATO on 1 August, and as a result when its personnel prepared for their third such trip to the South Atlantic since becoming operational in October 1991, they had ceased to be part of Leeming's air defence assets. This was sadly to be the last tour of duty of any sort for the Squadron prior to its disbandment in early 1996, immediately after its return to Leeming. The news that this third tour would come around had actually surfaced at the time when the Squadron returned from their second visit to the Falklands, and was a true indication of the uncertainties of Service life in the Nineties. The news of that third tour came as a shock to the Squadron but also showed that words can have a habit of "coming back to haunt". The

words in question were spoken just prior to 15 Squadron's first journey to the South Atlantic, when the Station Commander was unwise enough to comment that it would be their only trip to that outpost!

The year also saw the arrival of the European Fighter Aircraft (EFA) at Leeming, albeit in prototype form, and though of interest to many the occasion was not a planned one. It landed with its GR1 escort on 24 May because the weather at the British Aerospace airfield at Warton, near Blackpool, was outside of limits for the aircraft's return. A landing at a secure base was needed and with the EFA low on fuel it had to divert into Leeming, from where it was recovered, but only after groundcrew from the factory drove across country in order to provide the "starter crew", because the RAF were not permitted to use its engineers for that task! The word of its arrival did not take long to get out though and very soon there were approximately 100 "spotters" at various positions around the Station boundary.

The month of June in 1995 was a particularly busy one for the Station with the annual Leeming Air Fair taking centre stage for most people.

The work that goes into such an undertaking is almost incalculable, beginning many months in advance, with a great deal of time and effort given by a large number of people to ensure its success. In particular, the weekend of the event requires the involvement of almost everyone on the Station, but each year it was becoming more and more difficult to follow the achievements of the previous years, particularly in the area of fund raising. For example in 1994, after all sources had been tapped from the 93 Air Fair, a total of more than £120,000 was handed over to various charities, so it was unfortunate that for the 95 Fair, the weather was poor at the start and got worse by the afternoon. This curtailed some of the flying activities, but despite the weather the British public still turned up in their thousands, and the final estimate for attendance was somewhere in excess of 30,000.

Throughout the week that followed the Air Fair

the Station remained busy with visiting aircraft, especially in preparation for the Queen's Birthday Flypast on Saturday 17 June. Included amongst the visitors were 20 Tornado GR1 aircraft from Bruggen and they played their part in a successful celebration on the day. At approximately the same time, the Station was in the middle of playing host to Yorkshire Television and its TV drama which was to be named "Strike Force". A number of airmen and airwomen were given small parts to play, and the paid actors received their coaching from somewhere, but just like in real life the stars were the jets! The sorties were flown by XI Sqn to obtain the airborne footage, and many felt that this was the only area that prevented the programme from becoming pure "soap". Dramatic licence is perhaps the term!

On 18 Sep 1995, Hawk aircraft, sporting the distinctive skull and crossbones badge of No.100 Squadron, began to arrive at Leeming from their previous base at Finningley, with their official arrival being celebrated three days later with a Diamond Nine flypast.

No.100 Squadron

No 100 Squadron was formed in February 1917 at Hingham, as the RFCs first night bomber unit. Following a move to France and equipping with FE2Bs and BE2Es, operations commenced on 5 April against the airfield containing Richthofen's Flying Circus. In October, it was chosen to form the nucleus of the Independent Air Force under Major General Hugh Trenchard, paying particular attention to the raiding of German airfields. In August 1918 it converted to Handley Page 0/400 heavy bombers and the last aircraft to return to base on the night before the Armistice belonged to 100 Sqn. After returning to England in 1919, the Squadron was disbanded, but reformed at Baldonnel in January 1920 to operate against Sinn Fein. These operations, in Bristol Fighters, consisted mainly of leaflet dropping so it was almost a natural progression when the Squadron found itself delivering a great deal of mail. A move to Grantham in 1922 coincided with a change of aircraft and the DH9 and the Vimy were taken on strength. These in turn were replaced within two years with the Squadron receiving the newly built light bomber, the Fawn. In 1930 the Unit moved to Donibristle and converted to the torpedo-bomber role with Horsley's before receiving, in 1932, the first aircraft designed as a torpedo bomber, namely the Vildebeeste. No.100 Sqn was moved to Singapore in 1934 and in 1942 had to face the Japanese with their ageing biplane. In only two attacks the Squadron lost all of its aircraft, with the crews either dead or captured, but in December 1942, was reborn in Bomber Command flying from Grimsby where until the end of the war its Lancasters played their part in the bombing offensive. In 1946, Lincolns came as replacements and the Squadron was kept busy in Malaya, Egypt and Kenya, until 1955 when it returned to England. It then re-equipped with Canberras at Wittering where it served until it was disbanded on 1 September 1959, until 1 May 1962, when it reformed at Wittering with the Victor. It was again disbanded on 30 September 1968, but in February 1972 it came back to life as a target

towing squadron with Canberras at West Raynham. Other moves followed, first to Marham and then Wyton in 1976 and 1983, then in 1991 the Squadron converted to the Hawk before moving to Finningley in 1993.

In its role as a Target Facilities Squadron, the Hawks are required to act as subsonic silent targets for the School of Fighter Control, the Tornado F3 Operational Conversion Unit, the Sentry Training Squadron, Air Defence Fighter squadrons and SAM squadrons, with taskings coming from the Ministry of Defence and HQ Strike Command. The Squadron has also to tow banner targets for the Air Defence squadrons, a task previously carried out at Leeming in September 1953 when 228 OCU used the Mosquito Mk35 for towing the banner targets. The arrival of 100 Sqn at Leeming was also a reminder and possibly the first taste for many people of the way that some of the large scale reductions in Service strength were being met by the use of a civilian workforce. The Squadron had operated as a conventionally Service manned unit whilst at its previous base at Finningley, but appeared at Leeming with its groundcrew made up from employees of Hunting Aviation Limited.

At the same time the Joint Forward Air Controller Training and Standards Unit also moved into Leeming. Its task is to train the forward air controllers from all 3 Services and NATO, to direct the close support air strikes that may be called up during any future battles. The job of an FAC requires frequent practice to enable the skill to be retained, partially to prevent the air strike from impacting on friendly forces, but also because an aircraft that has to go around twice is in considerably more danger than in a single pass. The Unit has 2 Hawks from 100 Sqn to assist in this task, where the controller has got to give speedy and accurate instructions to direct the pilot to a target to ensure that the first run is sufficient. To this end the training brings into use laser designators, as well as the older methods of smoke or flares.

The latter months of 1995 saw the Station in a state of turbulence, and with its involvement with the Immediate Reaction Force (Air) (IRF(A)) just around the corner, everyone's mind was focused on the amount of preparation needed to meet this challenge. In addition there were to be major deployment exercises in January and February, both designed to test the Station's ability to deploy and operate, to be closely followed by a Tactical Evaluation by a NATO team. This was to take place over a ten day period commencing 12 March, with the aim of evaluating the Station while it performed its deployed role. The Gulf War, followed by the initial commitment to Operation Deny Flight, had shown that the Station could deploy and operate when called upon. Moreover, many of those involved in those operations were still at Leeming in 1996 and would have provided the core for any call on the IRF(A), so there could have been little doubt in the Station's ability to respond. Even so, when decisions were made to postpone the exercises, then the TACEVAL, the news came as a relief to many.

The "New Year" also brought with it rumours about the continuation of the deployment in Italy and it was not long before the supposition was seen to be based on fact. Neither of the two F3 squadrons at Leeming were involved at that time, but the Station had continued with its large involvement in the task by providing all aircraft replacements when any in-depth maintenance was scheduled on those in Italy. This had been a significant responsibility due to the fact that the duration of the sorties flown over Bosnia Hercegovina quickly used up the flying hours available to each aircraft. In turn, this meant the relatively frequent rotation of aircraft followed by the requisite work on the returned aircraft. Both tasks being fundamental to the continued success of the operation. Consequently, any decision to withdraw the F3 presence was going to reduce the workload for many at Leeming, but when it was made, the date for its implementation left many people surprised and with little time for anyone to think about anything but effecting the orders. The necessity for the "special fits" on the deployed aircraft meant that Leeming based F3s had always to be used in Italy, irrespective of the squadron using them. To balance that loan when their squadrons were "in theatre" both Coningsby and Leuchars had supplied the substitutes necessary to enable Leeming to continue with its flying in the UK. Therefore, the imminent restoration of its original assets meant that Leeming had to ensure that its holding of aircraft on loan were prepared, and if unserviceable repaired, to be ready for their return to their home base. Notwithstanding the short notice given, when the activation order for the planned return was announced for 5 February, No.43 Sqn crews flew the 8 aircraft from Italy into Leeming on the very same day, only experiencing a slight delay with their return to Scotland because of bad weather in the area of their base at Leuchars. As could be expected this exchange was only the first step in the withdrawal, with the Station being employed for a number of weeks at both ends of the supply chain while dealing with the large quantities of the Service's spares and ground equipment held at the Italian Air Force base.

Within weeks of the return of the aircraft from Gioia the Station had said its goodbyes to 15 Sqn RAF Regt which disbanded on 1 March, to be followed soon afterwards on the thirteenth by the publication of the names of those who were to be made redundant during the coming year. Quotas for redundancy had been announced in advance and the selection process had been geared to ensure that the RAF as a whole retained its best mix of skills and abilities to enable it to meet its future commitments. However, in most branches and trades throughout the RAF the requests far exceeded the places available, a fact that reflected the uncertainty felt by many at that time. At Leeming a total of 96 personnel received notice of redundancy, along with 61 who were granted it in the first phase in September 1995.

The month of March also saw the most recent

of Leeming's new arrivals make their appearance, when the advance party of No.34 Squadron RAF Regt began to arrive from their previous base in Cyprus. After 40 consecutive years located in that country the Squadron's move to Leeming was planned to ease its integration into the IRF (Air).

No.34 Squadron RAF Regiment

The Squadron had been formed on 19 November 1951 at RAF Yatesbury as a light anti-aircraft unit equipped with the Bofors Gun, but was soon moved to Egypt where it operated until early 1956. It then received its squadron number, which was followed by a move to Cyprus for the LAA defence of the airfield at Nicosia, along with internal security duties against the Greek-Cypriot nationalist organisation, EOKA. In November 1960 the Squadron moved to RAF Akrotiri from where during the next 14 years it undertook lengthy operational detachments to Libya, Aden and Iran, as well as carrying out its duties in Cyprus. These were particularly arduous during the Turkish invasion in 1974 when the Squadron was on constant standby in manning its gun positions for a period of four months. In January 1975 the Squadron was designated as a Field Squadron, a role that was changed again in 1982 when it received armoured vehicles to become a Light Armoured Squadron. Throughout the eighties 34 Sqn still continued to operate from Akrotiri, and in 1990 its experience in the region meant it was the first RAF Regiment field unit chosen to deploy to the Gulf area. It operated first from Bahrain then Dhahran, before being relieved and returning to Cyprus in 1993 where it was permanently employed on internal security duties, although this time as a Field Squadron again.

The years following the Gulf War were busy ones for the RAF, with Leeming personnel shouldering their share of the burden. The fact that they were successful in managing it demonstrated the professionalism and flexibility of everyone concerned, aided by the fact that the Royal Air Force has always fostered a "can do" attitude towards problems. However, in addition to this increase in the tasking, the reduction in the numbers of personnel in itself caused the Station to become much busier in many areas. Consequently, it was with some relief that the postponement of the NATO evaluation and the cancellation of the 1996 Leeming Air Fair showed that the problem was being recognised and addressed.

The reduction in the numbers of personnel has also imposed itself on other areas of life in the RAF, with sport but one example. While the Service has remained fully committed to competitive sport, opportunities for such activity have become slightly more difficult, especially on a front line station such as Leeming. It is almost paradoxical to say therefore, that notwithstanding this reality the sporting success of the Station between 1990 and 1996 was particularly notable, with the cricketers being almost unbeatable. The team lifted the RAF Cup four times, shared it on another occasion and were champions of the

Yorkshire Services League, also on four occasions. The golfers too were successful in their form of that League, topping it in 1994 and 1995, as well as winning five other trophies in the years to 1996. In 1996 the Station's athletes became champions in three competitions: the RAF Inter-Station Cup, the RAF Indoor Championship and the Strike Command Outdoor Championship. The football team cannot be left out either, running out as champions of the Yorkshire Services League in the 1995/96 season, but 1996 came to a close with some significant results from the Station's newest arrivals. In October a six man team from 34 Sqn RAF Regt came away with the team trophy from the Lord Wakefield's Boxing Championships, along with the featherweight title won by SAC Charley. Another member of the Squadron, SAC Henderson followed this up by being awarded the McDonalds Trophy as the RAF Boxer of the Season after winning six out of seven major bouts.

In attempting to draw parallels with other stations within the RAF, Leeming may perhaps be seen as a junior partner despite its 56 years of history. A junior partner however, that has an unbroken line of service dating back to those days of innocence in 1940 when it was still felt necessary to declare that an explosion would signify an air raid. From its original role as a "bomber base" the basic function of the Station has only been altered on two occasions – first to flying training, then to air defence. However, in certain fields within these functions Leeming has seen constant change and it is with this aspect of Service life that anyone who has served in the Royal Air Force will have an affinity with those who served at Leeming. Today, the Station remains an integral part of the RAF, ready to play its part in whatever challenge the future may hold.

THE FUTURE

The date of 1 January 1996, marked a significant, yet necessary change in the role of RAF Leeming with its nomination as the mounting base for the deployment of NATOs Immediate Reaction Force (Air), (IRF(Air)). When Leeming was being rebuilt as a fighter base between 1986 and 1988 there was no end in sight to the Cold War, and it was planned that the RAF would fight any future aggression from the hardened facilities of its home bases. It would have been a war fought on home ground and was known as the Citadel Concept. The sudden and dramatic end to the Cold War, followed in quick succession by the Gulf War, and then the peacekeeping operations over Bosnia, meant that the RAF had to move away from the home base philosophy to operate in a more flexible role. Mobility came to the fore and Leeming the focal point for the Tornado F3 contribution to IRF(Air). Throughout 1995 and 1996, all tasks, functions, exercises and operations were conducted with mobility very much in people's minds, possibly leading to an evaluation of the F3 force by NATO during 1998. It is a well known fact that RAF squadrons have had routine deployments to operate with friendly forces of other nations for the past 30 years or more. This in turn has enabled the Service to become well practised at moving aircraft and people over long distances for operations that might last for several weeks.

However, all of those routine deployments have been in peacetime with the support of a sometimes long but stable supply chain from the UK. It is in this area therefore, the area of support, where lies the huge difference that exists between static and deployed operations. The supply chain cannot be guaranteed during hostilities and deployed forces must take with them all of the support they might need to sustain operations; this could mean everything from teabags to tyres or washers to weapons. This represents a dramatic increase in anything that has been attempted before by fighter squadrons and to give a feel for the size of the increase a comparison can be made. In the past, a routine squadron detachment of 12 aircraft would have involved about 150 personnel and the load carrying capability of possibly 4 or 5 Hercules transports. The deployment of the IRF(Air), of which Leeming would be an integral part, would need the movement of approximately 1000 personnel and the load carrying capacity of the equivalent of some 100 Hercules. This then is the future for RAF Leeming: to provide quality and cost-effective mobile air defence to meet UK, and NATO commitments. To achieve this, the Station will operate with the Tornado F3 for the remainder of the century, then with the Eurofighter 2000 when it becomes the replacement aircraft for air defence operations. A challenging, yet interesting future looks to be assured for North Yorkshire's only remaining operational airfield.

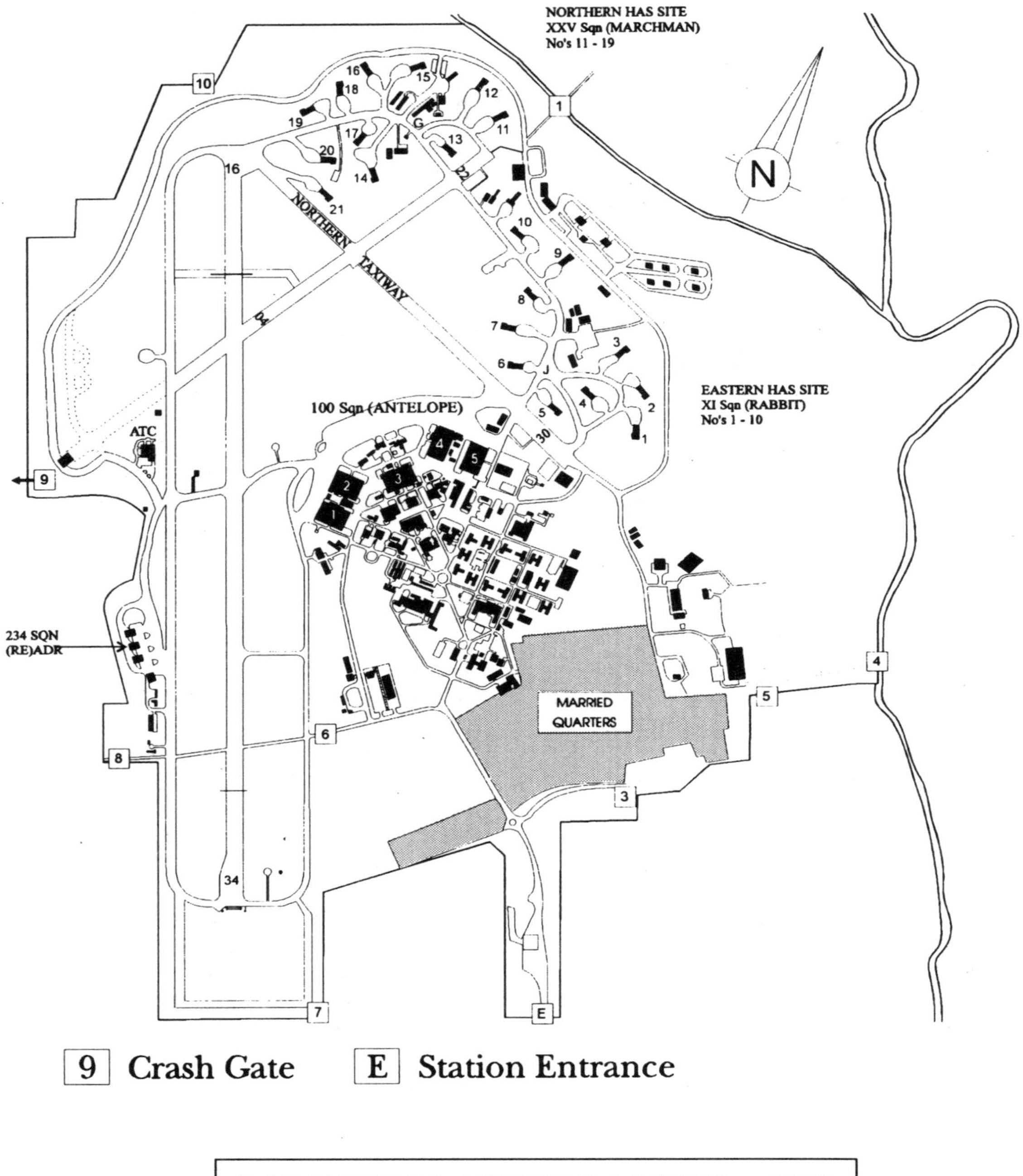
NORTHERN HAS SITE
XXV Sqn (MARCHMAN)
No's 11 - 19
EASTERN HAS SITE
XI Sqn (RABBIT)
No's 1 - 10
100 Sqn (ANTELOPE)
NORTHERN TAXIWAY
ATC
234 SQN
(RE)ADR
MARRIED
QUARTERS
N
9 Crash Gate
E Station Entrance

RAF LEEMING AIRFIELD LAYOUT – 1996

NOTES

1   In late 1941 Bufton was a Group Captain and the Director of Bombing Operations at the Air Ministry. It was largely due to his efforts in a long drawn out dispute with Sir Arthur Harris, who was against the idea, that a target finding force (to be known as the Pathfinders) was brought into being. The force was to be commanded by another ex CO of "Shiny Ten", D C T Bennett.

2   On 12 August 1940, P4965 took off from Abingdon to bomb the Fiat Aero Engine works at Turin. The aircraft was badly damaged over the target by a fighter attack, when one engine was put out of action and the starboard aileron almost shot away. After a long struggle to get home, the Whitley crashed into the sea when the aileron broke off while the pilot was trying to land on the beach at Dymchurch, Kent. Three of the crew escaped but both pilots, Plt Off Parsons DFC and Sgt Campion, died in the crash. The bodies were washed up on the French coast and are buried in the Eastern Cemetery in Boulogne. This was to be the first of many combat losses suffered by squadrons from Leeming.

3   When Plan WA11 for setting fire to German forests was proposed, it was at first dropped because of the Government's reluctance to aggravate the Germans. In opposing it the Secretary of State for Air, Kingsley Wood

questioned, "Are you aware it is private property?"

4   Whitley T4130 took off at 1804 for an operation over Berlin, and when it crashed both pilots were killed. Included in the crew but made POW was Sgt Chamberlain, who had survived Leeming's first loss of an aircraft due to enemy action (P4965), and Sgt Nicholson, who rescued his pilot from a crash at Leeming minutes before the wreckage caught fire (P5094).

5   Aircraft N1483 took off at 1800 to bomb the Air Ministry in Berlin but lost its way on return before finally coming down in the Irish Sea at 0640. The crew was rescued by a trawler off Waterford, and late that evening it put into Holyhead with five safe but very shocked crew members who were admitted to hospital for observation.

6   A blind bombing aid, rumoured to be thus named when a very senior officer, who being extremely suspicious of the scientists' claims, reputedly said, "It smells: call it H2S." (Hydrogen Sulphide)

7   "In June 1941 LAC Griffin was the first fitter of a Sunderland aircraft which, in the course of an operation, was attacked by an enemy Focke-Wulfe Condor aircraft. After the engagement it was found that the Sunderland

was losing large quantities of oil, and LAC Griffin crawled into the wing to discover two large holes in the bottom of the oil tank. Returning to the hull he obtained tools, plugs and a five gallon drum of oil which he took into the wing, and, after plugging the holes and piercing the top of the oil tank, he poured in the oil by means of a small tin; in this way he succeeded in maintaining a continuous supply of oil to the engine. He made four trips into the wing, and in all spent two hours nursing the engine in the noise, heat and in a very cramped position. He displayed great devotion to duty and materially contributed to the safe return of his aircraft."

8   Gp Capt Graham was born in Glasgow in 1895, first going to sea at the age of 14 as a cabin boy in a cargo ship. Then as an ordinary seaman he stayed with the sea until he enlisted as a private soldier in the Cameron Highlanders when the Great War broke out. He was commissioned into the Royal Highlanders in 1916, and in 1917 had won a Military Cross, when, despite being shot in the knee, he displayed conspicuous gallantry while leading a night attack. After being invalided out of the army he was commissioned into the RAF in 1919, where he trained as a pilot and as an engineer. In 1927 he crashed in the mountains of the North-West Frontier of India and though badly injured, was extremely fortunate that the local tribesmen observed that he was carrying a "goolie chit". This promised a reward for his safety, so they were prepared to look after him until a fellow pilot arrived to fly him back to the squadron. This proved more difficult than it sounds, because he had one leg encased in a splint and was unable to get into the cockpit. The solution the two pilots came up with was to have him rolled up in a bamboo stretcher, then strapped to the lower surface of the wing for the two hour flight back to base! Once

there, it took three days for his temperature to return to normal.

His brushes with death were not over though. In January 1943 he had been posted from Leeming to Cottesmore, again as Station Commander, where on 31 March he helped rescue the three survivors from a crashed Wellington. This aircraft had crashed while landing and then collided with another of its type, before both had finished up ablaze against a hangar. He was aware that one of the Wellingtons carried a 250lb bomb, but ignoring the danger from the petrol fed fire as well as the exploding ammunition and oxygen bottles, he first led the rescue, then the fire fighting. He was badly cut when the bomb finally exploded, but returned after receiving first-aid treatment to continue directing operations until the fire was extinguished. He was subsequently awarded the George Medal and was particularly proud that the evidence for the citation came from airmen involved with him that day.

9   Just after its departure from RAF Leeming one of 77 Squadron's aircraft attacked U-705 and sank it with depth charges.

10   The first of these losses, which occurred in December 1942, started a chain of events for one man that tends to underline the vagaries, or perhaps even the certainty, of fate. Following the accident where the aircraft overshot the runway, the Halifax was written off and the AOC recommended that Sgt Chambers, the pilot, be removed from four-engined training. As could be expected he was withdrawn, but as he was still considered a competent pilot he returned to twin engined bombers. He was killed in July 1943 when shot down in a Wellington during a raid on Cologne while flying with 432 Sqn from Leeming's satellite base of Skipton-on-Swale.

11 An interesting footnote on one of the Halifaxes of 427 Squadron shot down on the night of 24/25 June 1943, came to light 24 years later when the Rotterdam Europort was being developed. Some areas were being flooded, others reclaimed, and in August 1967 the wreck of DK135 was found while excavations were taking place for oil storage tanks. When one of the two survivors, Vern White, heard about it in 1976 he thought it was a hoax. As he related:

. . . I had believed that the aircraft had exploded into the North Sea. When I baled out of the blazing aircraft after 2 fighter attacks I was knocked unconscious and did not see what was left of the Halifax plough into a swamp on the island of Rosenburg just off the coast south-west of Rotterdam.

White later compulsively returned to Holland from Canada to talk with the RNethAF officials who had been involved in the recovery. There he found that two crew members had been found dead at the time of the crash and were buried in Rotterdam. Two others, including his friend the pilot, had been found during recovery operations and interred in the Canadian Military Cemetery near Nijmegen. The rear gunner remained missing, leaving White and the other air gunner as the only survivors. The Canadian was presented with the de-briefing report prepared by Wilheim Johnen, the Luftwaffe night-fighter ace who had shot him down, but he gave high praise to the Dutch Officers, for the care and reverence with which they dealt with this and many other similar recoveries in the post-war years.

12 In the New Year's Honours List of 1978, the British Empire Medal went to two sisters from Teesdale, who had reported to Leeming since 1937 on the weather conditions in their area.

The Redfearn sisters had first been approached by the Met Office in December of that year, when the official involved had requested that they took detailed notes of the wind speed, visibility, rainfall and cloud heights. In fact, anything that might affect flying operations. When RAF Leeming was opened, the requirement changed and involved them in making hourly reports by telephone to the Station, as well as supplying comprehensive written reports on a daily basis. Although they were looking forward to retirement in 1978 they were still carrying out their task when they received individual recognition for their 40 years of dedication.

13 Interestingly, Mr Percy Raine, the son of the farmer who carried out the rescue, was himself present at the crash (although his father stopped him from approaching). He recollects that his father was recommended for an award for his bravery, but on receipt of the instructions requesting his attendance at Buckingham Palace, he decided that as an ordinary farmer he could not go and the medal was never awarded. Unfortunately it has been impossible to confirm what this award might have been, but his actions that night certainly deserved some form of recognition. Strangely enough, many years after the war, Mr Raine senior died while he was out farming and his body was found in the same part of the field where the aircraft had crashed.

14 The Northrop P-61A was a large, twin engined, twin boomed night-fighter which was always painted black. For a time in 1944, they were used by 422 Sqn, US Army Air Force, operating from Scorton near Catterick.

15 The RCAF ensign, which flew at Leeming from 1943 to 1946, still flies on special o-ccasions, although now it is in the USA. It is in the possession of ex-Cpl Walter Martindale,

who worked in the MT Section at Leeming during the same three years. As one of the rear party responsible for closing down the Station he found himself as the last RCAF man to leave. He had been tasked with returning certain documents to Canada, but when he saw that the RCAF ensign was still flying, he lowered it so he could return it with the documents. When he delivered the records there was no one who wanted to take responsibility for the flag, so he decided to look after it himself. He now lives in the USA and flies it from his own flagpole to mark special Canadian memorial days, as well as for the VE celebrations in 1995.

16 The attitude of serving airmen was investigated between 4 October and 30 November 1948 by a working group consisting of service and civilian members, and including a representative from the Trades Union Council. They interviewed 1150 personnel of all ranks up throughout the Service, and one of their conclusions was that there was no appreciable difference between the reactions of conscripts or regulars to the problems associated with life in the RAF at that time. This was perhaps surprising given that the report indicated:

. . . there was a feeling that the conscripts do not belong.
. . . he is not expected to want to work, is rarely given responsibility and feels no sense of corporate life.

There was also clear evidence of many conscripts being repeatedly posted, some as often as 11 times in 20 months. It was also found that 70% of all NCOs and airmen were seriously disgruntled and thought that morale was low/fairly low, with only 4% showing enthusiasm for the service as it was at that time. The least affected were found to be the junior aircrew and some very senior officers.

17 The Station Commander at the time, Gp Capt Lowe, was often in print making such pronouncements, and if they are viewed as they are written, as some of them undoubtedly must be, then he must have been somewhat of a reactionary. However, when commenting on the effects of the Station's inappropriate and inadequate establishment, along with the lack of replies to proposals made to the Air Ministry Establishment Committee, he unbends by quoting Matthew Arnold, who remarked on his experience with a higher authority:

. . . we ask and ask, thou smilest and art still.

'T was always thus!

18 A "roller" landing is one where a pilot, in practising approaches to the runway, carries out all of the procedures for landing, but instead of slowing the aircraft after touchdown he opens the throttle and the aircraft takes-off again.

19 Possibly the crews of 10 Sqn would have been of the same mind in 1941 when over a period of four months, three out the 14 aircraft lost by the Squadron had been given the suffix "O".

OPERATIONS RECORDS

No. 4 Group (RAF) Bomber Command – RAF Leeming

DATE	SQN/ No AC	TARGET	AC U/S	AC ABORT SORTIE	AC LOST	REMARKS
20.07.40	10/9	1. Wenzendorf (Ac Factory) 2. Hamburg (Oil Refinery) 3. Borge (Aerodrome)	–	2	–	
22.07.40	10/8	1. Bremen (Ac Factory) 2. Hamburg (Oil Refinery) 3. Paderborn (Storage Hangar)	–	–	–	
24.07.40	10/9	1. Hamburg (Bismarck) 2. Wilhelmshaven (Tirpitz) 3. Emden (Oil Tanks)	1	7	–	
27.07.40	10/6	Cancelled – bad weather Germany				
02.08.40	10/7	1. Salzbergen (Oil Refinery) 2. Emmerich 3. Schipol (ADIEU)	1	1	–	
05.08.40	10/7	1. Wismar (Dornier Ac Factory) 2. Liel (Oil Fuel Depot) 3. ADIEU	–	1	–	
08.08.40	10/6	Cancelled				
11.08.40	10/8	1. Gelsenkirchen 2. Hattingen (Power Station)	–	1	–	Razzle Op
13.08.40	10/10	1. Turin (Ac Factory) 2. Any Mil Objective Identified (AMOI)	2	2	1	Via Abingdon P4965
15.08.40	10/4	Any Military Objective (AMO)	Cancelled			
15.08.40	10/9	1. Milan (Ac Factory) 2. Mannheim (Explosive Factory)	5	–	1	Via Abingdon N1497

DATE	SQN/ No AC	TARGET	AC U/S	AC ABORT SORTIE	AC LOST	REMARKS
16.08.40	10/9	1. Jena (Zeiss Works) 2. Kolleda (Storage Hangar)	–	–	1	Via Bridlington P4955
18.08.40	10/10	1. Rheinfelden (Aluminium Factory) 2. Friedburg (Aerodrome)	–	2	–	
24.08.40	10/10	1. Milan (Electric Factory) 2. Sesto Callende (Ac Factory) 3. Any Military Objective (AMO)	4	–	–	Via Abingdon
26.08.40	10/6	1. Milan 2. Sesto Calende 3. AMO	–	1	1	Via Harwell P4990
28.08.40	10/11	1. Dortmund (Oil Plant. Alternate Power Station) 2. Reisholz (Oil Refinery) Alternate. Essen (Krupps) 3. Dessau (Ac Factory) Alternate. Bernberg (Ac Factory)	–	–	–	
31.08.40	10/6	1. Wesseling (Oil Plant) Alternate Leverkusen (Chemical) 2. Self Evident Military Objective (SEMO) 3. Military Objective Previously Attacked (MOPA)	–	–	–	
03.09.40	10/7	1. Berlin (Power Station, Gas Works, West Harbour) 2. SEMO/MOPA	–	–	1	P4967
06.09.40	10/5	1. Berlin (Oil Depot) 2. SEMO/MOPA	–	–	1	P4935
08.09.40	10/6	1. Ostend (Harbour) 2. SEMO/MOPA	–	3	1	P5094
11.09.40	10/7	1. Bremen (Naval Yards) 2. Wilhelmshaven (Docks) 3. Emden (Docks, Fuel Installation)	–	–	–	Report any sign of invasion shipping
14.09.40	10/10	1. Antwerp (Barges) 2. Flushing (Shipping) 3. SEMO/MOPA	–	–	1	P4966
17.09.40	10/10	1. Hamburg (Bismarck) 2. Wilhelmshaven (Tirpitz) 3. Emden (Petrol Sheds)	2	–	–	
19.09.40	10/9	1. CC 24 (Le Havre) (Barges, Shipping)	Cancelled – Weather			
20.09.40	10/6	1. Hamm, Schwerte, Soest, (Marshalling Yards)	–	–	–	

DATE	SQN/ No AC	TARGET	AC U/S	AC ABORT SORTIE	AC LOST	REMARKS
20.09.40	10/4	1. Ehrang (Marshalling Yards)	–	–	–	Razzle Op
22.09.40	10/5	1. Lauta (Aluminium Works) 2. SEMO/MOPA	1	–	–	
22.09.40	10/1	Cancelled				
23.09.40	10/3	CC29 (Boulogne)(Docks, Barges) Any Invasion Port (AIP)	–	–	–	
24.09.40	10/12	1. Finkenheerd (Power Station) 2. Charlottenburg (Power Station) 3. Berlin (Siemens Factory) 4. SEMO/MOPA	–	–	–	Razzle Op
27.09.40	10/10	1. CC26 (Lorient) (Shipping, Docks) 2. Cherbourg (- " -) 3. AIP	–	–	–	
27.09.40	10/1	1. Le Havre (Shipping)	–	–	–	
30.09.40	10/10	Berlin (Air Ministry, W. Power Station, BMW Factory)	–	1	2	T4130 N1483
30.09.40	10/2	Le Havre, (Shipping, Docks) AIP/SEMO/MOPA	–	–	–	
05.10.40	10/5	Cancelled – bad weather				
07.10.40	10/4	1. Amsterdam (Fokker Ac) 2. Schipol (Aerodrome) 3. SEMO/MOPA	–	–	–	
07.10.40	10/5	1. Lorient (Barges, Shipping) 2. Le Havre (– " –)	–	–	–	
10.10.40	10/4	1. Cologne 2. Wesserling (Oil Factory) 3. SEMO/MOPA	–	–	–	
14.10.40	10/5	1. Stettin (Synthetic Oil) 2. Hamburg (Oil Refinery) 3. SEMO/MOPA	–	–	2	P4952 T4143
14.10.40	10/3	1. Le Havre (Docks, Shipping) 2. AIP	–	–	1	P4993
17.10.40	10/3	Skoda, Lunen cancelled				
17.10.40	10/2	Wesseling, Reisholz cancelled				
19.10.40	10/2	1. Osnabrück (Marshalling Yards) 2. Flushing (Docks, Shipping)	–	1	–	Nursery Op
21.10.40	10/4	1. Mannheim (Petrol Installation) 2. Stuttgart (Ac Factory)	–	1	1	T4152

DATE	SQN/ No AC	TARGET	AC U/S	AC ABORT SORTIE	AC LOST	REMARKS
21.10.40	10/2	1. Reisholz (Oil Refinery, Power) 2. SEMO/MOPA	1	–	–	Nursery Op
24.10.40	10/1	Hamburg (Oil Refinery, Ship Building)	–	–		Nursery Op
25.10.40	10/4	1. Magdeburg (Synthetic Oil Plant) 2. Hannover (– " – " –)	–	1	–	
25.10.40	10/1	1. Reisholz (Oil Refinery) 2. Duisburg/Ruhrort (Inland Port) 3. SEMO/MOPA	–	1	–	Nursery Op
27.10.40	10/4	Hamburg cancelled				
27.10.40	10/2	1. Lorient (Submarines) 2. Brest (Shipping, Docks) 3. SEMO/MOPA	–	–	–	Nursery Op
29.10.40	10/4	1. Magdeburg (Synthetic Oil Plant) 2. Hannover (Oil Refinery)	–	–	–	
29.10.40	10/2	1. Wilhelmshaven 2. Bremen (Shipbuilding) 3. SEMO/MOPA	–	–	–	Nursery Op
01.11.40	10/2	Rotterdam cancelled				
02.11.40	10/5	Milan, Aosta cancelled				
02.11.40	10/2	CC26, CC49 cancelled				
05.11.40	10/2	Bremen cancelled				
06.11.40	10/3	Milan	–	–	1	P5001
07.11.40	10/1	1. Wesseling (Synthetic Oil) 2. SEMO/MOPA	–	–	–	
08.11.40	10/6	1. Stuttgart (Ac Factory) 2. Lunen (Aluminium Works) 3. SEMO/MOPA	–	–	–	Via Honington
11.11.40	10/5	Polita, Hamburg cancelled				
11.11.40	10/4	CC26, CC24, AIP cancelled				
12.11.40	10/2	Lorient, Le Havre, AIP Docks	–	–	1	Nursery Op T4232
13.11.40	10/5	1. Merseburg (Oil Plant) 2. Sterkraim (Synthetic Oil Plant)	1	–	1	T4230
13.11.40	10/2	1. Hagen (Naval Arm Stores) 2. Herdecke (Power Station)	–	–	–	Nursery Op
15.11.40	10/5	Hamburg (Shipyards)	1	–	–	
15.11.40	10/2	Eindhoven (Aerodrome)	–	–	–	Nursery Op
17.11.40	10/5	Gelsenkirchen (Synthetic Oil)	1	1	–	

DATE	*SQN/* *No AC*	*TARGET*	*AC* *U/S*	*AC ABORT* *SORTIE*	*AC* *LOST*	*REMARKS*
17.11.40	10/1	Lorient, Le Havre (Docks, Shipping)	–	–	–	Nursery Op
21.11.40	10/5	Magdeburg (Synthetic Oil), Bremen (Oil Refinery) cancelled				
26.11.40	10/5	1. Turin (Royal Arsenal) 2. Aosta (Steel Works)	1	1	–	via Wyton
26.11.40	10/2	1. Antwerp (Docks, Shipping) 2. Boulogne (– " – " –)	–	1	–	Nursery Op
27.11.40	10/2	Le Havre, Boulogne (Docks, Shipping)	1	–	–	Nursery/Topcliffe
29.11.40	10/4	Bremen (Docks, Shipping)	–	–	–	Nursery/Linton
02.12.40	10/4	Lorient (Submarines)	1	2	–	
05.12.40	10/4	Gelsenkirchen cancelled				
07.12.40	10/5	1. Düsseldorf (Marshalling Yards) 2. Any railway or large fire	–	–	–	
07.12.40	10/1	Boulogne (Docks, Shipping)	–	–	–	Nursery Op
10.12.40	10/1	Duisburg (Port Area)	–	–	–	ex Linton
11.12.40	10/5	Mannheim (Power Station, any fire)	1	1	–	
14.12.40	10/5	Wilhelmshaven cancelled				
14.12.40	10/1	Boulogne cancelled – Nursery Op				
16.12.40	10/7	Mannheim	1	1	–	
17.12.40	10/5	Mannheim	1	–	–	
17.12.40	10/1	Boulogne, CC13 (Shipping) cancelled – Nursery Op				
20.12.40	10/6	Berlin SEMO/MOPA	–	–	1	P4961
20.12.40	10/1	Ostend, Boulogne (Shipping)	1	–	–	Nursery Op
21.12.40	10/1	Dunkirk AIP	–	–	–	Nursery/Linton
23.12.40	10/3	Mannheim (Naval Arm)	–	–	–	
23.12.40	10/3	Boulogne, Ostend, AIP	–	1	–	Nursery Op
26.12.40	10/4	Bordeaux (Ac Factory) Beo d'Ambes (Ac Oil Refinery) AIP – cancelled				
26.12.40	10/5	Boulogne, Le Havre, AIP cancelled				
27.12.40	10/6	Lorient, Cherbourg, AIP	–	–	–	Nursery Op
29.12.40	10/6	1. Frankfurt (Port Area) 2. Soest (Railway Sidings) 3. SEMO/MOPA	2	–	–	
01.01.41	10/7	Bremen	1	2	–	
03.01.41	10/4	Bremen	1	–	–	
04.01.41	10/2	Hamburg recalled				

DATE	SQN/ No AC	TARGET	AC U/S	AC ABORT SORTIE	AC LOST	REMARKS
04.01.41	10/2	Z3D, CC28, AIP cancelled				
04.01.41	10/4	Brest	–	1	–	
07.01.41	10/5	Duisburg cancelled				
10.01.41	10/6	Brest (Battle Cruiser) Lorient (Shipping, Docks) AIP	–	–	–	ex Linton
13.01.41	10/6	Boulogne, Calais, AIP	6	–	–	ex Linton
16.01.41	10/8	Wihelmshaven, Emden	–	2	1	ex Linton T4220
26.01.41	10/8	Hannover, SEMO, MOPA cancelled				
31.01.41	10/6	Friedrichshafen Railway cancelled				
01.02.41	10/6	Hamburg, Kiel Docks cancelled – ex Linton				
03.02.41	10/5	Brest (Battle Cruiser)	1	–	–	ex Linton
04.02.41	10/2	Calais, AIP	–	–	–	ex Linton
06.02.41	10/6	Dunkirk, Dieppe AIP, Shipping	–	–	–	ex Linton
07.02.41	10/2	CC25 Shipping cancelled – ex Linton				
10.02.41	10/7	Hannover, SEMO, MOPA Germany	–	–	–	ex Dishforth
10.02.41	10/2	Rotterdam, AIP	–	1	–	Nursery Op
11.02.41	10/6	Bremen, SEMO, MOPA cancelled – ex Dishforth				
15.02.41	10/6	Sterkrade, Duisburg (Oil, Power Station)–	–	–		ex Dishforth
15.02.41	10/4	Boulogne, Le Havre, AIP	–	–	–	ex Dishforth
23.02.41	10/7	Calais	–	2	–	ex Dishforth
26.02.41	10/7	Cologne (Trout)	1	–	–	ex Dishforth
01.03.41	10/8	Cologne	–	–	1	ex Dishforth T4265
03.03.41	10/7	Cologne	1	2	–	ex Dishforth
10.03.41	10/1	CC29, CC25, AIP cancelled – Nursery Op				
12.03.41	10/8	Hamburg SEMO, MOPA	–	1	–	ex Dishforth
13.03.41	10/4	Hamburg, SEMO, MOPA	–	–	–	ex Dishforth
14.03.41	10/6	1. Rotterdam (Oil Storage, Tanks) 2. Ostende, AIP	1	–	–	ex Dishforth
15.03.41	10/4	Polecat, CC49, CC24 cancelled – ex Dishforth				
17.03.41	10/5	Rotterdam, Ostende, AIP cancelled – ex Dishforth				
18.03.41	10/7	Kiel (Minnow)	1	–	1	ex Dishforth T4202
20.03.41	10/1	Lorient, Brest, AIP	–	–	–	Nurs. ex Topcliffe
21.03.41	10/5	Lorient, Brest, AIP cancelled – ex Dishforth				

DATE	SQN/ No AC	TARGET	AC U/S	AC ABORT SORTIE	AC LOST	REMARKS
27.03.41	10/7	Düsseldorf, SEMO, MOPA	2	2	1	ex Topcliffe Z6477
08.04.41	10/10	Kiel, Hamburg (Dace), SEMO, MOPA	–	3	–	5 ex Dishforth 5 ex Linton
09.04.41	10/8	Berlin (Whitebait) SEMO, MOPA	2	–	–	2 Linton 6 Dishforth
11.04.41	10/9	Chub, SEMMO, MOPA cancelled – ex Dishforth				
12.04.41	10/5	Brest (Battle Cruiser)	–	–	–	ex Dishforth
14.04.41	10/5	Brest (Scharnhorst, Gneisenau)	–	–	–	ex Dishforth
16.04.41	10/7	Bremen (Salmon)	–	–	1	ex Dishforth Z6557
18.04.41	10/3	Chub, SEMO, MOPA cancelled – ex Dishforth				
18.04.41	10/4	CC25, AIP cancelled – ex Dishforth				
20.04.41	10/3	Cologne, SEMO, MOPA	–	–	–	
20.04.41	10/4	Rotterdam, Ostend, AIP	–	–	–	
23.04.41	10/8	Brest	1	3	–	
25.04.41	10/2	Roach, Emden (Herring) AIP	–	–	–	Nursery Op
26.04.41	10/5	Dace B, SEMO, MOPA cancelled				
29.04.41	10/7	Mannheim, SEMO, MOPA	–	–	–	
29.04.41	10/1	Rotterdam	–	–	–	
03.05.41	10/9	Cologne, SEMO, MOPA	–	2	–	
05.05.41	10/6	Mannheim, Frankfurt, SEMO, MOPA	–	–	–	
05.05.41	10/4	Boulogne, AIP	1	–	–	Nursery Op
07.05.41	10/12	Brest (Battle Cruisers)	–	–	–	4 Nursery Op
08.05.41	10/14	Bremen, SEMO, MOPA	1	–	1	7 Nursery Op P4946
10.05.41	10/11	Hamburg, SEMO, MOPA	1	2	1	P5048
12.05.41	10/7	Mannheim, SEMO, MOPA	1	1	–	
15.05.41	10/7	Hannover (Eel), SEMO, MOPA	–	1	–	
15.05.41	10/4	Dieppe, AIP	–	–	–	Nursery Op
18.05.41	10/7	Kiel, SEMO, MOPA	–	–	–	
18.05.41	10/3	Emden, SEMO, MOPA	–	–	–	Nursery Op
27.05.41	10/10	Cologne, SEMO, MOPA	–	–	–	
02.06.41	10/14	Düsseldorf, SEMO, MOPA	–	–	–	4 Nursery Op
05.06.41	10/7	Kiel, SEMO, MOPA cancelled				

DATE	SQN/ No AC	TARGET	AC U/S	AC ABORT SORTIE	AC LOST	REMARKS
08.06.41	10/14	Dortmund, AIP	–	1	–	
12.06.41	10/16	Schwerte, SEMO, MOPA	2	2	1	Z6721
13.06.41	10/12	Schwerte, Dortmund, SEMO, MOPA	1	–	–	Nickel Op
16.06.41	10/13	Cologne, SEMO, MOPA	–	1	–	
18.06.41	10/11	Bremen, SEMO, MOPA	–	–	1	Z6671
21.06.41	10/10	Düsseldorf (Perch) MOPA	–	–	–	
24.06.41	10/11	Cologne, SEMO, MOPA	–	–	–	
27.06.41	10/12	Bremen, SEMO, MOPA	–	1	4	P5016 P5055 T4179 Z6561
30.06.41	10/10	Duisburg (Cod), SEMO, MOPA	–	–	2	P5018 Z6584
03.07.41	10/8	Essen, Duisburg, SEMO, MOPA	–	2	–	
05.07.41	10/9	Münster (Rudd), SEMO, MOPA	–	–	1	Z6793
07.07.41	10/9	Osnabrück, SEMO, MOPA	1	–	1	Z6816
08.07.41	10/10	Hamm, SEMO, MOPA	–	3	1	Z6627
10.07.41	10/8	GD1097, SEMO, MOPA cancelled				
13.07.41	10/8	Bremen, Wilhelmshaven cancelled				
17.07.41	10/4	Cologne, SEMO, MOPA cancelled				
17.07.41	10/3	Herring (Emden), AIP cancelled – Nursery op				
20.07.41	10/5	Cologne, SEMO, MOPA	–	–	–	
20.07.41	10/4	Rotterdam	–	–	–	Nursery Op
23.07.41	10/9	La Pallice (Scharnhorst), AIP	–	–	–	
25.07.41	10/6	Hannover, SEMO, MOPA	–	–	2	T4231 Z6624
27.07.41	10/3	Dunkirk, AIP	–	–	–	Nursery Op
30.07.41	10/6	Boulogne, AIP	–	6	–	
03.08.41	10/8	Frankfurt, SEMO, MOPA	1	–	–	
03.08.41	10/3	Calais, AIP	–	–	–	Nursery Op
05.08.41	10/12	Frankfurt, SEMO, MOPA	–	1	–	
05.08.41	10/1	Boulogne, Dieppe, AIP	–	–	–	Nursery Op
06.08.41	10/2	Frankfurt, SEMO, MOPA	–	1	–	
06.08.41	10/2	Calais, Boulogne, AIP	–	1	–	Nursery Op
08.08.41	10/12	Kiel, SEMO, MOPA	–	1	1	Z6815
12.08.41	10/13	Poodle B, SEMO, MOPA cancelled				
16.08.41	10/12	Cologne, SEMO, MOPA	–	–	3	Z6586 Z6794 Z6805

DATE	SQN/ No AC	TARGET	AC U/S	AC ABORT SORTIE	AC LOST	REMARKS
18.08.41	10/7	Cologne, SEMO, MOPA	1	–	2	Z6564 Z6672
18.08.41	10/2	Dunkirk, Ostend	–	–	–	Nursery Op
22.08.41	10/2	Le Havre, AIP	–	1	1	Nursery Op T4234
26.08.41	10/8	Cologne, SEMO, MOPA	1	1	–	
26.08.41	10/1	Le Havre, AIP				
29.08.41	10/8	Frankfurt, SEMO, MOPA	–	–	–	
31.08.41	10/8	Essen (Stoat), SEMO, MOPA	1	–	–	
02.09.41	10/7	Frankfurt, SEMO, MOPA	–	–	–	
02.09.41	10/2	Ostend, AIP	–	–	–	Nursery Op
06.09.41	10/2	Berlin, Huls	–	–	2	Z6478 Z6942
06.09.41	77/3	Huls	–	–	3	Z6824 Z6668 Z6654
07.09.41	10/4	Boulogne	–	–	–	
	77/3	AIP	–	–	–	
08.09.41	10/4	Kassel, SEMO, MOPA	2	–	–	
	77/5		–	–	–	
08.09.41	10/1	Not recorded				
11.09.41	10/8	Warnemünde	–	–	2	P5109 Z6867
12.09.41	77/8	Frankfurt, SEMO, MOPA	2	–	–	
12.09.41	10/3	Cherbourg, AIP	–	–	–	Nursery Op
17.09.41	10/5 77/8	Karlsruhe, SEMO, MOPA cancelled				
20.09.41	10/6	Berlin, SEMO, MOPA	2	–	1	Z6802
	77/6		–	1	2	Z6934 Z6827
22.09.41	10/2 77/4	Boulogne, AIP cancelled – Nursery Op				
26.09.41	10/5 77/6	Mannheim, SEMO, MOPA recalled				
28.09.41	10/1 77/4	Emden, AIP cancelled				
29.09.41	10/8	Stettin (Tarpon), SEMO, MOPA	–	1		
	77/11		–	3	2	Z9147 Z9150
29.09.41	77/1	Hamburg, SEMO, MOPA	–	–	–	
30.09.41	77/3	Cherbourg, Le Havre, AIP	–	–	–	Nursery Op
30.09.41	10/3 77/5	Hamburg, SEMO, MOPA	–	1	–	

DATE	SQN/ No AC	TARGET	AC U/S	AC ABORT SORTIE	AC LOST	REMARKS
01.10.41	10/5 77/7	Stuttgart (Railways), SEMO, MOPA	–	–	1	Z6941
01.10.41	10/1 77/1	Boulogne, AIP	– –	–	–	Nursery Op
03.10.41	10/6	Dunkirk, Ostend, AIP	–	–	–	Nursery Op
05.10.41	10/6 77/11	Wilhelmshaven, SEMO, MOPA cancelled				
09.10.41	10/4 77/6	Grayling B, SEMO, MOPA cancelled				
12.10.41	10/6 77/9	Nuremberg, SEMO, MOPA	– –	– –	– –	
12.10.41	10/3 77/3	Bremen, SEMO, MOPA (Nuremberg)	– –	– –	– 1	Z6801
13.10.41	10/2	Boulogne, AIP cancelled – Nursery Op				
15.10.41	10/5 77/9	Cologne, SEMO, MOPA cancelled				
16.10.41	10/4 77/3	Ostend, AIP	– 1	4 2	– –	Nursery Op
18.10.41	10/5 77/7	Emden, SEMO cancelled MOPA cancelled				
20.10.41	10/9 77/8	Wilhelmshaven (Kipper), SEMO, MOPA	— –	2 1	– –	
22.10.41	10/4 77/3	Le Havre, SEMO, AIP	– 1	– 1	– –	
23.10.41	10/10 77/9	Kiel, SEMO, MOPA	– 1	1 –	– –	
25.10.41	10/4 77/3	Emden, SEMO, cancelled MOPA cancelled				
26.10.41	10/8 77/8	Hamburg, SEMO, MOPA	– –	1 –	– –	
26.10.41	10/2	Cherbourg, AIP cancelled – Nursery Op				
28.10.41	10/5 77/3	Cherbourg, AIP	1 –	3 2	– –	Nursery Op
31.10.41	10/9 77/7	Hamburg, SEMO, MOPA	– –	– –	– 2	Z6950, Z6953
31.10.41	10/4	Dunkirk, AIP	1	1	–	Nursery Op
03.11.41	10/3	Cherbourg, AIP cancelled – Nursery Op				

DATE	SQN/ No AC	TARGET	AC U/S	AC ABORT SORTIE	AC LOST	REMARKS
06.11.41	10/5	Kiel (Deutche Werke) cancelled				
	77/5	AIP cancelled				
07.11.41	10/5	Berlin, SEMO, MOPA	–	–	–	
	77/6		–	2	–	
07.11.41	10/5	GN3814, SEMO, MOPA	–	–	–	
	77/2		–	1	–	
08.11.41	10/3	Ostend, AIP	–	–	–	Nursery Op
08.11.41	77/4	Essen, SEMO, MOPA	1	–	–	
15.11.41	10/2	Emden, AIP	–	1	–	
	77/3		–	–	–	
26.11.41	10/4	Dunkirk, AIP cancelled – Nursery Op				
27.11.41	10/3	Emden, SEMO, cancelled				
	77/4	MOPA cancelled				
27.11.41	10/9	Bremen, SEMO cancelled				
	77/9	MOPA cancelled				
30.11.41	10/4	Emden, AIP	–	–	1	Z9166
	77/4		–	–	1	Z9299
01.12.41	10/9	GH733, SEMO, MOPA cancelled				
	77/10					
07.12.41	10/8	GH733, SEMO, MOPA	–	–	–	
	77/11		–	1	–	
07.12.41	10/2	Dunkirk, AIP	–	2	1	Nursery Op Z9162
	77/1		–	1	–	
08.12.41	10/4	Calais, AIP cancelled				
11.12.41	10/2	CC24A, AIP cancelled – Nursery Op				
11.12.41	10/4	Cologne, SEMO, MOPA	2	–	1	Z9188
	77/6		3	–	–	
14.12.41	77/2	Cherbourg (Channel ports between Boulogne and Dunkirk not to be attacked 22.30 – 03.00) cancelled – Nursery Op				
15.12.41	77/4	Ostend, AIP	2	2	–	Nursery Op
16.12.41	77/13	Wilhelmshaven, Bremen, SEMO	1	–	–	
17.12.41	77/2	Le Havre, AIP	–	2	–	Nursery Op
18.12.41	10/6	Veracity (Battle Cruiser Brest)	–	–		
18.12.41	77/9	Toads (Brest/Battle Cruisers) cancelled				
22.12.41	77/12	Wilhelmshaven	–	–	–	
27.12.41	77/12	Düsseldorf, SEMO, MOPA	–	–	3	Z9306 Z6956 Z9226

DATE	SQN/ No AC	TARGET	AC U/S	AC ABORT SORTIE	AC LOST	REMARKS
29.12.41	77/6	Rotterdam, AIP cancelled. Two Halifaxes from 10 Sqn collided on take-off				
30.12.41	10/5	Veracity (Battle Cruisers Brest)	1	–	1	R9374
04.01.42	77/2	Brest AIP cancelled – Nursery				
04.01.42	77/9	Brest cancelled				
05.01.42	10/4	Brest	–	–	–	
05.01.42	77/2	Cherbourg, AIP	–	2	–	Nursery Op
06.01.42	77/5	Vichy cancelled – Nickel Raid				
06.01.42	77/6	Stavanger	1	1	–	
07.01.42	10/4	St Nazaire, AIP	1	–	–	Nursery Op
07.01.42	77/2	St Nazaire AIP cancelled – Nursery Op				
08.01.42	77/12	Brest	–	2	–	
09.01.42	10/5	Toads (Brest) Battle Cruiser cancelled				
09.01.42	77/1	Cherbourg cancelled – Nursery Op				
13.01.42	10/4	St Nazaire, Brest cancelled				
13.01.42	77/12	St Nazaire, Toads, AIP cancelled				
13.01.42	77/2	Cherbourg, AIP cancelled – Nursery Op				
15.01.42	10/3	Hamburg, SEMO, MOPA	1	–	1	L9622
15.01.42	77/13	Emden, SEMO, MOPA	–	–	–	Nickel Op
17.01.42	10/2	Bremen, SEMO, MOPA	–	–	–	
21.01.42	10/1	Bremen, SEMO, MOPA	–	–	–	
21.01.42	10/3	Emden, SEMO, MOPA cancelled – Nursery Op				
21.01.42	77/3	Dunkirk, AIP cancelled – Nursery Op				
22.01.42	10/3	Münster, SEMO, MOPA cancelled				
22.01.42	77/3	Rotterdam, SEMO, MOPA cancelled				
28.01.42	77/12	Rotterdam, AIP	–	1	–	
26.01.42	10/3	Hannover, SEMO, MOPA	–	–	–	
30.01.42	77/3	Cherbourg cancelled – Nursery Op				
31.01.42	77/3		–	3	–	Nursery Op
10.02.42	77/2	Emden	–	1	–	Nursery Op
11.02.42	77/12	Mannheim, SEMO, MOPA	–	–	–	
12.02.42	20/7	Operation Fuller	–	6	–	German battle cruisers in Channel Dash

DATE	SQN/ No AC	TARGET	AC U/S	AC ABORT SORTIE	AC LOST	REMARKS
13.02.42	77/12	Aachen	5	2	–	
13.02.42	77/1	Le Havre	–	1	–	Fresher Op
13.02.42	10/6	Cologne, SEMO, MOPA	2	–	–	
15.02.42	10/4	St Nazaire, AIP	–	1	1	L9619
15.02.42	77/12	St Nazaire	–	8	2	Z9229 Z9231
17.02.42	77/1	Special Nickel Oslo	–	–	–	
22.02.42	10/6	Mandal (Airport)	3	–	–	
25.02.42	77/14	Norway (Aluminium Factories)	–	14	–	Returned without bombing
26.02.42	10/6	Kiel, SEMO, MOPA	–	–	1	V9986 Gneisenau severely damaged
27.02.42	77/13	Wilhelmshaven	–	1	3	Z9148, Z6943, Z9280
03.03.42	10/3	Billancourt (Renault Factory)	–	–	–	
03.03.42	10/4	Advance Force (Tirpitz)	–	–	–	
03.03.42	77/12	Billancourt	–	–	–	
12.03.42	77/12	Emden	–	4	2	Z9293 Z9312
13.03.42	77/2	Boulogne, AIP	–	1	1	Fresher Op Z6975
25.03.42	77/4	Special Nickels over Paris	–	–	–	
25.03.42	77/9	St Nazaire, AIP	–	–	–	
27.03.42	77/12	St Nazaire	–	–	1	Z9221. In support of naval and commando raid
30.03.42	10/10	Tirpitz in Aasen Fjord	–	–	2	ex Lossiemouth W1043 W1044
01.04.42	77/12	Poissy (Matford Works)	–	1	–	
05.04.42	77/11	Gennevilliers	1	3	–	
12.04.42	77/14	Genoa, Turin	1	6	–	ex Wattisham
14.04.42	10/8	Dortmund (Sprat), SEMO, MOPA	–	–	2	R9492 W1045
15.04.42	77/9	St Nazaire	2	–	–	
16.04.42	77/3	Lorient	–	–	–	
17.04.42	77/10	St Nazaire	–	–	–	
22.04.42	77/2	Le Havre	–	–	–	Fresher Op

DATE	SQN/ No AC	TARGET	AC U/S	AC ABORT SORTIE	AC LOST	REMARKS
23.04.42	77/8	Rostock	1	1	1	Z9363
24.04.42	10/2	Dunkirk	–	–	–	
24.04.42	77/3	Rostock	–	1	–	
25.04.42	77/8	Rostock	–	1	–	
26.04.42	10/1	Dunkirk	–	1	–	
26.04.42	10/2	Rostock	–	1	–	
	77/2		–	–	1	Z9386
27.04.42	77/2	Dunkirk	–	–	–	
27.04.42	77/2	Dunkirk	–	–	–	Nursery Op
27.04.42	10/10	Tirpitz	–	–	2	ex Lossiemouth W1037 W1041
29.04.42	10/1	Ostend	–	–	–	Nursery Op
03.05.42	10/10	Hamburg	1	1	–	
05.05.42	10/1	Nantes	–	–	–	Fresher Op
05.05.42	10/6	Stuttgart	–	–	–	
06.05.42	10/2	Stuttgart	–	1	–	
08.05.42	10/5	Warnemünde	–	–	1	W7674
19.05.42	10/9	Mannheim	–	2	1	W1057
19.05.42	10/2	St Nazaire	–	–	–	
22.05.42	10/2	St Nazaire	–	2	–	Fresher Op
29.05.42	10/5	Gennevilliers	–	1	–	
30.05.42	10/22	Cologne	–	4	1	First 1000 bomber raid. Total 1053 ac W1042
01.06.42	10/20	Essen	2	1	3	Total 938 ac L9623 W1098 W1143
02.06.42	10/9	Essen, Cologne	–	2	–	
03.06.42	10/5	Bremen, Essen	1	–	–	
05.06.42	10/14	Essen	2	4	1	W7696
08.06.42	10/9	Essen	–	3	–	
16.06.42	10/11	Essen	–	3	–	
19.06.42	10/8	Emden, Osnabrück	1	–	1	W1158
20.06.42	10/7	Emden	1	1	1	BB201

DATE	SQN/ No AC	TARGET	AC U/S	AC ABORT SORTIE	AC LOST	REMARKS
25.06.42	10/15	Bremen	–	2	–	Total 907 ac
02.07.42	10/2	Bremen	–	–	1	Total 352 ac W1056
19.07.42	10/2	Vegesack	–	–	1	ex Topcliffe W1106
21.07.42	10/2	Duisburg	–	–	–	– " –
23.07.42	10/2	Duisburg	–	–	–	– " –
25.07.42	10/1	Duisburg	–	–	–	– " –
26.07.42	10/3	Hamburg	–	–	–	– " –
29.07.42	10/3	Saarbrücken	–	1	–	– " –
31.07.42	10/2	Düsseldorf	1	1	–	– " –
06.08.42	10/2	Duisburg	–	–	–	– " –
11.08.42	10/2	Wiesbaden	–	–	–	– " –
11.08.42	10/3	Le Havre	–	–	–	– " –
05.10.42	420/9	Aachen	–	1	–	
06.10.42	420/9	Osnabrück	–	2	–	
13.10.42	420/12	Kiel	2	4	2	X3963 DF636
01.01.43		RAF Leeming and satellite Skipton handed over to 6 Group (RAF) Bomber Command				

No. 6 Group (RCAF) Bomber Command – RCAF Leeming

DATE	SQN/ No AC	TARGET	AC U/S	AC ABORT SORTIE	AC LOST	REMARKS
09.01.43	408/8	Minelaying (Area Nectarines Frisians)	–	–	–	Mines 12 x 1500lbs
14.01.43	408/13	Lorient	–	1	–	Short notice
15.01.43	408/6	Lorient	–	–	–	PFF assisted
21.01.43	408/5	Minelaying (Frisians)	–	–	–	
23.01.43	408/5	Lorient	–	–	1	DT678
29.01.43	408/10	Lorient	–	2	1	HR662
02.02.43	408/7	Minelaying (Silverthorn – Norway)	–	3	1	DT682
03.02.43	408/14	Hamburg	–	4	1	PFF Skymasters DT680

DATE	SQN/ No AC	TARGET	AC U/S	AC ABORT SORTIE	AC LOST	REMARKS
04.02.43	408/10	Turin	–	1	–	
06.02.43	408/6	Minelaying (Frisians)	–	1	–	
07.02.43	408/8	Lorient	–	–	1	HR655
13.02.43	408/12	Lorient	–	4	–	PFF flares accurate
14.02.43	408/9	Cologne	–	2	1	DT750
16.02.43	408/11	Lorient	–	1	–	
17.02.43	408/7	Minelaying (Frisians)	–	1	–	
17.02.43	408/1	Wilhelmshaven	–	–	–	
19.02.43	408/12	Wilhelmshaven	–	–	–	
24.02.43	408/13	Wilhelmshaven	–	–	–	
25.02.43	408/4	Minelaying (Frisians)	–	2	–	
26.02.43	408/14	Cologne	–	–	–	
27.02.43	408/7	Minelaying (Frisians)	–	2	–	
01.03.43	408/9	Berlin	–	2	1	DT797
03.03.43	408/9	Hamburg	–	1	–	
05.03.43	408/10	Essen (Krupps)	–	3	–	
08.03.43	408/9	Nuremberg (Siemens Elect)	–	–	–	
09.03.43	408/9	Munich	–	1	–	
11.03.43	408/9	Stuttgart (Bosch Engine)	–	2	2	HR656 DT790
12.03.43	408/8	Essen	–	2	–	
13.03.43	408/3	Sea Search	–	–	–	
21.03.43	408/1	Weather recce over North Sea	–	–	–	
22.03.43	408/15 405/10	St Nazaire	– –	– 3	– –	
26.03.43	408/10 408/8	Duisburg	– –	– 2	– –	
27.03.43	408/11 405/11	Berlin	– –	1 2	1 –	BB332
28.03.43	408/2 405/5	St Nazaire	– –	– –	– –	
29.03.43	408/10 405/7	Berlin	– –	8 5	1 1	DT679 HR654
02.04.43	408/2 405/2	St Nazaire	– –	– –	– –	

DATE	SQN/ No AC	TARGET	AC U/S	AC ABORT SORTIE	AC LOST	REMARKS
03.04.43	408/12	Essen	–	2	3	HR713 JB866 DT 673
	405/5		–	1	2	DT723 DT808
04.04.43	408/10	Kiel	–	–	1	BB336
	405/10		–	–	1	DT704
06.04.43	408/4	Minelaying (Area Cinammon	–	–	–	
	405/6	La Rochelle)	–	1	1	DT699
08.04.43	408/4	Duisburg	–	1	–	4 crew members
	405/4		–	2	–	bailed out of one aircraft which returned safely
10.04.43	408/8	Frankfurt	–	1	–	
	405/3		–	–	–	
14.04.43	408/10	Stuttgart	–	2	2	JB909 BB311
	405/5		–	1		
16.04.43	408/12	Pilsen, Czech (Skoda Works)	–	–	4	JB854 DT752 BB343 JB925
20.04.43	408/8	Stettin				
26.04.43	408/10	Duisburg	6	–		
27.04.43	408/9	Minelaying (Frisians)	–	2	–	
28.04.43	408/11	Minelaying (Silverthorn – Norway)	–	1	–	
01.05.43	408/6	Essen (Krupps Works)	–	1	–	
04.05.43	408/14	Dortmund	–	1	2	HR658 JB898
12.05.43	408/9	Duisburg	–	3	–	
13.05.43	408/11	Bochum	–	1	1	JB931
23.05.43	408/12	Dortmund	–	–	1	Total 826 ac JB841
25.05.43	408/9	Düsseldorf	–	–	–	
27.05.43	408/12	Essen (Krupps Works)	–	–	1	DT674
29.05.43	408/12	Wuppertal	–	6	–	
	427/13		1	–		
11.06.43	408/18	Düsseldorf	–	2	1	JB972
	427/17		–	–	–	
12.06.43	408/12	Bochum	1	–	1	JB790
	427/12		1	1	1	DK183
19.06.43	408/13	Le Creusot (Schneider Works)	–	–	–	JD107
	427/17		–	–	–	

DATE	SQN/ No AC	TARGET	AC U/S	AC ABORT SORTIE	AC LOST	REMARKS
21.06.43	408/13	Krefeld	–	–	3	BB375 DT772
	427/14		–	–	–	JD209
22.06.43	408/8	Mulheim	–	–	–	
	427/14		–	–	4	DK225 DK141 DK191 DK139
24.06.43	408/9	Wuppertal	–	–	–	
	427/11		–	–	2	DK180 DK135
25.06.43	408/8	Gelsenkirchen	–	–	1	JB858
	427/9		1	–	3	DK190 1 DK 144 1
28.06.43	408/10	Cologne	–	–	–	
	427/9		–	1	2	DK183 EB 148
02.07.43	408/4	Minelaying (Frisians)	–	–	–	
	427/4		–	–	–	
03.07.43	408/12	Cologne (Kalk & Deutz)	–	–	2	JB796 JB913
	427/9		–	–	–	
09.07.43	408/11	Gelsenkirchen	–	–	2	JB922 JB216
	427/10		–	–	–	
13.07.43	408/11	Aachen	–	1	2	DT769 JD174
	427/12		–	1	1	DK142
24.07.43	408/14	Hamburg	–	–	–	
	427/12		–	–	–	
25.07.43	408/15	Essen	–	–	–	
	427/11		–	–	–	
27.07.43	408/15	Hamburg	–	–	1	DT749
	427/15		–	–	–	
29.07.43	408/12	Hamburg	–	–	–	
	427/15		–	1	–	
30.07.43	408/12	Remscheid	–	–	1	JD365
	427/12		–	–	1	EB242
02.08.43	408/11	Hamburg		–		Thunderstorm/
	427/13			4		icing
06.08.43	408/5	Bullseye Exercise				
	427/5					
09.08.43	427/9	Mannheim	–	3	1	EB247
10.08.43	427/11	Nuremberg	–	1	–	
12.08.43	427/9	Milan	–	1	–	One ac diverted to N Africa
15.08.43	429/4	Command Bullseye Exercise				

DATE	*SQN/ No AC*	*TARGET*	*AC U/S*	*AC ABORT SORTIE*	*AC LOST*	*REMARKS*
17.08.43	427/12	Peenemünde (Radiolocation)	–	1	2	DK243 DK 227 V Weapons Site
18.08.43	429/3	Command Bullseye Exercise				
22.08.43	427/13	Leverkusen	–	–	–	
23.08.43	427/17	Berlin	–	2	2	DK184 EB243
27.08.43	427/13	Nuremberg	–	1	–	
30.08.43	427/13	Mönchen Gladbach	1	2	1	LK629
31.08.43	427/12	Berlin	–	2	1	EB251
02.09.43	427/6	Minelaying	–	2	–	
02.09.43	429/4	Bullseye Exercise				
03.09.43	429/3	Bullseye Exercise				
05.09.43	427/12	Munich, Mannheim	–	1	1	LK636
06.09.43	427/10	Munich	–	4	2	LK628 DK255
15.09.43	427/13 429/8	Montluçon (Dunlop Factory)	–	3	1	DK253
16.09.43	427/9 429/10	Modane (Marshalling Yards, Fr/It frontier)	–	6	–	Diverted to US AAF Base Thurlie, Beds
22.09.43	427/15 429/10	Hannover	–	–	–	Ex Skipton
23.09.43	427/11 429/9	Mannheim	–	–	–	– " –
27.09.43	427/14 429/15	Hannover	–	–	–	– " –
29.09.43	427/8 429/7	Bochum	–	–	–	– " –
03.10.43	427/15 429/15	Kassel, Hannover	– –	1 2	– –	– " –
04.10.43	427/12 429/11	Frankfurt	– –	– –	1 1	– " – LK920 JD327
08.10.43	427/11 429/13	Hannover, Bremen (Diversion)	– –	1 1	1 1	– " – LK900 JD323
22.10.43	427/16 429/12	Kassel	– –	7 7	4 2	DK182 LK959 DK234 LK633 JD332 JD363
03.11.43	427/13 429/15	Düsseldorf	– 1	– 4	– 1	JD326

DATE	SQN/ No AC	TARGET	AC U/S	AC ABORT SORTIE	AC LOST	REMARKS
11.11.43	427/5	Cannes (Marshalling Yards)	–	–	–	
	429/5		–	–	–	
16.11.43	427		Air Sea Rescue Sweeps			
	429					
17.11.43	427		Empty Dinghy Sighted			
	429					
18.11.43	427/14	Mannheim	6	–	1	LK976
	429/16		12		1	JD275
19.11.43	427/12	Leverkusen	2	–	–	
	429/13		5			
22.11.43	427/14	Berlin	–	–	–	
	429/12		1	–	–	
25.11.43	427/17	Frankfurt	7	–	–	
	429/17		10	–	3	LK995 JD325 JD411
26.11.43	427/10	Stuttgart	5	–	–	
	429/8		3	–	2	JD164 JD333
03.12.43	427/14	Leipzig	2	1	1	DK181
	429/14		7	4	2	JD361 JD374
20.12.43	427/16	Frankfurt	–	–	2	LK627 LK644
	429/13		–	–	–	
24.12.43	429/8	Minelaying (Frisians)				
29.12.43	427/16	Berlin	7	4	–	
	429/17		6	–	1	JD318
02.01.44	429/4	Command Bullseye Exercise	–	–	1	LK734
20.01.44	427/15	Berlin	–	–	2	LL191 EB246
	429/15		–	–	1	LL197
21.01.44	427/12	Magdeburg	–	2	4	LL139 LL169
	429/13		–	–	–	LL176 LK923
28.01.44	427/15	Berlin	–	–	–	LK697 LK746
	429/15		–	–	2	
08.02.44	429	Group Bullseye Exercise	–	–	–	
15.02.44	427/14	Berlin	2	–	–	
	429/15		1	–	–	
19.02.44	427/12	Leipzig	4	–	1	LV829
	429/16		4	–	3	LK974 LK662 LK993
20.02.44	427/14	Stuttgart	1	2	1	LK 836
24.02.44	427/12	Schweinfurt	–	–	–	

DATE	SQN/ No AC	TARGET	AC U/S	AC ABORT SORTIE	AC LOST	REMARKS
24.02.44	429/9	Minelaying	–	–	–	
25.02.44	427/8	Augsburg	2	–	1	LK759
25.02.44	429/2	Minelaying (Kiel)	–	–	–	
01.03.44		Ops Cancelled – Icing condition on runways and ac				
02.03.44	429/13	Meulan les Mureaux (Aircraft Factory)	–	–	–	
06.03.44	427/14 429/5	Trappes (Marshalling Yards)	1 –	– –	– –	
07.03.44	427/14 429/8	Le Mans (Marshalling Yards)	– –	– –	– –	
13.03.44	427/8 429/8	Le Mans	– 1	1 –	– –	
15.03.44	427/16 429/16	Stuttgart	– –	1 3	2 1	LW558 LW559 LW690
18.03.44	427/14 429/16	Frankfurt	– –	– –	2 –	LW551 HX279
22.03.44	427/15 429/15	Frankfurt	– 5	– –	– –	
24.03.44	427/15 429/14	Berlin	– 5	– –	3 3	LW574 LW577 LK752 LW688 LK805 LV914
25.03.44	427/2 429/4	Aulnoye	– –	– –	– –	Fresher Op
26.03.44 –	427/14	Essen	–	–	–	
29.03.44	427/1	Vaires (Paris Railway Yards)	–	–	–	Fresher Op
30.03.44	427/16 429/13	Nuremberg	– –	1 –	3 2	LW618 LV898 LV923 LK800 LK804
09.04.44	427/14 429/16	Villeneuve-St-Georges	– –	– –	1 –	LV960
10.04.44	427/14 429/15	Ghent	– –	– –	1 –	LV883
18.04.44	427/15 429/13	Noisy-Le-Sec (Marshalling Yards)	– –	– –	1 –	LV789
20.04.44	427/16 429/16	Lens	– –	– –	– –	

DATE	SQN/ No AC	TARGET	AC U/S	AC ABORT SORTIE	AC LOST	REMARKS
22.04.44	427/16	Düsseldorf	–	–	–	
	429/16		1	–	–	LK802 LV963
24.04.44	427/15	Karlsruhe	2	–	1	LV960
	429/15		1	–	–	
26.04.44	427/16	Villeneuve-St-Georges	–	–	–	
	429/13	Essen	–	–	–	
27.04.44	427/16	Aulnoye	–	–	–	Master Bomber late
	429/12		–	–	–	but clearly heard
30.04.44	427/16	Somain (Marshalling Yards)	–	–	–	
	429/16		–	–	–	
01.05.44	427/14	St Ghislain (Marshalling Yards)	–	–	–	
	429/14		–	–	1	LW415
07.05.44	427/8	St Valery-en-Caux	–	–	–	
	429/8	(Coastal Gun Battery)	–	–	–	
09.05.44	427/11	St Valery-en-Caux	–	–	–	
	429/11	(Coastal Gun Battery)	–	–	–	
10.05.44	427/14	Ghent	–	–	1	LV986
	429/14	(Railway Yards)	–	–	–	
11.05.44	427/14	Boulogne (Marshalling Yards)	–	–	1	LW114
	429/14		–	–	–	
12.05.44	427/14	Louvain	–	–	–	
	429/14	(Railway Yards)	–	–	–	
19.05.44	427/15	Le Clipon	–	–	–	
	429/15	(Coastal Gun Battery)	–	–	–	
22.05.44	427/14	Le Mans (Marshalling Yards)	–	–	–	
	429/14		–	–	1	LV989
24.05.44	427/15	Aachen	–	–	–	
	429/15		–	–	3	HX352 LW124 LW137
27.05.44	427/18	Bourg Leopold (Military Camp)	–		2	LV831 LW365
	429/16				1	MZ295
31.05.44	427/16	Au Fevre (Wireless	–	–	–	
	429/15	Transmitting Stn)	–	–	–	
04.06.44	427/14	Calais (Heavy Coastal Battery)	–	–	–	
	429/14		–	–	–	
05.06.44	427/17	Merville/Franceville	–	–	–	
	429/19	(Coastal Gun Battery)	–	–	–	
06.06.44	427/18	Condé sur Noireau	–	–	–	
	429/19	(Crossroads)	–	–	–	

DATE	SQN/ No AC	TARGET	AC U/S	AC ABORT SORTIE	AC LOST	REMARKS
07.06.44	427/11	Achères (Marshalling Yards)	–	–	1	LV987
	429/11		–	–	1	LW128
08.06.44	427/10	Mayenne (Railways)	–	–	–	
	427/10		–	–	–	
10.06.44	427/10	Versailles/Matelots (Railways)	–	–	–	
	429/10				1	LV973
12.06.44	427/15	Arras (Railways)	–	–	3	LV995 LW135
						LW165 Fighter
	429/15		–	–	–	activity intense
14.06.44	427/14	Cambrai (Railways)	–	–	–	
	429/15		–	–	–	
15.06.44	427/13	Boulogne Port (E-Boats)	–	–`	–	
	429/13		–	–	–	
16.06.44	427/17	Siracourt (V-1 Site)	9	–	–	First daylight raid
	429/18		–	–	–	
17.06.44	427/11	Oisement/Neuville-aux-bois	–	–	–	
	429/12	(V-1 Sites)	–	–	–	
18.06.44	427/14		Cancelled			
21.06.44	427/17	Oisemont/Neuville-aux-bois	–	–	–	
	429/17	(V-1 Sites)	–	–	–	
24.06.44	427/17	Bonnetot (Construction Works	–	–	–	Daylight
	429/17	for V-1 Site)	–	–	–	
25.06.44	427/18	Gorenflos (Construction Works	–	1	–	Daylight
	429/19	for V-1 Site)	–	–	–	
27.06.44	427/18	Wizernes (Construction Works	–	–	–	
	428/18	for V-2 Site)	–	–	–	
28.06.44	427/20	Metz (Marshalling Yards)	–	2	1	LV938
	429/20		–	1	1	MZ302
04.07.44	427/16	Villeneuve-St-Georges	–	–	1	LW166
	429/16	(V-1 Site)	–	–	–	
05.07.44	427/15	Siracourt (V-1 Site)	–	–	–	Daylight
	429/15		–	–	–	
09.07.44	427/15	Ardouval	–	–	–	Daylight
	429/15					
12.07.44	427/17	Acquet	–	–	–	
	429/17					
14.07.44	427/13	Anderbelk (Construction Works	–	–	–	
	429/13	for V-1 Site)	–	–	–	

DATE	SQN/ No AC	TARGET	AC U/S	AC ABORT SORTIE	AC LOST	REMARKS
18.07.44	427/17	Mondeville	–	–	–	Daylight T/O 03.15 LV985
	429/17	Operation GOODWOOD	–	–	1	LW127
18.07.44	427/14	Wesseling (Synthetic Oil Plant)	–	–	–	Night T/O 22.00
	429/14		–	–	–	
20.07.44	427/	Ferme-de-Grande-Bois (Construction	–	–	–	Daylight T/O 13.04
	429/	Works for V-1 Site)	–	–	–	
20.07.44	427/4	Anderbelck (V-1 Site)	–	–	–	Night T/O 19.32
	429/4		–	–	–	
23.07.44	427/15	Donges (Oil Refinery)	–	–	–	Night
	429/14		–	–	–	
24.07.44	427/13	Stuttgart	–	–	1	MZ316
	429/14		–	–	1	MZ362
28.07.44	427/18	Hamburg	–	–	1	MZ757 Fighter
	429/19		–	–	–	activity intense
30.07.44	427/15	Amaye-sur-Seulles (Caumont)	–	–	–	Daylight. Support
	429/15		–	–	–	of US ground forces
31.07.44	427/13	Coquereaux	—	–	–	
	429/13		–	–	1	LV950
02.08.44	427/12	Le Hey (V-1 Site)	–	12	–	Master Bomber
	429/12		–	12	–	order ac back without bombing
03.08.44	427/21	Fôret-de-Nieppe (Construction	–	–	–	
	429/19	Works for V-1 Storage)	–	–	–	
04.08.44	427/15	Bois du Cassan (Construction	–	–	–	
	429/15	Works for V-1 Storage)	–	–	–	
05.08.44	427/19	St-Leu-d'Esserant	–	–	–	
	429/17	(V-1 Storage Site)	–	–	–	
07.08.44	427/21	Normandy (Strong points)	–	–	–	Support of ground
	429/21		–	–	–	forces
08.08.44	427/15	Chantilly (Oil Storage)	–	–	–	
	429/16		–	–	1	LW132
09.08.44	429/11	Prouville (V-1 Site)	–	–	–	
09.08.44	427/17	La Neuville (V-1 Site)	–	–	1	MZ363
	429/6		–	–	–	
12.08.44	427/11	Brunswick	–	–	1	LV821
	429/7		–	–	1	MZ825
13.08.44	427/8	La Breteque, (V-1 Site)	–	–	–	
	429/12	Cinammon Area (Minelaying)	–	–	–	

DATE	SQN/ No AC	TARGET	AC U/S	AC ABORT SORTIE	AC LOST	REMARKS
14.08.44	427/11 429/20	Caen/Falaise Highway Operation TRACTABLE	– –	– –	– –	Support of Canadian ground forces
15.08.44	427/15 429/15	Soersterberg (Aerodrome – Night Fighter)	– –	– –	– –	Disable runways
16.08.44	429/6	U-Boat Bases (Mining Approaches)	–	–	–	
17.08.44	429/5	Kiel Bay (Minelaying)	–	–	–	
17.08.44	427/15 429/10	Kiel	– –	– –	– –	Master Bomber Frequency Jammed
18.08.44	427/8 429/4	Le Hey, (V-1 Site) Minelaying (Biscay)	– –	– –	– –	
18.08.44	429/4	Bois St Remy (V-1 Site)	–	–	–	
18.08.44	427/10 429/10	Connantre (Marshalling Yards)	– –	– –	– –	
25.08.44	427/18 429/18	Brest (Coastal Gun Battery West)	– –	– –	– –	
27.08.44	427/15 429/15	Mimoyecques	– –	– –	– –	See Note 1
28.08.44	427/2 429/10	Ferme du Forestal, Fresnoy	– –	– –	– –	Unmarked Target Experiment
28.08.44	429/6	Minelaying (La Pallice)				
29.08.44	427/3 429/5	Bullseye Exercise	– –	– –	– –	
31.08.44	427/14 429/16	Île de Cézembre/St Malo (Coastal Gun Battery)	– –	– –	– –	
03.09.44	427/15	Volkel Airfield	–	–	–	Disable Runways
06.09.44	427/15 429/15	Emden	– –	– –	– –	
10.09.44	429/19	Le Havre (Enemy Defences)	–	–	–	In support of ground forces
11.09.44	427/19 429/10	Le Havre (Enemy Defences) Minelaying (Kattegat)	– –	– –	– –	
12.09.44	427/12 429/9	Dortmund (Synthetic Oil Plant)	– –	– –	– –	
12.09.44	427/5 429/7	Minelaying (Oslo Harbour)	– –	– –	– 1	MZ864
12.09.44	429/8	Sea Search				
14.09.44		Wilhelmshaven Attack Turned Back				

DATE	SQN/ No AC	TARGET	AC U/S	AC ABORT SORTIE	AC LOST	REMARKS
15.09.44	427/8	Kiel	–	–	–	Night Attack
	429/11					
15.09.44	427/5	Minelaying (Oslo Harbour)	–	–	–	
	429/5		–	–	–	
17.09.44	427/16	Boulogne Area (Strong points)	–	–	–	In support of ground forces
	429/15		–	–	1	MZ900
17.09.44	427/5	Bullseye Exercise	–	–	–	
	429/5		–	–	–	
20.09.44	427/13	Calais defences	–	–	–	In support of ground forces
	429/13		–	–	–	
24.09.44	427/15	Calais defences	–	–	–	
	429/16		–	–	1	LW136
25.09.44	427/15	Calais defences	–	–	–	
	429/15		–	–	–	
27.09.44	427/21	Sterkrade – (Duisburg)	–	–	–	
	429/20	(Oil Plant)	–	–	–	
28.09.44	427/19	Cap Gris Nez	–	19	–	Mission Cancelled.
	429/17	(Heavy Coastal Battery)	–	16	–	One ac bombed
04.10.44	427/6	Minelaying (Oslo)	–	–	1	MZ756
	429/7		–	–	–	
05.10.44		Sea Search for Missing ac; Dinghy and Wreckage sighted				
06.10.44	427/22	Dortmund	–	–	–	
	429/22		–	–	–	
09.10.44	427/15	Bochum	–	–	–	
	429/15		–	–	1	LV965
12.10.44	427/14	Wanne – Eickel	–	–	–	
	429/14	(Oil Refinery)	–	–	–	
14.10.44	427/20	Duisburg	–	–	–	Daylight
	429/16		–	–	1	MZ453
14.10.44	427/19	Duisburg	–	–	–	Night
	429/18		–	–	–	
15.10.44	427/10	Wilhelmshaven	–	–	–	Night
	429/16		–	–	–	
22.10.44	427/10	Minelaying	–	–	–	
23.10.44	427/19	Essen	–	–	–	
	429/21		–	–	1	MZ906
24.10.44	429/6	Minelaying (Kattegat)	–	–	–	

DATE	SQN/ No AC	TARGET	AC U/S	AC ABORT SORTIE	AC LOST	REMARKS
25.10.44	427/19	Hamburg	–	–	–	
	429/12	(Oil Plant)	–	–	–	
28.10.44	427/15	Cologne	–	–	–	
	429/18		–	–	–	
30.10.44	427/19	Cologne	–	–	–	All ac diverted to
	429/18		–	–	–	Spilsby on return
01.11.44	427/16	Oberhausen	–	–	–	3 fighters destroyed
	429/15		–	–		2 bomber crew died
02.11.44	427/16	Düsseldorf	–	–	–	
	429/13		–	–	–	
04.11.44	427/16	Bochum	–	–	–	
	429/14		–	–	–	
06.11.44	427/16	Gelsenkirchen	–	–	–	
	429/16		–	–	–	
11.11.44	427/6	Minelaying	–	–	–	
16.11.44	427/14	Jülich (Lines of communication)	–	–	–	In support of US
	429/14		–	–	–	ground forces
18.11.44	427/14	German Targets (Münster)	–	–	–	
	429/14		–	–	–	
21.11.44	427/19	Castrop – Rauxel (Oil Refinery)	–	–	–	
	429/12		–	–	1	MZ377
21.11.44	429/6	Minelaying (Oslo)	–	–	–	
24.11.44	427/5	Minelaying (Denmark)	–	–	1	MZ304
	429/3		–	–	–	All ac diverted Scotland on return
27.11.44	427/14	Neuss	–	–	–	Ac diverted on
	429/14		–	–	–	return
29.11.44	427/15	Duisburg	–	–	1	MZ288
	429/4		–	–	1	MZ314
02.12.44	427/10	Hagen	–	–	–	
	429/10		–	–	–	
04.12.44	427/12	Karlsruhe	–	–	–	
	429/12		–	–	–	
05.12.44	427/14	Soest	–	–	–	
	429/13		–	–	–	
06.12.44	427/12	Osnabrück	–	–	1	MZ463
	429/12		–	–		

DATE	SQN/ No AC	TARGET	AC U/S	AC ABORT SORTIE	AC LOST	REMARKS
17.12.44	427/20	Duisburg	–	–	–	
	429/16		–	–	–	
20.12.44	427/3	Minelaying	–	–	–	
	429/3		–	–	–	
24.12.44	427/3	Minelaying (Oslo)	–	–	–	
	429/3		–	–	–	
26.12.44	427/16	St Vith (German troop positions)	1	–	–	Ardennes offensive,
	429/17		–	–	–	ac diverted Scotland on return
27.12.44	427/14	Opladen	–	–	1	MZ291
	429/13		–	–		
28.12.44	427/4	Minelaying (Skagerrak)	–	–	–	
	429/4		–	–	1	NR197
29.12.44	427/14	Oberlar (Railway Yards)	–	–	–	
	429/11		–	–	–	
29.12.44	429/3	Minelaying (River Elbe)	–	–	–	
30.12.44	427/13	Cologne	–	–	–	
	429/13		–	–	1	MZ493
31.12.44	427/4	Minelaying (Kattegat)	–	–	–	
	429/4		–	–	–	
02.01.45	427/16	Ludwigshaven (Chemical Works)	–	–	–	
	429/15		–	–	–	
05.01.45	427/15	Hannover	–	–	1	NR257
	429/15		–	–	1	LV964
06.01.45	427/15	Hanau	–	–	–	
	429/14		–	–	–	
12.01.45	427/3	Minelaying (Kiel)	–	–	–	
	429/3		–	–	1	NR173
13.01.45	427/14	Saarbrücken	–	–	–	
	429/4		–	–	–	
14.01.45	427/10	Grevenbroich (Railway Yards)	–	–	–	
	429/14		–	–	–	
14.01.45	427/4	Minelaying (Oslo)	–	–	–	
	429/3		–	–	–	
16.01.45	427/15	Magdeburg	–	–	–	
	429/15		–	–	1	MZ427
16.01.45	427/3	Minelaying (Oslo)	–	–	–	
	429/3		–	–	–	

DATE	SQN/ No AC	TARGET	AC U/S	AC ABORT SORTIE	AC LOST	REMARKS
28.01.45	427/16	Stuttgart	–	–	–	
	429/15		–	–	–	
01.02.45	427/14	Mainz	–	–	–	
	429/14		–	–	–	
02.02.45	427/17	Wanne-Eickel	–	17	–	1 ac bogged down
	429/5		–	5	–	blocked others taking off
04.02.45	427/4	Osterfeld (Benzol Plant)	–	–	–	
	429/4		–	–	–	
04.02.45	427/6	Minelaying (River Elbe)	–	–	–	
	429/6		–	–	–	
07.02.45	427/17	Goch (Synthetic Oil Plant)	–	12	–	Master Bomber
	429/17		–	–	–	called off strike
13.02.45	427/14	Bohlen	–	–	–	
	429/14		–	–	–	
14.02.45	427/5	Minelaying (Kadet Channel)	1	1	1	MZ355
	429/4		–	–	1	MZ865
14.02.45	427/3	Chemnitz	–	–	1	MZ422
	429/3		–	–	–	
15.02.45	427/3	Minelaying (Oslo)	–	–	–	Ac diverted on
	429/3		–	–	–	return to Charter Hall
17.02.45	427/13	Wesel	–	–	–	Ac diverted on
	429/13		–	–	–	return
18.02.45	427/2	Minelaying (German Bight)	–	–	–	
	429/2		–	–	–	
20.02.45	427/14	Monheim (Oil Refinery)	–	–	–	
	429/14		–	–	1	NP942
21.02.45	427/11	Worms	–	–	1	NR288
	429/15		–	–	–	
23.02.45	427/11	Essen	–	–	–	
	429/16		–	–	1	LW139
24.02.45	427/10	Kamen nr Dortmund	–	–	–	
	429/14	(Synthetic Oil Plant)	–	–	–	
25.02.45	427/5	Minelaying (Oslo)	–	–	–	
	429/5		–	–	1	MZ452
27.02.45	427/7	Mainz	–	–	–	RG347
	429/13		–	–	1	
01.03.45	429/13	Mannheim	–	–	–	

DATE	SQN/ No AC	TARGET	AC U/S	AC ABORT SORTIE	AC LOST	REMARKS
02.03.45	427/14	Cologne	–	–	–	
	429/14		–	–	–	
02.03.45	427/6	Minelaying (Norway)	–	–	–	
	429/1		–	–	–	
05.03.45	429/4	Chemnitz	–	–	1	LV996
07.03.45	429/15	Hemmingstedt (Oil Refinery)	–	–	–	
08.03.45	429/5	Minelaying (Rivers Elbe + Weser)	–	–	–	
08.03.45	429/8	Hamburg (U-Boat Yards)	–	–	–	
09.03.45	429/10	Minelaying (Oslo)	–	–	–	
11.03.45	427/14	Essen	–	–	–	427 first trip
	429/10		–	–	–	Lancaster. Now fully converted
12.03.45	427/14	Dortmund	–			
	429/10				–	
12.03.45	427/2	Minelaying (Kattegat)	–	–	–	
	429/3		–	–	–	
13.03.45	429/13	Wuppertal	–	–	–	
14.03.45	427/12	Zweibrücken	–	–	–	
	429/14		–	–	–	
15.03.45	427/12	Hagen	–	–	–	Enemy fighters
	429/10	Catrop – Rauxel	–	–	–	still active
16.03.45	427/5	Minelaying (Heligoland)	–	–	–	
18.03.45	427/3	Exercise Sweepstake	–	–	–	
20.03.45	427/15	Heide	–	–	–	
22.03.45	427/15	Hildesheim	–	–	–	
24.03.45	427/11	Mathial Stimnes	–	–	–	
25.03.45	427/14	Hannover	–	–	–	
31.03.45	427/10	Hamburg (U-Boat Yards)	–	–	–	429 now with Lancasters
	429/10		–	–	1	NG345
04.04.45	427/13	Leuna (Synthetic Oil Plant)	–	–	–	
	429/11		–	–	–	
04.04.45	427/3	Minelaying (Oslo)	–	–	–	
	429/4		–	–	–	
08.04.45	427/11	Hamburg	–	–	–	
	429/11		–	–	–	

DATE	SQN/ No AC	TARGET	AC U/S	AC ABORT SORTIE	AC LOST	REMARKS
09.04.45	427/5 429/4	Minelaying (Kiel)	– –	– –	– –	
10.04.45	427/11 429/14	Leipzig (Marshalling Yards)	– –	– –	– –	
13.04.45	427/10 429/8	Kiel (Dock Area)	– –	– –	– –	
13.04.45	427/4 429/6	Minelaying (Kiel)	– –	– –	– –	
16.04.45	427/45 429/15	Schwandorf (Marshalling Yards)	– –	– –	– –	
21.04.45	427/5 429/5	Minelaying (Kattegat)	– –	– –	– –	
22.04.45	427/10 429/10	Bremen	– –	– –	– –	
25.04.45	427/10 429/10	Wangerooge Island: (Coastal Gun Battery)	– –	– –	– –	
03.05.45	427/9 429/9	Minelaying – mission recalled				
08.05.45	427/13 429/13	Operation Exodus 599 POW from Brussels to Westcott				
09.05.45		23 ac 599 POW Juvincourt to Wing				
10.05.45		31 ac 742 POW Westcott				
09.06.45		Incendiaries dropped at sea				
26.06.45	427	Ac to Tholthorpe for Bomb Disposal Duties from this date				
30.06.45	427 429	From now ground personnel passengers on trips over continent to view effects of bombing				
08.08.45	429	Ac to Tholthorpe for Bomb Disposal Duties from now				
20.08.45	427 429	To date 300 personnel on trips over Germany				
10.09.45	427/2 429/2	Operation Dodge: transporting Service personnel from Italy 80 passengers				
13.09.45	5 ac	Operation Dodge: transporting Service personnel from Italy 100 passengers				
14.09.45	5 ac	Operation Dodge: transporting Service personnel from Italy 100 passengers				
17.09.45	427 429	Operation Dodge from Italy 100 passengers				
27.09.45	427	Operation Dodge from Italy 100 passengers				
05.10.45	429	Operation Dodge from Italy 100 passengers				

DATE	SQN/ No AC	TARGET	AC U/S	AC ABORT SORTIE	AC LOST	REMARKS
08.10.45	427/10	Operation Dodge from Italy 180 passengers				
10.10.45	427/10	Operation Dodge from Italy 180 passengers				
18.10.45	427/4	Sightseeing to Berlin				
05.11.45	4 ac	2 Cross Country/2 Local Training Flights				RA571
27.11.45	427/4 429/3	Operation Dodge				
Dec, Jan, Feb	427 429	Training flying			1 1	RF257 RF259
20.03.46	427	Operation Dodge				
26.03.46	429	Operation Dodge				
27.03.46	427	Operation Dodge				
02.04.46	429	Operation Dodge				
04.04.46	427 429	Bullseye Exercise				
09.04.46	427 429	Operation Dodge				
17.04.46	427 429	Operation Dodge				
May 1946	427 429	Aircraft ferried to Maintenance Units				
31.05.46	427 429	Sqns Disbanded				

Note 1. The site at Mimoyecques was first considered to be that of a rocket launching structure, but after it had been taken by the Allies it was found to have another purpose. It was to house the 50 extremely long barrels that were to make up the High Pressure Pump gun. This was designed to fire finned shells at London every few seconds but in reality the theory was flawed and it would not have worked.

AIRCRAFT LOSSES
Suffered by RAF Leeming

In obtaining the details relating to the aircraft losses suffered by Royal Air Force Leeming, reference has been made to the Operations Record Books (Form 540 and Form 541) held at the Public Record Office, Kew, along with the Loss Cards and Accident Cards held by the Air Historical Branch at the Ministry of Defence.

During World War II, the aircraft flying on night operations were often on sorties that took place over two separate dates. That is to say that the aircraft were scheduled for take-off during the evening of one day for a return during the early hours of the following morning, and where an aircraft had been lost on a raid, the date given by the ORB or Loss Card usually refers to the date when the aircraft left the home base. Where it has been possible to discover the time of the loss and consequently the precise date, I have done so. Inevitably there are occasions where no trace of an aircraft has ever been found, and here I have made a judgement relative to take-off times, distance to target, aircraft speeds, last sightings etc. The losses are set out in date order, with aircraft type and mark, serial, squadron and where available, some detail relating to the loss and location.

All take-offs from Leeming unless specified.

P4965   10   WHITLEY V
Took off from Abingdon to bomb the Fiat aero engine works at Turin, but was badly damaged by a fighter attack while over the target – one engine was put out of action and severe damage sustained to the starboard aileron. When almost safe, and while the pilot was trying to land on the beach at Dymchurch, Kent, the aileron broke off and the aircraft crashed into the sea. Three of the crew escaped but both pilots, Plt Off Parsons DFC and Sgt Campion died. 14/8/40.

N1497   10   WHITLEY V
Took off from Abingdon to bomb an aircraft factory in Milan, but crashed in Italy after completing its mission. The pilot was killed in the crash and the remaining four in the crew became POW. 16/8/40.

P4955   10   WHITLEY V
Took off 2034 to attack Zeiss works in Jena, but hit by flak and crashed near Breda in Holland. The crew of five became POW. 17/8/40.

L8692   219   BLENHEIM 1.F
Over-ran the edge of Leeming airfield while practising a flapless landing. The pilot retracted the undercarriage to prevent the aircraft running into the Great North road. The Blenheim was severely damaged and later categorised as a write-off. 20/8/40.

P4990   10   WHITLEY V
Took off from Harwell to bomb an aircraft factory in Milan, and believed shot down near that city where all five in the crew are buried. 27/8/40.

N1489   102   WHITLEY V
Crashed on Silsden Moor, N Yorks, while on a training flight. Four of its crew were killed and one injured. 28/8/40.

P4967   10   WHITLEY V

Took off at 2026 for an operation to Berlin. Ran out of fuel on return and crash landed at 0645 in a field at the foot of the Cleveland Hills, 5 miles east of Northallerton, Yorkshire. 4/9/40.

P4935   10   WHITLEY V

FTR from an operation to Salzhot oil depot, Berlin. No trace of the aircraft or its crew of five was ever found. 7/9/40.

P5094   10   WHITLEY V

Following an operation to bomb the harbour at Ostend, the aircraft crashed on landing and finished astride the Great North Road. The pilot's leg was fractured, but he was pulled clear by the wireless operator Sgt Nicholson, minutes before the wreck caught fire. 9/9/40.

P4966   10   WHITLEY V

Outbound to bomb the invasion barges at Antwerp, but following engine failure ditched in the sea near Spurn Head. The crew was rescued by a trawler and taken into Grimsby. 14/9/40.

N3640   7   STIRLING MK 1

Hit by AA fire over the Isle-of-Man while on a cross-country navigation exercise. The aircraft got back to the mainland before it crash landed in Lancashire and was wrecked when it hit a stone wall. 29/9/40.

T4130   10   WHITLEY V

FTR from an operation to bomb the Air Ministry in Berlin. Two of the crew were killed, but included in those made POW was Sgt Chamberlain, who survived 10 Sqn's first loss from Leeming on 13 August, and Sgt Nicholson who rescued his pilot from a crash on 9 Sept. 30/9/40.

N1483   10   WHITLEY V

Following the operation to bomb the Air Ministry in Berlin, the crew became lost on return, finally coming down in the Irish Sea off Waterford at 0640. The crew of five were rescued by a trawler and landed in Anglesey. 1/10/40.

P4993   10   WHITLEY V

Whilst on an operation to bomb the docks at le Havre, the aircraft collided with a balloon cable near Weybridge, Surrey, and the crew of five were killed. 14/10/40.

T4143   10   WHITLEY V

Took off at 1727 to attack a synthetic oil plant at Stettin, and crashed near Thirsk at 0430 on return. The crew had been ordered to bale out but two failed to do so and were killed. The pilot had escaped from the crash landing of P4967 in September. 15/10/40.

P4952   10   WHITLEY V

Took off at 1733 to bomb a synthetic oil plant at Stettin, but on return the pilot was unable to break cloud cover and the aircraft was abandoned over the hills North of Hexham, Northumberland after almost 12 hours in the air. 15/10/40.

T4152   10   WHITLEY V

Crashed in open country near town of Scwabisch Hall while on an operation to bomb an aircraft components factory in Stuttgart. The bomb load exploded and killed the crew of five. 22/10/40.

P4957   10   WHITLEY V

After arriving over the 'drome following a training flight, the pilot was given permission to land but lost sight of the beacon and lights. He then failed to maintain sufficient height when flying blind and flew into a hillside three miles from Slaggyford Stn, Northumberland. It was later discovered that the pilot had been given a reciprocal heading (which caused him to fly in the opposite direction) by OC Leeming who had been in the air traffic control section when the aircraft flew over! The crew escaped serious injury. 30/10/40.

P5001   10   WHITLEY V

Took off at 1838 for an operation to Milan. Distress signals, received at 0610, plotted the aircraft close to the UK, but no trace of it or the crew of five was ever found. 7/11/40.

T4232   10   Whitley V
Took off at 2312 for a Nursery operation to the docks at Lorient, but after becoming lost over Wales crashed and caught fire at 0142. One crew member was killed and four were injured. 13/11/40.

T4230   10   Whitley V
FTR from an operation against an oil plant at Merseburg and probably crashed in the North Sea. The crew of five were killed. 14/11/40.

P4961   10   Whitley V
Aircraft abandoned near Honington in Suffolk while returning from an operation over Berlin. The wireless operator, Sgt Marshall, had survived the crash of the first aircraft lost from Leeming. 21/12/40.

P4994   10   Whitley V
Hit the roof of a house in Greengate Lane, Londonderry, while taking off on a training sortie. The aircraft caught fire, the Canadian 2nd pilot was killed, as was a child in the house. Her parents and three of the crew were injured. 22/12/40.

In January 1941, the airfield was "closed" for the laying of concrete runways, which meant that while the aircraft still operated from Leeming, they flew to Linton, Topcliffe or Dishforth for bombing up, returning "home" after the raid.

T4220   10   Whitley V
FTR from an operation, Linton-on-Ouse to Wilhelmshaven. The crew of five were killed. 16/1/41.

T4265   10   Whitley V
FTR from an operation, Dishforth to Cologne, though a distress signal indicated the bomber was returning on course for Suffolk. The crew of five were killed. 2/3/41.

T4202   10   Whitley V
Took off from Dishforth and carried out a raid on Kiel, but the crew were ordered to abandon after it caught fire on return. The bomber crashed near Masham, N Yorkshire, but the pilot was unable to escape and his body was found in the wreckage. 19/3/41.

Z6477   10   Whitley V
Took off from Topcliffe for an operation to Düsseldorf. Abandoned near Grantham after return and crashed near Cottesmore in Rutland. One of the crew was injured. 28/3/41.

Z6557   10   Whitley V
The aircraft was lost on a raid from Dishforth to Bremen and its crew of five were killed. 16/4/41.

P4946   10   Whitley V
Ditched off the Dutch coast after completing an operation to Bremen. The crew of five were made POW. 9/5/41.

P5048   10   Whitley V
FTR after completing a mission to Hamburg. the crew of five were killed. 11/5/41.

Z6721   10   Whitley V
After failure of the port engine caused the operation to Schwerte to be aborted, the aircraft ditched near the Dutch coast. The sea was running a heavy swell but the crew managed to clamber onto their overturned dinghy, where they were spotted after dawn by the crew of a Heinkel He.111. The German crew, and not without some risk to themselves, directed an RAF rescue launch to the location of their stricken fellow aviators, before finally flying off. All of the RAF crew were rescued and landed at Gt Yarmouth. 12/6/41.

Z6671   10 Whitley V
FTR from a raid on Bremen. The crew of five were killed. 19/6/41.

P5016   10   Whitley V
Lost on a raid on Bremen. Four of the crew were killed. FS E P Lewis, the wireless operator, became a POW. He escaped in March 1944 but was recaptured, handed over to the SS and shot on 1 August 1944. 28/6/41.

P5055   10   Whitley V
FTR from a raid on Bremen. The crew of five were killed. 28/6/41.

T4179   10   Whitley V
FTR from a raid on Bremen. The crew of five were killed. 28/6/41.

Z6561   10   WHITLEY V
Abandoned after being hit by flak near Kiel, while on an operation to Bremen. Four of the crew were rescued from the water to become POW, but the tail gunner was found dead. The second pilot, Sgt D Nabarro, escaped in November 1941, and after making his way back to the United Kingdom was awarded the DCM. 28/6/41.

P5018   10   WHITLEY V
Lost during an operation to Duisburg. Two of the crew were killed and three made POW. 1/7/41.

Z6584   10   WHITLEY V
On return from an operation to Duisburg, was shot down by an intruder and crashed near Thetford, Norfolk. Two of the crew of four were killed. 1/7/41.

Z6793   10   WHITLEY V
Shot down by a night-fighter and crashed in Holland while on an operation to Münster. The crew of four were killed. 6/7/41.

Z6816   10   WHITLEY V
Lost over the sea, presumed near Flamborough Head, on return from a raid on Osnabrück. The crew of four were killed. 8/7/41.

Z6627   10   WHITLEY V
Lost without trace on a raid to Hamm. The crew of four were killed. 9/7/41.

T4231   10   WHITLEY V
Crashed in Belgium while on an operation to Hannover. The crew of five were killed. 26/7/41.

Z6624   10   WHITLEY V
Crashed in the sea while on an operation to Hannover. The crew of five were killed. 26/7/41.

Z6815   10   WHITLEY V
Crashed near the target when raiding Kiel. The crew of five were killed. Plt Off M Littlewood, a Canadian, had been the pilot in the crew rescued after the intervention of the German He.111 in June. 9/8/41.

Z6586   10   WHITLEY V
Crashed in Belgium while on an operation to Cologne. The crew of five were killed. 17/8/41.

Z6794   10   WHITLEY V
Lost while on an operation to Cologne. Two of the crew were killed, but three were made POW after baling out. 17/8/41.

Z6805   10   WHITLEY V
Lost during an operation to Cologne. The crew of four were made POW, but Sgt H P Calvert was shot by police in Dresden after escaping from Stalag IIIE in May 1942. 17/8/41.

Z6564   10   WHITLEY V
Crashed in Belgium while on a raid to Cologne. The crew of five were killed. The rear gunner, Sgt T H Park RCAF, was a US citizen. 19/8/41.

Z6672   10   WHITLEY V
Crashed near the Belgium/Dutch border while on a raid to Cologne. Three of the crew were killed and two made POW. 19/8/41.

T4234   10   WHITLEY V
Crashed into high ground near Kendal in Westmoreland when almost four hours into a Nursery operation to le Havre. Two of the crew were killed and three injured. 23/8/41.

Z6932   10   WHITLEY V
Landed at Acklington, Northumberland after getting lost on an air test. It then crashed after taking off to return to Leeming, following a collision with some power lines. Three of the four man crew were killed and the fourth was injured. 6/9/41.

Z6478   10   WHITLEY V
Shot down by a night-fighter at 2300 and crashed in Holland while on an operation to Huls. The crew of five were killed. The pilot, Sgt A Poupard, had been the 2nd pilot of the crew who were rescued from their dinghy in June after the intervention of a He.111. 6/9/41.

Z6824   77   WHITLEY V
Shot down by a night-fighter at 2315 and crashed in Holland while on an operation to Huls. Four of the crew were killed and one made POW. 6/9/41.

Z6942   10   WHITLEY V
Lost while on an operation to Huls. The crew of five were made POW. 6/9/41.

Z6668   77   WHITLEY V
Crashed in Germany while on an operation to Huls. The crew of five were killed. The 2nd pilot, Sgt D W Mercer, was a US citizen. 7/9/41.

Z6654   77   WHITLEY V
Crash landed on Cromer beach, Norfolk, at 0240 after being damaged by a night-fighter while on an operation to Huls. 7/9/41.

P5109   10   WHITLEY V
Crashed in the North Sea while on an operation to Warnemünde. The crew of five were killed. 11/9/41.

Z6867   10   WHITLEY V
Ran out of fuel on return from an operation to Warnemünde and ditched in the sea just off Flamborough Head. The crew of five were rescued by the destroyer HMS Wolsey, although the rear gunner was injured. 12/9/41.

Z6827   77   WHITLEY V
Ditched near Bridlington at 0350, while returning from a raid on Berlin. The crew of five were rescued within the hour. 21/9/41.

Z6934   77   WHITLEY V
Lost over Berlin while on an operation to that city. The crew of five were killed. 21/9/41.

Z6802   10   WHITLEY V
Damaged by flak while bombing Wismar, the alternative target to Berlin, then ran out of fuel and ditched at 0500 off Withernsea, Yorkshire. The crew of five were rescued by a high speed launch from Grimsby. 21/9/41.

Z9150   77   WHITLEY V
Lost near Kiel while on an operation to Stettin. The crew of five were killed. 30/9/41.

Z9147   77   WHITLEY V
Crashed in a small wood near base after return from an operation to Stettin. One of the crew of five was slightly hurt. 30/9/41.

Z6941   10   WHITLEY V
Became lost while returning from a raid on Stuttgart, and after running out of fuel ditched in the Bristol Channel at 0530. The crew of five were rescued. 2/10/41.

Z6801   77   WHITLEY V
Crashed in Belgium, near Namur, while on an operation to Nuremberg. The crew of five were killed, and were afforded military honours by the Germans at their burial at the Military Cemetery at Dinant. 12/10/41.

Z6950   77   WHITLEY V
Crashed in the sea near Kiel while on an operation to Hamburg. The crew of five were killed. 30/10/41.

Z6953   77   WHITLEY V
Lost without trace while on an operation to Hamburg. The crew of five were listed as missing believed killed. 30/10/41.

Z9166   10   WHITLEY V
Lost without trace while on an operation to Emden. The crew of five were listed as missing believed killed. 30/11/41.

Z9299   77   WHITLEY V
Lost while on an operation to Emden. Four of the crew were killed and the fifth made POW. 30/11/41.

Z9162   10   WHITLEY V
Crashed through the roof of a house on the edge of the airfield after taking avoiding action to prevent a collision with Whitley from 77 Sqn. It followed a return with the bomb load intact from a Nursery operation to Dunkirk. The crew of five sustained minor injuries. 7/12/41.

Z9188   10   WHITLEY V
Crashed near Ripon, Yorkshire, after being caught in a severe down draft while returning from a raid on Cologne. One crew member was killed and four injured. This was the last Whitley lost by 10 Sqn before it converted to the Halifax. 12/12/41.

Z6956   77   WHITLEY V
Lost while on an operation to Düsseldorf. The rear gunner was killed and the other four in the crew were made POW. 27/12/41.

Z9226   77   WHITLEY V
Lost while on an operation to Düsseldorf. The crew of five were killed. 27/12/41.

Z9306   77   WHITLEY V

Shot down by a night-fighter over Holland, while on an operation to Dusseldorf. Four of the crew were killed and one made POW. 27/12/41.

L9614   10   HALIFAX II

Took off on the wrong runway while on a night training exercise and hit another Halifax. Two of the crew were killed. 29/12/41.

V9981   10   HALIFAX II

Collided with L9614 while taking off for an air test. No injuries were sustained by the crew which was captained by Wg Cdr Tuck, the Sqn CO. 29/12/41.

R9374   10   HALIFAX II

Ditched off Cornwall on return from Brest following Operation Veracity II, the second raid in 12 days on the Scharnhorst & Gneisenau. Badly damaged by flak which destroyed the port outer engine, hit by cannon fire from a Me109 which killed the rear gunner and put both inner engines out of action. The Halifax was successfully ditched by its pilot, FS L Whyte, some 80 miles south of Lizard Point. Rescued by an RN MTB five hours later and taken into Falmouth. This was the first successful rescue of a crew from a Halifax following a ditching. FS Whyte was later commissioned, and in August 1942 awarded the DFC. 30/12/41.

L9622   10   HALIFAX II

Crashed at 2330, near Northallerton, on return from an operation to Hamburg. Six of the crew were killed and the pilot very seriously injured. 15/1/42.

Z9229   77   WHITLEY V

Crashed at 0020 near Warwick, while returning to base on one engine from a raid on St-Nazaire. The 2nd pilot parachuted to safety, but the four others in the crew were killed. 16/2/42.

Z9231   77   WHITLEY V

Crashed while attempting an emergency landing at Colerne, Wiltshire, on return from a raid on St-Nazaire. The crew of five were killed. 16/2/42.

L9619   10   HALIFAX II

Abandoned after becoming lost and running out of fuel on return from St Nazaire. Crashed near Keld, Yorks. 16/2/42.

V9986   10   HALIFAX II

FTR from an operation to bomb the battle-cruiser Gneisenau at Kiel. Lost without trace along with its crew of seven. 26/2/42.

Z9280   77   WHITLEY V

Shot down by night-fighter at 2258 over Holland while on an operation to Wilhelmshaven. Four of the crew were killed and one made POW. 27/2/42

Z6943   77   WHITLEY V

Lost without trace with its crew of seven while on an operation to Wilhelmshaven. 27/2/42.

Z9148   77   WHITLEY V

Crashed while on an operation to Wilhelmshaven, killing the crew of five. The pilot, Plt Off M McCarthy RNZAF, was only 19 and had two brothers who also died on active service. 27/2/42.

R9371   10   HALIFAX II

Following brake failure after returning from a training flight and landing on a very wet runway at Lossiemouth, the crew were unhurt when the aircraft overshot, hit a hangar, and was later written off charge. 9/3/42.

Z9293   77   WHITLEY V

Lost without trace with its crew of five while on an operation to Emden. The pilot, Plt Off J Spalding, had been the sole survivor from a crash near Warwick less than a month before. 13/3/42.

Z9312   77   WHITLEY V

Presumed lost in the North Sea with its crew of five while on an operation to Emden. One body was washed ashore near Whitby, Yorkshire. 13/3/42.

Z6975   77   WHITLEY V

Stalled and crashed on return to base at 2325, after a Fresher operation to Boulogne. Four of the crew were killed and the fifth fatally injured. The aircraft hit the roof of Grimescar

House while on approach to the short runway. It was considered that icing of the windscreen had been a factor in the accident. 13/3/42.

Z9221   77   WHITLEY V
Crashed near Ripon, Yorkshire, at 0400 after jettisoning its bomb load into the sea. It followed an aborted mission in support of the major RN/Commando raid on the dock installations at St-Nazaire. The observer was killed and the four others in the crew were injured. 28/3/42.

W1043   10   HALIFAX II
Took off from Lossiemouth and FTR from a raid against the Tirpitz in Aasenfjord, Norway. The crew of seven were killed. 31/3/42.

W1044   10   HALIFAX II
Took off from Lossiemouth and FTR from a raid against the Tirpitz in Aasenfjord, Norway. The crew of seven were killed. 31/3/42.

R9492   10   HALIFAX II
Crashed near Hindhead, Surrey after running out of fuel while returning from a raid on Dortmund. The pilot had attempted an emergency landing after his crew of six had successfully baled out, but the aircraft spun in from 7,000 ft and he was killed. 15/4/42.

W1045   10   HALIFAX II
Ditched off Beer Head, Devon, after running out of fuel while returning from a raid on Dortmund. The crew of seven were rescued from their dinghy. 15/4/42.

Z9363   77   WHITLEY V
Crashed at 0111 near Neumünster while on a raid to Rostock. The crew of four were killed. 24/4/42.

Z9386   77   WHITLEY V
Damaged by flak while on a raid to Rostock, and ditched in the Baltic, near Kiel. This was the Squadron's final loss while operating from Leeming. The crew of four became POW, although one died in captivity two weeks before the war ended in Europe. Three days before their ditching, while returning from Rostock with engine trouble, the same crew

had survived a crash landing near Leeming. 27/4/42.

W1037   10   HALIFAX II
Took off from Lossiemouth but FTR from a raid against the Tirpitz in Aasenfjord. Two of the crew were killed and five made POW. 28/4/42.

W1041   10   HALIFAX II
Took off from Lossiemouth but FTR from a raid against the Tirpitz in Aasenfjord. Four of the crew were made POW, but three, including Wg Cdr D Bennett, OC 10 Sqn, evaded capture and escaped into Sweden. A month later he was back in command of the squadron at Leeming. 28/4/42.

W1054   10   HALIFAX II
Ground looped while landing on the crosswind runway at 1210 after a transit flight from Lossiemouth. The u/c collapsed and the aircraft was later categorised as "E" and written off charge. The "in use" runway had been obstructed by a steamroller, but the air traffic controller ordered the landing rather than wait to have the obstruction removed. 30/4/42.

W7673   10   HALIFAX II
Ground looped while landing after an air test. The u/c collapsed and the aircraft was wrecked, but the crew escaped with slight injuries. This was the second serious accident in 8 days for the pilot, Flt Lt Hacking, and with his ditching of Whitley Z6867 in September 1941 was his third escape from crashes while with 10 Sqn. 8/5/42.

W7674   10   HALIFAX II
FTR from Warnemünde. Its crew of seven were killed. 9/5/42.

W1057   10   HALIFAX II
FTR from Mannheim. Its crew of seven were killed. The aircraft had just been repaired after sustaining damage while on an operation against the Tirpitz on 30/4/42 when with a different crew. Heavy flak damage had caused the flaps to come down, so the return journey had been made at 110 mph. The aircraft just

made it to Sumburgh on the southern tip of the Shetlands. 20/5/42.

W7666   10   HALIFAX II
Undershot while landing from a three engined approach during an air test at Leeming. Four of the crew were slightly injured. 24/5/42.

W1042   10   HALIFAX II
Shot down by a night-fighter and crashed near Eindhoven on an operation to Cologne on the first 1000 bomber raid. Three of the crew were killed and four made POW. 31/5/42.

L9623   10   HALIFAX II
FTR from Essen and ditched off the Dutch coast. Six of the crew were rescued, but the rear gunner's body was not found. 2/6/42.

W1098   10   HALIFAX II
FTR from Essen and crashed at Oeding. The pilot, Plt Off Joyce, came from Argentina, and was killed along with five of his crew. The observer survived and became a POW. 2/6/42.

W1143   10   HALIFAX II
FTR from Essen and crashed near Rotterdam. The aircraft had been borrowed from 78 Sqn for the operation. Six of the crew were killed but the flight engineer survived to become a POW. 2/6/42.

W7696   10   HALIFAX II
FTR from Essen and crashed near Cologne. Three of the crew were killed and four made POW. 6/6/42.

W1158   10   HALIFAX II
The aircraft suffered hydraulic failure after take-off for an operation to Emden. With no flaps and with the u/c stuck down, the aircraft crashed at 2357 and burnt out at Maunby near Leeming, but with no serious injuries to the crew. 19/6/42.

BB201   10   HALIFAX II
FTR from Emden, with its crew of seven listed as missing believed killed. The pilot Plt Off Senior, had recently survived a ditching off the Dutch coast. The flight engineer Flt Lt Jackson was 42 and well over the average age for those on operations. FS Jones, one of the air gunners,

had flown previously with 77 Sqn and had been awarded the DFM in 1941. 21/6/42.

W1155   10   HALIFAX II
Control was lost during an air test and the aircraft crashed on the north side of Leeming airfield. Crossed control cables to the elevator trim tab were found to be partially responsible. Five of the six man crew were killed and one injured. 25/6/42.

W1056   10   HALIFAX II
FTR from Bremen and crashed in the sea off the Dutch coast. The crew of seven were killed. 3/7/42.

W7695   10   HALIFAX II
Crashed in the sea, 20 miles East of Alexandria, during the ferry flight for a detachment to the Middle East. The crew of seven were rescued with two of them injured. 9/7/42.

W1106   10   HALIFAX II
Took off from Topcliffe and FTR from Vegesack. No trace of the aircraft and its crew of seven was found. 19/7/42.

X3963   420   WELLINGTON III
Crashed in Norfolk at 0100 while returning from an operation to Kiel. Four of the crew of five were slightly injured. 14/10/42.

DF636   420   WELLINGTON III
On return from a raid on Kiel, crashed into a house near to the airfield while attempting to overshoot. The crew of five were killed. 14/10/42.

W1052   1659   HALIFAX II
Overshot the runway during take-off on a training flight. The aircraft was written off. 3/12/42.

RAF Leeming handed over to No.6 Group (RCAF) on 1/1/43.

W1150   1659   HALIFAX II
While returning at 300 feet from Catfoss, in E Yorkshire, with only a two man crew, the aircraft suffered a double engine failure and was crash-landed in a ploughed field. The

flight engineer was slightly injured, and the aircraft written off. 13/1/43.

DT678   408   HALIFAX II

While on an operation to Lorient, suffered the failure of both starboard engines. It returned, but crash-landed at Ossington, Notts, with no injuries to the crew. 23/1/43.

W1146   1659   HALIFAX II

Crashed into a hill when in cloud, six miles NW of Thwaite, Yorks, while on a cross country training exercise. Four of the crew were killed and three injured. 28/1/43.

HR662   408   HALIFAX II

FTR from Lorient. The crew of seven were killed. 29/1/43.

BB275   1659   HALIFAX II

Crashed at 1240 near Holyhead, Wales, during a flying exercise. The crew of eight were killed. 1/2/43.

DT682   408   HALIFAX II

After its port outer engine caught fire while on a mining operation, the aircraft crashed on a road near Long Dinnington, Notts, colliding with some trucks in the process. The crew of seven received a variety of injuries. 2/2/43.

DT680   408   HALIFAX II

FTR from Hamburg, where it was shot down by flak. The pilot was killed, five of the crew became POW, but one evaded. 3/2/43.

HR655   408   HALIFAX II

FTR from Lorient, and the crew of seven were killed. 8/2/43.

DT750   408   HALIFAX II

While outbound on an operation to Cologne, crashed at Kirby Wiske, near Thirsk, after the port outer engine caught fire. The crew baled out but one was killed when his parachute failed. 14/2/43.

DT797   408   HALIFAX II

Shot down by a night-fighter while on a raid to Berlin and crashed near Bathmen, Holland, just after midnight. Six of the crew were killed but one air gunner became a POW. 2/3/43.

W1241   1659   HALIFAX II

Stalled in circuit, then crashed and burned at 1410 in SE corner of Leeming airfield. The crew of eight were killed. 10/3/43.

HR656   408   HALIFAX II

Shot down by a Me 110 while on a raid to Stuttgart and crashed at Rozières in France. Three of the crew were made POW but four evaded capture. 11/3/43.

DT790   408   HALIFAX II

Returned early from the Stuttgart raid after being damaged by flak. The port engines cut out over Leeming and the aircraft came down nearby at 0047. The following day it was written off charge as being damaged beyond repair. 13/3/43.

BB332   408   HALIFAX II

Sustained flak damage over Berlin; with the fuel tanks holed and engines damaged, the bombs were jettisoned in the target area. The aircraft crashed at Blidberg, Sweden, after the crew of seven baled out. The crew were interned but in April 1943 returned to England. 28/3/43.

DT679   408   HALIFAX II

FTR from Berlin and crashed south of Leer. The crew of seven were killed. 30/3/43.

HR654   408   HALIFAX II

FTR from Berlin. Shot down by a night-fighter over Flensburg before bombing. Five were killed in the crash, one died later and the navigator was made a POW. 30/3/43.

DT808   405   HALIFAX II

FTR from Essen. Shot down from below by a night-fighter over Holland before reaching the target. Five of the crew were killed and two became POW. 3/4/43.

HR713   408   HALIFAX II

FTR from Essen. The crew of seven were killed. 3/4/43.

JB866   408   HALIFAX II

Shot down by a night-fighter at Opheusden, Holland, while on an operation to Essen. The crew of seven were killed. 3/4/43.

DT723   405   HALIFAX II

Shot down near Rotterdam while returning from a raid on Essen. The bomb aimer was killed and seven crew members were made POW. 4/4/43.

DT673   408   HALIFAX II

On return from an operation to Essen, the u/c failed to lower and the aircraft crash-landed on Leeming airfield. It was later written off as damaged beyond repair. 4/4/43.

JB906   405   HALIFAX II

Struck off charge on 13/4/43 as being damaged beyond repair after being hit on the ground by Halifax JB893 on 4/4/43.

DT704   405   HALIFAX II

FTR from Kiel. The crew of seven were killed when it crashed in the target area. 4/4/43.

BB336   408   HALIFAX II

Set on fire by flak while on a raid to Kiel. The pilot ordered his crew to abandon the aircraft but six were killed when it exploded over the sea. The rear gunner survived to become a POW. 4/4/43.

DT699   405   HALIFAX II

Crashed in the sea when mining off La Rochelle, killing the crew of seven. 6/4/43.

JB914   405   HALIFAX II

Stalled while landing in a cross-wind at Leeming. The u/c was torn off but only one of the crew was injured. 13/4/43.

JB909   408   HALIFAX II

Shot up by a night-fighter over the Rhine on return from Stuttgart and crashed near Reims, France. The pilot was killed in the crash and two of the six made POW were wounded, but the flight engineer evaded capture. The pilot, Plt Off Mackenzie RAAF, was seen to steer the Halifax away from la Neuvillette. After the war the inhabitants of the village erected a memorial to the gallant Australian. 15/4/43.

BB311   408   HALIFAX II

Shot down by a night-fighter while returning from Stuttgart and crashed near St-Quentin, France. The wireless operator was killed but the six others in the crew became POW. 15/4/43.

JB854   408   HALIFAX II

Crashed near Bar-le-Duc in France while on raid to Pilsen. The crew of seven were killed. 16/4/43.

BB343   408   HALIFAX II

FTR from Pilsen and crashed near Laon, France. The crew of seven were killed. 16/4/43.

JB925   408   HALIFAX II

FTR from Pilsen. Crashed near Bierfeld and the crew of eight were killed. 16/4/43.

DT752   408   HALIFAX II

Shot down by a night-fighter at 0408 near Nassogne, Belgium, after an operation to Pilsen. The crew of seven were killed. 17/4/43.

HR658   408   HALIFAX II

FTR from Dortmund. The crew of seven were killed, becoming the first all Canadian crew lost from the Squadron. 5/5/43.

JB898   408   HALIFAX II

FTR from Dortmund. Hit by a night-fighter firing from below. Set on fire and crashed at Leeuwarden in Holland. Three of the crew were killed in the crash, five baled out and were made POW. 5/5/43.

JB931   408   HALIFAX II

Shot down by a Me 210 near Flushing on the way to target at Bochum. One air gunner was killed in the attack, the pilot, flight engineer and the other air gunner drowned, with the four survivors becoming POW. 13/5/43.

JB841   408   HALIFAX II

Shot down close to the target while on a raid to Dortmund. The crew of seven were killed. 24/5/43.

DT674   408   HALIFAX II

FTR from Essen. Hit by a night-fighter which killed both air gunners and started a fire. Five crew members baled out and were made POW. 28/5/43.

JB972   408   HALIFAX II

Hit by flak over Ruhr on a raid to Düsseldorf, crashing near Krefeld. Both air gunners were killed when the aircraft was hit and the pilot was unable to get clear after the survivors of his crew had baled out. The four became POW. 12/6/43.

JB790   408   HALIFAX II
On fire after a night-fighter attack during a raid on Bochum, all seven in the crew baled out. Five were made POW but the Germans reported that the other two were found dead. The pilot, Fg Off Large, was killed on 16/4/45 when he was in a column of prisoners that was fired on by Allied aircraft. 13/6/43.

DK183   427   HALIFAX V
Hit by shells from a night-fighter while on a raid to Bochum. While attempting to ditch, the aircraft crashed near Texel and four of the crew were killed. There were three survivors who became POW. 13/6/43.

DK140   427   HALIFAX V
Ground looped on landing after avoiding a party of airmen. The u/c collapsed but no injuries were reported. 16/6/43.

JD107   408   HALIFAX II
FTR from Le Creusot. Hit first by a night-fighter near Caen, then by flak. Four of the crew were killed, and two of the three made POW were wounded. 20/6/43.

JD209   408   HALIFAX II
Shot down in area of target while on a raid to Krefeld. Four of the crew were killed and three made POW. 22/6/43.

BB375   408   HALIFAX II
FTR from Krefeld. An attack from a night-fighter killed the rear gunner, but after two of the crew had baled out to be made POW, the aircraft exploded before crashing into the River Lop, killing the four who remained. One of the survivors, Sgt Pridham RCAF, who lost a leg when a cannon shell had exploded, was repatriated 11 months later. 22/6/43.

DT772   408   HALIFAX II
Shot down near Zeist in Holland while on a raid to Krefeld. The crew of seven were killed. The pilot, a Frenchman from Marseilles, had the

Germanic surname of Blum and flew under a *Nom-de-Guerre* as Sgt Brooke. 22/6/43.

DK139   427   HALIFAX V
Crashed near Rheinhausen, on the west bank of the Rhine while on a raid to Mulheim. The crew of seven were killed. The pilot, Plt Off Cadmus, was from Argentina, and with this in mind had named his aircraft *Pampers*. 23/6/43.

DK191   427   HALIFAX V
FTR from Mulheim. Crashed at Wichmond, Holland, killing the crew of seven. 23/6/43.

DK225   427   HALIFAX V
Shot down by a night-fighter while on a raid to Mulheim, and crashed west of Mijzen, Holland. Six of the crew were killed but the navigator survived to become a POW. 23/6/43.

DK141   427   HALIFAX V
Shot down by a night-fighter while on a raid to Mulheim, and crashed near Berlicum, Holland. Six of the crew were killed. The flight engineer became a POW. 23/6/43.

DK135   427   HALIFAX V
Shot down by a night-fighter and crashed on the Rozenburg polder, near Rotterdam, while on an operation to Wuppertal. Five of the crew were killed and two became POW. 24/6/43

DK180   427   HALIFAX V
FTR from Wuppertal. After maintaining control to allow his crew to escape the pilot was killed in the subsequent crash. Unfortunately the flight engineer and the navigator baled out too late and were killed. Four of the crew did survive and were made POW. 24/6/43.

DK144   427   HALIFAX V
Ground looped on take-off at 2345 for an operation to Gelsenkirchen. The u/c collapsed but no injuries were reported among the crew, captained by Wg Cdr Burnside, OC 427 Sqn. 25/6/43.

JB858   408   HALIFAX II
Shot down by a night-fighter while on a raid to Gelsenkirchen, and crashed near Coesfeld, Germany. Seven members of the crew were

killed, with the flight engineer becoming a POW. 26/6/43.

DK190   427   Halifax V

Shot down by a night-fighter while on a raid to Gelsenkirchen and crashed on the east bank of the Ijssel, near Gorssel in Holland. The seven members of the crew were killed. 26/6/43.

427 Halifax V

FTR from Gelsenkirchen. Shot down by a night-fighter near Altmaar. The crew baled out but the pilot drowned after landing in a canal. His crew of six were made POW. (The loss card in the AHB indicates that this aircraft was DK135 but other evidence shows that aircraft as being lost while on the raid to Wuppertal, on the previous night.) 26/6/43.

DK183   427   Halifax V

Raked by cannon fire from a night-fighter while on an operation to Cologne. Crashed at Igleham, Suffolk, after turning back. The crew of seven baled out successfully. 28/6/43.

EB148   427   Halifax V

Attacked by a night-fighter near Bruges while outbound for an operation to Cologne. The bombs were jettisoned and the badly damaged aircraft managed to reach E Anglia where it came down west of Mildenhall in Suffolk. Two of the crew of seven were injured. 29/6/43.

JB796   408   Halifax II

Shot down over France while on a raid to Cologne. Six of the crew were killed and the mid-upper air gunner was made a POW. 4/7/43.

JB913   408   Halifax II

Shot down by a night-fighter while on a raid to Cologne and crashed near Hasselt in Belgium. Five of crew became POW, but two more evaded. 4/7/43.

JB959   408   Halifax II

Take-off for an operation to Gelsenkirchen was abandoned after an air speed indicator fault occurred, closely followed by the collapse of the u/c and crash of the aircraft. 9/7/43.

JB922   408   Halifax II

Shot down near Bochum while on raid to Gelsenkirchen. The pilot ordered the crew to abandon the aircraft, but he died in the crash along with two of his crew. The four who escaped became POW, but one died in April 1945 while still a prisoner. 10/7/43.

JD216   408   Halifax II

FTR from Gelsenkirchen. The crew of eight were killed. 10/7/43.

DK142   427   Halifax V

FTR from Aachen. The crew of seven became POW. 14/7/43.

DT769   408   Halifax II

Hit by gunfire from a night-fighter near Tilburg while on a raid to Aachen. The aircraft was set ablaze and the pilot, flight engineer, and wireless operator were killed in the attack. Both of the air gunners were then killed after baling out too low, but the navigator and the bomb aimer survived and were made POW. 14/7/43.

JD174   408   Halifax II

Hit by a night-fighter while on a raid to Aachen. The aircraft was abandoned successfully 12 miles from Leeming, and then, with its bomb-load still intact, crashed into a hillside and exploded. The pilot was injured. 14/7/43.

DT749   408   Halifax II

FTR from Hamburg. Shot down by a night-fighter, crashing near Neumunster. Five of the crew were killed in the crash but the remaining three baled out to become POW. 28/7/43.

DK242   427   Halifax V

Ground looped on landing at Leeming from a training flight, collapsing the u/c. No injuries were reported. 29/7/43.

DK189   427   Halifax V

Categorised "E" and written off following battle damage. 29/7/43.

EB242   427   Halifax V

Shot down near the target of Remscheid. The pilot was unable to follow his crew in baling out and was killed in the crash. His crew of six became POW. 31/7/43.

JD365   408   HALIFAX II
FTR from Remscheid and crashed at Duren. Five in the crew were killed and two became POW. 31/7/43.

EB247   427   HALIFAX V
Attacked by a night-fighter over Mannheim, and after getting their severely damaged aircraft back to England, the eight man crew abandoned it successfully over Hartford Bridge, Hampshire. Three of the crew received immediate awards of the DFM for their efforts that day. 10/8/43.

DK243   427   HALIFAX V
FTR from the Peenemünde V Weapons site and crashed at Wusterhusen. Five of the crew were killed and two became POW. 18/8/43.

DK227   427   HALIFAX V
Attacked and shot-up by a Me109 while returning from the raid on Peenemünde. The rear gunner shot the enemy aircraft down and the badly damaged bomber got back to England where it had to crash-land at Mildenhall, Suffolk. It was struck off charge the following day. The raid was the final one in the crew's tour of operations, making them the first crew in the Squadron to achieve this goal. The pilot, navigator and rear gunner were subsequently decorated. 18/8/43.

DK184   427   HALIFAX V
Shot down near Germandorf while on a raid to Berlin. Six of the crew were killed but the flight engineer survived and became a POW. 24/8/43.

EB243   427   HALIFAX V
Shot down near Gortle-Gernay on a raid to Berlin. The crew of seven were killed. Included among them was the flight engineer, Sgt Norreys RAF who was only 18. 24/8/43.

DF471   427   OXFORD
Crashed in bad weather and burnt out, NE of Kirkby Lonsdale while ferrying groundcrew to repair a Halifax. The pilot and the three passengers were killed. 29/8/43.

LK629   427   HALIFAX V
Shot down near Antwerp while on a raid to Moenchen Gladbach. Its crew of seven were killed. 31/8/43.

EB251   427   HALIFAX V
Shot down by a night-fighter while on raid to Berlin. The aircraft was carrying a second pilot that night, but the remainder of the crew were on their thirtieth operation. Six were killed and two made POW. 31/9/43.

LK636   427   HALIFAX V
FTR from Mannheim. The crew of seven were killed. 5/9/43.

LK628   427   HALIFAX V
Shot down by a night-fighter near their target of Munich. An experienced crew, with three previously awarded the DFM, five were killed and three became POW. 7/9/43.

DK255   427   HALIFAX V
FTR from Munich, and crashed near Chartres, France. Six of the crew of seven, who were all killed, were from the RAF. 7/9/43.

DK253   427   HALIFAX V
Crashed at Harmondsworth, Middlesex after an operation to Montluçon. The crew of seven were killed. 15/9/43.

LK920   427   HALIFAX V
FTR from Frankfurt, and crashed at Haut-Fays, Luxembourg. The navigator, a USAAF officer was one of the crew of seven killed. 4/10/43.

JD327   429   HALIFAX II
Crashed and burnt out at Heathfield Park, Sussex, after an operation to Frankfurt, where it had been badly hit by a night-fighter. Six of the crew baled out but two others died in the crash. Seven were from the RAF. 5/10/43.

JD323   429   HALIFAX II
FTR from Hannover, and crashed near Blomberg. Its crew of seven were killed. 9/10/43.

LK900   427   HALIFAX V
FTR from Hannover. The crew of seven were killed. 9/10/43.

DK182   427   HALIFAX V
Crashed at Newton Kyme, Yorks at 2115 after

turning back from an operation to Kassel. The crew of seven, all from the RAF, were killed. 22/10/43.

LK959   427   HALIFAX V
FTR from Kassel, and crashed SE of Rosendaal, Holland. Its crew of eight were killed. 22/10/43.

JD363   429   HALIFAX II
FTR from Kassel. The crew of seven were killed when it crashed near Antwerp. 22/10/43.

JD332   429   HALIFAX II
FTR from Kassel. Four of the crew were killed and three became POW. 22/10/43.

DK234   427   HALIFAX V
FTR from Kassel and crashed near Düsseldorf.The crew of seven were killed. 22/10/43.

LK633   427   HALIFAX V
FTR from Kassel and crashed SW of Lügde. Three of the crew were killed in the crash, but four baled out and were made POW. 22/10/43.

JD326   429   HALIFAX II
FTR from Düsseldorf. The crew of seven were killed. 4/11/43.

JD275   429   HALIFAX II
Shot down while on an operation to Mannheim. Two of the crew were killed in the crash and five became POW. Two days later the rear gunner died from his wounds. 18/11/43.

LK976   427   HALIFAX V
FTR from Mannheim. The body of the navigator was washed up on the French coast and it is believed that the aircraft came down in the Channel. The crew of seven were killed. 19/11/43.

JD325   429   HALIFAX II
Crashed in flames near Sedan in France while on an operation to Frankfurt. The crew of seven were killed. 26/11/43.

JD411   429   HALIFAX II
FTR from Frankfurt and crashed near Prüm. The crew of seven were killed. 26/11/43.

LK995   429   HALIFAX V
Hit by a night-fighter S of Namur, Belgium while on a raid to Frankfurt. The rear gunner was killed in the attack, the incendiaries set alight in the bomb bay and the aircraft abandoned. Five of the six who baled out were made POW, but the navigator evaded capture after parachuting to safety. 26/11/43.

JD333   429   HALIFAX II
Crash landed at Burneston, the decoy site for Leeming, after both port engines failed on take-off for an operation to Stuttgart. 26/11/43.

JD164   429   HALIFAX II
Hit by flak before reaching Stuttgart and with a damaged engine made it back to the English coast where a successful ditching was made just off Thorney Island, Sussex. 26/11/43.

DK181   427   HALIFAX V
Turned back from an operation to Leipzig after the starboard inner engine caught fire, followed by the port outer failing when back over England. The crew were ordered to abandon the stricken aircraft, but the pilot, Plt Off Cozens, was then able to bring it in for a crash landing at Woodbridge, Suffolk, even though he was only on one engine. The only injury was sustained by the rear gunner who broke his ankle when he hit the ground. 4/12/43.

JD361   429   HALIFAX II
FTR from Leipzig and crashed SW of Stendal. Six from the crew were killed and two became POW. One of those who lost his life was Sgt G Hooper RCAF who was only 18. 4/12/43.

JD374   429   HALIFAX II
FTR from Leipzig. Four of the crew were killed and three became POW. 4/12/43.

LK644   427   HALIFAX V
FTR from Frankfurt. Its crew of seven were killed. 20/12/43.

LK627   427   HALIFAX V
FTR from Frankfurt. The crew of seven became POW. 21/12/43.

JD318   429   HALIFAX II
Shot down from below by a night-fighter while on a raid to Berlin. Crashed near Almelo in Holland at 2145. Five of the crew were killed

and two made POW, one of whom evaded until April 1944. 29/12/43.

LK734   429   HALIFAX V

Tasked for a Bullseye exercise, force-landed on the edge of Leeming airfield following an engine fire after take-off, and failure of the u/c to retract. The aircraft was burnt out, but the crew were unhurt. 2/1/44.

LL191   427   HALIFAX V

Crashed and burned near N Walsham, Norfolk, after hitting telephone wires, a house and trees at 2345, when making its third approach to Coltishall on return from a raid on Berlin. Four of the crew were killed and three injured. 20/1/44.

EB246   427   HALIFAX V

FTR from Berlin. The crew of seven were killed. 21/1/44.

LL197   429   HALIFAX V

FTR from Berlin. Six of the crew were killed and one made POW. 21/1/44.

LL139   427   HALIFAX V

Attacked by a night-fighter after bombing Magdeburg. The rear gunner was killed in the attack and the aircraft exploded before anyone could bale out. The bomb aimer was thrown clear and became a POW, but seven others were killed. 22/1/44.

LL169   427   HALIFAX V

Attacked by a night-fighter over Magdeburg before bombing the target. The aircraft was abandoned in flames and its crew of seven became POW. 22/1/44.

LL176   427   HALIFAX V

FTR from Magdeburg. Six of the crew were killed and one made POW. 22/1/44.

LK923   427   HALIFAX V

Attacked and damaged by a night-fighter en route to Magdeburg. The captain chose to continue and bombed the target but the aircraft ran out of fuel on its return journey. Three of the crew, including the pilot, failed to bale out and were killed, with four becoming POW. 22/1/44.

LK697   429   HALIFAX V

FTR from Berlin. The crew of seven were killed. 29/1/44.

LK746   429   HALIFAX V

Shot down before bombing Berlin by a Ju88 night-fighter armed with *Schräge-Musik*. Five of the crew were killed and two made POW after the crash. 29/1/44.

LL196   429   HALIFAX V

Ground looped on take-off and the u/c collapsed. 1/2/44.

LV828   427   HALIFAX III

Crashed and burnt near Grafton Underwood, Northants, after engine failure. The Sqn had just received the new Mk IIIs and this was one of the first training flights with them. The pilot, a US citizen in the RCAF, was killed and two of the crew were injured. 1/2/44.

LK758   427   HALIFAX III

Crashed during an uncontrollable turn near Leeming, killing its crew of six. 7/2/44.

LK974   429   HALIFAX V

FTR from a raid on the Heinkel works in Leipzeg. Six of the crew were killed and one made POW. 20/2/44.

LK662   429   HALIFAX V

FTR from a raid on the Heinkel works in Leipzig. Three of the crew were killed and four became POW. 20/2/44.

LK993   429   HALIFAX V

FTR from a raid on the Heinkel works in Leipzig. The crew of eight were killed. 20/2/44.

LV829   427   HALIFAX III

FTR from a raid on the Heinkel works in Leipzig. The crew of eight were killed. 20/2/44.

LK836   427   HALIFAX III

The pilot lost control a few minutes after take-off for an operation to Stuttgart. The aircraft was seen to dive straight into a field 1 mile NW of Northallerton, killing the crew of seven. 21/2/44.

LK759   427   HALIFAX III

FTR from Augsburg. Six of the crew were

killed, one was wounded and became a POW. 26/2/44

LW685   429   HALIFAX III
Ditched in the sea off Aberdeenshire after the port outer engine caught fire during a cross-country exercise. The crew of seven were rescued. 10/3/44.

LW558   427   HALIFAX III
FTR from Stuttgart. Six of the crew were killed and one became a POW. 16/3/44.

LW559   427   HALIFAX III
Attacked by a night-fighter while on approach to Stuttgart, and one engine was put out of action. An attack from a second enemy aircraft damaged two more engines and set the aircraft on fire. The bombs were jettisoned and the seven man crew baled out to become POW. 16/3/44.

LW690   429   HALIFAX III
Shot down and crashed in France while on a raid to Stuttgart. Three of the crew were killed, one became a POW and three evaded. 16/3/44.

LW551   427   HALIFAX III
Shot down by a night-fighter over Frankfurt. The pilot was killed in the crash but his crew of six baled out and were made POW. Following major surgery, one man died in captivity on 11 May 1945 on the morning of his supposed repatriation. 19/3/44.

HX279   427   HALIFAX III
FTR from Frankfurt. Five of the crew were killed and two became POW. 19/3/44.

LW574   427   HALIFAX III
Shot down by flak over Althaus on raid to Berlin. Five of the crew were killed and two became POW. 25/3/44.

LW577   427   HALIFAX III
FTR from Berlin. Five of the crew were killed and two became POW. 25/3/44.

LK752   427   HALIFAX III
FTR from Berlin. Four of the crew were killed andthree made POW. 25/3/44.

LW688   429   HALIFAX III
Shot down near Kiel after a raid to Berlin. Five

of the crew were killed and two made POW. 25/3/44.

LK805   429   HALIFAX III
FTR from Berlin. Four of the crew were killed and three made POW. 25/3/44.

LV914   429   HALIFAX III
FTR from Berlin. The crew included a Flight Commander (the navigator and Captain of the aircraft), the Signal Leader and the Flight Engineer Leader. Fg Off Conroy, the pilot, who was killed, had, following a previous raid, parachuted to safety, evaded capture and returned to the UK. The six who survived were made POW. 25/3/44.

LV898   427   HALIFAX III
Shot down by a night-fighter at Herhahn, S of Aachen, on an operation to Nuremberg. The crew of eight were killed, seven of whom were on their second tour of operations. 31/3/44.

LW618   427   HALIFAX III
Crashed at Hohenroth after being attacked by a night-fighter after an operation to Nuremberg. The crew of seven were killed on what was their first operation. 31/3/44.

LK800   429   HALIFAX III
Shot down by a night-fighter near Luxembourg after an operation to Nuremberg. Five of the crew were made POW, but two evaded. 31/3/44.

LV923   427   HALIFAX III
Collided with Lancaster ND767 of 622 Sqn while over Nuremberg and crashed at Rathecourt, nine miles SW of Arlon. Six of the crew were killed, one died as a POW and one evaded. 31/3/44.

LK804   429   HALIFAX III
Ditched in the Channel after an operation to Nuremberg where it sustained damage from a night-fighter attack which caused it to run out of fuel. The pilot was killed, but his crew of six were rescued from their dinghy. 31/3/44.

LV960   427   HALIFAX III
Abandoned in the climb after take-off from Leeming following a collision with Halifax LW437 from 424 Sqn, Skipton-on-Swale, while

on an operation to Villeneuve-St-Georges. Crashed and burnt one mile from Goole. Three of the crew were slightly injured, but the other four were unhurt. 9/4/44.

LV883   427   HALIFAX III
Hit by flak over the French coast on return from a raid on Ghent, then abandoned successfully near Ipswich. 11/4/44.

LV789   427   HALIFAX III
FTR from a raid on the railway marshalling yards at Noisy-le-Sec. It crashed in the target area and the crew of seven were killed. 18/4/44.

LK802   429   HALIFAX III
FTR from Düsseldorf. Three of the crew were killed and four became POW. 23/4/44.

LV963   429   HALIFAX III
Shot down by a night-fighter after bombing Düsseldorf. The aircraft was abandoned in flames and crashed in a flooded area killing five of the crew. Three others survived to become POW, but one was shot while trying to escape from Stalag III on 13/4/45 and died within hours. 23/4/44.

LV973   429   HALIFAX III
Written off as damaged beyond service capability for repair after it returned with severe cannon shell damage sustained on the aforementioned raid on Düsseldorf. 24/4/44.

LV960   427   HALIFAX III
Abandoned after losing control E of Saarbrücken on a raid to Karlsruhe when icing jammed the controls. Two of the crew failed to escape from the aircraft and were killed, five became POW. 24/4/44.

LW415   429   HALIFAX III
Shot down on a raid on St Ghislain railway marshalling yards. The aircraft exploded and the pilot was blown clear to become a POW, his crew of six were killed. 1/5/44.

LV986   427   HALIFAX III
Assessed as damaged beyond repair after landing at Woodbridge following an attack from a night-fighter over Ghent. 11/5/44.

LW114   427   HALIFAX III
FTR from a raid on Boulogne railway marshalling yards. The navigator was a USAAF officer and was one of the crew of seven who were killed. 11/5/44.

LV989   429   HALIFAX III
Stalled and spun into the ground near Snape, Yorks, after take-off for an operation to Le Mans. The Crash Tender was at the scene when an explosion injured five of the crash-crew, so the fires were left to burn out. The crew of six in the bomber were killed in the crash. 22/5/44.

HX352   429   HALIFAX III
FTR from Aachen. Six of the crew were killed and one was made POW. 25/5/44.

LW137   429   HALIFAX III
Shot down by a night-fighter on a raid to Aachen. Four of the crew were killed and three became POW. 25/5/44.

LW124   429   HALIFAX III
Hit by flak on a raid to Aachen. Four of the crew were killed and three became POW. 25/5/44.

LW365   427   HALIFAX III
Attacked by a night-fighter on a raid to Bourg Leopold military camp, Belgium. The bomber exploded, and the crew of seven were killed. 28/5/44.

LV831   427   HALIFAX III
FTR from Bourg Leopold military camp, Belgium, after a collision with Halifax MZ295, SE of Brussels. The crew of seven were killed. 28/5/44.

MZ295   429   HALIFAX III
FTR from Bourg Leopold military camp, Belgium, after collision with Halifax LV831, SE of Brussels. The crew of seven were killed. 28/5/44.

LV987   427   HALIFAX III
FTR from Achères railway marshalling yards. Two of the crew became POW, but five evaded. 7/6/44.

LW128   429   HALIFAX III
Hit by flak on operation to Achères, the pilot was fatally wounded and three of the crew

baled out under his orders. The aircraft was flown back to the UK by the flight engineer, but the pilot did not survive when it was abandoned. The flight engineer received the CGM and the air gunners the DFM for their courage in attempting to save their pilot. 7/6/44.

LV973   429   HALIFAX III
FTR from Versailles, and crashed near Chartres. One of the crew was killed, three became POW and three evaded. 10/6/44.

LV995   427   HALIFAX III
FTR from Arras. Four of the crew were killed, two became POW and one evaded. 12/6/44.

LW135   427   HALIFAX III
FTR from Arras. Five of the crew were killed, one became a POW and one evaded. 12/6/44.

LW165   427   HALIFAX III
Shot down by a night-fighter on a raid to Arras. Crashed and burst into flames on impact killing the crew of seven. 12/6/44.

LV938   427   HALIFAX III
Hit by flak over Evancourt on a raid to the railway marshalling yards at Metz. The aircraft caught fire and was abandoned. Six of crew became POW, but one evaded. 28/6/44.

MZ302   429   HALIFAX III
FTR from Metz railway marshalling yards. Three of the crew became POW and four evaded. 28/6/44.

LW166   427   HALIFAX III
FTR from an operation to Villeneuve-St-Georges. Its crew of seven were killed. 4/7/44.

LV913   429   HALIFAX III
Both outer engines cut on take-off for a test flight, causing the aircraft to swing. The pilot, who was the new OC 429 Sqn, raised the u/c to try to prevent a collision with three other aircraft. He was one of the two crewmen who were injured when the aircraft subsequently crashed and burned. 13/7/44.

LV985   427   HALIFAX III
FTR from Mondeville, near Caen on an operation in support of ground troops. The crew of seven were killed. 18/7/44.

LW127   429   HALIFAX III
Struck by bombs from another Halifax while attacking Mondeville, lost its starboard tailplane and crashed. The crew baled out into the target area, where three were killed, and four became POW. 8/7/44.

MZ316   427   HALIFAX III
Hit by flak on return from an operation to Stuttgart and abandoned over Normandy. Two of the crew were killed, but five evaded. 25/7/44.

MZ362   429   HALIFAX III
FTR from Stuttgart. The crew of seven were killed. 25/7/44.

MZ757   427   HALIFAX III
FTR from Hamburg. The crew of seven were killed. 29/7/44.

LV950   429   HALIFAX III
FTR from Coquereaux. The crew of seven were killed. 31/7/44.

LW132   429   HALIFAX III
While returning from a raid on an oil storage depot at Chantilly the starboard outer engine caught fire at 12,000 ft. The aircraft spun towards the sea before exploding some 10 miles off Littlehampton, Sussex. The navigator survived after being blown clear with his parachute, but his six comrades were killed. 8/8/44.

MZ363   427   HALIFAX III
FTR from La Neuville and crashed in the sea near the French coast, killing the crew of seven. 9/8/44.

MZ825   429   HALIFAX III
FTR from Brunswick. The crew of seven were killed. 13/8/44.

LV821   427   HALIFAX III
FTR from Brunswick. The crew of seven were killed. 13/8/44.

MZ864   429   HALIFAX III
Hit by flak while mining off Oslo and ditched in the sea. The crew of seven were rescued. 12/9/44.

MZ900   429   HALIFAX III
Hit by flak while on an operation to Boulogne

and abandoned over the Channel. The crew of seven was rescued by a Walrus aircraft, then transferred to an ASR launch, and returned to England. 17/9/44.

LW136   429   HALIFAX III
Hit by flak over Calais, and crashed SW of Quer Camp, killing the crew of seven. 25/9/44.

MZ756   427   HALIFAX III
FTR from minelaying off Oslo. Leeming launched 22 aircraft to search for the crew of this aircraft, but no trace of them was found. The crew of seven was a very experienced one, with all of them having completed at least 23 operations. 5/10/44.

LV965   429   HALIFAX III
While landing at USAAF Old Buckenham in Norfolk, after a raid on Bochum. A fire in the port outer engine caused the aircraft to ground loop on landing and the u/c to collapse. 9/10/44.

MZ453   429   HALIFAX III
Hit by flak over Duisburg and abandoned successfully near Brussels, which by then was in Allied hands. 14/10/44.

MZ906   429   HALIFAX III
FTR from Essen, and the crew of seven were killed. 23/10/44.

MZ866   427   HALIFAX III
Burnt out after incendiary bombs dropped out during refuelling at Leeming. 28/10/44.

MZ903   427   HALIFAX III
Ground looped while landing at Leeming in a cross wind after an operation to Cologne. The u/c collapsed and the aircraft written off. 30/10/44.

NP954   429   HALIFAX III
Landed at Spilsby, Lincs, after an operation to Cologne. Was damaged beyond repair when hit by Lancaster PD290 of 518 Sqn which had swung on take-off before exploding. 1/11/44.

MZ424   429   HALIFAX III
Landed at Spilsby after an operation to Cologne. Was wrecked by Lancaster PD290 when it caught fire and exploded. 1/11/44.

MZ824   429   HALIFAX III
Landed at Spilsby after an operation to Cologne. Was damaged beyond repair when Lancaster PD290 exploded. 1/11/44.

MZ880   429   HALIFAX III
Landed at Spilsby after an operation to Cologne. Was damaged when Lancaster PD290 exploded, but was later re-categorised as being damaged beyond repair. 1/11/44.

NR203   429   HALIFAX III
Abandoned and crashed at Myton-on-Swale, after the starboard outer engine failed. 21/11/44.

MZ377   429   HALIFAX III
FTR from Castrop Rauxel. Five of the crew were killed and two became POW. 21/11/44.

MZ304   427   HALIFAX III
Crashed at Dallachy, Scotland while returning from a mining operation off Denmark. The crew of seven were killed. 25/11/44.

MZ867   427   HALIFAX III
Ground looped into a mound of earth following a three engined landing at Leeming. The u/c snapped off and the aircraft was later written off. 27/11/44.

LV945   427   HALIFAX III
Swung and hit a tree after being bogged down in the mud at Leeming. 28/11/44.

MZ288   427   HALIFAX III
FTR from Duisberg. The crew of seven were killed. 30/11/44.

MZ314   429   HALIFAX III
FTR from Duisburg. Crashed in Holland following a probable collision with Halifax NR193 of 578 Sqn. The crew of seven were killed. 30/11/44.

MZ463   429   HALIFAX III
FTR from Osnabrück. The crew of eight were killed. 6/12/44.

MZ291   427   HALIFAX III
After a tyre burst on take-off for a raid on Opladen, the aircraft ground looped, caught fire and was destroyed. 27/12/44.

NR197   429   HALIFAX III
Hit by flak and crashed while mining in Sandefjord. The crew of seven were killed. 28/12/44.

MZ493   429   HALIFAX III
After an operation to Cologne, overran on landing at Tholthorpe and the u/c collapsed. 30/12/44.

LV964   429   HALIFAX III
FTR from Hannover, and crashed near Wachendorf, killing the crew of seven. 6/1/45.

NR257   427   HALIFAX III
FTR from Hannover. Four of the crew were killed and three became POW. 6/1/45.

NR173   429   HALIFAX III
FTR from mining off Flensburg. The crew of seven baled out and were made POW. 12/1/45.

MZ427   429   HALIFAX III
FTR from Magdeburg. The crew of seven became POW. 17/1/45.

MZ355   427   HALIFAX III
FTR from mining in the Kadet Channel. Two of the crew were killed but five were rescued. 15/2/45.

MZ865   429   HALIFAX III
FTR from mining in the Kadet Channel. Crashed NW of Falsterbo, Sweden, killing the crew of seven. 15/2/45.

MZ422   427   HALIFAX III
FTR from Chemnitz. Four of the crew were killed and three made POW. 15/2/45.

NP942   429   HALIFAX III
FTR from Mannheim. Two of the crew were killed and five made POW. 21/2/45.

NR288   427   HALIFAX III
FTR from Worms. Six of the crew were killed but the seventh survived and evaded capture. 22/2/45.

LW139   429   HALIFAX III
While carrying out a three engined overshoot after an engine had failed on take-off for Essen, the aircraft spun, stalled and crashed at Londonderry, on the edge of the airfield. Four

of the crew were killed and three injured. 23/2/45.

MZ452   429   HALIFAX III
FTR from mining near Oslo. The crew of seven were killed. 25/2/45.

RG347   427   HALIFAX III
After a tyre burst on take-off from Leeming for an operation to Mainz, the aircraft crashed on one wing and exploded. Six of the crew were killed and the tail gunner injured. 27/2/45.

LV996   429   HALIFAX III
Crashed into high ground at 0212 near Upper Hulling, Kent, while returning from an operation to Chemnitz that had lasted for almost nine hours. The crew of seven were killed. 6/3/45.

NG345   429   LANCASTER I
Attacked and shot down by jet fighters on a raid to Hamburg. Five of the crew were killed but two evaded capture. 31/3/45.

RA571   429   LANCASTER I
Crashed into a hill while in cloud N of Ilkley. Four in the crew were killed and four injured. 5/11/45.

RF257   427   LANCASTER III
Crashed on overshoot at Leeming. 10/1/46.

RF259   429   LANCASTER III
Crashed on take-off from Leeming. 14/2/46.

54 OTU

NY266   MOSQUITO MkXXX
Lost control while in cloud, with ice accretion a possible contributory factor. Crashed five miles from Helmsley, N Yorks killing the crew of two. 8/11/46.

MM809   MOSQUITO MkXXX
Seen to dive steeply out of cloud, struck the ground and blew up near Thirsk, N Yorks. The crew of two were killed. 9/11/46.

228 OCU

RS647   MOSQUITO MkVI
Abandoned after complete electrical failure,

but the jettisoning of the cockpit door caused the aircraft to dive steeply and crash in Nottinghamshire. Both crew members baled out but the pilot left it too late and was killed. 27/1/48.

RS654   MOSQUITO MKVI
Forced landing in a field near Leeming after the port engine overspeeded. The aircraft was later categorised as a "Write-off". 25/2/48.

RH803   BRIGAND B.I.
Aircraft yawed and stalled after full-flap was selected in error after the port engine had been feathered for a practice single engined approach. 14/10/48.

RL197   MOSQUITO NF36
While flying under full power on a night cross-country exercise, the aircraft impacted into high ground near Grassington, Yorks. The crew of two were killed. 13/12/48.

RL265   MOSQUITO NF36
Carried out a wheels-up landing after engine failure and was later written off. 21/1/49.

RL247   MOSQUITO NF36
Force landed in a field after the port engine failed at 200 feet during approach to Leeming. The pilot had failed to transfer from the outer to the inner fuel tanks and the engine was starved of fuel. 15/3/49.

RL260   MOSQUITO NF36
The crew baled out successfully near Catterick, N Yorks following a suspect fire in the rear fuselage. 4/1/50.

RS528   MOSQUITO MKVI
Spun off steep turn, failed to pull out and crashed in the range in Druridge Bay, Northumberland. The crew of two were killed. 20/4/50.

RK993   MOSQUITO NF36
The starboard engine cut during take-off, the aircraft ground looped, struck the ground and broke up in flames. The crew of two were injured. 15/6/50.

HJ983   MOSQUITO T3
While landing at Acklington the pilot lowered the flaps too soon and lost control. The u/c was then retracted to prevent a collision with the ATC building and the aircraft was wrecked. 31/7/50.

RL156   MOSQUITO NF36
Ran off the runway after the port engine cut out during take-off and finished up in an adjacent field with its u/c collapsed. 25/1/51.

RP414   WELLINGTON T.XVIII
Crashed near Carthorpe after the spinner came off the airscrew during take-off. It struck the canopy, shattering the perspex and slightly injuring the pilot. He was attended to at the crash site by a doctor who took time off from a local hunt in order to assist! 26/2/51.

ND109   WELLINGTON T.XVIII
Categorised as unrepairable after a fire in a hangar. 26/4/51.

RK984   MOSQUITO NF36
While carrying out an asymmetric landing ran across the main road and collided with a lorry. The student pilot sustained a broken ankle. 3/5/51.

WA604   METEOR T7
Crashed near Leeming. The pupil was killed and the Sqn Cdr, who was injured, died a few weeks later. 29/5/51.

RL246   MOSQUITO NF36
Written off after a wheels up landing following overspeeding of the starboard engine and the subsequent failure of the port. 11/7/51.

PG367   WELLINGTON T.XVIII
In mid-air collision with Martinet NR570. Six in the crew were killed, but one passenger parachuted to safety after being saved by Flt Lt Quinton who, posthumously, was awarded the George Cross. 13/8/51.

NR570   MARTINET
In mid-air collision with Wellington PG367. The pilot and his passenger were killed. 13/8/51.

RL184   MOSQUITO NF36
Hit a tree while on approach at night in thick fog. The pilot had been given diversions but

considered he could make a safe landing at his home airfield. Both crew members were killed. 14/11/51.

RK979   Mosquito NF36

The starboard engine lost power on take-off after the u/c had retracted. The aircraft crash landed, slightly injuring the crew. 1/12/51.

HJ993   Mosquito Mk3

Ground looped on landing and later written off charge. 7/1/52.

WD716   Meteor NF11

Ditched in Saltwick Bay after both engines cut. The pilot was drowned while attempting to swim ashore and the navigator's body was never found. 20/7/52.

WF793   Meteor T7

Hit high ground in cloud near Leyburn while under control of GCA. The crew of two were killed. 7/8/52.

WD714 Meteor NF11

A mid-air collision with WD772 resulted in the deaths of the two man crew. 19/8/52.

WD772   Meteor NF11

After a mid-air collision with WD714 both crew members baled out safely. 19/8/52.

WD723   Meteor NF11

While on a flight over the N Sea, the aircraft went missing with its crew of two and no trace of them was ever found. 17/11/52.

WD761   Meteor NF11

Crashed after it ran out of fuel and the crew had baled out. 2/12/52.

WD713   Meteor NF11

Written off after a wheels-up landing following a tyre burst on take-off. 30/3/53.

WD778   Meteor NF11

Lost radio contact while returning from a night sortie. Unable to find its base it crashed seven miles from Appleby, Westmoreland, killing the crew of two. 24/3/54.

WH239   Meteor T7

A student on his first solo flight crashed three minutes after take-off, after his failure to lock the canopy shut allowed it to rip away from the airframe. He abandoned the aircraft at low altitude, but died from his injuries and shock. 28/6/54.

WD650   Meteor NF11

When three miles from Leeming the pilot was told to break off his approach. The aircraft crashed shortly afterwards, killing both crew members. 23/3/55.

XA662   Javelin FAW5

Crashed after engine failure 30 miles west of Leeming. The crew of two ejected safely. The navigator was an exchange officer from the USAF. 29/9/59.

XA706   Javelin FAW5

After experiencing an airborne fire, the aircraft was landed safely but was later found to have been damaged beyond repair. 29/6/60.

No 3 FTS

XN642   Jet Provost T3

Crashed two miles from Leeming after the engine flamed-out on take-off. The crew ejected, but the student was killed. 19/2/63.

XM368   Jet Provost T3

Crashed near Pately Bridge, N Yorks after failing to recover from an intentional spin. The crew ejected safely. 29/4/63.

XP621   Jet Provost T4

After a fire warning would not extinguish, the crew ejected and the aircraft crashed five miles from Catterick Camp. Investigation later proved that the warning had been spurious. 15/11/65.

XN631   Jet Provost T3

After a mid-air collision with XM428 the instructor was able to eject but the pupil was killed. 20/4/65.

XM428   Jet Provost T3

Following a mid-air collision with XN631 the crew ejected safely. 20/4/65.

XN575   Jet Provost T3

Crashed on the airfield after one wing touched

the ground during take-off. The student, who was flying solo, was killed. 30/9/69.

XP576   JET PROVOST T4

Crashed near the River Swale after the engine flamed-out. The crew ejected safely. 16/3/70.

XN465   JET PROVOST T3

Crashed in a field one mile north of Easingwold, N Yorks after control was lost in a spin. The crew ejected safely. The student, Plt Off Spears, was the great-nephew of Major James McCudden VC, DSO, MC, MM, who was one of the top scoring "aces" in World War I. Spears also had two other uncles who were pilots in the RFC and his father was a pilot in the RAF in 1939. 24/2/71.

XM418   JET PROVOST T3

The aircraft caught fire when ready for take-off at the end of the runway. The crew vacated and the aircraft burnt out. 25/3/71.

XN558   JET PROVOST T3

Crashed in sugar beet field near the A1 trunk road at Dishforth, N Yorks, after a bird strike to the engine. The crew ejected safely. 29/6/71.

XW331   JET PROVOST T5

Crashed on the runway at Leeming while carrying out a "roller" landing. The crew were unhurt. 11/4/73.

XS211   JET PROVOST T5

Crashed close to the northern perimeter of the airfield after engine failure. The crew ejected at low level but one was seriously injured. 13/2/76.

XW414   JET PROVOST T5A

Came down in a field alongside the A1 trunk road after suffering engine failure on completion of a "roller" landing at Dishforth. The pilot, who was flying "solo", ejected safely. 28/6/78.

XX530   BULLDOG

Crashed near Billsdale Radio Mast, on the North Yorkshire Moors, killing the crew of two. 21/9/78.

XX542   BULLDOG

Crashed two miles NW of Topcliffe. The crew baled out safely. 16/11/79.

XW329   JET PROVOST T5

Crashed on the airfield, with the crew uninjured. 16/6/81.

XM453   JET PROVOST T3A

Crashed on remote moorland in the Pennines. The crew ejected safely. 21/11/83.

RAF LEEMING

ZE833   23   TORNADO F3

Crashed into the sea off Newcastle. The crew ejected, but the pilot was dead when picked up from the water by a "Search and Rescue" helicopter. 21/7/89.

ZE809   XI   TORNADO F3

Crashed into the sea after suffering mechanical failure at high speed and low level. The crew ejected and were rescued by a "Search and Rescue" helicopter. 7/6/94.

HONOURS, AWARDS AND DECORATIONS

1940

30 Jul	Squadron Leader G W PEARCE RAAF		DFC	10 Sqn
30 Jul	Flying Officer M T G HENRY		DFC	
30 Jul	Pilot Officer E I PARSONS		DFC	
30 Jul	Sergeant W S HILLARY		DFM	
30 Jul	Sergeant A S JOHNSON DFM	Bar to DFM		
30 Jul	Sergeant J G MacCOUBREY		DFM	
13 Sep	Squadron Leader W N GIBSON		DFC	
13 Sep	Squadron Leader D P HANAFIN		DFC	
13 Sep	Flight Lieutenant J A COHEN		DFC	
22 Oct	Squadron Leader W H GARING		DFC	
22 Oct	Flying Officer G W PRIOR		DFC	
22 Oct	Flying Officer R V WARREN		DFC	
22 Oct	Sergeant D T WITT		DFM	
22 Nov	Wing Commander S O BUFTON		DFC	
22 Nov	Wing Commander J N WHITWORTH DFC	Bar to DFC		
22 Nov	Flying Officer W M NIXON		DFC	
22 Nov	Pilot Officer J C CAIRNS		DFC	
22 Nov	Pilot Officer K J SOMERVILLE		DFC	

1941

1 Jan	Warrant Officer W C STEEL		MBE
17 Jan	Squadron Leader D C TOMLINSON		DFC
17 Jan	Pilot Officer J H STEYN		DFC
17 Jan	Sergeant T S W TOWELL		DFM
7 Mar	Pilot Officer K D BRANT		DFC
7 Mar	Pilot Officer A BRIDSON		DFC
18 Apr	Sergeant A F ELCOATE		DFM
18 Apr	Pilot Officer J A S RUSSELL		DFC
18 Apr	Sergeant G F DOVE		DFM
18 Apr	Sergeant M S MAAS		DFM
9 May	Pilot Officer J N FORREST		DFC
9 May	Sergeant A COWIE		DFM
6 Jun	Sergeant P F HICKLING		DFM

6	Jun	Sergeant M A NIMAN	DFM	
1	Jul	Squadron Leader H M BIRCH RAAF	DFC	
18	Jul	Flight Lieutenant K HUMBY	DFC	
18	Jul	Flying Officer H J HEAL	DFC	
18	Jul	Sergeant L R JOHNSON	DFM	
25	Jul	Pilot Officer E H BAGNALD	DFC	
25	Jul	Leading Aircraftsman M T GRIFFIN RAAF	DFM	
23	Sep	Sergeant J F BASSETT	DFM	10 Sqn
23	Sep	Sergeant C L GOLDSMITH	DFM	
23	Sep	Sergeant R E GRIFFIN	DFM	
23	Sep	Sergeant A J JONES	DFM	
23	Sep	Sergeant I PHILLIPS	DFM	
23	Sep	Sergeant L ZALSBERG	DFM	
	Sep	Pilot Officer T W G GODFREY	MiD	
24	Oct	Wing Commander V B BENNETT	DFC	
24	Oct	Sergeant F SCOTT	DFM	77 Sqn
24	Oct	Sergeant R E WHEATLEY	DFM	
21	Nov	Sergeant C J FARNERY	DFM	10 Sqn
21	Nov	Sergeant D WILKINSON	BEM	
21	Nov	Sergeant L FISH	DFM	77 Sqn
21	Nov	Sergeant T A MATTHEWS	DFM	
21	Nov	Sergeant L F SANDFORD	DFM	
23	Dec	Pilot Officer N E ROSCOE	DFC	
23	Dec	Sergeant E W BURGESS	DFM	
23	Dec	Sergeant J R T HAZLETON	DFM	
23	Dec	Sergeant R N P LUFF	DFM	
23	Dec	Sergeant S R MAYSTON	DFM	

1942

1	Jan	Wing Commander E G KNOX-KNIGHT RAAF	OBE	10 Sqn
2	Jan	Squadron Leader I S PODGER RAAF	DFC	
9	Jan	Squadron Leader F D WEBSTER	DFC	
30	Jan	Sergeant C S GEORGE	DFM	
13	Feb	Sergeant D V FLAVELL	DFM	77 Sqn
13	Feb	Sergeant S A E MUNNS	DFM	
13	Mar	Squadron Leader P W F LANDALE	DFC	10 Sqn
13	Mar	Sergeant J K CORKE	DFM	
13	Mar	Squadron Leader L H W PARKIN	DFC	77 Sqn
14	Apr	Flight Lieutenant F A DRURY	DFC	
14	Apr	Flight Lieutenant H H LAWSON	DFC	
23	Apr	Squadron Leader F W THOMSON	DFC	10 Sqn
26	May	Sergeant G E MORTIMER	DFM	
29	May	Flight Sergeant W J PORRITT	DFM	
29	May	Flight Sergeant P G ROCHFORD	DFM	

29 May	Sergeant M D GRIBBIN		DFM	
2 Jun	Flying Officer J B JEWELL RAAF		DFC	
16 Jun	Wing Commander D C T BENNETT		DSO	
16 Jun	Sergeant H WALMSLEY		DFM	
30 Jun	Flight Lieutenant S R C WOOD RAAF		DFC	
30 Jun	Warrant Officer H V PETERSON DFC	Bar to DFC		
7 Jul	Flight Lieutenant H G POCKLEY RAAF		DFC	
4 Aug	Flight Lieutenant T W G GODFREY		DFC	
4 Aug	Flight Lieutenant J V WATTS		DFC	
4 Aug	Pilot Officer L G A WHYTE		DFC	
4 Aug	Sergeant C E DARBY		DFM	
22 Sep	Sergeant R G BELL		DFM	408 Sqn
23 Sep	Pilot Officer H A HITCHCOCK		DFC	408 Sqn
29 Sep	Flight Lieutenant D J WILLIAMS		DFC	
27 Oct	Flight Lieutenant D S H CONSTANCE		DFC	
24 Nov	Flight Lieutenant G C FISHNER		DFC	
24 Nov	Flight Lieutenant VAN DEN BOK DFC	Bar to DFC		
29 Dec	Pilot Officer K J METHERAL		DFC	
29 Dec	Pilot Officer R J REYNOLDS DFM		DFC	
29 Dec	Flight Sergeant N C TURNOUR		DFM	
29 Dec	Sergeant D S LEECH		DFM	
29 Dec	Sergeant G E GALLOWAY		DFM	

1943

12 Jan	Flight Lieutenant W C SANDERSON		DFC
12 Jan	Flying Officer W F PARKE		DFC
12 Jan	Sergeant A NORMAN		DFM
Jan	Flight Sergeant P R G GUYATT		MiD
Jan	Flight Sergeant J A WALTERS		MiD
Jan	Sergeant J G BECKETT		MiD
Feb	Warrant Officer G S YOUNG		MiD
Feb	Flight Sergeant J K BELL		MiD
Feb	Sergeant E A GRANT		MiD
6 Apr	Squadron Leader E G GILMORE		DFC
6 Apr	Pilot Officer D F ALLEN		DFC
6 Apr	Pilot Officer P E MITCHELL		DFC
6 Apr	Flight Sergeant M MARMENT		DFM
6 Apr	Flight Sergeant A L ROSS		DFM
6 Apr	Sergeant J W T MASON		DFM
6 Apr	Sergeant H E PARRATT		DFM
20 Apr	Flight Lieutenant R H G BOOSEY		DFC
23 Apr	Flight Lieutenant A J G JARVIS		DFC
14 May	Pilot Officer D C FERGUSON		DFC
14 May	Pilot Officer T C KAYE		DFC

14 May	Pilot Officer J K KNIGHTS	DFC	
14 May	Pilot Officer R C MOYER	DFC	
28 May	Wing Commander W D FERRIS	DFC	
25 May	Flight Sergeant F J HIGGINS	DFM	427 Sqn
15 Jun	Pilot Officer J K BELL	DFC	408 Sqn
15 Jun	Pilot Officer R C BERRY	DFC	
15 Jun	Pilot Officer J R PRICE	DFC	
15 Jun	Pilot Officer T H REEVES	DFC	
6 Jul	Pilot Officer C C STOVEL	DFC	
6 Jul	Flight Sergeant R L M SMITH	DFM	
23 Jul	Flight Lieutenant V F GANDERTON	DFC	427 Sqn
6 Aug	Flying Officer G BENNETT	DFC	408 Sqn
6 Aug	Sergeant A ROGERS	DFM	
13 Aug	Squadron Leader C H EARTHROWL	DFC	427 Sqn
17 Aug	Pilot Officer G T CROSSMAN	DFC	
17 Aug	Pilot Officer P DORMAND	DFC	
17 Aug	Pilot Officer E F FLANAGAN	DFC	
17 Aug	Pilot Officer D B ROSS	DFC	427 Sqn
17 Aug	Pilot Officer G P VANDEKERCKHOVE	DFC	
10 Sep	Flight Lieutenant B G CREW	DFC	
10 Sep	Flight Sergeant W BIGGS	DFM	
10 Sep	Sergeant J ELLIOT	DFM	
10 Sep	Sergeant L E MOYLER	DFM	
14 Sep	Pilot Officer E A JOHNSON	DFC	
14 Sep	Pilot Officer G B WHYTE	DFC	
14 Sep	Sergeant E B CARLETON	DFM	
10 Sep	Flight Sergeant J BOLE	DFM	429 Sqn
10 Sep	Flight Sergeant T S HEYES	DFM	
14 Sep	Warrant Officer G L KENNEDY	DFC	
23 Oct	Flight Lieutenant G L LAIRD	DFC	427 Sqn
23 Oct	Sergeant W H CARDY	CGM	
25 Oct	Flight Lieutenant C H TUBMAN	DFC	
25 Oct	Pilot Officer A H FERNAND	DFC	
25 Oct	Pilot Officer W H SCHMITT	DFC	
25 Oct	Sergeant R McNAMARA	DFM	
25 Oct	Flight Lieutenant L C DILWORTH	DFC	429 Sqn
23 Oct	Flight Lieutenant B F N RAWSON	DFC	
23 Oct	Flying Officer B G D JACKSON	DFC	
23 Oct	Sergeant F C EDMUNDS	DFM	
21 Nov	Flight Sergeant J P DUVAL	DFM	427 Sqn
21 Nov	Flight Sergeant H NELSON	DFM	
21 Nov	Flight Sergeant R L SKILLEN	DFM	
21 Nov	Sergeant A L D'EON	DFM	
7 Dec	Flight Lieutenant G L VOGAN	DFC	

7 Dec	Flight Lieutenant I F MACINTOSH		DFC	429 Sqn
7 Dec	Pilot Officer H W MITCHELL		DFC	

1944

1 Jan	Wing Commander R S TURNBULL DFM		AFC	427 Sqn
14 Jan	Flight Lieutenant A RODWELL		DFC	
14 Jan	Flying Officer C L HUGHES		DFC	
14 Jan	Flight Sergeant J CLIBBERY		DFM	
14 Jan	Sergeant R E QUALLE		DFM	
18 Jan	Squadron Leader D H ARNOT		DFC	
Jan	Flight Lieutenant J CHACANOFF		MiD	
Jan	Flight Lieutenant J E DUROCHER		MiD	
Jan	Flight Lieutenant S A HONSBY		MiD	
Jan	Flight Lieutenant L D IZZARD DFM		MiD	
Jan	Flight Lieutenant G E MORRISON		MiD	
Jan	Warrant Officer M DERBYSHIRE		MiD	
Jan	Flight Sergeant T A COLLINS		MiD	
Jan	Sergeant P PURA		MiD	
19 Apr	Flight Lieutenant A M STOCKDALE		DFC	429 Sqn
19 Apr	Sergeant H GLASS		DFM	
16 May	Wing Commander R S TURNBULL AFC DFM		DFC	427 Sqn
19 May	Squadron Leader J G CRIBB		DFC	
19 May	Squadron Leader F N MURRAY		DFC	427 Sqn
18 May	Flight Lieutenant L V POLLARD		DFC	429 Sqn
18 May	Flying Officer W W TUCKER		DFC	
18 May	Pilot Officer G F CLARK		DFC	
18 May	Flight Sergeant S POOLE		DFM	
25 May	Wing Commander J D PATTISON DFC	Bar to DFC		
25 May	Flight Lieutenant J ATKINS		DFC	
25 May	Flight Lieutenant R H V HUNT		DFC	
25 May	Flight Lieutenant A P SMITH		DFC	
2 Jun	Flying Officer G A WELDON		DFC	427 Sqn
7 Jun	Squadron Leader W B ANDERSON		DFC	429 Sqn
7 Jun	Pilot Officer T B F JELDSTED		DFC	
7 Jun	Warrant Officer O D McCLEAN		DFC	
14 Jun	Flight Lieutenant T RAWLINSON		DFC	
14 Jun	Flight Sergeant J MANGIONE		DFM	
14 Jun	Flight Sergeant G J M RITCHIE		DFM	
14 Jun	Sergeant G E J STEERE		CGM	
16 Jun	Flying Officer R J HAWORTH		DFC	
16 Jun	Flight Sergeant A R WOOLSEY		DFM	
Jun	Flight Lieutenant A R H RILEY		MiD	
Jun	Flying Officer P G F MONEY		MiD	
Jun	Flying Officer E GARLICK		MiD	

14 Jul	Pilot Officer J DAVIS	DFC	
14 Jul	Pilot Officer C GARGETT	DFC	
14 Jul	Warrant Officer L N T MURIE	DFC	
14 Jul	Flight Sergeant A MARSHALL	DFM	
14 Jul	Flight Sergeant P A WEST	DFM	
21 Jul	Sergeant J B SULLIVAN	DFM	427 Sqn
28 Jul	Flight Lieutenant W A CORY	DFC	
28 Jul	Flying Officer M S STRANGE	DSO	
28 Jul	Sergeant D F WALKER	DFM	
15 Aug	Flying Officer W R RAND	DFM	
15 Aug	Warrant Officer J HEATON	DFC	
18 Aug	Flight Lieutenant W D STEPHEN	DSO	
18 Aug	Flying Officer J A McLURE	DFC	
29 Aug	Squadron Leader G F ARBUCKLE	DFC	429 Sqn
29 Aug	Pilot Officer K M EVANS	DFC	
29 Aug	Pilot Officer M N McLEAN	DFC	
29 Aug	Pilot Officer W R STEWART	DFC	
29 Aug	Pilot Officer W H WARDELL	DFC	
5 Sep	Squadron Leader L G NEILLY	DFC	
5 Sep	Flight Sergeant E J LEFAVE	DFM	
11 Oct	Flight Lieutenant R R KINGSLAND	DFC	
11 Oct	Pilot Officer J H R COURTOIS	DFC	
16 Oct	Flying Officer J R CALDERBANK	DFC	
16 Oct	Flying Officer J C LAKEMAN	DFC	
16 Oct	Flying Officer G W LINCKNER	DFC	
21 Oct	Flight Lieutenant K E JOHNSTON	DFC	
21 Oct	Flight Lieutenant D W MORRISON	DFC	
29 Oct	Flight Lieutenant A F CHILDS	DFC	
28 Oct	Flying Officer L E J MURRAY	DFC	427 Sqn
28 Oct	Flying Officer W C WHITE	DFC	
28 Oct	Flying Officer F E WOODLAND	DFC	
28 Oct	Pilot Officer W J ELLWOOD	DFC	
28 Oct	Warrant Officer W W NASH	DFC	
8 Nov	Flying Officer J T BARLOW	DFC	429 Sqn
15 Nov	Flying Officer J L WIDDIS	DFC	
15 Nov	Pilot Officer E APPLETON	DFC	
15 Nov	Pilot Officer W R GOODHUE	DFC	
15 Nov	Pilot Officer G S JAMES	DFC	
15 Nov	Pilot Officer J A McCRARY	DFC	
15 Nov	Pilot Officer N L THOMPSON	DFC	
22 Nov	Flying Officer J C HALL	DFC	
22 Nov	Pilot Officer R W MEREDITH	DFC	
22 Nov	Flight Sergeant H J VENN	DFM	
25 Nov	Pilot Officer W K HAMMOND	DFC	427 Sqn

25 Nov	Pilot Officer P E REGINBALL	DFC	
30 Nov	Flight Lieutenant D C HENRICKSON	DFC	429 Sqn
30 Nov	Flying Officer D BELL	DFC	
30 Nov	Sergeant P F BOLDERSTONE	DFM	
8 Dec	Flight Lieutenant W DOBSON DFC	Bar to DFC	
17 Dec	Flying Officer V C SUNSTRUM	DFC	427 Sqn

1945

2 Feb	Squadron Leader R J LAWLOR	DFC	
2 Feb	Flight Lieutenant E E MORGAN	DFC	
2 Feb	Flight Lieutenant J M MORRICE	DFC	
2 Feb	Flight Lieutenant J M MURPHY	DFC	
2 Feb	Flying Officer J H GRIBBON	DFC	
14 Feb	Flight Lieutenant J E ROWE	DFC	429 Sqn
1 Mar	Flight Lieutenant J E CREEPER	DFC	
1 Mar	Flight Lieutenant H W McDONALD	DFC	
1 Mar	Flight Lieutenant A M McDONALD	DFC	
1 Mar	Flight Lieutenant R K MITCHELL	DFC	
13 Mar	Flight Sergeant R BROWN	DFM	
21 Mar	Squadron Leader H J HOGARTH	DFC	
21 Mar	Flight Lieutenant R D BUE	DFC	427 Sqn
21 Mar	Flight Lieutenant D T HEPBURN	DFC	
21 Mar	Flight Lieutenant J D V LARVIERE	DFC	
21 Mar	Flying Officer W B BRITTAIN	DFC	
21 Mar	Flying Officer W D BRITTON	DFC	
21 Mar	Flying Officer H L RUFFELL	DFC	
24 Mar	Flight Lieutenant R J GARVIN	DFC	
24 Mar	Flying Officer C E MONTY	DFC	
24 Mar	Flying Officer P SLIPEC	DFC	
24 Mar	Pilot Officer D R RUNCIMAN	DFC	
24 Mar	Pilot Officer J F WHONE	DFC	
8 Apr	Flight Lieutenant K D POWELL	DFC	429 Sqn
19 Apr	Flight Lieutenant W T GLASS	DFC	
19 Apr	Flight Lieutenant C S POPE	DFC	429 Sqn
28 May	Flight Lieutenant G D PARRY	DFC	
28 May	Pilot Officer L J JODRELL	DFC	
28 May	Flight Sergeant W H MAGILL	DFM	
29 May	Flying Officer G R KIRBY	DFC	427 Sqn
29 May	Flying Officer W MACKERACHER	DFC	
29 May	Flying Officer D B ROSS DFC	Bar to DFC	
29 May	Flying Officer T G WAGER	DFC	
29 May	Pilot Officer H M B MILLWARD	DFC	
30 May	Flight Lieutenant A E BEALS	DFC	
30 May	Flight Lieutenant J F SMART	DFC	

30 May	Flight Lieutenant J L STORMS		DFC	
30 May	Flight Lieutenant W M WALKER		DFC	
30 May	Flight Lieutenant F J WILGRESS		DFC	
30 May	Flying Officer J R THACKERAY		DFC	
30 May	Pilot Officer R R McKENNEY		DFC	
13 Aug	Flight Lieutenant J MACKAY		DFC	429 Sqn
5 Sep	Wing Commander J COMAR DFC	Bar to DFC		
12 Sep	Flying Officer A COLQUHOUN		DFC	
13 Nov	Flight Lieutenant R K TODD		DFC	

1946

1 Jan	Flying Officer S R WALLIS		DFC	427 Sqn

1948

1 Jan	Flight Officer S HARVEY WAAF		MBE	228 OCU
1 Jan	Sergeant J PERCIVAL WAAF		BEM	

1951

1 Jan	Flight Lieutenant C B L WARWICK		MBE
28 Oct	Flight Lieutenant J A QUINTON DFC		GC

1952

1 Jan	Wing Commander J G TOPHAM DSO DFC		OBE
1 Jan	Sergeant E E BARFF		AFM

1953

2 Jun	Squadron Leader F C BARTER		AFC
2 Jun	Warrant Officer A H HAMILTON		MBE

1955

1 Jan	Flight Lieutenant R M RAW		AFC

1957

13 Jun	Flight Lieutenant J ROSS		AFC

1958

12 Jun	Warrant Officer A W KEMP		MBE

1960

1 Jun	Flight Sergeant J A FAREY		BEM

1961

1 Jan	Squadron Leader R NEIL		QCVSA

1962

1 Jan	Squadron Leader K W HOLMES		MBE

1963

1 Jan	Flight Lieutenant R W KIMMINGS		QCVSA

1964

1 Jan	Flight Lieutenant C HORN	MBE
1 Jul	Squadron Leader P KENT	MBE
1 Jul	Sergeant W J HODSON	BEM
1 Jul	Mr G G MARRINER	BEM

1966

Jun	Warrant Officer T H ELLIS	MBE

1967

Jan	Warrant Officer A SCOON	MBE

1968

Jan	Squadron Leader R MACLACHLAN	AFC

1969

Jun	Squadron Leader D M HOLIDAY	AFC

1970

Jun	Flight Lieutenant P R RAYNER	AFC

1971

Jan	Corporal G L KEMP	BEM
Jun	Flight Lieutenant D F GARDNER	QCVSA

1972

Jan	Wing Commander D J PENMAN DSO DFC	CBE
Jun	Flying Officer R W B PATTISON QCVSA	
Jun	Flying Officer R A SARGEANT	QCVSA
Jun	Mr T E NUGENT	BEM

1973

Jan	Wing Commander W EDWARDS	OBE
Jan	Warrant Officer B T TAYLOR	MBE
Jan	Flight Lieutenant T F CARTER	AFC
Jan	Squadron Leader K R PETRIE	QCVSA
Jan	Flight Lieutenant J T GALYER	QCVSA

1974

Jan	Group Captain J R CARSON AFC	CBE
Jan	Warrant Officer R W CORNFORTH	MBE
Jan	Flight Lieutenant D M C TRUSLER	QCVSA
Jun	Flight Lieutenant C J THOMSON	QCVSA

1975

Jan   Corporal W E D DUNCAN   BEM

1976

Jan   Flight Lieutenant M A FOX   QCVSA

1977

Jun   Squadron Leader L MEADOWS   MBE
Jun   Sergeant C WOODWARD   BEM

1978

Jan   Flight Lieutenant R J H FALLIS   AFC
Jan   Lieutenant R V FREDERICKSEN RN   QCVSA
Jan   Lieutenant K G LAMPREY RN   AFC
Jun   Flight Lieutenant J CABLE   QCVSA
Jun   Flight Lieutenant D WALBY   QCVSA

1979

Jan   Flight Lieutenant J S MARCHANT   MBE
Jan   Warrant Officer R C A MORRIS   MBE
Jun   Lieutenant R BRADSHAW RN   QCVSA

1980

Jan   Flight Lieutenant M N SAWYER   AFC
Jan   Flight Lieutenant R A COLE   QCVSA
Jan   Flight Lieutenant E J SCOTT   QCVSA

1981

Jan   Flight Lieutenant N M NAYLOR   AFC
Mar   Flight Lieutenant T P McDONALD   QCVSA

1983

Jan   Warrant Officer W G WINTERBOURNE   MBE
Jan   Squadron Leader B A McDONALD AFC   Bar to AFC
Jan   Flight Lieutenant B S WALTERS   AFC
Jan   Chief Technician M R MYERS   BEM
Jan   Flight Lieutenant R G BRAITHWAITE   QCVSA

1984

Jan   Flight Lieutenant F A DA COSTA   QCVSA
Jun   Flight Sergeant R S TAYLOR   BEM

1989

Jun   Squadron Leader N BALGARNIE   MBE

1990

Jan	Warrant Officer L DEVLIN	MBE
Jan	Flight Sergeant G W DUTTON	BEM
Jun	Wing Commander D C SMITH MBE	OBE

1991

Jan	Group Captain J E ROOUM AFC	CBE
Jan	Wing Commander P W GILES	OBE
Jan	Squadron Leader N J E KURTH	MBE
Jun	Wing Commander T J PINK	OBE
Jun	Wing Commander A M DAVIS	OBE

1992

Jan	Chief Technician M F LYNSKEY	BEM
Jun	Flight Sergeant J D GRAHAM	BEM
Jun	Sergeant S M KAY	BEM

1993

Jan	Group Captain R S PEACOCK-EDWARDS AFC	CBE

1994

Jan	Warrant Officer M S COLEMAN	MBE
Jun	Wing Commander J A CLIFFE	OBE
Jun	Flight Sergeant G W DUTTON BEM	MBE
Jun	Chief Technician P C JAKES	MBE

1995

Jan	Chief Technician S M KAY BEM	MBE
Jun	Squadron Leader C A WYNNE	MBE
Jun	Flight Sergeant J SINCLAIR	MBE
Jun	Sergeant J P DUCKWORTH	MBE

1996

Jan	Senior Aircraftsman D MACKELL	MBE
Jun	Flight Lieutenant A J HALL	MBE

Notes:

1. The award of a "Mention in Despatches" (MiD) was promulgated in a monthly consolidated roll of honour and consequently does not have a specific date recorded.

2. From 1966, awards bestowed to persons in January or June relate to those appearing in the New Year's Honours List or the Queen's Birthday Honours List of that year.

STATION COMMANDERS
RAF Leeming

Jun	1940	–	Jul	1940	Wing Commander	K E WARD RAF
Jul	1940	–	Jan	1942	Group Captain	W E STATON DSO MC DFC ADC RAF
Jan	1942	–	Jan	1943	Group Captain	S GRAHAM MC RAF
Jan	1943	–	Apr	1943	Group Captain	C R DUNLAP RCAF
Apr	1943	–	Jun	1943	Group Captain	H M CARSCALLAN DFC RCAF
Jun	1943	–	Nov	1943	Group Captain	J L PLANT RCAF
Nov	1943	–	Jun	1944	Group Captain	J G BRYANS RCAF
Jun	1944	–	Oct	1944	Group Captain	W F M NEWSON DFC RCAF
Oct	1944	–	Apr	1945	Group Captain	J B MILLWARD DFC RCAF
Apr	1945	–	May	1945	Group Captain	A C HULL DFC RAF
May	1945	–	Jul	1946	Group Captain	E N EVANS RCAF
Jul	1946	–	Jan	1948	Group Captain	R S RYAN RAF
Jan	1948	–	Feb	1950	Group Captain	M LOWE CBE RAF
Feb	1950	–	Jul	1950	Group Captain	A E CLOUSTON DSO DFC AFC RAF
Jul	1950	–	Jan	1953	Group Captain	R V McINTYRE DFC RAF
Jan	1953	–	May	1955	Group Captain	P J SAUNDERS DFC RAF
May	1955	–	Mar	1957	Group Captain	J E INNES-CRUMP RAF
Mar	1957	–	Nov	1958	Group Captain	J M THOMPSON CBE DSO DFC AFC RAF
Nov	1958	–	May	1961	Group Captain	K P SMALES DSO DFC RAF
May	1961	–	Sep	1962	Group Captain	E JAMES DFC AFC RAF

Sep	1962	–	Mar	1964	Group Captain	D F HYLAND-SMITH MVO DFC AFC RAF
Mar	1964	–	Sep	1966	Group Captain	R S RADLEY DFC AFC RAF
Sep	1966	–	Jul	1967	Group Captain	J W ALLEN DSO DFC AFC RAF
Jul	1967	–	Jan	1970	Group Captain	S J RAWLINS DFC RAF
Jan	1970	–	Mar	1971	Group Captain	G W W WADDINGTON CBE DFC RAF
Mar	1971	–	Jun	1973	Group Captain	R J CARSON AFC RAF
Jun	1973	–	May	1975	Group Captain	J M A PARKER AFC RAF
May	1975	–	Nov	1976	Group Captain	M J HARDY RAF
Nov	1976	–	Nov	1978	Group Captain	P C VANGUCCI AFC RAF
Nov	1978	–	Nov	1980	Group Captain	J M CURRY RAF
Nov	1980	–	Aug	1983	Group Captain	G C BATT RAF
Aug	1983	–	Sep	1984	Group Captain	R G CURRY RAF
Oct	1984	–	Dec	1987	Wing Commander	D L BATES RAF
Dec	1987	–	Apr	1988	Wing Commander	D C SMITH MBE RAF
Apr	1988	–	Jun	1990	Group Captain	J E ROOUM AFC RAF
Jun	1990	–	Jun	1992	Group Captain	R S PEACOCK-EDWARDS AFC RAF
Jun	1992	–	Aug	1994	Group Captain	P W ROSER MBE RAF
Aug	1994	–	Feb	1997	Group Captain	E J BLACK RAF
Feb	1997	–			Group Captain	B P DOGGETT RAF

AIRCRAFT, SQUADRONS AND UNITS
Based at Royal Air Force Leeming

Aircraft Type	Function	Sqn	Date
	BOMBER COMMAND		
Blenheim I.F	Night-fighter operations	219	Jun 40 – Oct 40
Whitley V	No 4 Group operations	10	Jul 40 – Dec 41
	Training	102	Aug 40 – Sep 40
	No 4 Group operations	77	Sep 41 – May 42
Stirling I	Training	7	Aug 40 – Oct 40
Halifax B.I	Traning	35	Nov 40 – Dec 40
	Training	76	Apr 41 – Jul 41
	No 4 Group operations	10	Dec 41 – Aug 42
Wellington III	No 6 Group operations	419	Aug 42
	No 6 Group operations	420	Aug 42 – Sep 42
Halifax B.II	No 4 Group operations	10	Dec 41 – Aug 42
	No 6 Group operations	408	Dec 42 – Aug 43
	No 6 Group operations	405	Mar 43 – Apr 43
	No 6 Group operations	429	Aug 43 – Jan 44
Halifax B.V	No 6 Group operations	408	Sep 42 – Dec 42
	No 6 Group operations	427	May 43 – Feb 44
	No 6 Group operations	429	Nov 43 – Mar 44
Halifax B.III	No 6 Group operations	427	Jan 44 – Mar 45
	No 6 Group operations	429	Mar 44 – Mar 45
Lancaster B.I/ B.III	No 6 Group operations	427	Mar 45 – May 45
	No 6 Group operations	429	Mar 45 – May 46
54 OTU/228 OCU			
Mosquito T 3	Pilot training		Jun 46 – Dec 53
Mosquito VI	Light bomber training		Jun 46 – Dec 53
Mosquito XXX	Night-fighter training		Jun 46 – Dec 53
Mosquito NF 36	Night- fighter training		Sep 47 – Dec 53
Wellington T.10	Crew training		Jun 46 – Oct 51
Martinet	Target-tug		Jun 46 – Jun 52
Master III	Advanced training – pilot		Jun 46 – Feb 48

Aircraft Type	Function	Sqn	Date
Oxford	Advanced training – pilot		Oct 47 – May 54
Brigand B I	Light bomber training		Aug 47 – Jul 51
Buckmaster	Advanced training for Brigand		Oct 48 – Jun 51
Tiger Moth II	Elementary training – pilot		May 49 – Mar 51
Meteor T 7	Advanced jet training		Apr 51 – Jul 61
Brigand T 4	Radar training – navigator		Jul 51 – Jun 52
Meteor NF 11	Jet night-fighter training		Jan 52 – Dec 58
Mosquito TT 35	Banner target towing		Sep 53 – Apr 54
Vampire T 11	Advanced jet training		Apr 54 – Aug 59
Chipmunk T 10	Elementary training – pilot		Jun 54 – Sep 84
Prentice T I	Basic training – pilot		Sep 54 – Nov 56
Meteor NF 12	Jet night-fighter training		Oct 54 – Aug 59
Anson T 21	Navigator training		Aug 56 – Jul 59
Valetta T 3	Navigator training		Mar 57 – Apr 57
Valetta T 4	Navigator training		Jun 57 – May 59
Valetta C 1	Navigator training		Feb 57 – May 59
Meteor NF(T)14	Jet night fighter training		Oct 57 – Jun 61
Javelin FAW 5	Javelin conversion		Jun 57 – Aug 61
Canberra T 4	Canberra conversion		Apr 58 – Jul 61
Javelin T 3	Dual control Javelin conversion		Feb 59 – Aug 61
Canberra T 11	A.I. radar operator training		Feb 59 – Jul 61
3FTS			
Jet Provost T 3	Basic training – pilot		Aug 61 – Sep 84
Jet Provost T 4	Basic training – pilot		Jan 62 – Sep 84
Jet Provost T 5	Basic training – pilot		Jul 70 – Sep 84
Bulldog	Basic training – pilot		Sep 75 – Sep 84
Jetstream	Multi-engine training – pilot		Nov 76 – Apr 79
NUAS			
Chipmunk T 10/ Bulldog	Air experience – University students and ATC cadets		Sep 74 –
UK AIR DEFENCE			
Tornado F 3	UK air defence	XI	May 88 –
	UK air defence	23	Jan 89 – Feb 94
	UK air defence	XXV	Jul 89 –
Hawk	Target facilities	100	Sep 95 –

INDEX

Heinkel Helll, 157
Junkers Ju88, 42, 48
Junkers Jul88, 48
Lockheed C130 Hercules, 84, 89, 93, 103, 104, 117
Lockheed C141 Starlifter, 89
Lockheed Super Electra, 16
Lockheed Tristar, 105
McDonnell Douglas Phantom, 89, 93, 96, 97, 101
Messerschmit Me109, 14, 160, 167
Messerschmit Me110, 27
Messerschmit Me163, 47, 48
Messerschmit Me262, 48
Mikoyan MiG-21, 103
Mikoyan MiG-27, 107
Miles Martinet, 55, 58, 61, 63, 64, 175, 191
Miles Master, 55, 191
North American Harvard, 75
North American Mustang, 38
Northrop Black Widow, 121
Panavia Tornado GR1, 89, 93, 101, 112, 113
Panavia Tornado F2, 90, 92
Panavia Tornado F3, 89, 90, 95, 96, 97, 98, 99, 101, 103, 104, 105, 106, 107, 108, 109, 110, 111, 112, 114, 115, 117, 177, 192
Percival Pembroke, 93
Percival Prentice, 70, 75, 192
Percival Provost, 75
Republic Thunderbolt, 93
R100, xv
R101, xv
Scottish Aviation Bulldog, 83, 84. 86, 87, 91, 177, 192
Scottish Aviation Jetstream, 84, 85, 86, 192
Short Stirling, 11, 15, 156, 191
Short Sunderland, 119
Sikorski HH-3E 'Jolly Green Giant', 93
SNIAS/Westland Gazelle, 86
SNIAS/Westland Puma, 93
Sopwith Dolphin, 97
Sopwith Snipe, 97, 99

Supermarine Spitfire, 9, 14, 61, 93, 96, 100, 110
TSR2, 89
Tupolev Backfire, 101
Tupolev Bear D, 101, 107
Tupolev Blackjack, 107
Vickers Valetta, 65, 72, 192
Vickers Vildebeeste, 113
Vickers Vimy, 113
Vickers Wellington, 21, 22, 30, 34, 37, 55, 58, 60, 61, 63, 64, 162, 175, 191, 192
Westland Lynx, 92
Westland Wessex, 93
Westland Whirlwind, 100

Aerobatic Teams:
Red Arrows, 87
Swords, 84
Synchronised Pair, 84
Vintage Pair, 88, 90, 91

Stations:
Abingdon, 6, 9, 65, 78
Akrotiri, 99, 103, 116
Balderton, 22
Baldonnel, 113
Barkston Heath, 100
Benson, 41
Binbrook, 96
Boscombe Down, 14
Bruggen, 100, 102, 113
Catterick, 2, 11, 29, 62, 78, 96
Chivenor, 19
Church Fenton, 79, 90, 94
Colerne, 60, 65, 68
Coningsby, 92, 97, 103, 106, 109, 115
Coltishall, 65, 66, 67, 97
Cottesmore, 58, 120
Cranwell, 76, 87, 93
Croft, 18, 24, 25, 30, 94
Culdrose, 83
Dalton, 24, 25
Dishforth, 1, 3, 12, 14, 24, 25, 79, 91
Donibristle, 113
Driffield, 11, 13
East Moor, 24, 25, 33, 55, 56

Farnborough, 2
Finningley, 13, 87, 106, 113, 114
Ford, 35
Gosport, 97
Gransden Lodge, 29
Grantham, 75, 113
Grimsby, 113
Hawkinge, 99
Henlow, 97
Hingham, 113
Horsham St Faith, 97
Hullavington, 87, 102
Innsworth, 102
Kenley, 97
Khartoum, 62
Kinloss, 3
Laarbruch, 100
Leuchars, 65, 91, 96, 97, 106, 109, 115
Lindholme, 22, 80
Linton-on-Ouse, 3, 10, 11, 12, 13, 24, 25, 33, 90, 91, 98
Little Rissington, 84, 87
Little Snoring, 97
Lossiemouth, 15
Lyneham, 103
Manby, 79
Manston, 19, 61
Marham, 9, 65, 114
Marston Moor, 22
Melbourne, 21, 22
Middleton St George, 22, 24, 25, 37, 57, 61
Mildenhall, 22
Mount Pleasant, 97
Netheravon, 95, 102
Netherton, 102
Nicosia, 115
North Coates, 100
Northolt, 97
North Luffenham, 70
Oakington, 11
Odiham, 100
Ossington, 27
Patrington, 100
Pembrey, 9, 102
Pershore, 89
Pocklington, 21, 22

HARRY, WARRIOR PRINCE

"Make love not war."

Prince Henry of Wales, the royal less formally known as Prince Harry, was born in September 1984. He was educated at Eton and graduated from the Royal Military Academy Sandhurst in 2006. He then went on to serve in the Blues and Royals regiment in Windsor, rising to the rank of Captain. He retired from the army in 2016, having served two tours of Afghanistan.

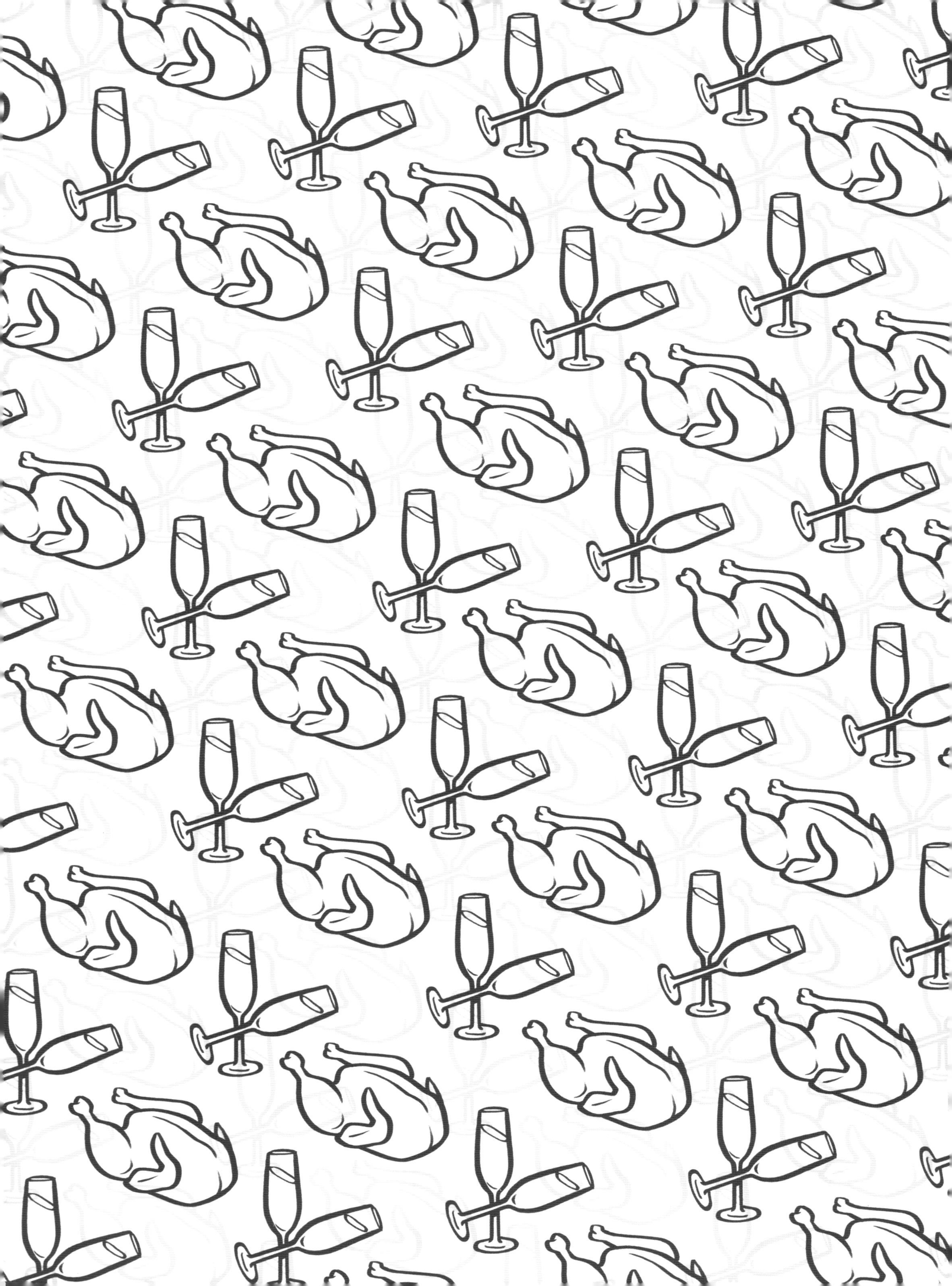

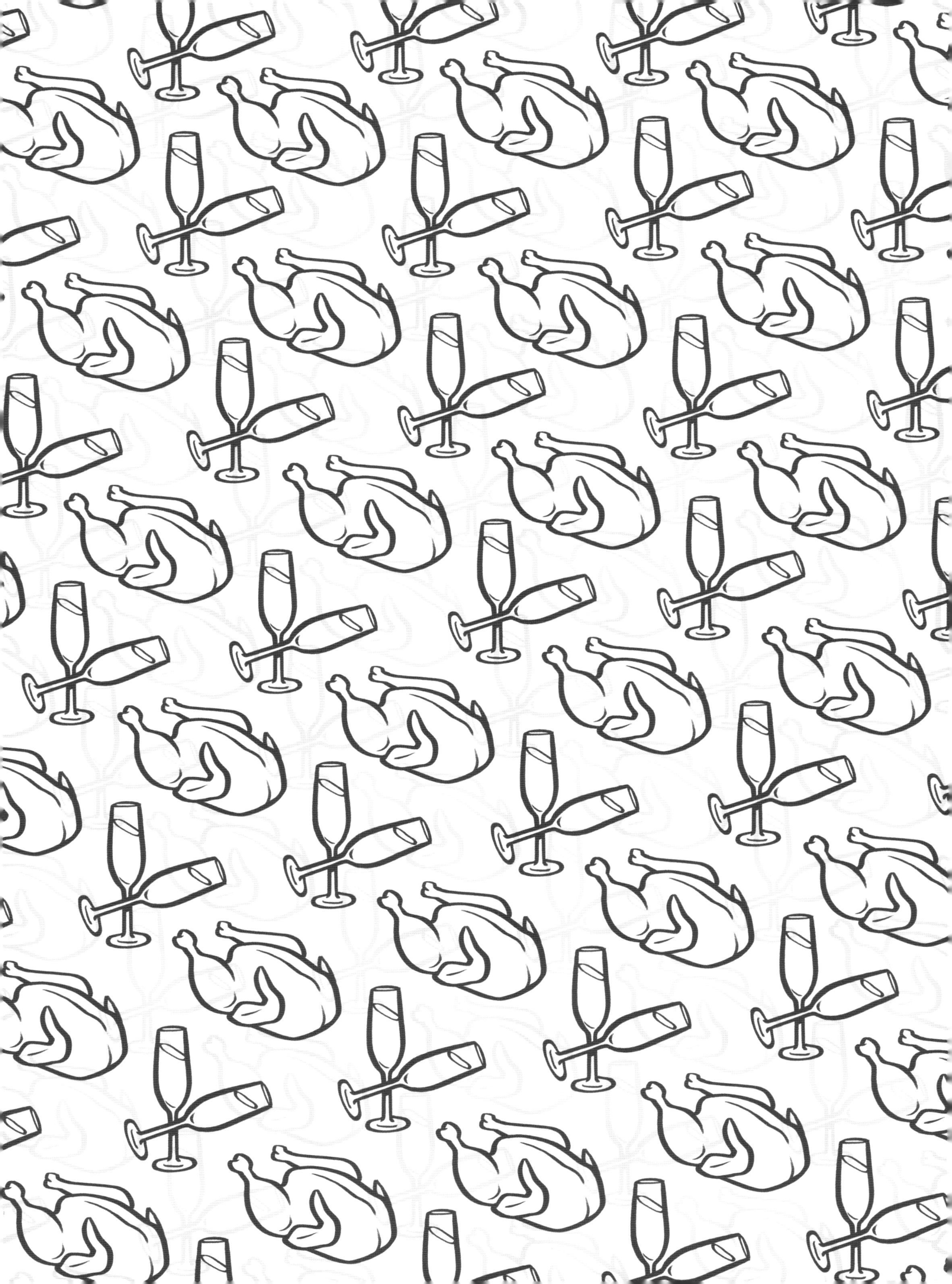

GREAT BALLS OF FIRE!

"Sports of kings."

Sports-mad Harry is equally
at home on the rugby pitch
and the polo field. In 2004,
he spent some time as a
volunteer rugby coach for
the Rugby Football Union.

FACT:
HARRY PLAYED POLO FOR THE YOUNG ENGLAND TEAM.

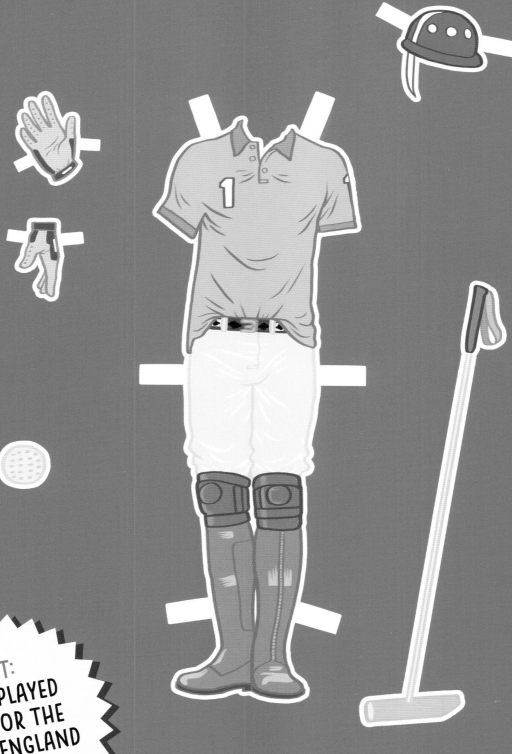

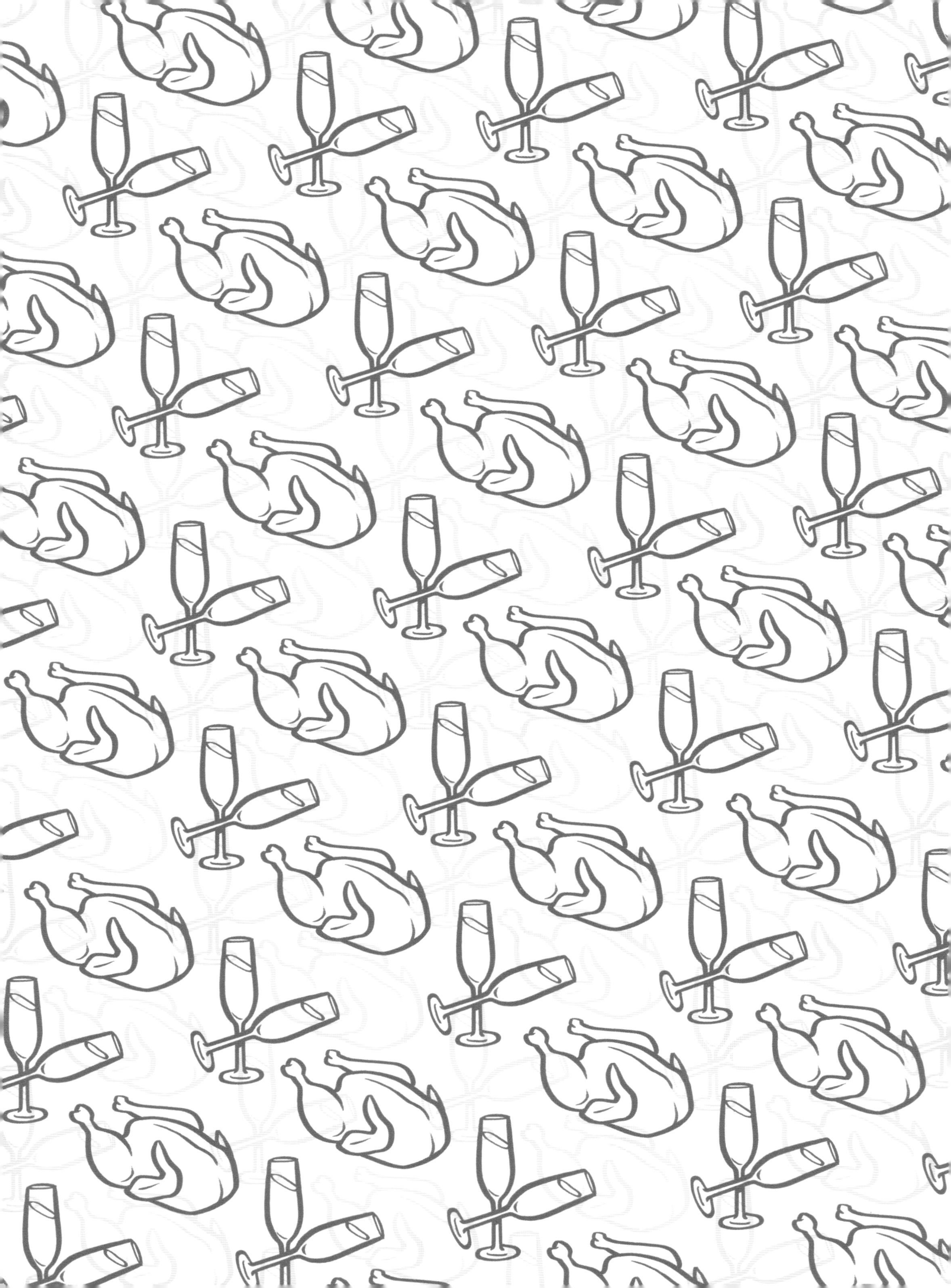

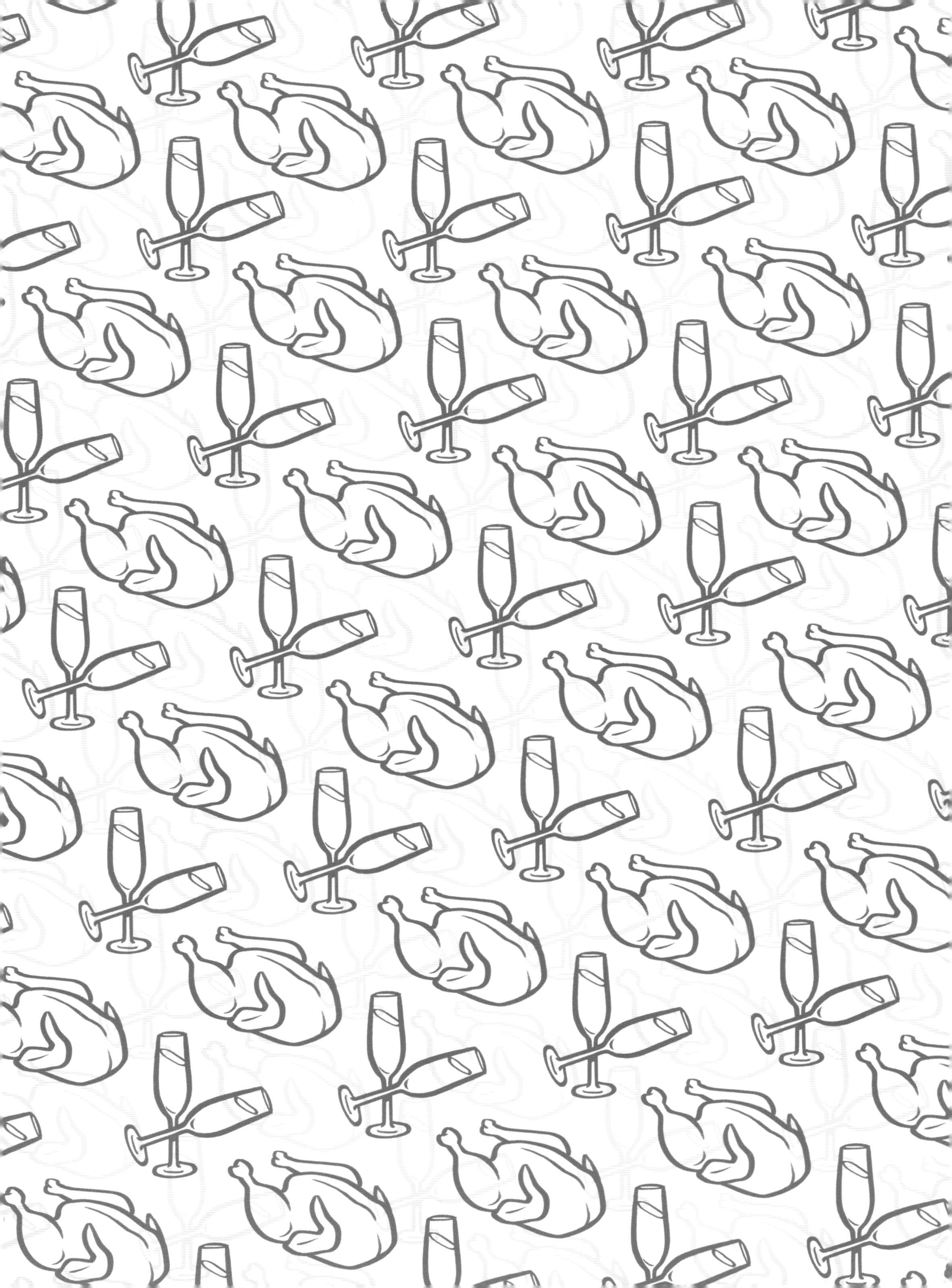

PRANCING

ON ICE

"There's no business like snow business."

FACT:
HARRY ONCE TREKKED TO THE SOUTH POLE FOR CHARITY.

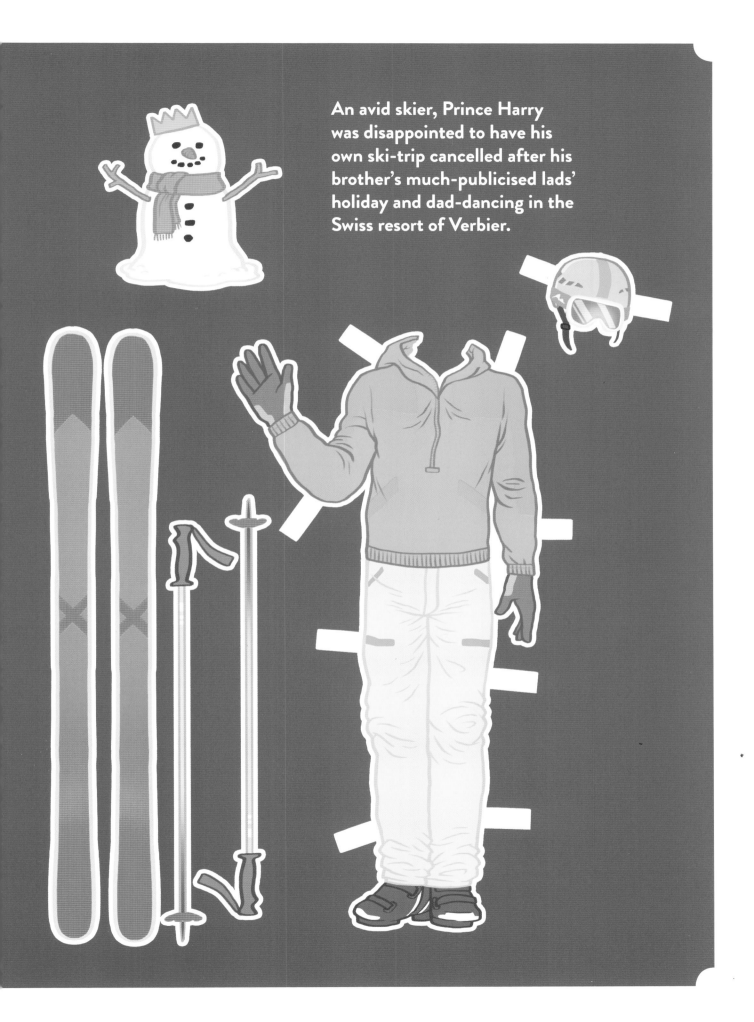

An avid skier, Prince Harry was disappointed to have his own ski-trip cancelled after his brother's much-publicised lads' holiday and dad-dancing in the Swiss resort of Verbier.

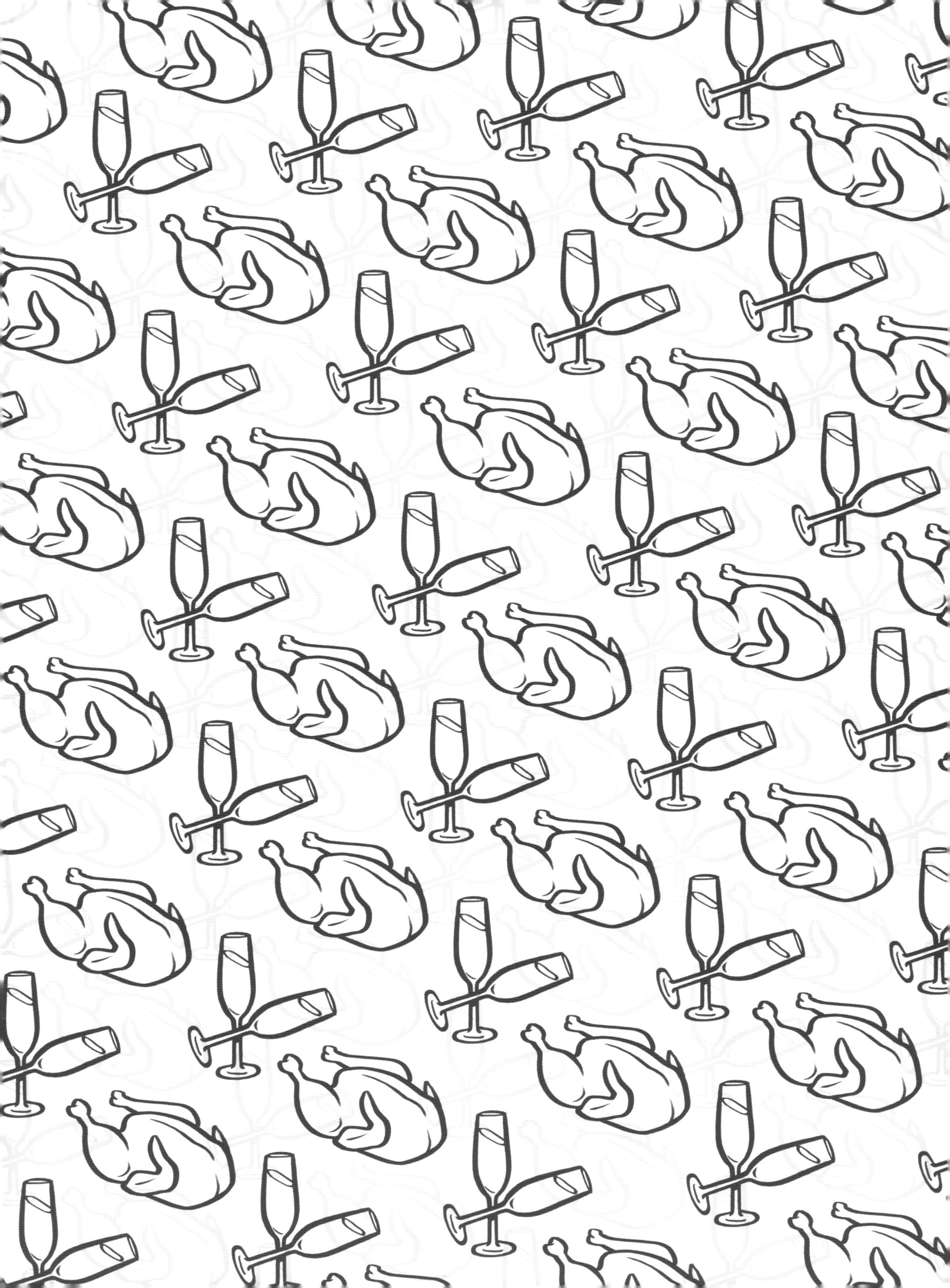

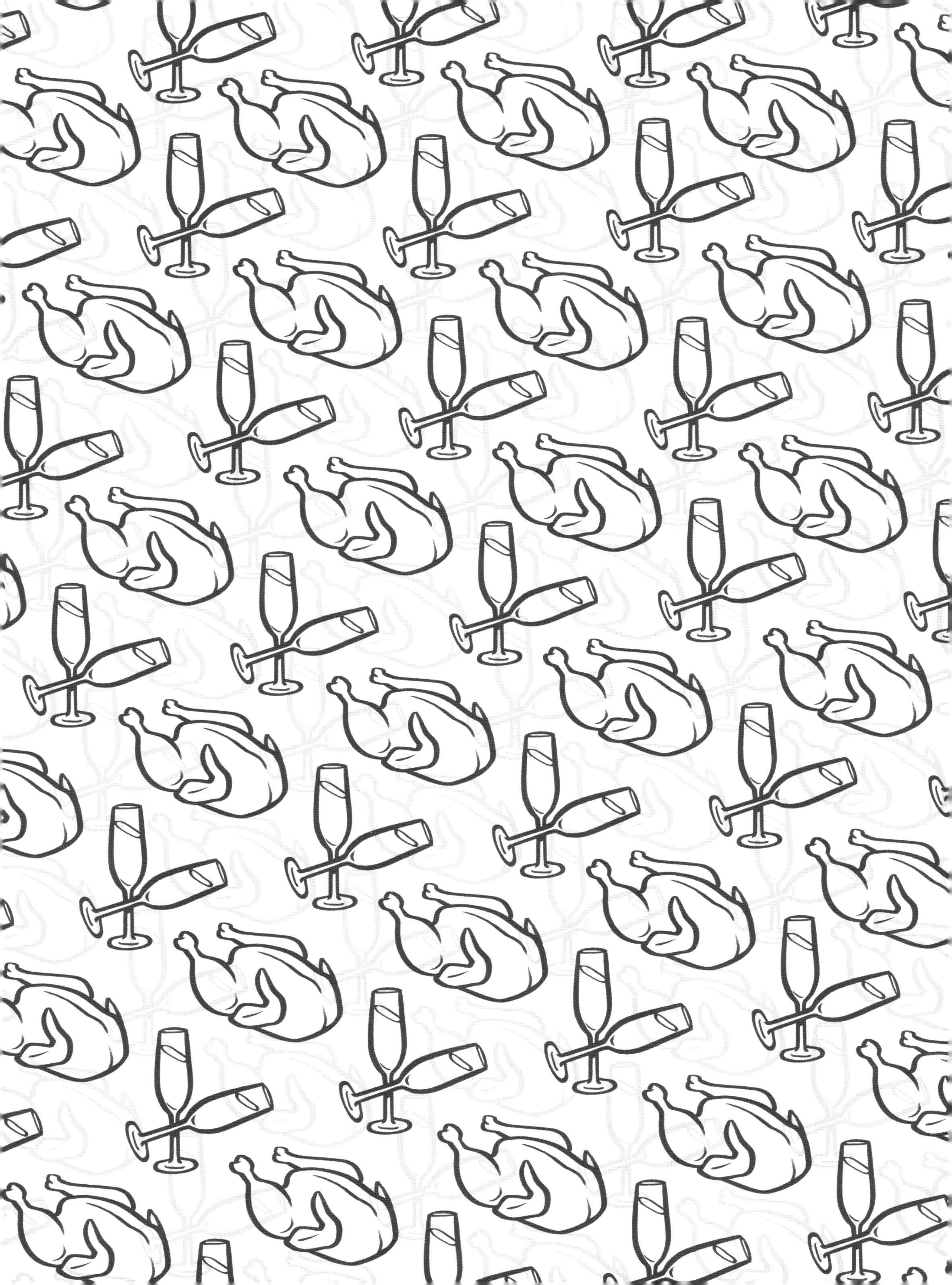

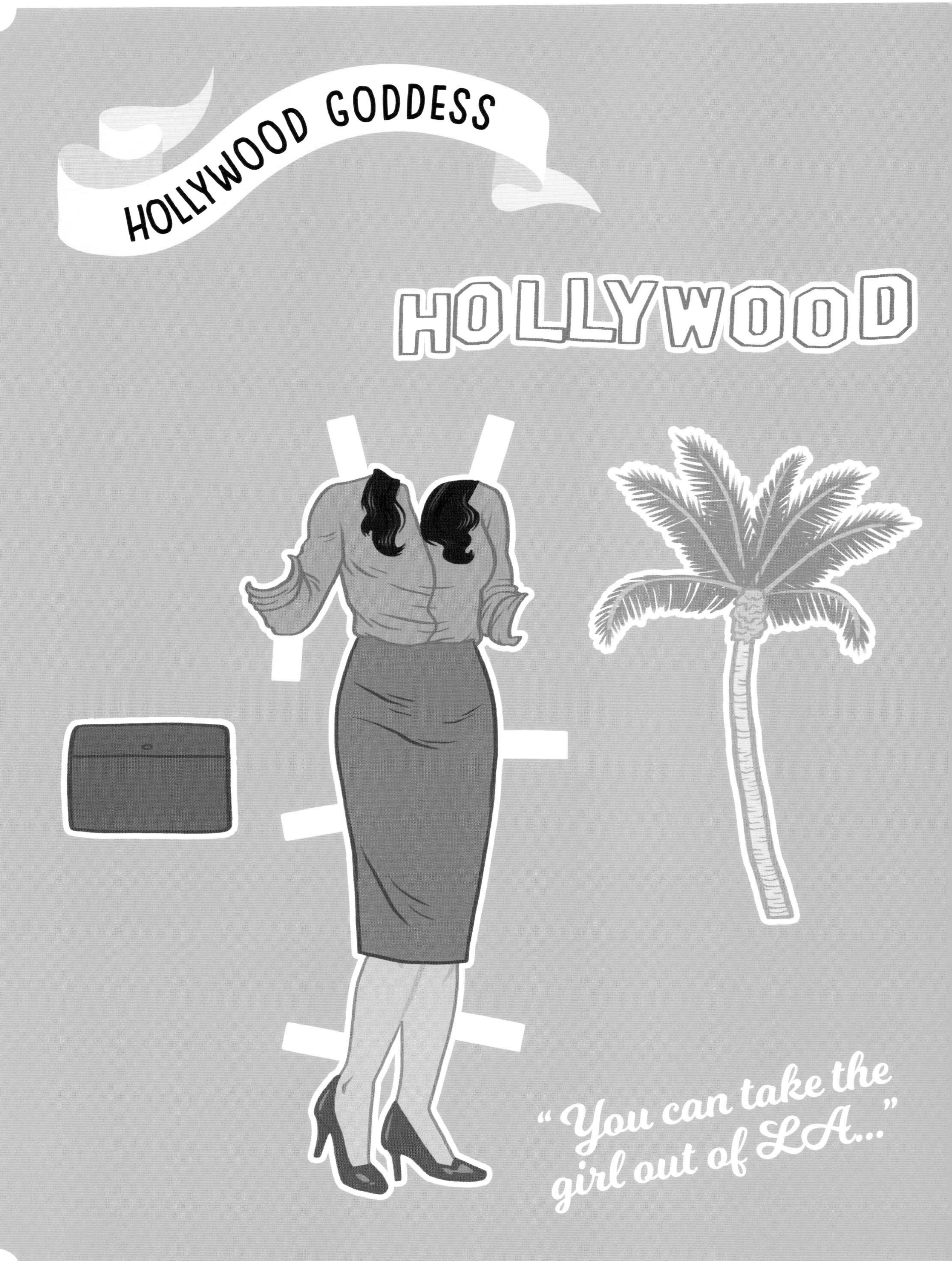
HOLLYWOOD GODDESS
HOLLYWOOD
"You can take the girl out of LA..."

FACT:
MEGHAN ONCE
WORKED AS
A FREELANCE
CALLIGRAPHER.

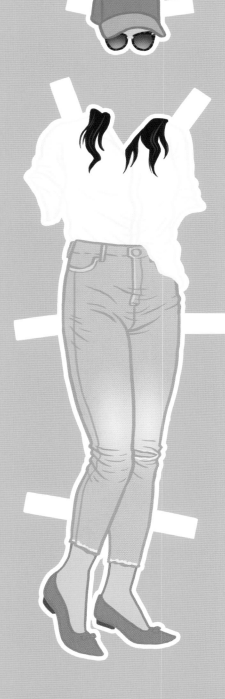

SCRIPT

American actress and humanitarian Meghan Markle grew up in Hollywood and starred in legal drama *Suits*. On her blog she said, "I was born and raised in Los Angeles, a California girl who lives by the ethos that most things can be cured with either yoga, the beach or a few avocados."

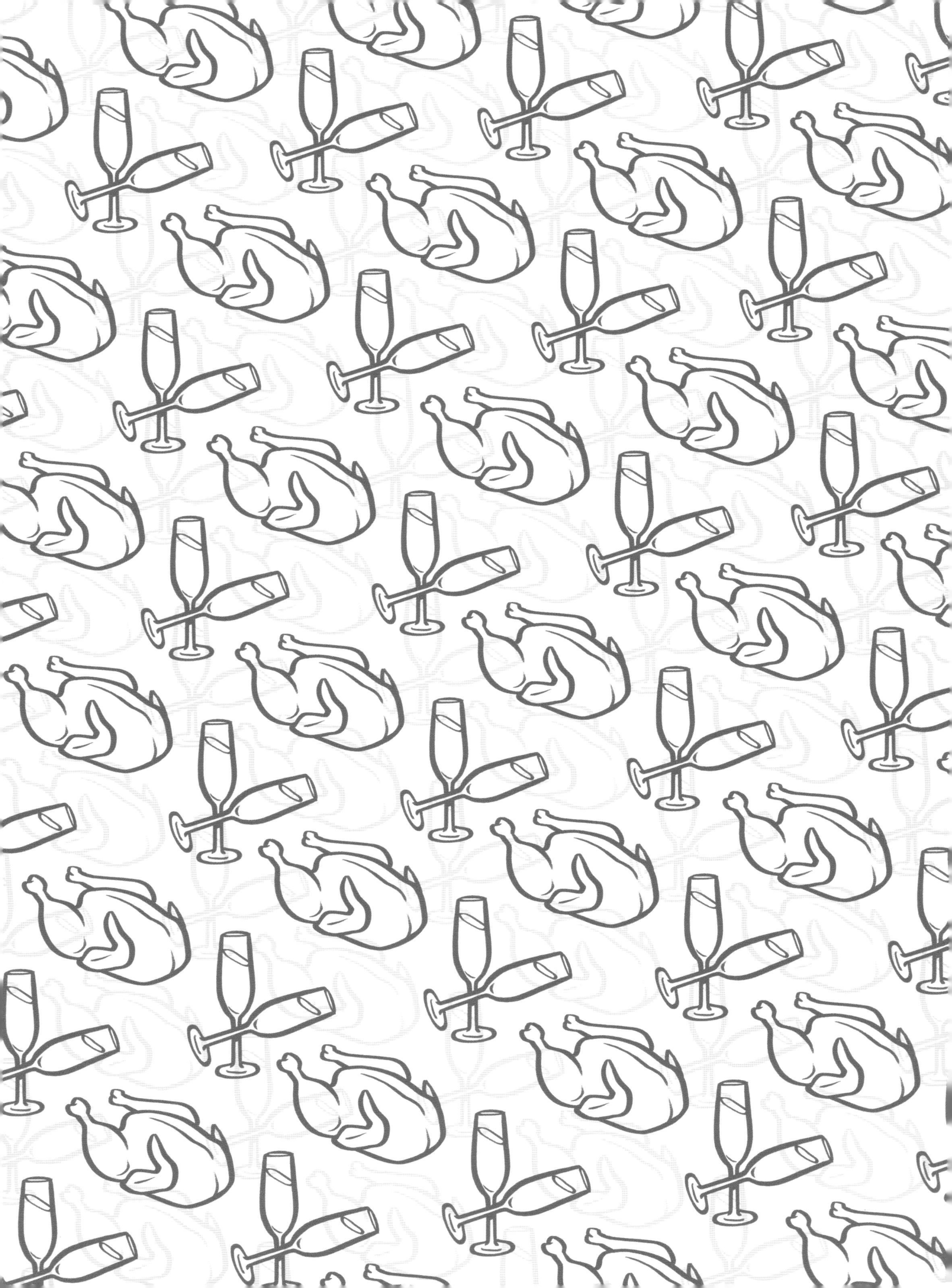

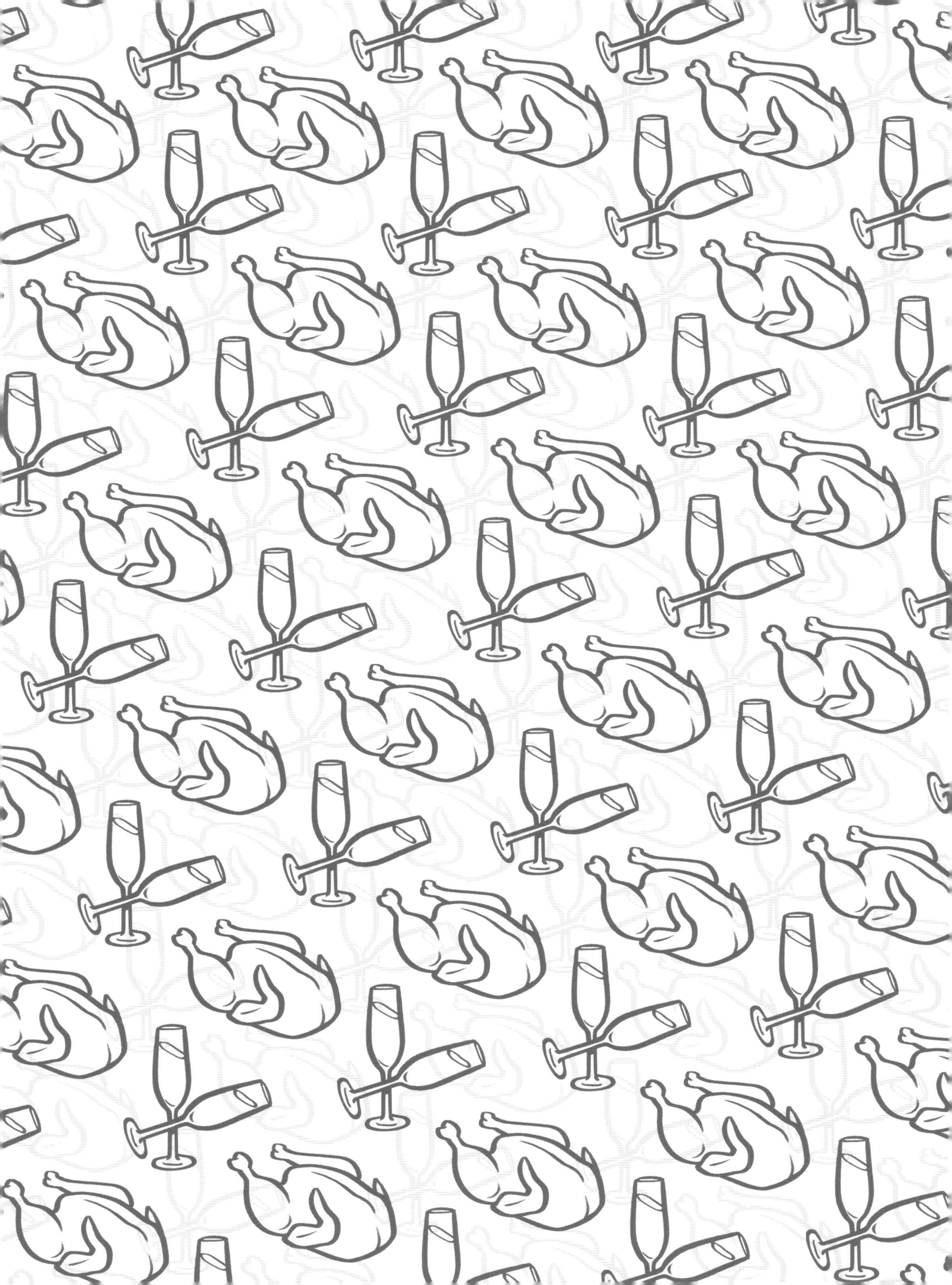

"MARRIAGE" HAS A NICE RING TO IT

"When two become one."

KISS THE COOK

Harry proposed to Meghan over a home-cooked dinner. "It was a cosy night, we were roasting chicken, and it was an amazing surprise," Meghan explained.

FACT:
HARRY DESIGNED
THE BESPOKE
RING HIMSELF.

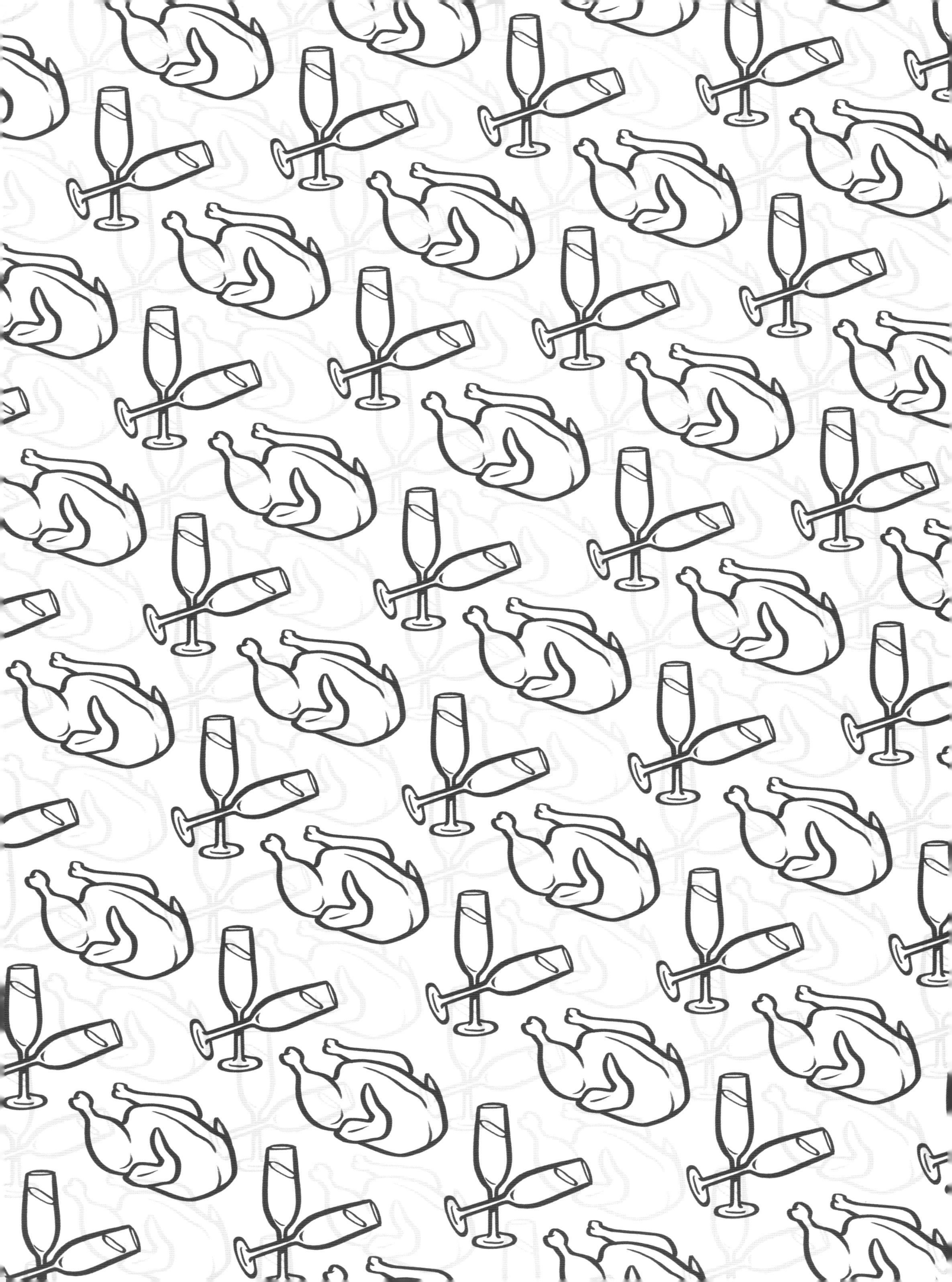

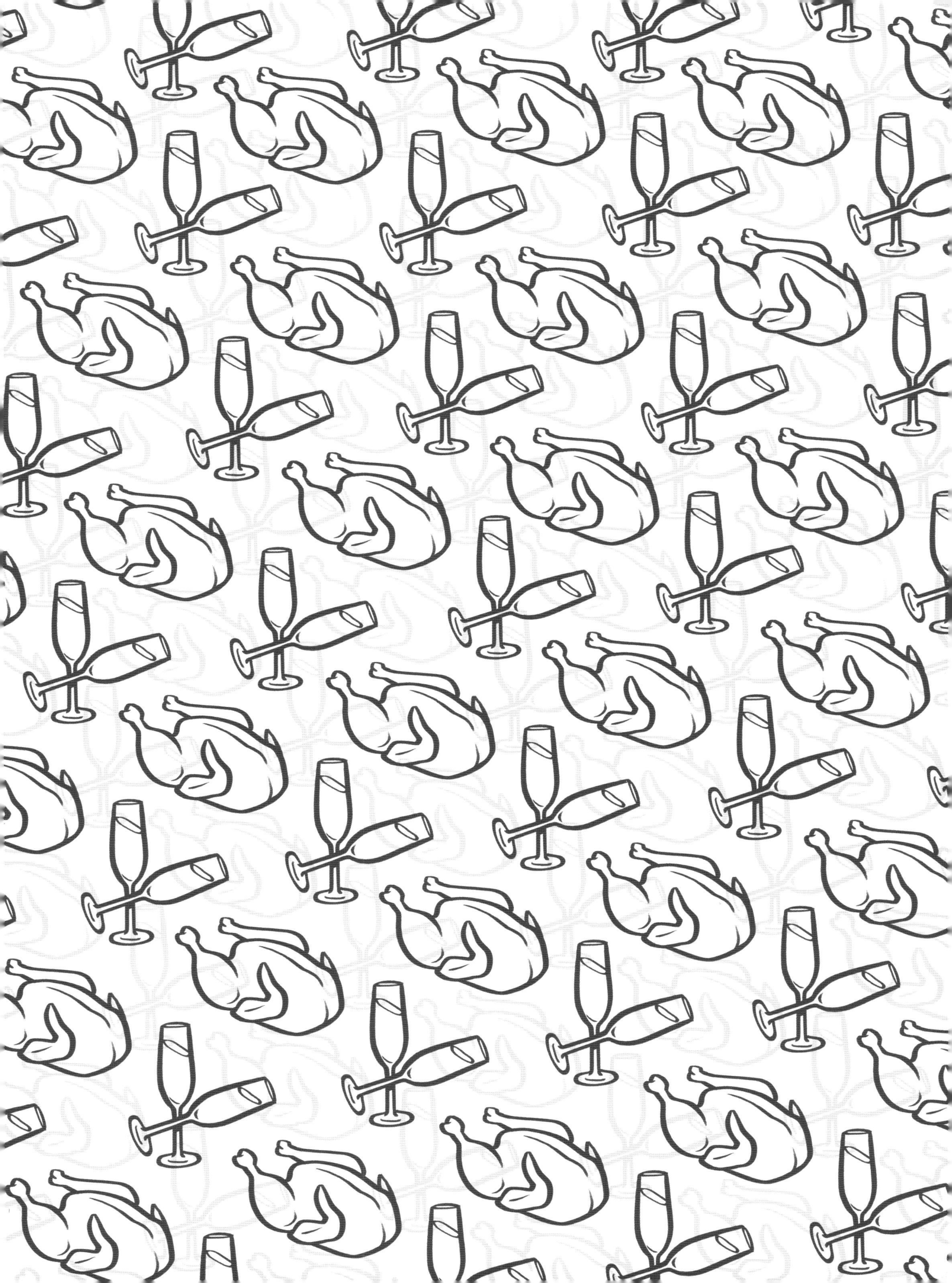

CHRISTMAS WITH THE FAM

Harry and Meghan spent Christmas with the Royal Family at Sandringham.

(POSSIBLE) FACT: MEGHAN GIFTED THE QUEEN A SINGING HAMSTER TOY.

"It's a wonderful wife."

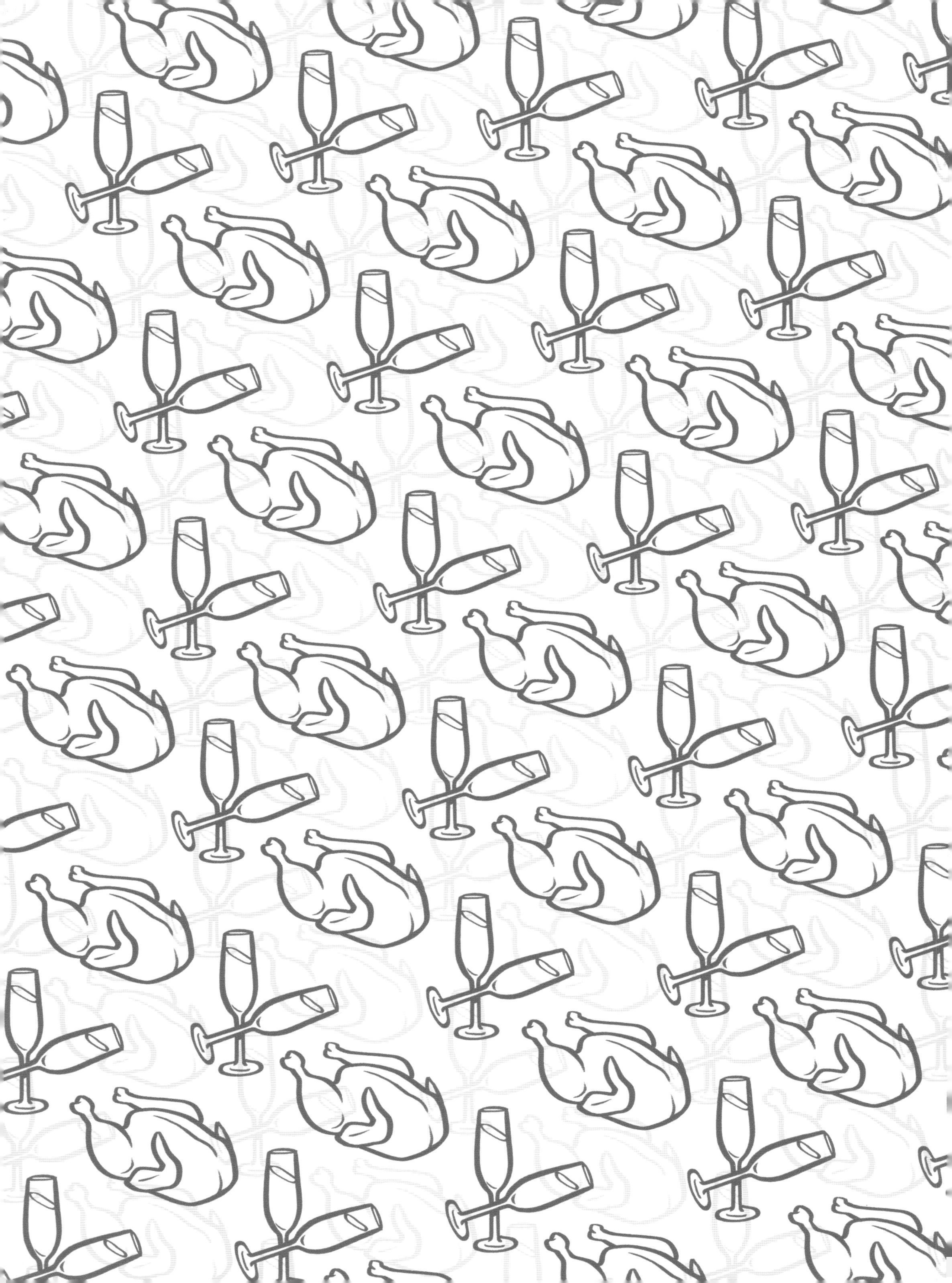

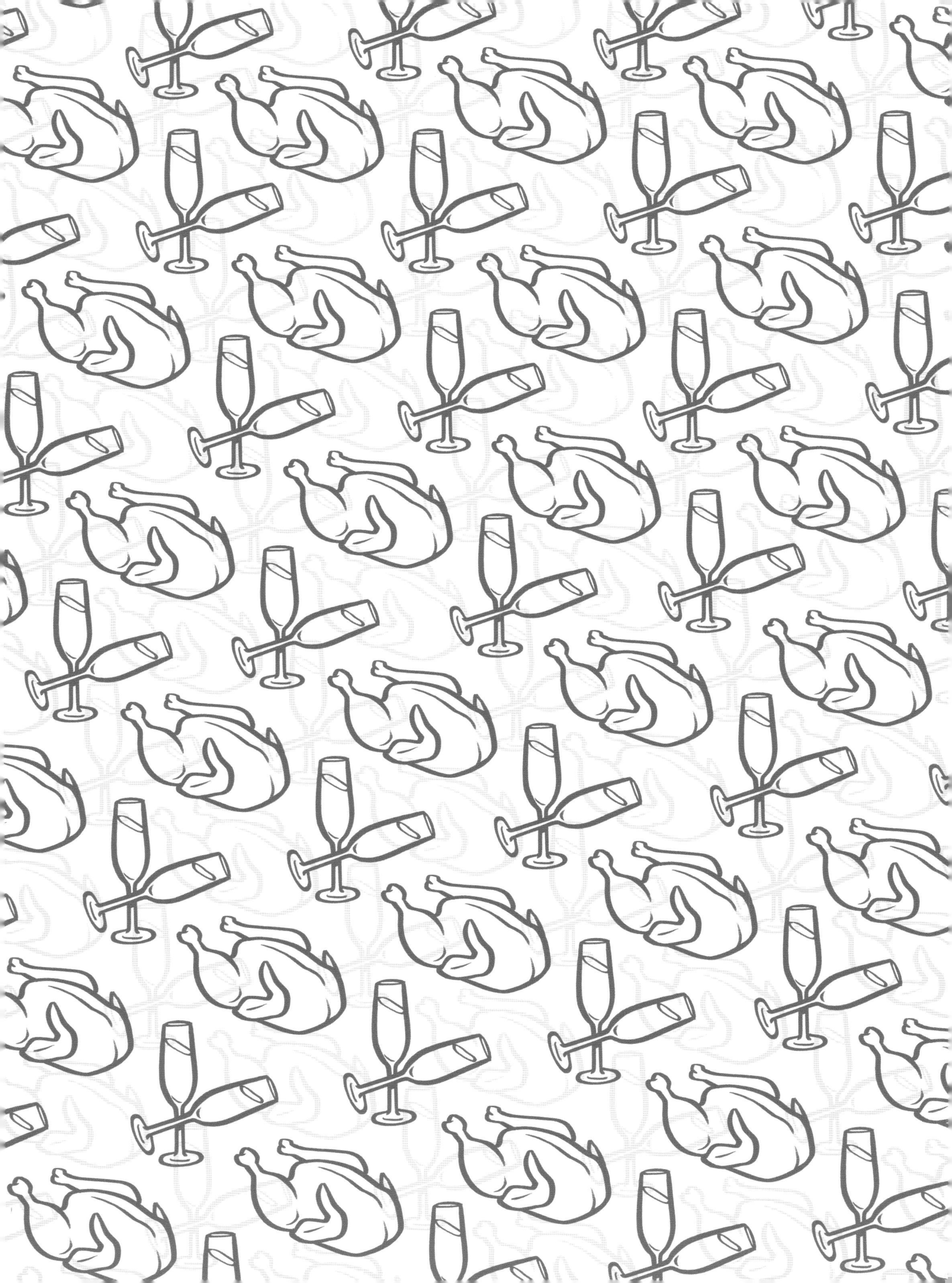

LAS VEGAS BACHELOR PARTY

Prince Harry loves to party. No matter where he goes for his final send off as a single man, it is bound to be epic.

(POSSIBLE)
FACT:
HARRY LOVES
TO TWERK.

"What happens
in Vegas, stays
in Vegas."

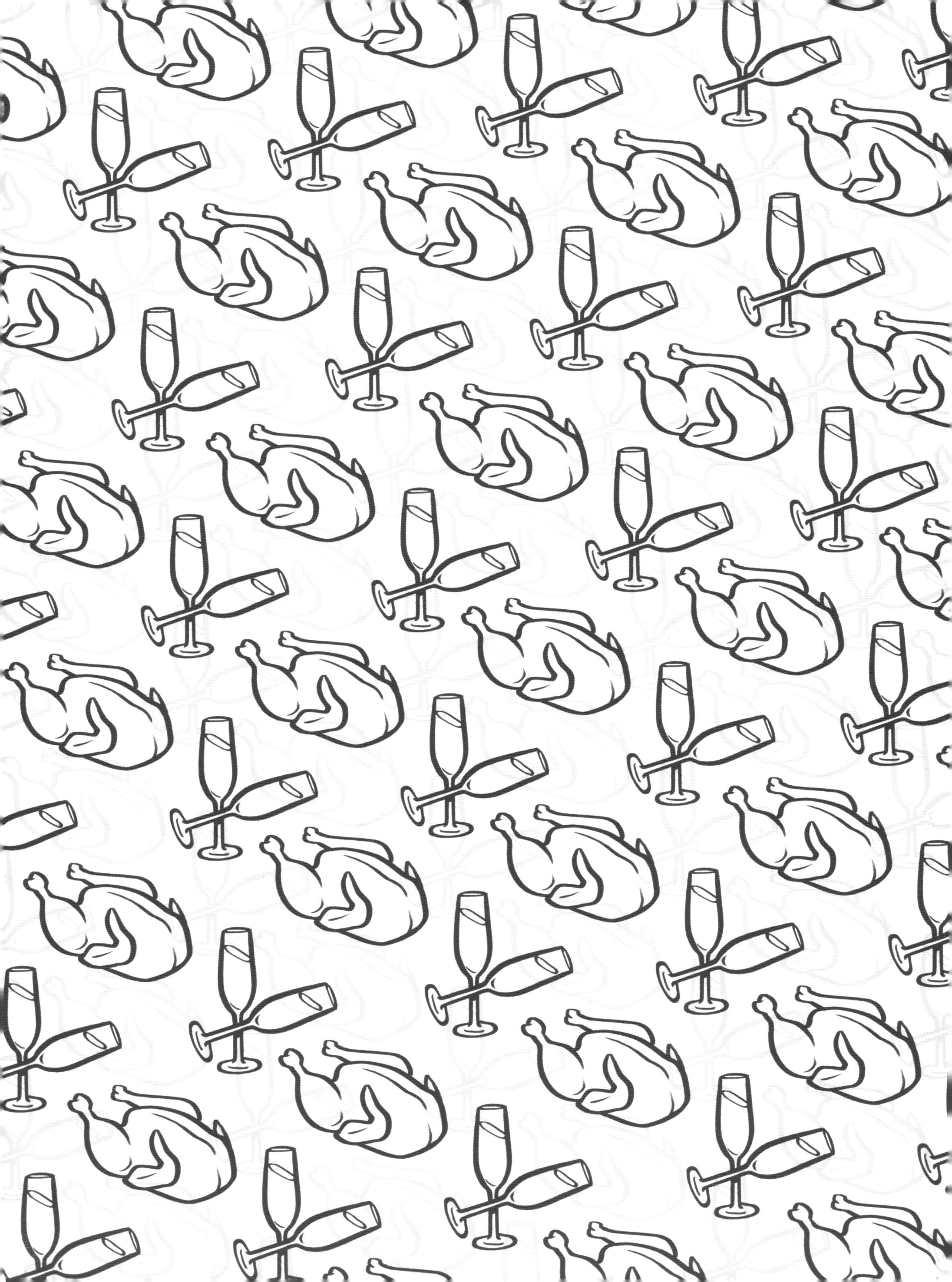

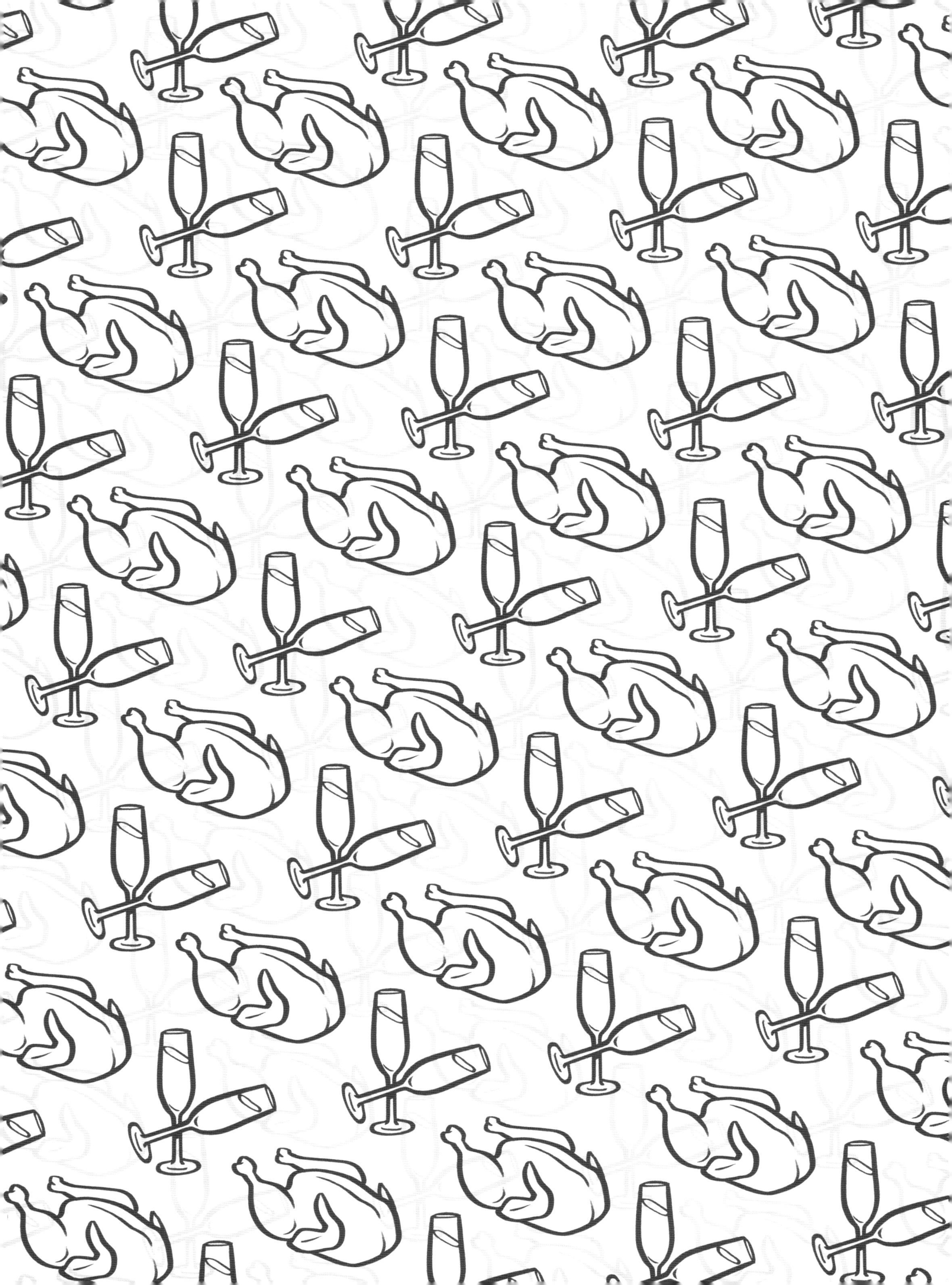

SAY "YES" TO THE DRESS

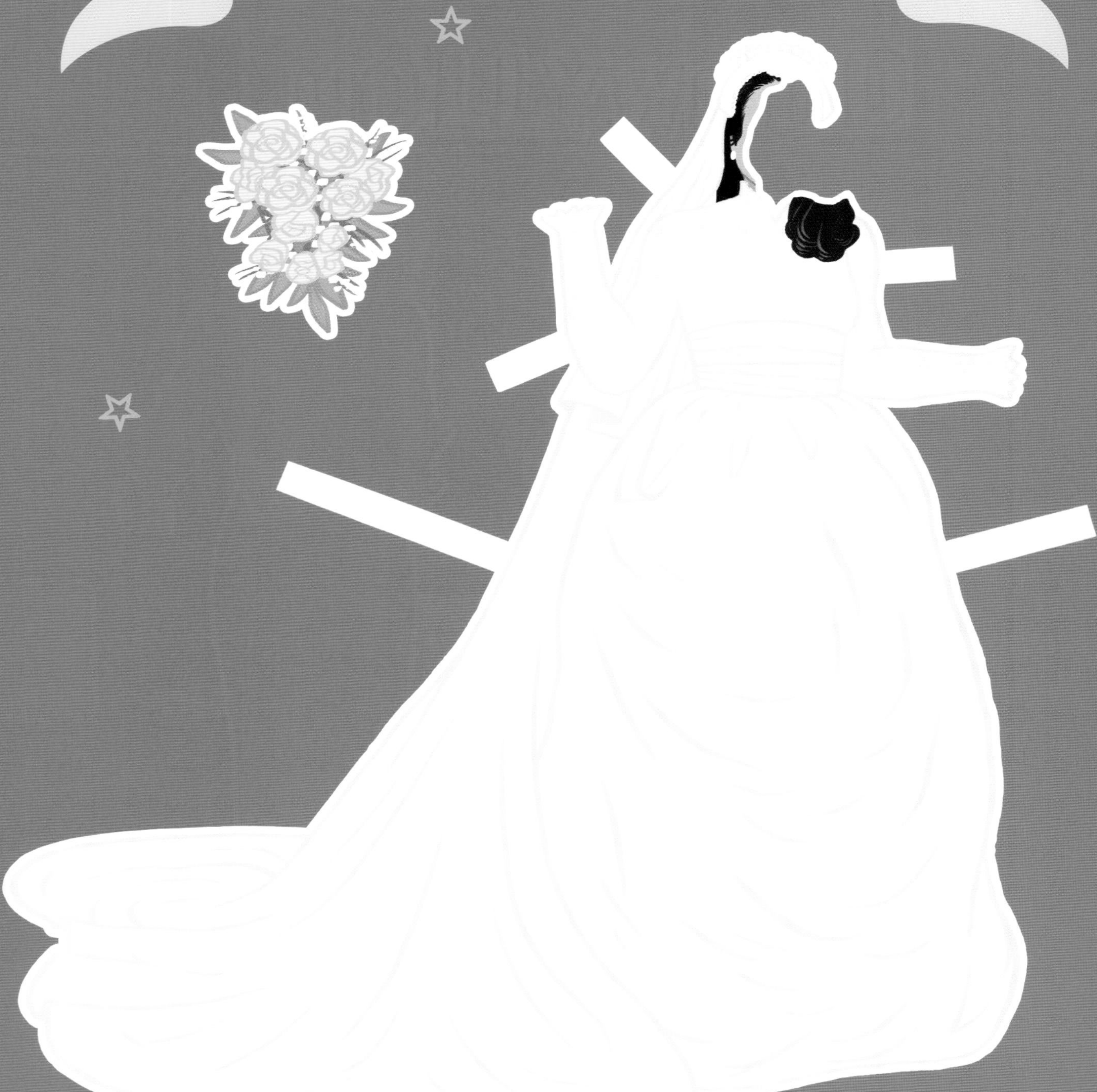

"Don't tell the bridegroom."

Meghan is known for her elegant sense of style. Try her in these dresses similar to the style of other famous American princesses Grace Kelly and Kim Kardashian.

FACT:
MEGHAN'S DREAM DRESS IS "CLASSIC AND SIMPLE".

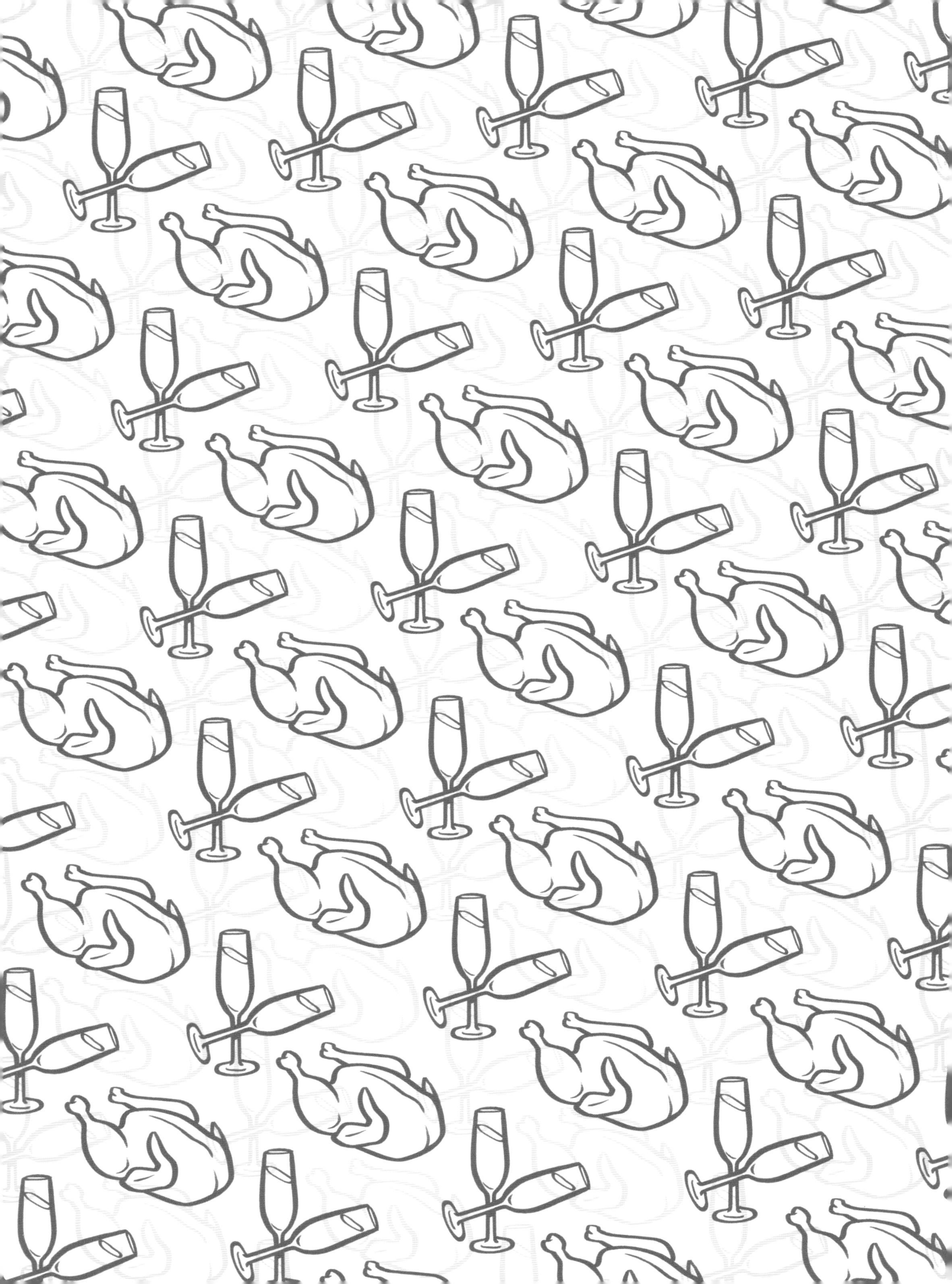

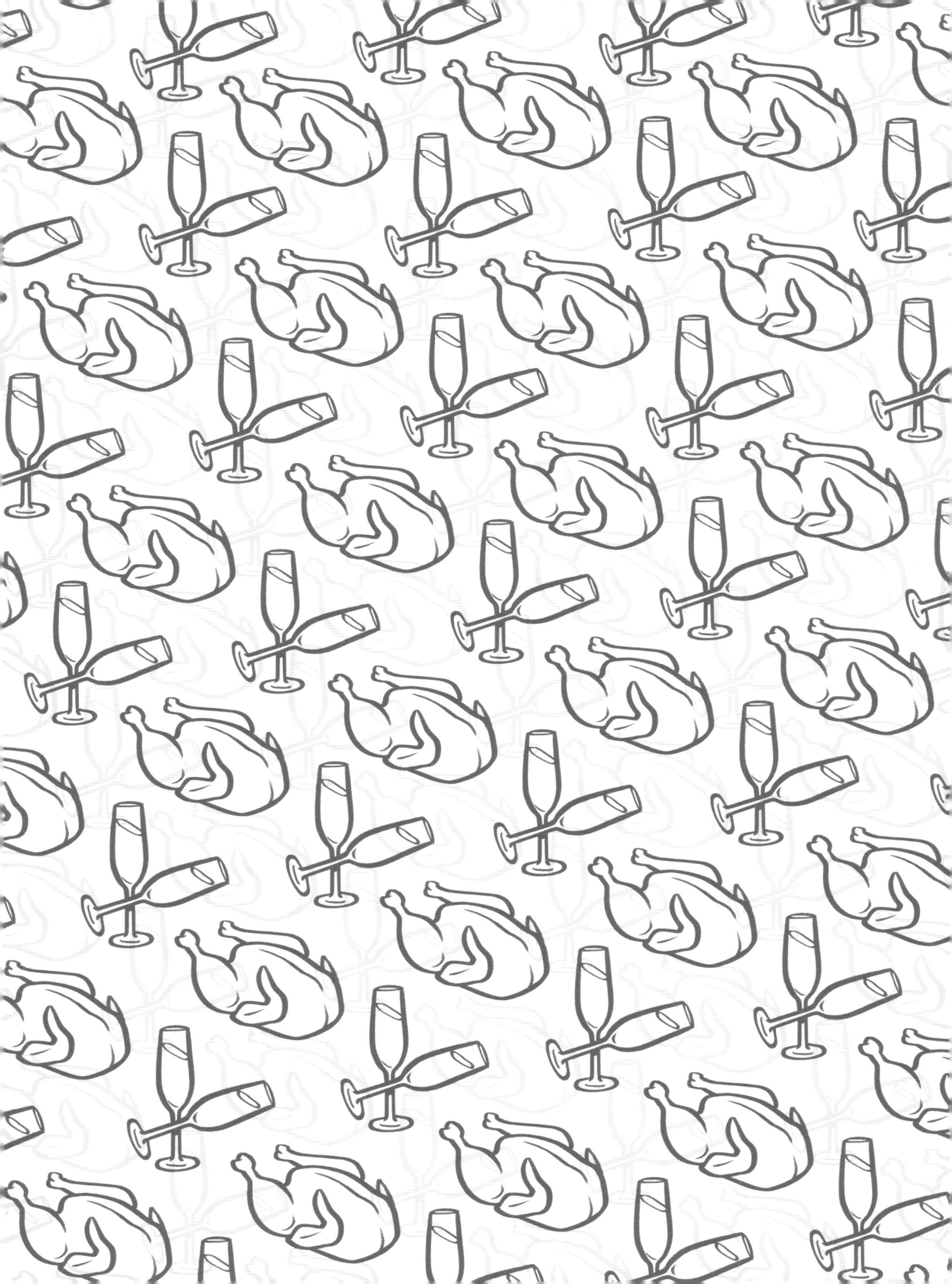

DOWNTOWN DOWNTIME

"Because yoga is for posers."

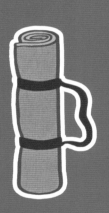

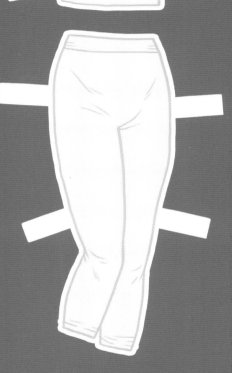

Born in California in 1984, Meghan Markle is an actress and all-round decent human being. She is well known for her work for the Clean Water Campaign in Africa and for promoting gender equality. She inherited her love of yoga from her mother Doria, who is a yoga teacher. "I love an intense vinyasa class — and even better if it's blasting hip hop and done in a dark room with candlelight."

FACT:
MEGHAN DOES HOT YOGA A COUPLE OF TIMES A WEEK.